ARISE AND RETURN

ARISE AND RETURN

Restoring the Ancient Paths of Authentic Discipleship to Impact the World

JOSIAH ARMSTRONG

RAISE A WARRIOR

Arise And Return: Restoring The Ancient Paths Of Authentic Discipleship To Impact The World.
Copyright © 2024 by Josiah Armstrong. All rights reserved.

Editor: Monique Ciccarone

No portion of this publication may be reproduced, distributed, or transmitted in any form or by any means, including photocopying, recording, or other electronic or mechanical methods, without the prior written permission from the publisher or author, except in the case of brief quotation embodied in reviews and certain other non-commercial uses as permitted by U.S. copyright law. For permission please email josiah@ariseandreturn.com or Josiah@forerunnerfitness.net

www.AriseandReturn.com   www.Forerunnerfitness.net

www.RaiseaWarrior.com   www.TheBushidobooks.com

www.JosiahArmstrong.org

All Scripture quotations, unless otherwise indicated, are taken from the Holy Bible, New International Version®, NIV®. Copyright ©1973, 1978, 1984, 2011 by Biblica, Inc.™ Used by permission of Zondervan. All rights reserved worldwide. www.zondervan.com The "NIV" and "New International Version" are trademarks registered in the United States Patent and Trademark Office by Biblica, Inc.™

ISBN: 979-8-89316-370-4 - eBook

ISBN: 979-8-89316-371-1 - Paperback

ISBN: 979-8-89316-372-8 - Hardcover

Contents

Preface xi
Introduction 1

Chapter 1: For Such a Time as this! 37
Chapter 2: Cultural Complexities and the Call 49
Chapter 3: Leadership is Critical 67
Chapter 4: Human Drives 87
Chapter 5: To Be or Not to Be: Being Before Doing 109
Chapter 6: Crisis- martial arts, dance, education…what? ... 143
Chapter 7: Where to start: "What's in your hand" 157
Chapter 8: Growing for the sake of the "Going" 179
Chapter 9: What's the Goal? 193
Chapter 10: Teaching isn't for me or is it? 217
Chapter 11: Make Impact, Leverage Influence 259
Chapter 12: Holistic Education & Making disciples 295
Chapter 13: Curriculums of Transformation 331
Chapter 14: Creating Transformational Environments—a leaders responsibility 397
Chapter 15: Fostering the "Flame of Intelligence" and the Passion of Christ 441
Chapter 16: Making the Shift and Counting the Cost 467
Chapter 17: Join the Mission! 487

12 Tips for Crafting Great Open-Ended Questions: 509
AI Dynamics 511

FREE VIDEO SUMMARY'S

WANT VIDEO SUMMARY'S OF EACH CHAPTER & MORE?

Transformational Tools & Resources

Think about this **FREE** resources as a training process and master class loaded with value and discussion prompts for your people and your own reflection.

ARISEANDRETURN.COM

CLAIM YOUR 75% OFF CODE:

"BOOKBONUS75XP"

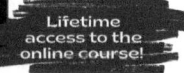

Lifetime access to the online course!

YOUR STRATEGIC PATH TO BREAKTHROUGH, CLARITY, AND ABUNDANT LIFE!

Transformational Tools & Resources

Discover your unique God given purpose, breakthrough your barriers, craft a strategic and prayer plan with a rule of life that leads to fruitfulness and fulfillment. Leave a transformational legacy!

FORERUNNERFITNESS.NET/BREAKTHROUGHXP

TRANSFORMATIONAL BREAKTHROUGH & HIGH PERFORMANCE COACHING

- PURPOSE
- WELLNESS
- LIFESTYLE
- LEADERSHIP
- CLARITY
- ENERGY
- COURAGE
- NECESSITY
- PRODUCTIVITY
- INFLUENCE

With Josiah Armstrong

CERTIFIED HIGH PERFORMANCE COACH

Set up a Call!

Fully Live, Fully Express Your God-Given Purpose! Take your Life, Business, & Ministry to the Next Level!

WWW.FORERUNNERFITNESS.NET

Foreword
Shawn Foster

It seems surreal that I first met Josiah as a 15 year old when he started attending the youth ministry I led at a church in Massachusetts. As a youth who had just come to Christ through a personal encounter alone in his room, Josiah exhibited an uncommonly intense devotion to God. As one who was forgiven much, he loved much. (Luke 7:47) It has been expressed in diverse ways ranging from radical, bold sharing of his faith, unwavering perseverance in the midst of persecution and trials, self-sacrificing devotion and loyalty to God and the leaders he served, vivacious hunger for Spirit and Truth, dedication to his wife and family, and the fruit of the Spirit, particularly joy. I have had the privilege of being a spiritual father in Josiah's life and witnessing firsthand the growth and maturity of his devotion over the past 25 years. I share this because this intense devotion clearly sources this book.

Josiah also has very creative and prophetic giftings. He lives from the heart. He has been given the nickname "The Scribe" by our leadership team because of his deep reflection, extensive journaling and thorough recording of spiritual happenings. This book is no exception: it is a lifework type of project where the whole of life and godliness is surveyed: identity and purpose, growth and discipleship, family and Church community, leadership development and influence. The book presents a compilation of many different voices, resources and practical approaches that have impacted Josiah personally. He is a learner and appreciates knowledge. He sees things broadly as a visionary. In the book, he surveys from 10,000 feet and then plunges down in elevation to speak to the heart and challenge the reader. Then, back up again!

This is the type of book that needs to be digested in parts and processed to truly produce the growth it summons.

Shawn Foster

Crossing LIFE Church, Senior Leader

Preface

While my hope is that the principles in this book impact people from all walks of life, I'm focusing on those who share a faith in Jesus Christ, and want to make a real impact in the world. I'm writing to parents, pastors, and leaders—educators and trainers of sorts. Those of you who love people and want or need a better process to help them grow, heal, mature. Yet, you have struggled with the present state of the Body of Christ, the mode of many the Church, and superficial Christianity. I'm speaking to those who burn to make an impact in culture and the church, and who see the need for radical change and reformation.

In truth, this book is not just for leaders, pastors, and parents. It is for every believer who is called to share the gospel and make disciples, but struggle knowing how to do it effectively. It's for those who are stuck thinking in the box of what they have always known; those who feel a subconscious conflict over "engaging culture in a relevant way vs involvement in the life of the Church" or " ministry vs workplace" and struggle finding their role in life and ministry. It's for people needing fresh inspiration and a compelling vision to put their gifts, and abilities to use for the Glory of God. It's for those who want to grow in leadership and effectiveness in teaching and discipling others—for educators, parents, pastors, creatives, martial artists, athletes, trainers, and coaches. People in places of influence.

The very fact you opened this book tells me a lot about you. I'd like to start with a huge thank you.

- For your investment in yourself and your trust in entering into a conversation with me.

- For being a passionate person who wants to make a real impact in this life— faithful to grow in God, to steward your life, gifts, and abilities well, and who desires to raise up the next generation.

- For being one who has eyes to see and ears to hear that the winds of change are blowing.

- For having a "yes" in your heart and a fight in your spirit to be the change the church and the world desperately needs.

- For taking delight in or aspiring to the honor of teaching and instruction.

- For choosing to live on mission and setting your heart on the great commission—to make disciples and love the Lord with all your heart, soul, and strength.

- For recognizing that something must change and being willing to be a part of the solution.

- For persevering through your pain, embracing the process of growth, and continuing to look with hope to Jesus and the future.

This book will inspire you, challenge you, and give wisdom and practical instruction concerning the call and concepts discussed in this book. Take your time through it. My prayer is that it becomes a useful tool and resource to the Body of Christ.

What to expect

I'm a preacher and exhorter, so you'll see that in my writing style. Through this book, you will gain:

- A compelling vision and call to pass on the faith to the next generation in biblical, creative, and intentional methods.

- A challenge to grow to the next level in life, faith, and your craft as an educator, parent, pastor, athlete, instructor or leader.

- Ways to level up and leverage your influence.

- Advice to stir and impart the joy and love of learning.

- Tools to leverage neuroscience for personal growth, education, and training.

- Tools and frameworks to craft your master plan for personal development, family culture and discipleship, and church based discipleship.

- Paradigm-shaping truths that destroy the false dichotomy of secular and sacred that keep Christians neutralized from making a greater impact in society.

- Knowledge of what it means to be a transformational leader who makes an impact both now and forever.

- Tips on how to integrate biblical truth into your everyday life, and in the instruction or teaching of others in a skillful way.

- Insight into the Socratic method and a Holistic learning approach to internalize truth and make disciples.

- Essential laws of leadership, personal growth, and progressive mastery.

- Understanding of the great commission for all believers, the present crisis in making disciples, and an actionable solution to effectively carry out the Lord's command.

- Some of my personal story, about coming to faith, personal healing and growth, and my journey into ministry, coaching, the arts, and education.

- Challenging questions and calls to action.

At the end of each chapter there will be a "**PAUSE. CAPTURE. APPLY - Prompts to help you process**" section. I would strongly encourage you to use this to help you assimilate the content. This doesn't have to be just another book.

Reformational Language

Some of the things said throughout this book could be perceived as critical or sharp. Although I am direct and will say some hard things, it is from love, compassion, and deep desire for Christ to have the reward of His suffering. I love God's people. I'm a pastoral leader, church planter, and convener. I earnestly seek to bring the Body of Christ together in the heart and spirit of John 17 unity. I'm deeply committed to serve and see the Bride of Christ come into maturity and everything Christ died for. I'm not just pointing the finger as a critic, aloof from deep involvement with leaders, parents, and the next generation. I'm in the thick of it. I'm being poured out and committed to my own ongoing personal transformation. I am pressing and calling others to lean in to the fullness God has purposed for us in Christ. I'm a prophetically oriented reformer, a revolutionary, a warrior, a father, a catalytic agent of change. That means this book will challenge the status quo, and for some, the content will not be easily accepted, at least initially. The concepts can feel radical, merely idealistic, or even impossible. But that is the nature of what it means to be a forerunner and pioneer, to move things forward as well as call us back to our roots.

We have to remember, what is revolutionary or radical in one generation becomes the norm in the next. Think about it. People have a hard time with change, when things don't fit their box. They are comfortable with what has been working. So when change comes, they resist it, ignore it, persecute it, and, sometimes, crucify it. Divine and necessary shifts all through time and history advanced through the challenge, commitment, sacrifice, faith, and blood of people, even the son of God Himself.

Consider some of these reformers and what was accomplished by their bold efforts; what we enjoy is a result of their sacrifice and challenge of the status quo:

- Martin Luther—the monk who revived the truth that we are saved by grace and not by works. He faced excommunication and threats for challenging the Catholic Church and translating the Bible into German, the language of common folk.

- William Tyndall—translated the Bible into English and was martyred for it.

- John Wycliffe—Condemned as a *heretic* for translating the Bible into English and criticizing church corruption.

- John Hus—Burned at the stake for promoting church reforms and Wycliffe's ideas in Bohemia.

- William Wilberforce— Faced opposition and threats for decades as he labored to abolish slavery in Britain—and ultimately prevailed.

- The 56 signers of the Declaration of Independence, our founding fathers in the United States, who stood for our God-given inalienable rights. Their possessions and wealth were confiscated. Some were tortured, imprisoned, and put to death for the stand they took to birth such a nation.

- Martin Luther King Jr—Key civil rights leader who contended for equality and an end to segregation. He was not only assassinated but suffered much alongside other black Americans standing for equality. Some of the conversations, prevailing mindsets, and institutional realities in America only 60 years ago are thought unthinkable today.

- Susan B. Anthony— played a pivotal role in the women's suffrage movement, laying groundwork for women's voting rights in the United States. She was arrested in New York for illegally voting as a woman in a presidential election. Without her voice, we might live in an America where women couldn't vote. It's laughable.

- Dorothea Dix—a 19th century reformer who campaigned tirelessly for 40 years to improve conditions and treatment of the mentally ill in asylums. People believed those with mental illness could not be helped. Her views of compassion and respect were radical in her time. That is a wild thought! Dix's work led to the founding or expansion of over 30 hospitals for the treatment of mental illness across the United States. She also advocated reforms in Canada and Europe.[1]

---

[1] Prison and Asylum Reform—USHistory.org https://www.ushistory.org/us/26d.asp, Dorothea Dix-Learning to Give https://www.learningtogive.org/resources/dorothea-

Preface

- Jesus and the Apostles—they redefined truth, brought forth salvation for humanity, and laid the foundation of the Church for all time. Eleven of the Apostles were martyred and the last one lived out his days in exile and prison on the Island of Patmos. The old saying goes, "the blood of the martyrs is the seed of the Church." Right in line with what Jesus taught when He said, "Truly, truly, I tell you, unless a kernel of wheat falls to the ground and dies, it remains only a seed; but if it dies, it bears much fruit. Whoever loves his life will lose it, but whoever hates his life in this world will keep it for eternal life...."[2]

Now consider these modern industry disruptors that have changed the game. Their inventors thought the unthinkable, and challenged the status quo:

- The airplane: The Wright brothers' first powered flight in 1903 revolutionized transportation and warfare. Many thought heavier-than-air flight was impossible. Today, the International Air Transport Association (IATA) predicts 4.7 billion passengers traveling by air in 2024.[3] The thought of not being able to travel by plane today is, again, laughable.

- The light bulb: In 1879, Thomas Edison's incandescent light bulb transformed indoor lighting and enabled widespread electrification. Today we see beautiful light shows in concerts, in our churches, in film and many other places.

- The automobile: Karl Benz's 1885 gasoline-powered car and Henry Ford's mass production techniques radically changed personal transportation and manufacturing. Today, we have

---

dix, Biography:Dorothea Dix—National Women's History Museum https://www.womenshistory.org/education-resources/biographies/dorothea-dix
2 John 12:24-25 BSB
3 Survey Predicts Air Travel Boom For 2024: What It Means ...—Forbes https://www.forbes.com/sites/rogerdooley/2023/12/06/air-travel-boom-predicted-for-2024/

xvii

electric cars and the work of Elon Musk. We've even seen transportation access change the rental car industry from taxis to Uber to Turo.[4]

- The telephone: Alexander Graham Bell's 1876 invention revolutionized long-distance communication. That has evolved to today's iPhone and Starlink satellite phones.

- The computer: From early mechanical computers to modern digital devices, computers have transformed nearly every aspect of society.

- The internet: Developed in the late 20th century, it has revolutionized information access, communication, and commerce globally. It evolved from early web browsers to apps on your phone. Using the internet, Amazon transformed shopping. Others transformed data access and storage in the "cloud." This intersects with the utilization of satellites for phones, navigation, and more. Now consider artificial intelligence: Machine learning and AI are transforming industries from healthcare to finance to personal development to graphic design, with potential impacts we're only beginning to understand.

- Inns for Travelers to Hotels to AirBnB's—From ancient times, the practice of hospitality was in effect. Inns became popular in ancient Greece and Rome. In the 1800's, hotels began to gain momentum. In 2008, Airbnb was founded in San Francisco by Brian Chesky, Joe Gebbia, and Nathan Blecharczyk. The company's rapid growth began disrupting the traditional hotel industry and by 2016, Airbnb was a

---

4 Turo: the Uber Model for Rental Cars https://d3.harvard.edu/platform-rctom/submission/turo-the-uber-model-for-rental-cars/, Uber Issues a Major Challenge to Popular Car Rental App Turo https://www.thestreet.com/automotive/uber-issues-a-major-challenge-to-popular-car-rental-app-turo

major player in the accommodation industry, forcing hotels to adapt and innovate. This shift has caused the hotel industry to evolve, focusing more on personalized experiences, local authenticity, and unique offerings to compete with the new paradigm introduced by Airbnb and similar platforms.[5]

- And more…

There are many other industrious and reformational shifts worthy of mention but I will pause for now so that we can move on. The point is: these inventions were often met with skepticism or disbelief initially but went on to fundamentally reshape society, industry, and human capabilities. They demonstrate how fighting for growth can produce transformative technologies that emerge from seemingly impossible ideas.[6]

Every bit of change and reform is the result of questioning and challenging the norm. In the face of the old adage, "if it ain't broke don't fix it", the great John Maxwell says, "if it ain't broke, break it!." We have to keep pressing onward and upward to the call of God, not camping out in the past or stagnating in the present. Analysis and critique is key to innovation and progress, not to be vilified or resisted. We may know this, but change is still hard for humanity. That's why we need great humility and teachable hearts. We need eyes that see, ears that hear and hearts that understand what the Lord is doing and saying in our time. We need to perceive the new thing, reform our ways, and respond to His invitation.

---

5 The 100-Year Timeline of Hotel History | RMC Asia Blog https://www.educationaltravelasia.org/the-100-year-timeline-of-hotel-history/, Change in the Hospitality Industry: New Paradigms, Frames: https://www.bu.edu/bhr/2017/06/12/hospitality-change-paradigm-and-perspective/, How the hotel industry has changed over the past 20 years https://www.hotelmanagement.net/own/how-hotel-industry-has-changed-over-past-20-years

6 34 Industrial Revolution inventions that changed the world forever https://interestingengineering.com/lists/34-industrial-revolution-inventions-that-changed-the-world, 28 Industrial Revolution Inventions—Science | HowStuffWorks https://science.howstuffworks.com/innovation/inventions/5-industrial-revolution-inventions.htm

Prepare your hearts and minds to stand with me at the crossroads; to cry out for the ancient paths that lead to the rest of soul. Get ready for God's revelation of His growth paradigms that bring the expansion of His kingdom in and through your life. For such a time as this, we must fight forward into His purpose and plan. Let us return to our roots in Christ and progress toward maturity and fullness in Him, for this is the way.

Introduction

> *"I have one desire now—to live a life of reckless abandon for the Lord, putting all my energy and strength into it."*
> —Elisabeth Elliot

> *"The greatest issue facing the world today, with all its heartbreaking needs, is whether those who are identified as 'Christians' will become disciples—students, apprentices, practitioners—of Jesus Christ, steadily learning from Him how to live the life of the Kingdom of the Heavens into every corner of human existence."*
> —Dallas Willard —From "The Great Omission"

> *"Every church (believer) needs to be able to answer two questions: What is your plan for making disciples? Does your plan work?"*
> —Dallas Willard

Pause for a second and consider that there is a crying need for a new breed of "Christian" on the earth! And in fact, it's not so much new as it is going back to the roots of our faith and the ancient paths of the early church.

The scriptures and history describe "the good way that leads to rest of soul," the manner of life that is well pleasing and God glorifying— the reality and rhythm of what it means to be an authentic follower and lover of Christ. The early Church of disciples were a people who shook and shaped the world with the power of the gospel. They changed nations with their intentional pursuit of holiness and obedience to the mission of Christ; The vibrant witness of their lives that modeled God's transforming power and grace was undeniable and catalytic.

Every aspect of life and culture was touched by the power of the gospel through them. Historical records and the present work of God throughout the earth testify to the effect of a people rightly responding to Christ's call to follow Him. From the small seed, sown among a small band of disciples living under Roman occupation, grew a massive multiplying work that took over the known world. This global work continues to expand to this very day by the power of the Holy Spirit and through a people committed to Christ and His cause. That divine seed has irrepressible power to fulfill the divine purpose for which it was sent. We find ourselves in another critical time of history with massive opportunity. Today, the eyes of the Lord are looking to and fro for those who will answer the call to wholeheartedness and take their stand in Christ and the mission. For such a time as this we must rise and fight the fight of faith.

The world needs authentic disciples of Christ now more than ever:

- Spiritual warriors with a burning love for Jesus and holy jealousy for His glory and fame in the earth.
- Those who are wholly given to the mission of Christ to preach the good news and make disciples; to plant and establish new churches patterned after the early church as seen in the book of Acts.
- Willing kingdom servants, able to operate as change agents to radically reform the existing Church; to call her back to

the ancient paths and her apostolic roots to shake the world with the gospel.
- Believers who effectively and boldly engage in every sector of society—from education to arts and entertainment to business, media to government— in every arena, as the light and salt of the earth that demonstrate the wisdom and goodness of God.
- People who have applied themselves to the truth in authentic faith, who have overcome their own bondages in the grace of God, are walking in freedom, and are truly living for God's will.
- Those who have been healed from their wounds, to become transformational agents to set other people free—to ignite spiritual hunger, and call people into authentic devotion to Christ.

Not only do we need spiritual awakening and revival in our day and age that leads to another reformation and return to radical and authentic Christianity, the rumblings are happening. *There is a great reconstitution happening in the Body of Christ to bring forth purity of devotion and clarity of moral character and divine purpose.*

There must be a recovery of the faith and the knowledge of God, and from that place, a restored vision to change the world. The first commandment must be first and married to the new commandment of Christ to love each other as He has loved us. Then, together, we can faithfully and effectively fulfill the great commission to disciple the nations and prepare the earth for the Lord's return.

It is not enough to just gain our own freedom, have a restored faith, and blessing in the Lord. We must have a vision for the freedom of others in Christ and for righteousness and morality to dwell in our land, looking forward, with longing, to the final day of restoration when Christ returns. We must burn to reach the lost and labor in the grace of God for the salvation of those the Lord loves and for speedy justice in the earth. Jesus has an inheritance among the nations and we have the privilege to co-labor with Him to receive it by being salt and light in society. Jesus plans to partner with us to win a harvest of souls, provoke Israel to jealousy and repentance, and add them to His family, the Church, His Bride, before He comes.

Our mission is to bring heaven to earth as we wait and long for His appearance. Until He comes we are to occupy by being busy with the Lord's work as agents of God's goodness, justice, wisdom, and salvation in the earth. We have a divine assignment to preach, pray, disciple, and be given to good works.

Every believer in Christ has been given the ministry of the Spirit and the message of reconciliation so that Christ Himself can plead through us to the world around us to be reconciled to God![7] We are all called to be active participants in rebuilding ruined cities and the desolations of many generations. The vision is big—bigger than many have thought. We cannot abdicate nor delegate our divine responsibility to obey the great commission. Every mission and ambition of our lives is to be subservient to "the mission," all else is secondary.

We all are to preach the good news in every place and at all times with both the words we say and in the lives we live. Those who come to believe, as the result of our testimony and witness, are to be baptized and added into the family of God. Thus, they continue to grow as a disciple of Christ and share in the mission of gospel advancement.

God's method is incarnation. That means He has called *us* as His body, in whom He dwells by His Spirit, to reach the world! It's not someone else's job, it's our job. *Pause.* Say to yourself out loud, "He's talking to me."

---

7 2 Corinthians 5:20

Introduction

As Christ was sent into the world, so He has sent us.[8] Wow! He lives in us and through us and wants to live through YOU in greater ways to reach the world and build His Church. Are you up for the adventure?

Don't check out, keep reading, my friend.

There's a Problem

Yet we must also pause to consider the critical hour we live in. There's a major disconnect from the call of God, our biblical mission, and the state of many the Church in the west. And, maybe, in you. Many are failing to thrive in authentic love for God, walk in obedience to scripture, and become mature in the faith. Too few are making disciples as commanded and failing to impact their communities. So much of the body of Christ is irrelevant in culture and has abdicated her voice and authority to make a real difference.

Before I share some not so encouraging statistics, understand that I share these with great hope and as an invitation to you to be part of the solution for such a time as this. God is raising up a standard and this book is to help you in the battle plan of turning the tide in our generation.

Approximately 80% of believers today have never led someone to Christ and over 70% of believers in America have not shared their faith with someone in the last 6 months.[9] Even more alarming, of the 96% who believe it's part of their faith to be a witness for Jesus and the 94% that believe "the best thing that could happen to someone is for them to come to know Jesus.", 47% also said, "It is wrong to share one's personal beliefs with someone of a different faith in hopes that

---

8 John 17:18
9 Accessed 6/4/24, https://www.Christianpost.com/news/two-thirds-of-Christians-dont-know-methods-for-sharing-jesus.html

they will one day share the same faith."[10] Over HALF of Christian millennials believe evangelism is wrong!

Do you see the disconnect?

Culture is in crises because the church has been in crisis.

Part of the problem is that the church in many ways has lost her first love for Christ Himself. She has been enthralled and distracted by other things. Oh, how far we have fallen! Paradigms and practices have undermined the mission and aims of Christ from being central and first place in our lives and in many Christian communities.

Many studies and mission workers' testimonies have revealed a real lack in a sound biblical worldview that leads to effective living in truth. People don't know the scriptures or actually think biblically. Many believers, both young (as in new believers) and "mature" believers, truly lack submitted lives to the Lordship of Christ. There's a major disconnect from knowing and doing, thus they possess shallow devotion, prayerlessness, and dull hearts void of the continual transforming and sanctifying power of God.

Many of the saints lack the experiential knowledge of God and an exalted vision of Christ. More than not, much of the Church is like the "foolish virgins" of Matthew 25 who lack the costly oil of intimacy and the corresponding fear of the Lord that leads to obedience to His voice. So many lack wisdom in the effective practice of truth that's expressed in well-ordered lives, marriages, parenting, passing on the faith to their children, and biblical community engagement. Lastly, outreach and evangelism that is both consistent and evidencing the power of the Holy Spirit to win souls, change lives, and impact their communities is not the norm or a way of life. The traditions of men have eclipsed the methods of Christ and missed the point and

---

10 "Almost Half of Practicing Christian Millennials Say Evangelism Is Wrong," Barna, February 5, 2019, www.barna.com/research/millennials-oppose-evangelism.

priorities of God. Friends, we need to return to the ancient paths, hunger for more, press into maturity, desire true and lasting fruit, and embrace a better way!

We need to recover the ancient paths.

Jeff Reed, founder of BILD International (Biblical Institute of Leadership development) writes,

> "Even though we have seen the gospel expand around the world in the last 150 years, most movements of churches planted by Western, colonial missions fail to become strong churches. By the second generation there is a desperate lack of leadership. By the fourth generation, they suffer from significant nominalism. Even in America we are losing ground. If one carefully examines bodies of work such as those by George Barna, it is not farfetched to conclude that we are losing almost an entire generation of children who are growing up in our fundamentalist and evangelical homes—children who are not carrying on the faith. Parents consistently demonstrate a significant deficiency when it comes to being strong in the Scriptures and the ability to think, instruct, and guide their children in the faith, in this ever complex, postmodern, pluralist culture."[11]

Recent reports and surveys estimate that 35 million youth raised in Christian families will disaffiliate from Christianity by the year 2050. You should read that stat again! These reports project the "single largest generational loss of souls in history" and "It is the largest and fastest

---

11 Jeff Reed, "First principles Series" booklet, intro, (BILD International, Ames, Iowa, 2003) pg 6

numerical shift in religious affiliation in the history of this country." Just to maintain the status quo by 2050 in America, we would need to plant 215,000 new churches. The hour and time is urgent and the work is great! These stats are utterly startling and yet will become a reality if we don't embrace a massive shift and reorientation. We must move toward biblical truth, passion for Jesus, and focused missional advancement that's biblical in its philosophy and methods, and energized with the power of the Holy Spirit. We need revival, awakening, and reformation on so many levels.

I am hopeful in the face of these reports. I see and hear what the Lord is doing in both the realm of the Spirit as I pray, in what I see happening in my local community, and also in the regional and global networks to which I'm connected. God is on the move!

Even now, spontaneous outbreaks of God's presence are breaking into churches and college campuses across the nation such as Asbury University in Kentucky. At the time of writing this, what started as a handful of young people skipping class to worship Jesus has turned into a visitation from the Spirit of God where thousands have been gathering for weeks straight, day and night. Our community as well, in Windham, NH, is experiencing an incredible movement of God. We have been day and night around the clock for months in worship and prayer experiencing the love, power, and presence of God. People are meeting Jesus in beautiful ways, confessing and repenting of sin, being healed, delivered, and renewed in faith, hope, and love. We are being poised and in the budding beginnings of one of the greatest movements of the Spirit of God the earth has ever seen. We all are being prepared for what will be unprecedented! We're pressing in and hungry for more.

Here's one more example of the present global impact of the Holy Spirit from a ministry called CFaN (Christ for all Nations), doing extensive work in Africa. Daniel Kolenda writes in his newsletter February 2023:

INTRODUCTION

> "This April will be our first full Operation Decapolis Campaigns, which means 10, five-night crusades simultaneously happening in 10 different cities. That's a total of 50 crusade meetings – and all in just two weeks! This is what we have been building up to for the last couple of years, expanding our team, our equipment, and our expertise to meet the challenge.
>
> This is a strategy that works. In the past two years, CfaN has held 21 Decapolis Crusades across Africa. We have seen more than 2.7 million in attendance, with <u>956,980 documented salvations</u>. We are expecting this 10—city push to be the biggest Operation Decapolis yet. In faith, we are preparing our follow-up system (with the local churches) to handle over a million new converts. Isn't that exciting?"

Think about the magnitude of this—but also the intentional work of people given to the mission and cause of Christ to preach the gospel, shake the nations with the truth, plant churches, and make disciples. As it has always been in revival history, it was in dark and desperate times that awakening broke out to turn the tide for the souls of men, and raise up a new standard of the Lord in a generation. This critical hour provides a great opportunity for real missional advancement for the heart and soul of a generation. This massive disaffiliation trend over the next 30 years actually represents the largest missional opportunity in U.S. history. We need to get focused and let the love of God grip us deeply, so that we are compelled by His love to not only live wholly for Him but to be given to His mission. You were born for such a time as this!

Society and all its institutions need reformation and the sweet influence of the Kingdom of God. Do you agree? God's plan and primary agent of grace and transformation in the earth is His people, the Church—who, being blessed by Him in every way, should bless and serve the world around them. What a calling!

This is for every believer and not a select few "professionals." The body of Christ is to be the light of the world and the salt of the earth. He gave us His precious Spirit, the Holy Spirit, to dwell with us and to endow us with power to be His witnesses and fulfill His mission![12] It's my passion to inspire and equip God's people for the works of service to which they are called and help them grow up to full spiritual maturity—to the fullness of Christ.

I'm a worshiping warrior, a lover of God and a disciple of Christ. I am on a mission to raise up warriors, authentic disciples, and transformational leaders: people who love God with their whole heart, who have the passion and ability to advance His cause in the earth with authenticity, character, Holy Ghost power, and excellence in their skill and craft. I'm talking about raising up adults and children, families & communities (churches), who are the real deal; transformational agents that effectively fulfill the great commission born out of the great commandment, who will do so wherever they are in life with whatever He has placed in their hands.

I want Jesus to receive the reward of His suffering among the nations. How about you? Are you with me?

We are called to occupy until Christ comes and to bear much fruit for His glory.

Are you in?

Let's keep reading.

---

12 Acts 1:8

Introduction

The Mission

The mission of every true believer in Christ is to be faithful to Him and fully participate in the mission of Christ; to love Him as biblically defined and to make disciples of all people, teaching them to obey, live, and practice everything the Lord has commanded us. The bottom line is that we are called to *know Him* and *make Him known,* to walk with Him personally and intimately, to participate in His mission to win souls and make disciples alongside our brothers and sisters in the Lord. We are to apprentice under Jesus, personally and collectively as a community.

I understand that some readers may have a hard time conceptualizing this in light of their present manner of life. How would this look in our day and age, and in light of the possible lack of solid examples? We know there has been so much hypocrisy, dead religion, and ineffective churches that are not producing authentic disciples of Christ. My heart genuinely grieves over this, but, there are also sincere, beautiful, authentic believers who affectionately love God, and are living consistent godly lives. There are churches that have woken up (not "woke") and returned (or are returning) to a biblical faith, authentic community, and missional living to change the world.

There is hope for restoring the witness and credibility of the Christian community, enabling it to effectively fulfill the Great Commission, which springs from the Great Commandment to love the Lord our God with all our being. Read that sentence again and take it in.

He's calling you to be part of this.

We are in radical times and the Lord is restoring the radical roots of what it means to be an authentic disciple of Christ.

As you read, I want you to understand that I aim to address your heart and the divine purpose and calling that every follower of Jesus Christ carries, regardless of your life role or status. I urge you to get out of the box and entrapments of religious thinking and the confines of "four walls." I want you to be free to be who you really are in Christ, to go into the places of your influence, passion, and gifting in culture to make an eternal impact.

For example, I am a pastor and senior church leader, a husband and father of 5 children. I am blessed with the opportunity and joy of impacting lives, spreading the gospel, and creating disciples in unconventional ways. Serving as a high performance and breakthrough coach, wellness pro, competitor, performer, and educator, I have been able to reach people and institutions who would not go to church or affiliate with something "religious" in fields such as martial arts, wellness and mental health, fitness, performing arts, and life empowerment.

That's the point. We have to be intentional and unconventional in our approach, without violating the truth and our character, to reach the people around us. Without building the bridges of relationship with those outside the faith in the context of our life, we can't expect people to just come to us in our church services. We have to become skillful fishers of men. Apostle Paul said, "I have become all things to all people so that by all possible means I might save some. I do all this for the sake of the gospel, that I might share in its blessing."[13] What a freeing, exciting way to live in the adventure of advancing the Kingdom of God! God wants to use us, use you, to bring the gift of Christ, reaching those in need. God uses the gifts He gave you to manifest His glory, bless humanity through service and good works, and extend an offer of both eternal salvation and abundant life to those around you!

We're all called in a unique way, with unique gifts, with unique assignments to fulfill on the earth. It is in the context of making

---

13 1 corinthians 9:22-23

INTRODUCTION

disciples that our gifts, abilities, and passions find the fullness of their meaning and purpose. This is the grand mission and obedience to God! The scriptures say, we were created in Christ for pre-ordained good works[14]. Doesn't that sound fun? No matter your cultural background, professional field, or age, you are called to work in service of God's Kingdom and purpose; to be a faithful witness for the Lord, and to energetically participate in spreading the faith, creating followers of Jesus in all corners, starting with your own household.

The command was "*as you are going*, make disciples...." This means that you don't have to leave where you are and what you're doing to venture into a remote jungle to reach an unreached people group in order to walk out the great commission. Some of you may be called to do that, but most of you are surrounded by unreached people in your homes, neighborhoods, workplaces, sports teams, classrooms, schools, Dojos, gyms, even in your churches. You simply need to lift up your eyes and see the harvest in front of you. It's simple, understand your role and purpose in the grace of God, and get to work. Those without Christ, matter to God and they should matter to us! Historic preacher and revivalist Charles Spurgeon said, "Every Christian is either a missionary or an imposter." To love Christ is to love people and stay on mission. His mission.

You were made for this mission, made to express the goodness of God on the earth—no matter where you are or what you're doing. Your circle of influence is your field of favor and a fishing hole for the gospel. This book will enlarge your vision to make an eternal impact on the world around you, remove "boxes" that compartmentalize your faith and mission, and inspire fresh action.

His mission is two-fold: He is forming His life on the inside of you, and He is advancing His life across the earth through you. We actively participate in both aspects through our faith, surrender, and

---
14 Ephesians 2:10

obedience. We must live as authentic disciples who are continually being transformed into His likeness, and we must be intentional about sharing His good news and making disciples of others.

The Path

My heart and passion is to know Christ intimately and be faithful and pleasing to Him in every way. But I'm also eager to help believers grow to full maturity in Christ and reach the potential He's called them to. All while ensuring we pass down a living and vibrant faith to the next generation, which includes raising our kids.

It's the principle *path* or *way* of development that is key to the success of the mission. The process for change and how people are trained and equipped matters. The right things applied in the wrong way become the wrong things and don't produce the right outcomes. You catch that?

The "HOW" we do it is just as important as "WHAT" we are doing and "WHY" we need to do it. The process of development and discipleship should not be random and haphazard, but intentionally designed with the end in mind. God can use anything and move in the midst of our weak attempts, but there is a better path that we should pursue.

Many parents, pastors, and educators of all kinds fail to have an ordered, strategic, and well integrated discipleship process. We need one that is holistic, relational, and effective in producing authentic disciples who love God and live in the freedom of the gospel. Those who have the fruit of wholesome lifestyles that actually adorn the gospel and are effective in the mission of advancing it. Many leaders and parents lack a clear vision of the outcomes to seek and what it truly means to apprentice or follow Christ in today's world.

INTRODUCTION

If we are not producing fruit of biblical proportion then we need to re-evaluate our own lives and faith and what we are reproducing. We need to grow and transform to become and foster disciples who embody Christ's likeness, of whom "the world is not worthy of; a people who turn the world upside down»[15]—those who radically change society through God's love and power, and who inspire and multiply others to do the same. Like the Apostles and disciples of the early church, we are to continue in the way and ministry of Jesus Christ as seen in the book of Acts.

Nothing has changed in terms of normal Christianity and what is expected of every one of us who trusts in Christ. Our internal bond with Jesus must manifest in an outward flow that looks like personal transformation, virtue and moral goodness, a disciplined life, and a brilliant, bold, active witness of the gospel to those around us, displaying all the Lord's grace, goodness, power, and hospitality.

In this book, we will weave between two realms: both influencing people to win them to Christ in your unique positions in life, as well as the process and educational path of discipling those who respond to the gospel, are in the faith, or are being raised in your household. How someone is established in the truth, trained, and prepared for life and mission is essential. Our methodologies should be effective to produce the fruit of transformed lives who are fully equipped to effectively serve. Our approach to training or mentoring people must result in authentic followers and lovers of Christ who are becoming more and more like Him in every way, or we are missing it!

We cannot afford to stay in spiritual infancy or extended adolescence. We need mature men and women of God who can change the world as faithful witnesses of Jesus Christ. We must live lives worthy of the gospel that inspire the next generation to want to serve the God that they can clearly see in our lives. We must lead by example. We must

---

15 Hebrews 11:38, Acts 17:6

fight to build our lives and the Kingdom of God rightly according to His word. As Nehemiah exhorted the people, we must not be afraid of our enemies, but remember the Lord, who is great and awesome. It's time to fight for your brothers, your sons and daughters, your wives and your homes.[16]

When biblical discipleship happens in the way the Scriptures actually instruct us, it produces good, lasting fruit, and a people who authentically love God; who live according to His word, and positivity change their world to the glory of God. When we live in alignment with God's kingdom, things work as they should and advance to the glory of God.

His ways are perfect and He always leads us in triumph, so we can press on in hope.

The Path is Holistic

Some of what we'll cover in the book is holistic development that thoroughly equips people to wholly love God, become like Him, and fulfill their life's calling in the abundance He's given. In essence, it is the biblical call to discipleship— to authentically apprentice Jesus in an integrated way alongside His people.

This process of training, education, and development has to be more than words and knowledge transferred in a classroom. It must be comprehensive, relational, grounded in practice and adherence, ultimately lifelong. It should be intentionally designed with the essential knowledge, character and skill development, and key experiences that foster wisdom and obedience to God through

---

[16] Nehemiah 4:14-15 —this passage is a call to not be intimidated and shrink back from the work God had called the people of God to in rebuilding the walls of Jerusalem. The call to fight and continue to build protective walls in the city was for the sake of God's people's purpose. We are in such a time of contending for our families and for future generations in the purposes of God for America.

every season of life. When we understand God's ways and how He sovereignly develops people over time, we learn to cooperate with His principles, processes, and presence, and teach others to do the same. This is the art of skillful living, born out of the fear of the Lord and sincere love for God.

This *holistic and Christ -centered approach to education and discipleship* is a matrix of formation that ought to be intentionally oriented toward the *presence of God and the mission of God. It has intrinsic and extrinsic factors, internal formation and external expression. We need to teach what it means to be with and abide in God,* while also teaching productivity in life and with the knowledge of Him (fruitful in the knowledge of God). These developmental discipleship aims should be played out in the *context of family and authentic biblical community (the local Church) in a spirit of worship and prayer.* That's a lot of terminology so let's briefly break that down for a moment:

- The *educational/discipleship* approach is the overall process and framework (wineskin) of passing on the faith and bringing believers to fullness and maturity in Christ. The faith is more than just biblical doctrinal statements. *It's a way of life*—a life architected and oriented around *knowing God, becoming like Him, and doing what He has called us to do.* The aim is conformity to the image and nature of Christ—living in the *new man*—formed in us and expressed through us.

- The transformative power and our source of life, joy, peace, righteousness, true knowledge, wisdom, and change, is found in *the presence of God,* specifically through the Holy Spirit, whom we also refer to as God with us. This divine presence is where we direct our attention and find our delight. All real growth comes from Him. Believers must learn to fellowship with Him in all things! We only actually "know" God experientially through fellowship with God, the Holy Spirit and His word. In every aspect of our lives and in all our endeavors, it is essential to recognize God, welcome His presence, and develop a deep sensitivity to the guidance of His Spirit. Intimacy with God should be the aim of our life and education. By remaining firmly connected to Christ, the Head, and dwelling in His teachings through the communion of the Holy Spirit, we will experience the growth that originates from God (Col 2:17-23). We must master beholding Him by the Spirit and honoring His presence in our lives. He is the one always working *in* us to will and do according to His good pleasure. He uses all things for good to conform us to His image (Philippians 2:13, Romans 8:28-29). God is omnipresent and in us as born again believers. Beyond this, there is also a reality of the tangible felt sense of God's presence that inhabits the places He is welcomed. The mystery of the Church is that we are His temple and God literally dwells among us by His Spirit (Eph 2:19-22). His Spirit of Truth leads us into all truth. We want Believers to be able to know, discern, fellowship with, and accommodate His presence wherever they are. Plus, to do the works we are called to do in this life requires the power and presence of God. We must learn to participate with His presence in reaching the world around us. The Kingdom of God is power and not mere talk.[17]

- *This is the spirit of worship and prayer:* the centrality of our focus and aim in life is to know, please, and Honor God in all things by abiding in the sweet fellowship of the Spirit. Our union with God is expressed through a life of prayer and devotion; a continual loving acknowledgement of His presence. We seek to foster a culture of such devotion and delight in His presence. We want to cultivate a soul

---

[17] 1 Corinthians 4:20

orientation that learns to behold Him in all things, at all times, and in all aspects of life. When our lives are oriented on pleasing God, we engage in devotional acts like singing, creating music for the Lord, expressing gratitude, offering praise, meditating on the Bible, and studying scriptures, along with other spiritual expressions. These disciplines align our hearts and minds to truly see and appreciate the Lord and the truth He embodies; through this beholding, we are transformed into what we admire. We become what we behold. Discipleship should center around both the personal and community experience of gazing upon and worshiping the Lord. Education without Christ at the center is humanistic.

- The context of *authentic biblical community* is that true believers are not an island nor can they serve God in truth apart from the rest of His Body, the Church. The believer is baptized into one body and one Spirit, one hope, one Lord, one faith one baptism; one God and Father of all, who is over all and through all and in all (Eph 4:4-6). The family of God is God's inheritance and mission in itself; but it is also His plan and design for the advancement of His mission on the earth. The Church has been given the responsibility to make disciples and pass on the faith as the foundation of the truth. Biblical discipleship that produces the right kind of results (fruit) cannot be carried out apart from the community of believers. God's plan to express His love that both transforms us into His likeness and reveals His glory to the world is accomplished through deep, open-hearted familial relationships in the local church. "By this, the world will know that you are my disciples and that I truly came from my Father, that you love one another and walk together being perfectly united."(John 13:35, 17:23). One of the mysteries and incredible realities of the Family of God is that we actually experience God in Christian community as we learn to love and serve one another with the very love and gifts of Christ at work within us. Christ lives in us and expresses Himself through us; Christ is incarnate in Christian community and thus central to the discipleship process. Together, by what each joint supplies, we grow into the fullness of Christ. The Church is called to reveal His manifold wisdom and bear witness to His name till the end of the age. We do this by walking together in Holy Spirit unity, embodying the oneness that Jesus prayed for in John 17 at a local and regional level. The Church is central to His heart and plan. Every believer must be vitally a part of Christian community and an active participant in the mission of the church. Holistic education and discipleship happens in this relational context.

I hope you can see that we need the Spirit and power of God fueling our growth and formation (for that's where transformation comes from). We need the truth and instruction of the scriptures training and equipping us for both right living and effective service. It's essential for us to belong in a community where we find accountability, love, support, and role models. Within this setting, we experience God in greater ways as we both serve and grow. The scriptures are God breathed. They are useful for teaching, rebuking, correcting, and training in righteousness and for equipping us for every good work (2 Tim 3:16-17). The living community of believers must properly model the faith expressed in love and the Spirit's power and to vocationally apprentice people for fruitful life work. The scripture tells us to consider the faith of our leaders and those that have gone before us and to look at the outcome of their faith, because it is about a *way* of life that is learned and lived.[18] The local community is an untapped gold mine of knowledge, skill, wisdom, resource, creativity and life experience.

---

18 Hebrews 13:7-8

Introduction

It's time to rediscover God's design for His people and embrace a new wineskin. The Church is a presence-centered family on mission. It is a living supernatural reproducing organism, a living temple inhabited by the Spirit of God. It is not a business and mere hierarchical institution or organization. It's a divinely ordered household wired to reproduce godly offspring (disciples) and fill the earth with the knowledge of God.

When it comes to training and discipleship, the old wineskins of education and teaching are ineffective and unbiblical. They are rooted in the simple transfer of knowledge and doctrinal truth fragmented from the other domains of knowledge and life, separated from a biblical worldview and detached from real life application and community. Christian education and the great commission need to embrace a new, fully integrated paradigm to effectively fulfill God's plan and express His wisdom to the powers of the air and the watching world. To raise up a generation of authentic believers who can impact the world with the gospel, we need to carefully consider HOW we are doing things. It's time to rediscover our radical roots in Christ.

Whether in a classroom, on a sports field, around the dinner table or in a small church group, we must connect the life lessons and insights we share with kingdom principles, the bigger picture of God's plan and will for us. The sad present reality is that most in the Church cannot do that. I believe this is partly due to how they were taught. It's been one dimensional, not holistic. We must become influencers and leaders who can shepherd people well. We must guide others into the experiential knowledge of God and the whole counsel of His word. Failure to do so could result in people who are nearsighted, deficient in truth, and susceptible to today's deceptive philosophies. Knowledge must become understanding and understanding must become wisdom.

When it comes to training people in the faith and mentoring them in life, we need to move towards apprenticeships and skill development from a relational context. Yet, also getting to the matters of the heart and fostering encounters with God, devotional lifestyles, and fascination with Christ. When we nurture and train people holistically it will lead to deep change from the inside out.

Our goal should be helping people connect from the heart to God, spiritual and relational impartation, and life transformation. This looks like life on life mentoring and equipping. It's inner healing and deliverance, character formation, and helping people identify and focus on their God given purpose, assignments, and active participation in the overall mission of Christ.

This approach is about coming alongside each other in the church to be disciples of Christ Himself, so that together we are embodying the truth we are declaring and passing on. We have to be able to bring together all the pieces of our activities and knowledge so that the big picture of God's plan and people's unique purpose and role in it becomes clear. People who can SEE this clearly can give themselves to it with wholehearted conviction. Without personal ownership of the truth and plan, we can't grow and be transformed, nor walk together in unity of purpose.

But It starts with you.

We are returning to wisdom-based models of education, embedded in the life and mission of the local Church, rooted in Christ. These are loaded statements that may not mean anything to you yet, but keep reading to learn more.

Wisdom Based Education

Wisdom based education is transformative, affecting the entirety of a person's being and productivity. It fosters a maturity of character and love with corresponding skills and competence necessary to perform well in its given objective. And, it can reproduce itself in others. It's the art of skillful living and the pursuit of both mastery and excellence. The results of such education should cause people to be confident in who they are and who their God is. Plus, it develops the skills to effectively serve and prosper in every area of life for kingdom impact. Sounds amazing right? It should!

Have you been discipled and taught in this way? Are you leading and teaching others this way? If not, you are not alone. Many have never been educated or discipled in this way. But it's time for a change—time to return to the ancient paths revealed in the word of God; to learn to walk in it effectively for ourselves, our children, and all those God has appointed for us to serve, influence, and disciple.

The time is now.

Billy Humphrey posted this online, and I fully agree: "We have been educated beyond our level of obedience, and this must stop." The gap between knowing and doing is being closed in this new era in the body of Christ. It's a new day and new season, so let's get started and raise up warriors!

When someone has been properly trained and has a real understanding of something they should also be able to teach others at some level (I understand that teaching is also a skill to be developed and a grace given by God). This is exactly what Jesus did with the twelve who followed Him. He gave us the model to follow. They were properly trained and then commissioned to go and do the same. To teach others in the way you have been taught, to produce particular outcomes is a test of true comprehension, competence, and obedience. This is our stewardship as Christians. We must pass on the deposit and entrust *the way* and truth to faithful people.

As a martial artist, teaching is also essential to the learning process to internalize and further understand technique. It is also an expectation for a black belt to pass on what he has learned—in other words, to go make apprentices. At the heart of the art is the responsibility to reproduce the stewardship we have been taught and benefitted from. It's also at the heart of our faith as Christians. We have a stewardship to give, even multiply, what we have received from God. Freely we have received, and freely we are to give and go into all the world to make disciples; to go love as we have been loved by Him.

In a similar manner, scripture guides families and the household of God. Fathers and mothers are called to teach their children. Older adults are called to teach younger ones to live pleasing to God, faithfully carry out their roles, and to maintain orderly households.

Wisdom based education speaks to the manner and skill sets in which we need to live well. It speaks to obedience and effective implementation of truth. We see that how to live, speak, act, and think were modeled and taught in a relational context. This type of teaching is not simply relaying the right facts and information. It is the facilitation of obedience. It's unto flourishing and fruitfulness in the lives and families we serve and influence.

When it comes to training other leaders in the church, we are instructed to find the faithful people we are to entrust the faith to who can teach and will be able to train others (2 Tim 2:2).

The strategy has not changed and will not change until the end of the age. We must identify leaders, develop leaders, and deploy them into action.

When people are properly trained and discipled, both their Church community and their other relationships benefit from the beauty and power of that person's identity in Christ. Proper equipping obliterates the problems of spiritual superficiality, moral depravity, broken homes, and ineffective mission efforts that leave society unchanged by the gospel.

INTRODUCTION

When it comes to training and discipling others, we need to think *quality* over quantity in the pursuit of transformation. As John Mark Comer said in his book *Practicing the Way,* "Transformation is possible if we are willing to arrange our lives around the practices, rhythms, and truths that Jesus himself did, which will open our lives to God's power to change. Said another way, we can be transformed if we are willing to apprentice ourselves to Jesus."[19]

The informal and formal training processes that forge spiritual warriors and authentic disciples are what we want to consistently implement for our children, our churches, and those we lead. We need to first be disciples of Christ who make disciples who teach others to continue the work of making disciples. You catch that? Sustainable and lasting fruit is built through the wisdom of obedience to the Lord's command to make disciples. You and I are called to do this no matter where we are in the world. In doing so, we are to use all the gifts, abilities, passions, hobbies, and opportunities God provides.

God knows we need to become and raise up mature and competent believers, both young and old. Those who can positively change the world, effectively fulfill the great commission, who will ready the earth for the coming of the Lord! God is raising up a standard in the earth and you are invited to be a part of it!

> "The solution to our ineffectiveness as churches *(and as believers)* involves following a clear and uncomplicated way to train people to be spiritually mature, fully devoted followers of Christ, and then in turn having those disciples make more disciples."[20]

---

[19] John Mark Comer, *"Practicing the way : be with Jesus, become like him, do as he did"*, Colorado Springs : WaterBrook, 2024, pg 16
[20] Robert Coleman, Jim Putnam, and Bobby Harrington—"Discipleshift: 5 Steps to help your church make disciples who make disciples", pg 22)

Wisdom based education does not leave the student with knowledge and "know how" but no action. It leads to a productive life in the plan and will of God, skillfully lived out in vibrant faith, a living hope and sincere love.

As we will talk about later, this type of education must take a holistic approach and integrate knowing, being, and doing goals in a reflective and practiced based learning process. Check out the image below to try to visualize it.

Introduction

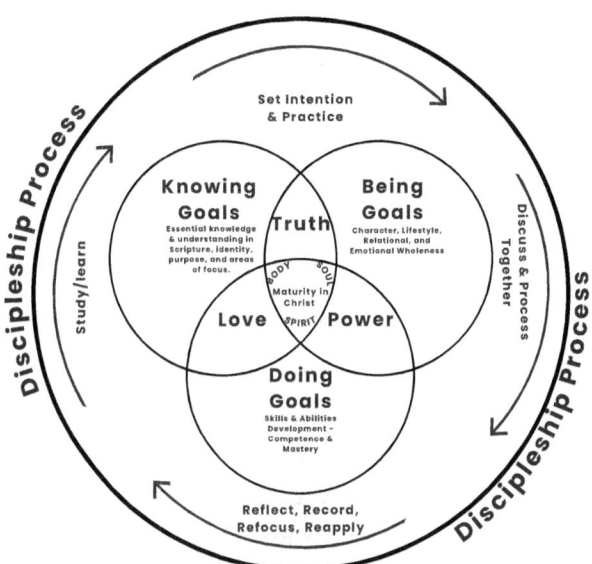

Daniel and The Next Generation

Our obligation and biblical call is to raise up and pass on the faith to the next generation. This must be a constant concern now, for our future and for the Church's future. We act on a multigenerational vision, knowing that youth can understand the deep and profound things of God's heart. In fact, they are hungry for it. We see people like Daniel and the Young David in scriptures who said, "Since my youth, God, you have taught me, and to this day I declare your marvelous deeds."(Psalms 71:17 NIV). It is time to get a conviction for what God will do in the hearts of the youth; to know that God has called us to nurture and raise up the next generation. There has been a major assault and agenda to pervert and destroy our children and youth and, therefore, our future.

We must engage the next generation and immerse them in the things and reality of God! Oh, may He encounter them and raise them up!

Consider these few scriptures:

- "For He established a testimony in Jacob and appointed a law in Israel, which He commanded our fathers to teach to their children, that the coming generation would know them—even children yet to be born—to arise and tell their own children that they should put their confidence in God, not forgetting His works, but keeping His commandments. Then they will not be like their fathers, a stubborn and rebellious generation, whose heart was not loyal, whose spirit was not faithful to God."—Psalm 78:5-8 (BSB)

- "Hear, O Israel: The LORD our God, the LORD is One. And you shall love the LORD your God with all your heart and with all your soul and with all your strength. These words I am commanding you today are to be upon your hearts. And you shall teach them diligently to your children and speak of them when you sit at home and when you walk along the road, when you lie down and when you get up. Tie them as reminders on your hands and bind them on your foreheads. Write them on the doorposts of your houses and on your gates....In the future, when your son asks, "What is the meaning of the decrees and statutes and ordinances that the LORD our God has commanded you?" then you are to tell him, "We were slaves of Pharaoh in Egypt, but the LORD brought us out of Egypt with a mighty hand. Before our eyes the LORD inflicted great and devastating signs and wonders on Egypt, on Pharaoh, and on all his household. But He brought us out from there to lead us in and give us the land that He had sworn to our fathers. And the LORD commanded us to observe all these statutes and to fear the LORD our God, that we may always be prosperous and preserved, as we are to this day. And if we are careful to observe every one of these commandments before the LORD our God, as He has commanded us, then that will be our righteousness."- Deuteronomy 6:4-9, 20-25 (BSB)

- "Children, obey your parents in the Lord, for this is right. "Honor your father and mother" (which is the first commandment with a promise), "that it may go well with you and that you may have a long life on the earth." Fathers, do not provoke your children to wrath; instead, bring them up in the discipline and instruction of the Lord."— Ephesians 6:1-4 (BSB)

Jesus prayed for the generations. He understood the seed of His life would be multiplied through the ages via the message and lives of His disciples: "For them I sanctify Myself, so that they too may be sanctified by the truth. I am not asking on behalf of them alone, but also on behalf of those who will believe in Me through their message, that all of them may be one, as You, Father, are in Me, and I am in You. May they also be in Us, so that the world may believe that You sent Me." -John 17:19-21(BSB)

There are many more New Testament passages on the role of older men and women in the church and what they are to teach younger men and women (Titus 2:1:-9). They outline what mature believers are to demonstrate in their families, to provide the rest of the church a model to follow (1 Timothy 3, 5, Titus 1). This emphasis to the next generation is not for the select few "called to youth." It's a community-wide responsibility and a call to fathers, mothers and mature older people. We must have a multigenerational vision.

So here's the deal. I'm passionate about training and inspiring the people of God to do everything for the Glory of God—to live worthy of the gospel. I want to see the people of God, achieving excellence in what they're called to do in life, making lasting kingdom impact where they serve, uncompromising in their devotion to God, and exercising leadership that effectively transforms the world around them. I'm not just talking about training adults and parents, but also young adults, teenagers, and children as well! Young people are always the catalyst for revival!

Discipleship and spiritual formation start when we're young and for our own children, even before they are born (it's so powerful to parent with a prayerful, intentional focus to disciple our kids). There's nothing like seeing young people with real passion for Jesus shake the world and lay down their lives to advance God's Kingdom! We need to coach and empower our youth to be warriors—authentic disciples who boldly impact the world for Christ, not merely coexisting in the flow and status quo of culture!

In the day of God's power, His people will volunteer freely and the youth will be to Him like the dew of the morning (Psalm 110). Daniel was brought into Babylonian captivity when he was young. He shone as an excellent one, being 10 times better than his contemporaries. He modeled excellence in body, soul, and spirit, both in his personal life and in his oversights. He lived a consecrated life before God and refused to compromise or defile himself. He arose at a critical time to bring forth the wisdom of God to those he served. He did so faithfully his entire life *from the days of his youth*. He modeled both the power of a supernatural life expressed through faithful and excellent service.

Introduction

He made a lasting and eternal impact on those he served in the darkest of times. He was wise and strong, knew His God and did mighty exploits! We need such people today that are both wise and strong in the Lord's might and ready to do the work of the Kingdom of God. These are warriors- disciples of Jesus Christ. Are you in?

His testimony still serves and inspires us today as a model of eternal impact wherever we're stationed, while living in uncompromised devotion. He was a captive from youth of an invaded and conquered land. Yet he rose to become one of the most powerful and influential leaders over the provinces and wise men of Babylon. Wow! Daniel was a transformational leader and His training started in childhood. Lord, help us to raise up Daniels!

Part of my mission is to be such a leader and to raise them up. If you choose to continue to read this, then you share my aspiration to be everything God intended for you and to faithfully raise up the next generation. I'm not talking about something presumptuous or grandiose but simply the biblical mandate for every believer to be salt and light wherever they are. We are called to make a lasting and eternal impact on the world around us no matter what we are doing; We are called to be "fishers of men." We do this by good works, authentically living our faith, and sharing the gospel message. And also by intentionally entering into relationships with others to help them know and follow Jesus, become like Him, and join His mission. It's a full and continuous cycle that reproduces itself. We must wholly rediscover this ancient path in order to become and raise up disciples and warriors who can shake and shape the world. You and I are called to bear fruit that remains.

There are many other biblical heroes that express a similar ethos as Daniel that may resonate more with you. I encourage you not to check out or say to yourself. "I'm not trying to raise up "transformational leaders or warriors…I just want to be the best I can be before God and raise up my kids to love God, be good people, and do what they are called to do in life." That's good, but there is more for the Believer and follower of Jesus Christ!

All leadership starts with self leadership; We must start with ourselves. But from there we are all called to make a positive impact on those around us. This starts at home and works out into our other relationships and places of influence.

The call to make disciples is for every believer. You and I have to wrestle with this until we have been submitted and subdued by its truth and decide to fully orient our lives and priorities around this purpose. If you want to answer the call to intimately know and follow Jesus, to become His disciple, then you must also be ready to share the gospel and make disciples as He has commanded us. This is an amazing and sacred charge—take it seriously!

Part of the problem in today's culture is an incomplete gospel that makes no demands on its people, a gospel of cheap grace void of the cost of discipleship. To believe in Christ means to be His disciple, to follow Him, to radically change and be transformed, to repent (change the way we think and behave), and live for His will and not our own.

As Dietrich Bonhoeffer said, "When Christ calls a man, He bids Him come and die."[21] Christ Himself wants to live through us to reach the world. This requires a surrendered life lived by reliance upon the power of His Spirit and grace.

Do you hear Him calling you?

We all long to make meaningful contributions in life. We were made to serve others and add value at the highest level. We were made to live a life of significance, leave a purposeful legacy, do what's right and pleasing to God, and live a full and well spent life. We all want to be

---

21 Dietrich Bonhoeffer, "*The Cost of Discipleship*", Touchstone, First published 1937

found faithful in the end. This cry and core motivation is in the heart of all of us, whether it's only a whisper in you now or an all consuming shout.

You were made for more and made to do things that have eternal significance and lasting impact in the here and now. You are called to be a warrior, a disciple, who like Christ, came to destroy the works of darkness, set captives free, and raise up authentic disciples who Glorify God by the life that they live and by the works they produce. Do you agree?

If so, say aloud with me, "YES AND AMEN!"

He chose us in Christ, He chose you....will you answer the call and follow wherever He may lead?

This great task and adventure await us!

Read on!

PAUSE. CAPTURE. APPLY - Prompts to help you process

This is your first prompt section, congratulations! I know it was just the introduction, but it was hefty. Answer the following prompts the best you can without getting bogged down.

1. What specific insights or concepts from this chapter resonated with you the most? Why do you think these stood out to you?

_____

_____

_____

2. How can you practically apply the principles discussed in this chapter to your daily life, relationships, or ministry? Identify at least one actionable step you can take this week.

_____

_____

_____

3. What potential challenges or barriers might you face in implementing these concepts? How can you overcome them?

_____

_____

_____

4. What are 3-5 quotes or points from this chapter that capture the essence of what it's communicating? Write them down.

_____

_____

_____

_____

_____

5. How can you involve your family, small group, or church community in the practices and principles outlined in this chapter? What steps can you take to foster a culture of discipleship and transformation within your circle of influence?

_____

_____

_____

6. Spend a few moments in prayer, asking God for the wisdom, strength, and courage to live out the truths you've learned. Write down a commitment or a prayer that reflects your desire to grow as an authentic disciple and transformational leader to impact the world.

_____

_____

_____

CHAPTER 1

For Such a Time as this!

"For if you remain silent at this time, relief and deliverance for the Jews will arise from another place, but you and your father's family will perish. And who knows but that you have come to your royal position for such a time as this?"

Esther 4:14

It is for such an hour of history that we were born. Extraordinary times call for extraordinary measures— and an extraordinary people. We live in a unique time of history, unprecedented in many ways, though we've seen similar historical patterns and critical junctures. God is shaking the nations and the Church in profound ways. He is readying His people for the greatest harvest of souls to come to faith in Christ as we have never seen throughout history. The world is our field to influence with the gospel, even more so now than ever before. Globalization and technology have put the world at our fingertips. With this kind of access, the question before us stands with an invitation: who will be about the work of the Kingdom, leveraging the opportunities before us for the love of Christ and the work of the gospel? Who is going to live for that which is eternal rather than temporal? Who's going to use their influence and catch the vision to develop influence for the cause of Christ?

Jesus said it Himself, the work is great but the laborers are few! Jesus said, "pray to the Lord of the harvest to send forth laborers." We need to do so and pray, and do our part to prepare our lives so that we can be useful in His hand.

I love what revivalist John Wesley said, " Give me a hundred people who desire nothing but God and fear nothing but sin, and I'll change the world." We need to understand that the world is not changed necessarily by many but by a few. Dawson Trotman said, "God can do more with one man who is one hundred percent dedicated to Him than with a hundred men who are only ninety percent." God is raising up consecrated people who burn with holy love, who are fully given to Him and His purposes in the earth. He's raising up warriors, authentic disciples, lovers of God; A people fashioned and forged for such a time as this.

Are you one of those people?

Will you be?

Will you follow Christ for real? Will you live a life worthy of the gospel? Worthy of your calling? A life aligned with the truth of scripture and the teachings of Christ and His Apostles?

This is the only way. To be what the scriptures call Christians or followers of "the Way" is to be a people on mission, called to change the world! Nothing less.

It is a noble and beautiful way but also a countercultural way, a supernatural way; a way of love, truth, and power.

The scriptures invite us into such a life, empowered by His Spirit, a life in which you and I become a people in whom the world is not worthy. We are called to be shining lights in the midst of a crooked and perverse generation.[22] We are called to be both bold and meek people who know their God—who do great things for both the Kingdom of God and the welfare of all.

In the complexity and turbulence of our day and age, a glorious Church must arise endowed with the wisdom of God, the power of God, and the love of God. It is time to take our place in life and culture to reach and speak into the people, families, communities, institutions, and industries we influence. This is our call and it's for such a time as this.

Many nations, including America, hang in the balance. We need you to arise and take your place in the story as part of the answer, right where you are.

The context and landscape of society is set for a fresh apostolic and authentic expression of the faith. The world, especially in the west, has had a poor representation of Jesus, the Church, and the gospel message of Jesus Christ. We have an opportunity to re-image and rightly represent the truth. The Lord must have a new and authentic witness, rightly expressed before the watching world. And you've been invited.

God will act in our generation for His own Name's sake, and He will establish a testimony for Himself! God will shine forth from among a glorious people—His Bride, His Family, His Church.

You in?

God is raising up an army, a Gideon's three hundred type, set apart to do His will and liberate the nations from the deceptive and oppressive powers of satanic forces.

---

22 Eph 4:1, Phil 1:27-30, 2:12-16, Heb 11:38

I can hear the sound of "dry bones rattling" and the scripture from the prophet Isaiah, heralding, *"Arise and shine your light has come and the glory of the Lord has risen upon you. See darkness covers the earth and thick darkness is over the peoples, but the Lord rises upon you and His glory appears over you. Nations will come to your light, and kings to the brightness of your rising."*[23]

The seasons have changed and the tides are turning, the glory of the Lord is rising upon His people!

Can you sense it?

Let's keep reading.

The Landscape Dynamics of Our Day

The scriptures are very clear on the moral and cultural dynamics as we continue to move closer to the end of the age. It will surely require both wisdom and endurance for the saints. Even at the cost of our lives or reputation, we must be able to stand on the rock of truth as unwavering, bold, and faithful witnesses, while being productive disciples in the midst of gross darkness. We must not be merely reactive to culture but proactive and prophetic, setting the trend, shaping culture, and pioneering the future.

In this hour, the night is far spent and the day is at hand; the light is already shining and the darkness has not overcome it! We have the victory no matter what is happening on the earth. NO MATTER WHAT.

Let that settle into your heart.

---

23 Isaiah 60:1-3

It's true that we are more than conquerors in Christ. We have the victory, and we know how the story ends, but we still need to be aware and alert to the things happening around us in our world. The time clock of the Lord is tied to the participation and preparation of His church. We can either hasten the Day of the Lord or prolong it, based on our response and cooperation with Him. It's part of our responsibility and stewardship in the earth to stay awake, alert, and relevant to our current times with the eternal word of God so that we can be an effective voice and witness.

In the face of technology and AI creating more complexity in relationships, social interactions, the workforce, and the moral fabric of society, we need not be silent spectators nor laggers. We can still become servants of all, able to provide real solutions, needed wisdom, and know-how to navigate such times and advancements. We have to be both relevant in the cultural conversation as well as productive in our callings and vocations, appropriately leveraging technology advancements for both our livelihood and the Lord's sake. This requires that we see what's going on around us, do our due diligence to understand, and get the Lord's mind on the matter, lest we be swept up in the agenda of men and distracted by the bewitchments of this age. We need to be intentional in acquiring both the wisdom of God and the knowledge of the world's advancements with a prayer heart and studious mind.

Things will continue to speed up in the realm of technology and we need to be able to not just keep up, but be ahead of the curve—and have sound biblical wisdom to navigate our ever-changing society while staying focused on the increase of God's Kingdom in our hearts and in the world around us. Remember, the mission and plan of God does not change. The call is to stay on mission with focus and diligence in making disciples, being salt and light in society, and keeping ourselves undefiled from the ways of the world as we wholly love the Lord.

The book of Daniel talks about how knowledge will increase but it is the wise who will shine and lead others to righteousness[24]. The technology and information revolution supports the schemes of man and seeks to replace God's design for humanity, relationships, the need for faith, and reliance on the Holy Spirit. I'm not vilifying technology, as I appreciate it and use it, but we must stay deeply rooted in the truth of God's plan for us.

If you want to read a few more thoughts on AI and the complexity it brings, see the Appendix.

In light of these dynamics, we must hold before us that we are called to be Christ's witness to the ends of the earth. The grand plan of God before the Lord's return has to do with a mature Church (the bride of Christ), the fullness of all nations (Jew and gentile) coming to a saving faith and being added to the Church, and the gospel preached to every tribe, tongue, and nation. This all occurs in the midst of God bringing measures of judgment on anti-Christ systems and injustice on the earth.

Things are getting and will get pretty wild. Glory and shaking go together.

The truth to remember is that in gross darkness, deception, immorality, and the sorceries of this age, the Church is to shine in the beauty of holiness as a bold witness in every place. The people of God are to serve as a prophetic voice of God to every sector of culture and society. God has things to say and do on the earth and He wants to use you to do it! Yes you.

We are called to live on mission and the mission of Christ. This is not for a select "qualified few" but for every believer in Jesus Christ who has been qualified by His blood and sacrifice! Oh, that's good news!

---

24 Daniel 12

Bold, Faithful, Ready

I love this recent Facebook post by Prophet and Pastor, Kris Vallotton:

> "It's time to unleash the Kingdom! I recently had a vision from God of a man walking down the street with a domesticated lion on a leash and I heard a voice in my spirit say, "Unleash the Kingdom!"
>
> As Christians, it's easy to become spiritually domesticated in today's society where criticism and cynicism rain down like silencing arrows at the sound of Truth being released into the Earth. Often the response is to become careful and calculated in speaking the Truth instead of sharing without fear of reproach. But, I'd propose that the Lord is letting the Lion of Judah off the leash!
>
> The time to mince words in the hope of reducing offense has come to an end. Now let me be clear- the goal should never be to offend, but the cost of minimizing the power of Jesus is too great. The Kingdom is RADICAL! In the Kingdom of God, the impossible is made possible. Anything can happen—anything."

So true! We are in such a landscape of change and technology and intense polarizations with tensions and efforts toward "harmony" or tower of babel type building, wokeism, aggressive liberal agendas, and one world order type stuff. Yet still, I see His people being strategically positioned in every sector of society to be an influence and witness for the gospel, as He has always done throughout time.

The scriptures give us precedence with people like Daniel, Joseph, Moses, Esther, Nehemiah, Nahaam's Jewish servant girl, and others who served in the world system or within "enemy territory." These people learned the ways of Babylon and Egypt in order to influence and make an impact for the kingdom without compromise and brought Glory to God. These things were written down in scripture to give us an example of those who remained set apart for the Lord, but who also engaged culture in a reformational and transformational way. They did not just stand apart from the world and point the finger and criticize the darkness, though they surely gave a clear prophetic witness of confronting wickedness and advocating for righteousness and justice. They served with excellence, had compassion and mercy, used their voice and abilities to provide wisdom and solutions, and trusted God to do what only He can do while not clinging to their own lives. They were on mission. They were bold, brave, they were faithful, they made an eternal impact!

We need to be of the same mind and become transformative agents wherever we find ourselves. Let us remember the great cloud of witnesses that have gone before us, and who are cheering us on to complete the unique work and task we've been given in our generation.

Let us pray, let us take action, and let us embrace the loving discipline of God in our lives that makes us ready and fit for effective service. As the Church has been experiencing the chastisement of God, let's remember His intention and heart is to prepare us for Himself and the works He's called us to. His loving discipline refines us, purifies us, and helps us order our lives in such a way that rightly represents Him to the world. Our lives and character must adorn the gospel and we must be ready to be effective witnesses and ministers in culture without eventual compromise. Celebrity Christianity is being crumbled in our day, calling people back to the purity of the truth, the humility of service, and the sincerity of faith. Jeremiah Johnson stated powerfully, "Church history is full of men and women who had been tested by obscurity but failed miserably the test of notoriety. The worst thing that can ever happen to a man or woman is for them to be promoted before they are ready." This is so true, whether you are called to be a visible public figure and influencer in culture or whether you are in the obscurity of a rural community and growing in leadership and influence within your local church or workplace. How we handle power, influence, and authority is critical. Thus we need to lean into God's refining process and be deeply consecrated to Him and His work.

For such a time as this we must be made ready for greater usefulness in the hand of God. Our character and the soundness of our faith must be able to stand under the pressures and seductions of this age that are waging war against the Kingdom of God. The enemy's plan is to rob, steal, kill, and destroy our lives and ruin the witness of the Church and undermine the power of the gospel, but the Lord's will is that we have an abundant and triumphant life that glorifies God and is above reproach. You are called to live in glorious freedom in Christ and express that to the world around you.

You can say "Amen!"

In the midst of gross darkness, the glory of the Lord rises upon His people and especially those who have said, "yes" to Him and yielded themselves to His training and development. If you desire to be used by God in mighty ways, get ready. The hour is late and the eyes of the Lord are searching to and fro throughout the earth looking for loyal hearts that are completely His that He might show Himself strong on their behalf.[25]

Will that be you? Your household…your community?

Will you let God use you for such a time as this?

I hope so. The time is now!

25

PAUSE. CAPTURE. APPLY
Prompts to help you process

1. What specific insights or concepts from this chapter resonated with you the most? Why do you think these stood out to you?

_____

_____

_____

2. How can you practically apply the principles discussed in this chapter to your daily life, relationships, or ministry? Identify at least one actionable step you can take this week.

_____

_____

_____

3. What potential challenges or barriers might you face in implementing these concepts? How can you overcome them?

_____

_____

_____

4. What are 3-5 quotes or points from this chapter that capture the essence of what it's communicating? Write them down.

_____

_____

_____

_____

_____

5. How can you involve your family, small group, or church community in the practices and principles outlined in this chapter? What steps can you take to foster a culture of discipleship and transformation within your circle of influence?

_____

_____

_____

6. Spend a few moments in prayer, asking God for the wisdom, strength, and courage to live out the truths you've learned. Write down a commitment or a prayer that reflects your desire to grow as an authentic disciple and transformational leader to impact the world.

_____

_____

_____

CHAPTER 2

Cultural Complexities and the Call

"The only thing necessary for the triumph of evil is for good men to do nothing."
COMMONLY ATTRIBUTED TO EDMUND BURKE

Let me continue to encourage you to consider the nature of our day and where to look first. The earth is groaning for the revealing of the sons of God. Those who sit in darkness need the light of the goodness of God that shines through His people.

The prevailing crises all over the land are the compounded effects of generations of spiritual, social, political, and economic dysfunction being further fueled and fortified by broken homes. It demands a response. We cannot sit by as though nothing is wrong or as if peace prevails, because it doesn't. For example, the epidemic of fatherlessness alone has had a massive destructive impact on the very fabric of society. I could give you lists of statistics to prove it as many people have previously written about, but just consider these:

- Children are 4 times more likely to be in poverty from a lack of a father in the home. (U.S. Census Bureau)

- 90% of runaway and homeless children are from fatherless homes. NJI (National Institute of Justice)

- 90% of teenage repeat arsonists come from an absent father household (Psychology Today)

- 85% of minors in prison who grew up without a father (Texas Department of Corrections)

- 85% of children with behavioral disorders are from homes without fathers (Center for Disease Control)

- 80% of rapist came from a fatherless home (NJI)

- 75% of adolescents in substance abuse treatment facilities are from fatherless homes (NJI)

- 71% of all high-school dropouts are from a fatherless household (National Center for Education Statistics)

- Even though these are damning numbers, you have to remember that only 24.7 million children (33%) live absent from their biological father. (U.S. Census Bureau, Current Population Survey).

There's more but I'll spare you for now.

Tim Kennedy says in reflection on our present cultural condition, "Boys are encouraged to be docile. Men are encouraged to be perpetual boys. Both are encouraged to be apathetic. While the situations may be complex and nuanced, the answers are simple.

1. Good men mentoring other good men.

2. Good men mentoring young men."

Today we can see clearly that people's core sense of identity has been misplaced and distorted in profound and demonic ways. This has been catalyzed by the absence of healthy fathers and households that should be imparting identity, the dignity of life, sound principles of character, courage, work ethic, justice, love and more. As a result of compounded brokenness, we see the pendulum swings of society and the complexity of sophisticated evil schemes of dehumanization through things such as human and child trafficking, abortion, rampant pornography, toxic masculinity and femininity, gross sexual immorality of all sorts, violence and lawlessness, gender and identity confusion, and a massive growing global occultic movement with grotesque satanic ritual abuse (SRA) of both children and adults. What we have is a systemic breakdown of the moral and spiritual fabric of society. America has become weak in many ways and must be awakened and saved from her depraved state. We need warriors and authentic disciples to help turn the tide!

Furthermore, we see immature adult adolescents, widespread narcissism, a young generation lost in the virtual vortex of gaming. They know little about, but are hungry for, real relationships and connection. They are altogether under challenged to do something great with their lives and stay crippled, co-dependent, or altogether lawless. Sure, there are many challenges for the generation at hand, but this is systemic and not helped by coddling, enabling, and abdicating our powers to change the status quo in our circles of influence. We have a generation void of moral foundations and hardly any sense of absolute truth which leads to folly and deceptive ideologies that spur on and spawn further evils in the name of "good." True as the scripture say, we are in times where good is called evil and evil is called good.

It's time to take our stand.

We need to become the solution. As men and women of God, rooted in truth and as a people of character, we must actively raise up a new generation and influence those in our trust with the ways of the Lord.

There is no room for neutrality and casual Americanized "Christianity." The gospel and a widespread spiritual awakening are a necessity to turn hearts back to the Lord and the way of righteousness again. You and I have a part to play and a massive amount of work ahead of us! We have to rebuild what has been devastated for generations. This is our biblical mandate and holy responsibility—to rebuild the desolations of many generations (Isaiah 61).

I hope you're up for the task.

We know all too well the passage of scripture out of second Chronicles 7:14, that says "if my people who are called by my name, will humble themselves and pray and turn from their wicked ways then I would hear from heaven, forgive their sins and heal their land." We stand in a time where the people of God are answering the appeal of this passage, and the Lord is responding.

Start at Home

The prophet Malachi said, Before the great and terrible day of the Lord He will send a messenger, an Elijah type figure or the spirit of Elijah, to turn the hearts of the fathers to the children, and the hearts of the children to the fathers, lest the land be totally destroyed.[26] God knows what is needed to reconstruct and heal a nation, He brings us back home.

It's easy to get distracted by secondary things that feed our anxieties, or are outside our control rather than what really matters regarding our faith and the call to make disciples and change the world. I love what Mother Theresa said, "What can you do to promote world peace? Go home and love your family." She had it right.

---

26 Malachi 4:5-6

Cultural Complexities and the Call

Building strong families that produce mature children in the faith create strong churches that become the base for penetrating nations with the gospel. When we think about the complexity and weight of brokenness in our world, we must first start with our own hearts and then those closest to us. If we want to turn the tides, we must start with our home and family.

The restoration and reordering of homes is key and essential to healing the land, rebuilding a healthy society, and restoring righteousness on the earth. Despite the many systemic issues, it starts in your heart and home, with the type of true Christian education and discipleship that passes on the knowledge of God to our children in a living way that informs all of life. Regardless of your role or place in the family, you have a call and a part to play in this!

Being established in the foundational ways of God and what the scriptures call the elementary principles of Christ, point us right back to the primary issue and centerpiece of family. God's family, the Church, and your biological individual family.

God gives us the structure, design and spirit of family that is both timeless and above cultural differences. This illustrates the wisdom and ways of God, for it is rooted in the very nature of God. Even if you are not yet married, a parent or oversee a home, it's crucial to understand God's design and plan for family if you intend to help rebuild what has been long devastated and work towards the restoration of all things. We need clear biblical thinking here.

Plus, to possess the love of God produces a parental heart of love, the heart of Father God, that compels us to serve the bigger picture of His people coming into the fullness of what He's intended for their lives. This starts by living into God's design at home and how you relate to your family.

We all must be part of the solution and contend for heaven on earth! Children and teens have a responsibility to contribute to a well ordered home according to God's design as well, though they will follow the lead of the parents who are to model and set the order.

Children are commanded in scripture to honor and obey their parents, for this is right in the Lord's eyes (Ephesians 6:1). This is part of their worship to God. It is key to their personal development as men and women of God who can become healthy change agents in society. This includes how older children honor and care for their elderly parents as well, not just youthful kids learning to honor and obey their parents' authority. This work and call to restore household order ranges through the generations. Powerful, right? Such ordering and healing the home according to God's design, can become a model and healing agent to society. It starts with the heart and life of the parents, the leaders of the household, and, particularly, fathers. Where we are dealing with many single parent homes, men in the church can be a real solution if they'll rise up to answer the call.

Believing households and the Church community, composed of many families, must be the forerunners that shine as living witnesses of God's restorative and redemptive work in our homes first. The world, our local communities and our neighbors are watching. This call to get our houses in order and God's shaking in His Church is calling us back to His divine design. In it, we can flourish as His people but also actually help disciple nations and heal communities as we are called. The lack of biblical order and healthy homes in the American church (and globally, really). is a crying need and reproach that's inviting the discipline and healing grace of the Father.

The winds of change are blowing and clarity to these issues are emerging.

The marriage relationship itself is to be the living embodiment of the mystery of the gospel concerning Christ and His Church. That's a powerful theological fact, but more than a concept or ideal, it is a truth and instructions to be practiced. Think about this. What are people seeing when they look at our marriages? What are you modeling your marriage ideas, roles, and behaviors after? How do you understand your role in it? Are you more culturally influenced in your attitudes, beliefs, and behaviors or is scripture and submission to Christ shaping your perspectives and practices?

Just saying. Pause and consider.

Our households should be habitations of heaven's culture where our families and other people experience the love, order, peace and joy of Heaven. The goodness of God should be experienced in our homes. Authentic and loving relationships with real connection and transparency and care that's deeply rooted in biblical truth and purpose, is becoming rare, even though it is what every soul is craving. We need to live this for ourselves and lead others into this as well. We can't settle for anything less than the fullness God has intended. The call to authentic discipleship and the practice of truth is our path here.

Healthy faith and Christianity will manifest as healthy well-ordered households. This is not idealism, it's our invitation to let the power of the gospel transform us, causing us to live wholesome ordered lives as the scriptures prescribe. We are to be agents of reconciliation and restoration starting in our marriages, families, and closest relationships. Hope and healing is our portion and gift in Christ. Isn't that good news?

Moms, dads, educators of all kinds with a heart for the next generation, take this quote in and let it inform how we teach and where we spend our energies:

"It takes more work to repair broken men than to raise strong children"—Fredrick Douglas. Oh, how we need to start in the homes and look to our children.

Statistics reveal that the Christian community is having more babies than others in America (atheists and agnostics). This is good, but many of the youth are not staying in the faith as they grow.[27] The godless are doing a better job indoctrinating and training our kids! Oh Lord, help us!! We must turn our hearts towards our kids and learn to effectively pass on a living faith while reaching out to win the lost and winning back those who have strayed.

The data and our own experience tells us that households are not taking advantage of the many resources available to train and disciple their family. In one survey, 99% of believing parents wouldn't consider discipling their own children in the top three priorities of their lives.[28] Yet 85% of parents know that they are supposed to be the primary disciplers of their children, but admit that they do nothing to develop their faith beyond taking them to church.[29]

Can I call us into a fresh vision and commitment to intentional and biblical action around raising up the next generation, discipleship, and personal transformation? We must start in our own hearts, lives, and homes. We need to get clear on the process and pathways we are going to train and develop others, especially our sons and daughters. If we don't, the spirit of the age and other people with their own agendas will disciple, shape, and use our kids for their own aims. O God, forbid it!! We need to live with intentionality and urgency, focus and passion. There is great work before us and the hour is late my friends, our salvation is closer now than when we first believed!! Revivalist John Wesley said, "I learned more about Christianity from

---

[27] Lyman Stone, "America's Growing Religious-Secular Fertility Divide", Institute for Family Studies, August 8, 2022, https://ifstudies.org/blog/americas-growing-religious-secular-fertility-divide.
[28] David Kinneman and Gabe Lyons, *UnChristian: What a generation really thinks about Christianity- and Why it matters.*" (Grand Rapids, MI: Baker books, 2007) pg 50.
[29] Timothy Paul Jones, "*The Task Too Significant to Hire Someone Else to Do,*" in *Perspectives on Family Ministry*: Three views, ED. Timothy Paul Jones, Nashville B&H academic, 2009) pg 22.

my mother than from all the theologians in England.³⁰" Parents, don't downplay your role or influence.

And young people, if you're reading this I want to encourage you to get established in your faith. Settle into home and your local church community, be discipled in the faith, submit to the process and be fully trained. It starts right where you are in the midst of the mundane. If you don't see people available to do this or they don't know how to mentor, you just might be the one to pioneer the conversation and initiate the process of growth with them. You both can learn together, become the example, and shift things for those who are to come after you. Catch the vision!

Changing The World By Making Disciples:

You are called to know Christ intimately, follow Him wholeheartedly, be deeply transformed, win souls for His name's sake out of deep compassion, and make disciples that multiply other disciples.

Positive generational impact is not possible without intentional and sacrificial investment in the great commission. This consists of more than just sharing the content of the message of the gospel. We are called to more than just sharing our faith and moving on or worse, merely coexisting living our own life with a "private faith" in the security" of our comfort. We are charged with the sacred stewardship to entrust the faith to others who in turn will do the same to others and advance the Kingdom of God no matter the cost or sacrifice. The faith we pass on exceeds mere doctrinal truth but holds a way of life, a way of being and doing that reveals the heart and nature of God. Thus, we are commanded to "teach them to *obey* everything I (the Lord) have commanded you.", not just memorize everything He commanded.

---

30 https://gracequotes.org/author-quote/john-wesley/ #7 accessed on October 19, 2024

Discipleship and making disciples comes out of burning love for Christ Himself. It is a soul orientation around His presence, being conformed to the likeness of Jesus Christ in our character through radical obedience to the will of the Father in and through the indwelling power of the Holy Spirit—not just knowing truths about Jesus and doing things for Him! "Anyone who claims to know Him (or live in Him) must live as Jesus did."—1 John 2:6.

We are called to live as Jesus did! Think about this.

Oh, may His will be done and not ours! May we learn to truly live and move and have our being in Him. May our food be to do the will of the Father, just as it was for the Son of God!

Read the words of these three amazing men of God. The revivalist, John Wesley, who's movement planted a church a day for 150 years (WOW!) said, "The church is called to change the world. The church changes the world not by converts but by making disciples"

This is our task my friends!

And he also said in speaking to his workers, "You have nothing to do, but save souls. Therefore, spend and be spent in this work."[31]

Richard Wurmbrand, persecuted minister in communist Russia and Nazie Germany and author of "*Tortured for Christ*" said, "We should never stop at having won a soul for Christ. By this, we have done only half the work. Every soul won for Christ must be made to be a soul-winner." We see the essence of the framework and process of a disciple who makes a disciple who can do the same.

And finally, read the words of Dr Robert Coleman, author of "The Master Plan of Discipleship & Evangelism", who is speaking to part of

---

31 "John Wesley Quotes," Quotlr 2023, https://tinyurl.com/3wfbd62n.

the problem today among the people of God. From the introduction of the book "DiscipleShift:"

"Something is missing in the life of the church. Today's institution has a polite form of religion, but it seems to lack power, the power to radically change the wayward course of society. This is not to say that nothing worthwhile is happening. In fact, all kinds of things are going on, and if success is measured by big meetings, big buildings, and big budgets, then the church appears to be doing quite well. But the real question has to be asked: is all this business actually fulfilling the mandate of Christ to make disciples and teaching them, in turn, to do the same? That's the mission of the church. Yes, we want churches to grow, but it is becoming painfully evident that getting more people on the roster has not resulted in a corresponding increase in transformed lives. Where do you find the contagious sacrifice and all-out commitment to the Great Commission? In our obsession with bigger numbers of converts, far too little attention has been given to the nurture of believers in how to live their faith. This neglect has created a crisis in the contemporary church. How we deal with it, I believe, represents the most important issue we face today."

The truth is we have an eternity to celebrate our victories but a few short moments in this life to win those victories. We need to give ourselves to the mission of becoming authentic disciples of Christ, who, out of love for Him and in the power of His presence, make disciples and change the world!

Let's become the answer to the crisis, and shift and shape a culture of authentic discipleship!

Paradigms

I hope that what you find within these pages resonates deeply within you and helps you bridge the gap between some paradigms and some how-to's in making that kind of impact. I hope to inspire you to action. More than that, to inspire you with informed and strategic action that helps us all hit the mark of God's plan for our lives, communities, and for passing on the faith to the next generation. We must all learn to become skilled "fishermen" when it comes to winning souls and effective disciple making, influencing people into the truth and into their next place of growth and development in Christ, especially our kids and the next generation.

Our methodologies and approaches to impact the world around us flow out of who we are and what we actually believe to be true: it's our character, emotional health, paradigms, and world views that shape and inform how we actually live and influence others.

The word paradigm comes from the Greek word *paradeigma,* which means example, model, pattern. Thomas S. Kuhn defines paradigm as "the entire constellation of beliefs, values, techniques and so on shared by the members of a given community."[32] Barker defines paradigms as follows: "…a set of rules and regulations (written or unwritten) that does two things: (1) it establishes or defines boundaries; and (2) it tells you how to behave inside the boundaries in order to be successful."[33] A paradigm is very similar to maybe your understanding of how we would define culture.

Our current paradigms and cultures must be shaken, some shut down and utterly dismantled. Something altogether new (yet ancient) must emerge for the hour we live in. The new thing the Lord is doing on the earth will require innovation and renovation in our thinking. Strategies and tactics without a shift of paradigm or culture will not prove effective or last. Paradigms and cultures trump strategy all the time.

---

[32] "The Structure of Scientific Revolutions", by Thomas S.Kuhn, (Chicago, 1970). Pg 75
[33] "Paradigms: The Business of Discovering the Future", by Joel Arthur Barker (HarperBusiness, 1992). Pg 32

I find that many sincere folks not only lack self awareness and are stuck in old and unquestioned paradigms. They get stuck on the "how" or the "what" needs to happen for the next level of growth or development for the people around them. They struggle to keep in focus the "why" and underlying causes of people's actions and feelings (much like they are not aware of their own). They get frustrated with the lack of real change or why the people they're teaching aren't "getting it" and able to faithfully follow through or get the personal breakthroughs they need to keep growing. They fail to go deep, get involved enough to know what's going on, and just keep pressing hard into their old paradigm assumptions, and external behavior modifications rooted in self will and just trying harder. What ends up happening is that they expend so much energy but with little effect and no lasting results. They stay irritated, loveless, overwhelmed, and stuck. Then they move on and tend to just blame those not getting results and continue their old methods in hopes that they work with someone else. There's a better way.

Behavior modification and memorization of information alone is not enough. Classes merely communicating information or sermons alone won't do it. If we don't get to the heart of the matter and help people see and understand their "why", their internal reasons, and way of thinking, they won't get to their underlying motivations and core beliefs for their actions or lack thereof. At that point the ability for real change, exchange with God by His Spirit, and transformation is delayed at best if not lost.

We need to stay on mission and stay future oriented in our approach in order to stay healthy and to continue to grow. But we must hold in tension the understanding that people will always default back to what they really think and believe in their hearts. Under pressure and duress people always default back to their most basic level of training or conditioning, the place of safety, present level of maturity, and sense of being. "As a person thinks in their heart so they will be"—Proverbs 23:7. So If we change how we think we change how we live. Taking the time to identify these things and apply energy here, we will see greater results. We all live from the inside out.

We have to go deep into people's stories and lives to really understand why and how they got stuck.. Behavior modification alone is insufficient for real change, and at best people are "performing" and trying to play a role but failing to truly grow from the inside out and renew their minds. Self discipline apart from renewing your mind and learning to think in a different way will only lead to striving and performance without the rest and peace that accompanies true transformation. Real freedom is born out of a renewed mind. Deliverance and breakthrough is accelerated when we can get to the roots of an issue first. Proper diagnosis is key before prognosis. Trying to fix the fruit of behavior without dealing with the root is a futile cycle that does not result in freedom or lasting change.

On the other hand, people get stuck just looking at the underlying motivations of action and the core belief systems that produce feelings and behaviors. They fail to keep the big picture vision and mission in front of them and they become overly introspective and self absorbed. Many times people have to just get their eyes off themselves and take the right actions to move them forward. Oftentimes, people fail to give the tools needed to shift and develop skills that help people move forward. Sometimes it's just a matter of missing skills and the need to form new habits and routines.

Just telling people what to do or what to believe is not enough. People also need the how and why with the accountability and coaching to implement new skills and behaviors. People have to know how to actually do and apply things. They need to develop actual competence that fosters confidence in life and the grace of God. People need to know that even if they have been victimized they are not victims anymore in Christ and that real freedom and healing is both available and something tangible to be walked out. God has given them power to overcome, develop internal and external skills, and get free from the habits, traumatic triggers, and patterns of thought that are not truly serving them or the world around them.

When it comes to shifting out of old, compartmentalized paradigms, we must move toward an integrated approach and thought process to minister holistically. Warriors, discipleship practitioners, everyday believers, and transformational Kingdom leaders must be able to do both and more (dealing with the internal and external factors pertaining to growth, healing, and maximizing potential) to see continual change and transformation in our own lives. And to be able to serve and create the environments, learning processes, and opportunities for others to grow into their full potential as well.

As you continue reading, we will dive into both the internal and external factors that foster real transformation and positive change which leads to lasting impact through participation in the great commission to make disciples. What we will cover will help you, challenge you, and make you hungry for more!

We will discuss what it means to be a transformational leader and what it means to continue to grow in leadership. We'll talk about what it looks like to use your gifts and abilities, and creative avenues to fulfill the great commission. We'll explore living our faith, leveraging our places of influence to reach the world and pass on the faith to the next generation; how to raise an authentic disciple, a kingdom warrior. I hope you are both inspired and challenged as you continue to read.

On with it!

PAUSE. CAPTURE. APPLY
Prompts to help you process

1. What specific insights or concepts from this chapter resonated with you the most? Why do you think these stood out to you?

_____

_____

_____

2. How can you practically apply the principles discussed in this chapter to your daily life, relationships, or ministry? Identify at least one actionable step you can take this week.

_____

_____

_____

3. What potential challenges or barriers might you face in implementing these concepts? How can you overcome them?

_____

_____

_____

4. What are 3-5 quotes or points from this chapter that capture the essence of what it's communicating? Write them down.

_____

_____

_____

_____

_____

5. How can you involve your family, small group, or church community in the practices and principles outlined in this chapter? What steps can you take to foster a culture of discipleship and transformation within your circle of influence?

_____

_____

_____

6. Spend a few moments in prayer, asking God for the wisdom, strength, and courage to live out the truths you've learned. Write down a commitment or a prayer that reflects your desire to grow as an authentic disciple and transformational leader to impact the world.

_____

_____

_____

CHAPTER 3

Leadership is Critical

"The greatest among you will be your servant."
— Jesus Christ (Matthew 23:11)

"A leader is one who knows the way, goes the way, and shows the way."
— John C. Maxwell

"Leadership is not about being in charge. It is about taking care of those in your charge."
— Simon Sinek (a principle rooted in biblical servanthood)

To be effective, raise authentic disciples, and live as an agent of transformation, leadership is critical. As leading global authority on leadership and personal development, Dr John Maxwell, says, "Everything rises and falls on leadership...and that the true measure of leadership is influence- nothing more, nothing less" And it's true. One of the things I love about Dr. Maxwell is that he unashamedly says that anything and everything he knows about leadership comes from the scriptures. From beginning to end, we see within scripture the impact and ramifications of quality leadership versus poor leadership on the individuals, families, churches, and nations. How our lives and oversights are led and managed makes all the difference in the world. This is true for our personal lives, the Church, the work place, our cities and towns, our nation.

All leadership and external influence starts with internal governance and self leadership. Every issue of life flows out from our hearts, and that's why scripture tells us this is the first place of stewardship before God.[34] Godly leadership starts with and demonstrates the choice of yielding its will to the headship of God. The mature children of God are those governed or led by the Spirit,[35] thus we must personally choose this daily. That's what I mean when I say "self leadership." "Today I place before you life and death, blessing and curses. Now choose life, so that you and your children may live."[36] Everything flows out of this place of surrender and acknowledgement of God, who alone is wise. Spiritual leaders must lead God's way, regardless of where they are serving in life.

The measure of capacity for making an impact on others requires that we first lead our *own* lives in the vision worthy of our lifeblood and energy-,a life worthy of the calling and gospel of God. Scripture exhorts shepherds, leaders, overseers, fathers and mothers. We are called to lead not as overbearing overloads but as servants and examples, using our influence to guide people into the knowledge, will, and ways of God. A big part of this requires that we can clearly communicate that vision and mission to those around us and influence them into it.

The scriptures say that people perish for lack of vision. One translation says they perish for lack of knowledge (or prophetic revelation) and without vision or proper insight people cast off restraint.[37] Vision and

---

34 Proverbs 4:23
35 Romans 8:14, Galatians 5:7-6:5
36 Deuteronomy 30:19. And elsewhere this language is used all over scripture. How we choose and lead our life has an effect on us and the people we lead.
37 Proverbs 29:18, Hosea 4:6

clear understanding drive our core motivations and empower us to be resilient, responsible, and sound decision makers under the pressures and temptations that try to divert us. As we shared in the introduction, it is evident that the mission and pervasive culture of the church lacks clarity on Christ's mission and the conviction to persevere in making the radical shifts necessary to come back into divine alignment. There's been a crisis in leadership.

As Jesus said, if the blind (those lacking vision) lead the blind, they fall into a ditch. The point is, we need clarity of vision and direction for our own lives and for those that we lead or influence. If we don't understand the plan of God, how can we confidently live a life worthy of the gospel or lead people in and toward that plan? We can't.

Any leader, especially those desiring to be a transformational leader, can only carry as much authority and power to create change for the Kingdom of God inasmuch as they know the will of God, can articulate it, and possess the wisdom to walk in it. His word, His will, His ways, His nature and plan, must be alive in our hearts and continually shaping how we live, our relationships, our priorities, our speech, and our approach to serving others. Otherwise we have mishandled the gift and responsibility of our leadership role and focused on secondary things.

How We Lead People

When it comes to the entrustment of leading others and our intentions to grow in influence in their lives, it's important that we don't think and see people simply as they are right now—but as who they *are to become*. We want to see the potential of people, and even better, we want to see them through the eyes of the Spirit, through the eyes of love and from the vantage point of the Lord. God relates to them, and us, based on His great love and mercy, and according to His divine purpose. We ought to do the same. Isn't that good news? We have to look past the dirt of humanity and find the gold in the lives of those we lead, and call it out. *Godly leadership should see, extract, and nurture the potential of people from a heart of compassion and humility without resenting their weakness or being short in patience.* You should write that one down. We can walk in the tension of nurturing people with both compassionate care and candor.

The difference between good leaders and bad leaders has to do with their values, character, capacity, and skills. You can be a great person and be a great example in character and values but lack the skill to actually help people. Or you can have amazing leadership skills but if you lack character and values, you'll end up manipulating people. John Maxwell breaks it down like this in his book "High Road Leadership."[38]

---

[38] John Maxwell, "*High Road Leadership: Bringing people together in a world that divides.*" 2024 Maxwell Leadership Publishing, pg 12.

RAISE A WARRIOR

GOOD SKILLS & GOOD VALUES	LEADERS RAISE UP THEIR PEOPLE
POOR SKILLS & GOOD VALUES	LEADERS CANT HELP THEIR PEOPLE
GOOD SKILLS & POOR VALUES	LEADERS MANIPULATE THEIR PEOPLE
POOR SKILLS & POOR VALUES	LEADERS DRAG DOWN THEIR PEOPLE

Maxwell's Good Leaders VS Poor Leaders
HIGH ROAD LEADERSHIP: BRINGING PEOPLE TOGTHER IN A WORLD THAT DIVIDES

As we'll read many times throughout this book, *we lead out of who we are.* Therefore, you and I need to know the kindness of God toward us in real ways so that we can rest in the hope and security of the Lord's love and lead from there. God relates to us in and through Christ—through love and mercy; the love that hopes all things, bears all things, suffers long and is still kind. God is enthusiastic about who

He made us to be in Christ and is working all things together for our good according to His purpose for us and to the good works He has planned for us. We are not defined by our weaknesses but by His great love for us in Christ Jesus. Wow! That's good news! We need to learn to lead others from this same place. When we lead from here, we have much more capacity to walk out the process without burning out, frustration, or resentment.

As leaders or aspiring leaders, we don't want to relate to people, or ourselves, based on their weaknesses alone (though we need to be aware of them) but on their potential and purpose in Christ. If we can learn to lead people according to their unique God-given purpose, identity and personal vision within God's divine plan, considering their unique motivations, we will strengthen the Body of Christ and advance God's kingdom. In this, our weaknesses and vulnerabilities are our opportunity to boast in God's mercy and kindness and are our escort into His strength and virtue. In our weakness, He is Strong! Plus, our weaknesses also provide us a personal focus for our own growth plan. Weaknesses highlight areas of potential growth and give us a direction for development. This is an essential ingredient to becoming a transformational leader—seeing opportunity and recognizing potential.

Effective leadership leads with clarity of purpose and guides people to God's desired outcome by *starting with the end in mind*. Leaders see into the future and exercise forethought. They perceive what could or should be. When the end vision directs how we lead our own lives and others, we live intentionally, make the most of our time, bear fruit to the Glory of God, and become transformational leaders.

Everything rises and falls on leadership. It can be a blessing or a curse. We can lift and liberate people or we can oppress and hinder people. What kind of leader will you be? Will people truly be better off under your leadership and influence, or worse off? If you're reading this, I trust your heart and intention is to be the best God has called you to be; that you aspire to be a force of good and make an eternal impact for the glory of God. No matter where you are as a person, your leadership capacity, skills, and maturity can grow and develop. Keep pressing on and God will bless you and increase you.

When we consider the call to arise and return and restore the ancient paths of authentic discipleship to impact the world, big picture clarity is key. The strategy, endgame, and big picture, though complex in execution with all life's variables, is not complicated. Our call is simply to love the Lord with all our hearts, soul, mind, and strength, love others with His love, preach the gospel, and make disciples as we speed the day of the Lord's return.

These realities should be at the core of our lives and what we are communicating and leading, regardless of our context and vocation in life. The main thing has to be the main thing. This is not compartmentalized to our "church life" or what we focus on on Sunday mornings and Wednesday nights when we gather with other Believers.

This is the way of life.

We Need to "See" It

People are inherently visionary and live towards the things they can see. As leaders, we must learn to meet the future horizon by personally crafting and continually communicating a compelling vision that people can "see" with their hearts, minds, and physically with their eyes. People need to see what we see so they can engage in it with conviction. Communication breakdown occurs when people can't see what we see or see something altogether different that what we intended. We make this harder when we fail to lead by example, not modeling the mission, culture, and strategy we seek to impart and reproduce. *Leadership must incarnate the message and values of the*

Kingdom of God. Leaders of organizations must model the message, mission, and values, if they intend to thrive.

To lead others in a mission or vision, and to keep people anchored in the call to be and make authentic disciples, you must keep people connected to the bigger picture and the main point of what and why you are doing what you're doing. It is very easy for people to get lost in the process, tasks, and struggle. Some people have said that "vision leaks," and that is exactly where leadership is critical. Leaders keep people anchored to the "why" behind what they are doing. Effective leaders always call people's minds and hearts back to the vision and purpose of who they are and what they are called to do. Alignment is essential. Their eyes have to be refocused in order to keep in unity of heart and effectiveness of service.

Connection to the "why" in the grind of getting "it done" is a game changer. It fuels motivation, engagement, and overall performance in life. People need to "see" the vision, find personal connection to it, and wholly buy in. Authentic disciples and transformational leaders are people of purpose, intention, and discipline, and that requires clarity of vision to curate such conviction. To stay the course in restoring the ancient paths of the way of Christ in an age of distraction, we must give special attention to generating and communicating vision—of who Christ is, what He has done for us, His power and life available to us, and the mission He calls us to.

Vision is breath and sight; it is vision that inspires, directs, and calls forth the needed energies for the journey of achieving the dream or goal at hand. It also gives people the determination to endure the process to get there; pain finds its purpose in the adventure of living into its desired outcomes. Clear vision makes it all worth it!

Getting On The Same Page

In leading others and accomplishing a mission together, we must communicate the vision, goals, methods, tasks, etc., in a manner that affirms you're on the same page. Otherwise, you may find you are working towards a different vision, different goals, and with different methods. That's called division, and no house, heart, team, church, ministry, or organization can stand divided that way nor be successful in their purpose and vision.

I have personally found, as have many others, it's not a lack of talent or ability, it's a lack of clarity and unity around the vision, mission, and execution plan that gets in the way. Clarity of vision helps create the needed organization, structures, and unity to execute on the plan. So as the Lord said to the prophet Habakkuk, "Write the vision and make it plain on tablets so that whoever reads it may run with it."[39]

To illustrate quickly, as a father and husband, if I don't provide vision, direction, and proper leadership to my family, all types of dysfunction and disorder would have its way in both my marriage and the flow of my family life. People would be unhappy, underdeveloped, and my kids would not be prepared for life. In the areas I oversee in the ministry or in any initiative in my business, if the vision and direction is not clear, there would be no unity of purpose, motivation would suffer, and proper skill sets, priorities, and tasks would be disorganized and productivity would suffer.

Clarity comes before productivity and without clarity of vision there is only confusion and distraction with no meaningful progress. Whether in sports teams, in preparation for a performance or for black belt testing in martial arts, if the vision and desired outcomes are not clear the developmental process suffers, performance would suffer, and nobody wins in the end. If I don't have clarity in my own life about

---
39 Habakkuk 2:2 NIV

what I'm doing, why I'm doing it, what needs to happen, what the problems are and what my next steps are, then I would be floundering, unintentionally un faithful, and probably pretty unhappy.

Pause.

In your gut-level-honest times of self-assessment, (in fact, take a moment even right now), ask yourself, is every person you're teaching, leading or working with on the same page? Is your household, your staff, your team, class, the leaders in your church, your client, etc.?. Do they all agree on what success measures look like right now for your goals and how you plan to achieve them? Has that conversation ever happened or even been considered as a need? What needs to happen to get connected and on the same page? Are you clear yourself?

Take the time to answer these questions for yourself and make sure to write down your responses. Then take the needed action to bring about unity of focus and purpose necessary.

It's worth the struggle and time to do this up front. In the long run, it will actually save you a lot of time, unnecessary frustration, and wasted resources.

The point is, leadership is critical and everything requires leadership of some sort. When we lead with a clear sense of purpose, we tap into a divine calling and stewardship that can transform not only our own lives but also the lives of those we lead. Clarity of purpose is more than a leadership principle; it's a spiritual compass and anchor for the soul that aligns our actions and life with God's desired outcome.

Let's consider and highlight a few points on leadership:

1. **Start to Lead Towards God's Desired Outcome:** Effective leadership begins with seeking God's guidance and aligning your vision with His will. As a leader, if your vision is not submitted and aligned

with God's will and kingdom principles, you have a problem and need to go back to the drawing board. To know Him intimately and make Him known, along with the core mission of making disciples who multiply must guide everything we do.

When we start with the end in mind and seek to discern His purpose, we become co-laborers with Him in achieving His plan. This not only empowers us as leaders and fills us with great joy, but also helps us lead those we serve toward God's desired outcome—maturity in Christ. The question is then, do you know the grand plan and mission of God? Can you confidently articulate it to others and see it expressed in the domains and circumstances of life? Are you living it yourself to be able to lead others in it?

2. **Leadership Should Be Transformational:** When leaders have clarity of purpose, it changes them into transformational figures who can catalyze comprehensive growth in others and lead people into the purpose of God. When we are crystal clear about the mission and vision God has placed in our hearts, our passion becomes contagious and the vision get's set in motion. We inspire others to join us in pursuit of a higher purpose and continual growth. This is the essence of transformational leadership: Catalytic inspiration and vision for purposeful action and growth in Christ and His cause. This comes with an inherent authority from God for the building up of His people and advancing His purposes in the earth.

Clarity of vision and purpose with a strategic and comprehensive plan builds momentum and moves through different realms of impact: from the individual, to the family, to the community, to the organization or team. It becomes all pervasive and self perpetuating from generation to generation. Transformational leadership thinks and acts beyond the here and now and calls us into the future with a multi-generational vision. Are you thinking big enough? Deep enough? Long term enough?

3. **Clarity Precedes Productivity:** When leaders are unsure of their purpose, it leads to confusion, indecision, unproductivity, and a lack of direction among those they lead. But when we have a clear sense of God's purpose and a plan of action, it becomes the guiding light that propels us forward, maximizing our effectiveness. When leaders are sure of their mission, they make choices that align with that mission, even in the face of difficult decisions. Such consistency builds trust and confidence among followers and fellow leaders. When you have trust with your people you can walk in unity, which empowers commitment, accountability, and the ability to produce the results that align with your predetermined purpose and mission. Where are you lacking clarity? What are you most sure about at this time in your life? Are those you are walking and working with on the same page?

4. **Inspiring and Serving Others:** Leadership is more than clarity of vision and purpose with setting goals; it's setting an example, inspiring hearts, and adding value to others through meaningful service. People are drawn to leaders driven by a deep sense of purpose and a clear vision of what God is calling them to do, and even more so to the leaders who serve them and add incredible value to their lives. We need to see people as the Lord would see them, otherwise we may violate love and relationship, leading like mere humans in the way of the world. We are called to lead like Christ and love others in the way He has loved us. When we demonstrate the nature and likeness of Christ in our leadership, though not always understood, health and inspiration follow that ignite a fire within the hearts of followers, motivating them to work passionately toward a common objective. If you lead others well, they'll willingly follow you through thick and thin. As the shepherd lays his life down for the sheep, the sheep lay their life down for the shepherd. It's a mutual bond of love and respect for each other further rooted in clarity of the truth and the shared mission. Ask yourself, are people invested and sacrificially serving with you? Out of fear, respect, duty, love, etc.? Are they going the extra mile? Is there love and a sense of joy in what you're doing and in your working dynamics? These little questions are a little litmus test.

People who are inspired, motivated, and feel loved and grateful, give of themselves willingly. We see the lives of those who gave themselves away sacrificially in both local and global mission efforts, even selling themselves into slavery in order to reach slaves with the gospel, simply because Jesus was worthy of the reward of His suffering. People gripped by the love and leadership of Jesus willingly gave themselves away for His sake, His gospel, and the saving of souls. Our leadership and example can help ignite hearts that willingly and completely give of themselves as well.

5. **Witness to God's Glory:** When leaders operate with clarity of purpose, aligned with God's will and lead well out of the integrity and authenticity of who they are, their leadership becomes a powerful witness to God's glory and nature. It demonstrates to others what is possible when we surrender to His guidance and work for His divine purposes. It also demonstrates the intentionality of God who has a plan and acts upon it with perfect wisdom and power to bring it to pass. God is not passive, disorganized, confused, or random. He's highly intentional, perfectly and profoundly organized, and joyfully acting with zeal according to His plan and purpose. We are to be as He is and as the scriptures say regarding those with a grace of leadership, "…he who leads, do it diligently."[40] Leadership is a gift of God and part of His very nature that we all possess in one degree or another. Let's acknowledge and step into this part of our identity as leader and exercise our influence to the Glory of God!

Transformational leaders:

- Express and embody the vision, mission, and nature of God.

- Function and focus on "being" over "doing." They value character over gifting but understand the value of both. They father and mother people into the character of

---

[40] Romans 12:8

Christ (exhorting, correcting, rebuking, teaching, training, comforting, nurturing, etc).

- Are satisfied and fulfilled in knowing they are living into the will of God, pleasing to Christ, and doing all things unto the glory of God.

- Are motivated by love and purpose and walk with a sense of divine stewardship, calling, and sacred responsibility.

- Understand the nature of process, as well as the needs and condition of humanity. They are concerned not only about their own ongoing growth and transformation, but the growth and transformation of others, according to the will of God (into the character and purposes of Christ).

- Commit to the action and implementation of the right things to achieve the vision and foster growth, regardless of the personal sacrifice required. They understand that costly sacrifice and measures of suffering are required to enter into transformational labor and maturation. Apostle Paul labored as like in the pains of childbirth to see Christ formed in individual believers, households, and communities. They were his joy and crown before God. Godly leaders possess this heart.

- Think and see the big picture, leading with the end in mind.

- Communicate clearly, continually, and courageously the vision, mission, and values of the Kingdom and their unique work to those running with them in order to keep everyone's mission aligned. They are creating and nurturing culture, and administrating necessary discipline for the wellbeing of their community.

- Remain humble, grateful, and joyful seeking to simply be faithful to the Lord, to love well and serve well those in their trust.

- Value others around them and are great at collaborating, pulling out the collective wisdom of others that is needed to make maximum impact. They are not insecure and freely share power in order to expand and accomplish the mission.

- They understand the wisdom of weakness and vulnerability and know how to utterly lean into and rely upon God's grace and power to do what they cannot. They live for God's glory and purpose, not their own.

- Are committed to the long game and focused on raising up and multiplying other leaders. They think strategically and multigenerational, are given to equipping and activating others in their gifts and callings, and are concerned with matters of legacy.

To wrap this up, leading with clarity of vision and purpose is not just a leadership strategy; it's a spiritual calling and necessity. It empowers leaders to guide their lives and the lives of those they lead toward God's desired outcome. Such leadership is transformational, inspiring, and effective. It aligns human effort with divine intention. In the words of the Apostle Paul, "I became its servant by the commission God gave me to fully proclaim to you the word of God, the mystery that was hidden for ages and generations but is now revealed to His saints. To them God has chosen to make known among the Gentiles the glorious riches of this mystery, which is Christ in you, the hope of glory. We proclaim Him, admonishing and teaching everyone with all wisdom, so that we may present everyone perfect in Christ. To this end I also labor, striving with all His energy working powerfully within me…..(so) whatever you do, whether in word or deed, do it all in the name of the Lord Jesus, giving thanks to God the Father through Him" (Colossians 1:25-29, 3:17 NIV)

You Are A Leader

Since everything we do requires leadership in some capacity, you are a leader! Do you believe that? Can you see that or accept that? I hope so (I'm smiling at you as I write this). Father, mother, brother, sister, friend, mentor, mature believer, CEO, coach, Pastor, team captain, department head, entrepreneur, team player. It doesn't matter, you possess a realm of influence and leadership, starting with your own heart.

But the leadership potential you possess must be cultivated and called upon in order to live into the next level of fruitfulness, faithfulness, and fulfillment. Your life and the lives of those you are leading and influencing will depend on it. And, here's the thing, you choose every day the type of influence you'll wield in any given moment. *We must forsake passivity and be intentional for the sake of love and the glory of God.* This is a powerful truth and somewhat sobering, right? We need to own this role as "leader" and step into it. Our life matters and has influence on those around us, over us, under us, those running alongside us, and even those on the outside observing from a distance.

I want to encourage and challenge you to exercise your leadership in a way that makes an eternal impact and learn to leverage your places of influence for the gospel of Jesus Christ, no matter what your station of life. Whether trying to influence your kids, your partner, your colleges, your peers, your team, your community, your business, industry, or your nation. Do it for the gospel's sake, the salvation and spiritual growth of others, and for the glory of God. We must be intentional about this.

If you are a true believer in Jesus Christ, this is part of your primary responsibility and core identity as belonging to His Church, the pillar and foundation of truth. We are called to be light and salt and to live on mission every day of our lives! This is not a compartmentalized "spiritual" or "religious" or "my faith" box to check. This is to be an all consuming reality and orientation of our lives. It's part of the reason for our existence and why we are still here after being born again. Ever think about that? Why didn't God just translate us to heaven and take us up like Enoch or Elijah after winning our hearts? Well, there's a few reasons but one of the main ones is that He wants us to join Him in His mission to see others saved too. He desires that none perish. That's also one of the reasons He has not returned yet either, because when He does, time is up. Now is the time to work while it is still called "today."[41]

My friend, you are called to know God intimately, be transformed into His character and likeness, and to make Him known passionately wherever you go! You are called to occupy until He comes, in and through your occupations and on all occasions. We are to be busy with the Lord's work and seeking first His Kingdom, not merely building our own lives or careers. You can learn to do this with grace and skill no matter where you are in life . It is one of our greatest joys and privileges to partner with the heart of God in loving, serving, and impacting others for His name's sake. This fires me up!

Leadership is critical, and we want to learn to do it well. Part of being a good leader requires good self awareness as well as empathy and understanding of what drives the human heart and human behaviors. In the next chapter we'll dive into some matters of the heart and identity that are critical for life, spiritual formation, and becoming a transformational leader.

---

41 Hebrews 3:13-15, 4:7, John 9:4, 2 Peter 3:8-18

PAUSE. CAPTURE. APPLY
Prompts to help you process

1. What specific insights or concepts from this chapter resonated with you the most? Why do you think these stood out to you?

_____

_____

_____

2. How can you practically apply the principles discussed in this chapter to your daily life, relationships, or ministry? Identify at least one actionable step you can take this week.

_____

_____

_____

3. What potential challenges or barriers might you face in implementing these concepts? How can you overcome them?

_____

_____

_____

4. What are 3-5 quotes or points from this chapter that capture the essence of what it's communicating? Write them down.

_____

_____

_____

_____

_____

5. How can you involve your family, small group, or church community in the practices and principles outlined in this chapter? What steps can you take to foster a culture of discipleship and transformation within your circle of influence?

_____

_____

_____

6. Spend a few moments in prayer, asking God for the wisdom, strength, and courage to live out the truths you've learned. Write down a commitment or a prayer that reflects your desire to grow as an authentic disciple and transformational leader to impact the world.

_____

_____

_____

CHAPTER 4

Human Drives

Leadership without understanding human drives only leads to shipwreck.

As we lead our own lives and others, it's important to know and understand people's basic needs, human drives, and psychology. We need to be self aware in order to lead our own "ship ," but without knowing what makes other people really "tick" or what drives them, our ability to really influence them will be limited. Connection starts in the common ground of our shared humanity. We have to be able to really *connect* with people or we will just find ourselves walking alone, detached from meaningful relationships and unable to do the greater things for God. He called us together for His name's sake to be one as He is one and to collectively do the work He has called us to. This requires teamwork and communication and connection.

You can have the best plan and vision and know what needs to happen in order to go where things need to get, but if people will not follow you, your desired impact and influence to move people into a better place or progress in the vision you're leading, it's going nowhere.

We have to touch the heart to move the hand. People "know stuff" in their head but often don't really "KNOW" stuff in their heart. The disconnect becomes evident in their attitudes, thinking, and actions. We need to get this. Not only that, but also grow to be able to help people "KNOW" in their hearts so that it transforms their life by causing them to take proper action from the heart. That's just a fuller, more godly, and human way to live. So the goal in understanding and appealing to our human drives and motivations is to get to the heart in order to foster the real work of transformation.

It's obedience to God from the *heart* that results in transformation and growth. The manifestation of a changed life is the fruit of an inward work and a true knowledge in the soul. When we consider discipleship and the how-to's, which we'll talk about later, it's all about learning to shepherd the heart. That's what transformational leaders do. When people respond out of love for Him, love for what they are doing, and love for who they are serving from the right motivations, great things happen. Powerful action is born out of love. When it comes to leading others and mobilizing them to action, we have to learn to get people to truly "buy-in" from the heart through the practice of the law of connection.

Connection starts by first understanding and touching the heart of people through relationship before asking for their hand in service. To touch the heart we need to understand the core human drives. This is what Jesus does too. As God, He knows what makes us tick and will pull on those things in His love and mercy to lead us to repentance and compel us to follow Him wherever He goes. Thus, He leads us to desire and love to be poured out in joyful and sacrificial service. He makes us feel alive, loved, known, honored, significant and more. We can learn to lead people in God's grace like this too.

There is a key paradigm regarding our own development as well as understanding and influencing others, especially when it comes to designing or walking out a process of development and discipleship.

Human Drives

This principle has to do with identity, and simply stated, it is: "*being precedes doing.*" It means that we live and do out of who we are. Who we are is our visible witness and power to influence others. We have to catch this. We cannot give what we do not possess, and we reproduce who we are, not just the things we say and teach. God is about shaping *who* we are more than what He can accomplish through us. Both are imperative but what God can do *through* us is hinged upon what we have allowed Him to produce *in* us. Being before doing.

We have to start here at the core of who we are and understand who the people are that we want to influence. Otherwise, we are going to miss it in more ways than one. Ideally, if we want to maximize impact in the heart and spirit of people that is pleasing to God, we should relate to them first on the basis of their God given identity and intrinsic value as people, beloved and precious to God. As a foundation, this comes first before relating to them based on what they can do for us or according to their weakness and present immaturities. Leading others requires assessment and seeing people from a sense of reality, both strengths and weaknesses. This all has to be framed and processed through the lens of love and faith and the new creation.[42]

Regardless of personality and leadership style, not only are we called to be like Christ in how we lead, we need skills and understanding of the way we have been wired in our core drivers and soul needs. Leaders who deeply understand human drives and motivations are better equipped to communicate effectively, engage their teams and families, resolve conflicts, make balanced decisions, and create organizational structures that bring out the best in people. This understanding allows

---

[42] When working with a Believer and or in relating to ourselves we need to see and operate from a lens of redemption. 2 Corinthians 5 talks about how the power of the gospel changes how we should understand and relate to each other not according to the flesh but according to the spirit, since we are new creations. The tension must be held of knowing people in their present state of maturity while seeing them through the eyes of faith and their God given call, potential, and belovedness before God. Plus, love and faith keep us tender to believe that people, like ourselves, have the ability to grow and change and not be confined to past failures.

them to adapt their leadership style to meet the diverse needs of their family, community, or team as a whole, ultimately driving better performance, growth, and outcomes.

Leaders in many fields of personal development see this issue of understanding and meeting human drives and needs as key to human flourishing, productivity, and high performance. Here are a few ways some leaders have categorized them before we touch on how the gospel and the call of discipleship satisfies them.

10 human drives that influence how we think, feel, and act. - BRENDON BURCHARD.

5 "BASELINE" Human drives:

1. Control-
2. Competence-
3. Congruence -
4. Caring-
5. Connection -

5 "FORWARD" Human drives:

6. Change-
7. Challenge -
8. Creative Expression-
9. Contribution -
10. Consciousness -

"DRIVE" - DANIEL H. PINK

""Human beings have an innate inner drive to be autonomous, self-determined, and connected to one another. And when that drive is liberated, people achieve more and live richer lives."

"The science shows that the secret to high performance isn't our biological drive or our reward-and-punishment drive, but our third drive—our deep-seated desire to direct our own lives, to extend and expand our abilities, and to make a contribution."

6 CORE DRIVERS - TONY ROBINS

1. **Certainty:** assurance you can avoid pain and gain pleasure
2. **Uncertainty/Variety:** the need for the unknown, change, new stimuli
3. **Significance:** feeling unique, important, special or needed
4. **Connection/Love:** a strong feeling of closeness or union with someone or something
5. **Growth:** an expansion of capacity, capability or understanding
6. **Contribution:** a sense of service and focus on helping, giving to and supporting others

Human Drives, Needs, & Motivations

We'll visit this concept a few times but let's get to the heart of the matter and identify some of these human drives.

The Search For Meaning

People need to feel and know that they are important and that their lives matter. As indicated above, we see and can relate to some of our core human drives around significance, connection, meaningful contribution, certainty, and growth. As a leader or aspiring leader/influencer, we need to know this is at the heart of so much. People are searching for significance, both believers in Christ and unbelievers alike. In the ways that people search to satisfy these desires and drives, they often fail to realize and come to rest in what the gospel declares to us.

A godly and transformational leader must first learn to see things from a point of reality, as God sees it. The gospel and word of God is that point of reality by which we can see, know, and understand all things. "In your (His) light we see light."[43] So it is very important we let the truth of God frame our minds and leadership approach. With that said, we need to know the truth of the gospel here in our deepest parts first. If we endeavor to really make an impact in other people's lives, we need to be able to communicate this truth effectively with deep conviction and in what we embody with our lives.

We are loved. You are loved.

When we see and experience the truth of God's love for us revealed in Christ, everything changes. Truth is, we are significant because we were made in God's image and likeness, and not because of the things we do. We are loved apart from our performance and not merely defined by the things we do. This is radically different from the way of the world and from the religious spirit that seeks to justify and find

---

43 Psalm 36:9

value and validation from their own righteousness and good works. The gospel truth declares that we are NOT righteous on our own and are justified by faith in Christ, so that no one can boast before God. Most believers would nod their head in agreement and say "amen" to this biblical truth. However, at this present time, the hearts, attitudes, and devotion of many of those same believers say something else.[44] Oh, how we need the depths of the soul persuaded by the love of God revealed in the gospel!

Let me go on for a moment and boast on God. We are so deeply loved by Him, so much so, that He gave Jesus to die on our behalf so that we could be free from the corrupting power of sin and death, be forgiven, liberated and healed from the pains of our past, and reconciled back to God as His Royal children. Wow! He gave us a lasting and eternal inheritance as Heirs of God and co-heirs with Christ, while we were still His enemy. This is wild! We were once hopeless in this life and without purpose, cut off from Christ, deserving of wrath, and without eternal life, hostile in our minds and enemies of God. But now, because God is rich in mercy, in Christ we have been given new life, a unique purpose and a mission alongside other brothers and sisters in God's very own family, the Church. Not only that, God's very power enables us to live an abundant life now and have eternal life in the age to come. What? This is amazing! God literally comes to live in us by the Holy Spirit, makes us a partaker of His nature, gives us supernatural gifts, and grants us perpetual access to His love and presence. We have been called into friendship, more than friendship, fellowship, Sonship, and union with God! We are not orphans left alone, but sons

---

[44] On the other side of the performance based Christianity epidemic, the truth of the matter is, when we are living authentically in the truth what we do is a manifestation of who we are. How else could Jesus say, "you will know people by their fruit"…? In the end we are judged by the good and bad we have done in the body and are repaid for our deeds. We are accountable for what we do. People tend to swing to extremes and many have resisted anything that feels like "works" or effort to do or meet a standard in resistance to their own inner turmoil and lack of establishment in their identity as sons and daughters of God. God's grace is not cheap and He does expect a return on His investment—that we produce fruit.

and daughters of God himself! Did you catch that? Not to mention that God also fully restores who we are as men and women in the truest sense. We are not left in a broken and confused state in this life with just a distant hope in the future for wholeness and healing. We experience a living hope now through our faith in Christ. This allows us to walk in the freedom and wholeness Christ purchased for us at the Cross and resurrection. Our true masculinity & femininity is restored and empowered to give an authentic and healed expression to the image of God in which we were created. This is amazing! Someone once said, "Man fully alive is the glory of God." And in Christ, this is what He has made available to us as an INCREDIBLE gift of grace. This is so good! If you're not shouting, I don't know what to tell ya, but my heart is shouting with how good God is right now!

Let me ask you, did you know these things? Are these truths alive in you and motivating your life and heart? Is Christ your greatest joy and reward? Is our biblical hope real to you? If so, AWESOME! Keep burning, growing, and giving away the good news to others! If not, settle your heart and mind on these things, meditate on them until the Spirit of God lights up your heart with the fire of His love, goodness, and truth! I want to encourage you, if you are not already connected, connect with other authentic believers who are pursuing God and the mission of changing the world for His glory!

And here's the other thing to ask, if these truths are alive in you, are they coming out of you and being shared with others? Are you being moved with love for the people you lead, influence, and serve, encouraging them deeper into these truths? Is evangelism flowing out of your life to the world around you? Are you making disciples and intentionally passing on/entrusting the faith to others? Helping them get deeply rooted and ordering their lives around Christ and His teachings? Do you know that this is the primary responsibility of every parent and every true believer? This is not just for "clergy" or the "professional minister." The people of God are all royal priests with the same mission, the same faith, the same Father, the same Spirit. If you consider yourself a Christian, this is for YOU!

> Quick rant: I know many great Christian leaders (or leaders who are Christians) who add awesome value to people and promote things that are good, wholesome and better people's lives in business and industry. But they fall short of making an eternal impact in that they don't leverage their influence for the gospel and bring people into the true knowledge and saving grace of God. There are many reasons for this which we'll explore some later, but let me just say as the apostle Paul said, "if we have hoped in Christ for this life alone, we are most to be pitied."(1 Cor 15:19) and as Jesus said, "what does it matter if someone gains the whole world but loses their soul" (Luke 9:25). There is more to this life than the here and now! Mere human goodness alone won't cut it when it comes to eternal things, so we need to think bigger and look to influence others deeper. Life is a vapor and the people around you will die at some point. Maybe unexpectedly and suddenly. My point is, God has you in their life for a reason and the greatest gift you can give them is the gospel and a bridge into a living faith.

You may be one of those amazing leaders who do great good for your people but do not share the faith nor intentionally use your influence for the gospel. This book is for you! You can amplify your influence and make a lasting impact for both this life and the life to come for the people you serve and love. This task of sharing the faith is not just for "clergy" or some religious domain of life relegated to a compartmentalized spirituality or a private faith. Authentic faith in Jesus is not private at all, even the requirement of baptism declares this. Being an actual follower of Christ means that you have signed up to become like Him, sharing His message, living on mission, and making disciples (just a reminder)! There is no division of secular & sacred. For the believer, all things are to be done to the glory of God as an act of worship. Something to think about. Some people think that if they bring their faith into their business they will lose business. The truth is you may lose some business but you more likely will also grow in abundance and have greater impact, especially as you learn to be an authentic witness of the faith and love people well. The truth is attractive when it is lived and expressed well in the spirit of truth and not in dead religion. And on the other end, we have to settle the issue whether we are serving God or money. You can't serve both, and God has commissioned us to spread the good news about Him. We cannot be ashamed of the gospel and we must learn to make the most of every opportunity in the places we serve. And if you are hated and rejected because of your faith, remember that Christ was hated and rejected first. Be happy that you would suffer as a Christian. You need to prepare yourself for the days we are in because they are becoming more polarizing, as good is called evil and evil is called good. If you want to live for Christ and live righteously, the scriptures tell us, we will be persecuted[45].

---

45 2 Timothy 3:12—read the context as well—all chapter 3 and chapter 4

Ok, I'll end my rant and get back to talking about the need for leaders to understand people's search for significance.

As leaders, we have to know and understand the nature of man in terms of their needs, wants, and desires. To positively influence people and move them in a good and godly direction, into their full potential, we have to know how to appeal to the core of who they are and what motivates them. We have to love people well by accommodating and honoring who they are, what they want (at times), and what they need. Some call this social and emotional intelligence, and it is important at every level of life.

The search for meaning or significance is at the core of our hearts. The desire to make meaningful contributions in life is essential to the heart of humanity, as we were created for both love and service. And the desire to be known and to be loved as you are, unconditionally, is a fundamental need of the soul. It's the way God created us.

We all have this hard wired into the fabric of our being. This need will be satisfied one way or another, legitimately or illegitimately, in a healthy way or unhealthy way, in truth or in falsehood. But either way, it will be satisfied because the core desires of our hearts and beliefs ultimately direct and guide the things we choose in life. It's just the truth. As leaders, we need to always look to the deeper reasons of why people do things and remain aware of why we are doing the things we do as well.

Much, if not all, the destructive things in life, in our relationships, and in society stem from illegitimate attempts to satisfy these internal wants, needs, drives, and desires.[46]

Often in our search for meaning and love, whether our family was healthy or dysfunctional, we go through phases of trying to define our value by what we do and how we perform in life. We seek affirmation

---

[46] James 3:13-16

and validation from people around us to try to solidify our sense of confidence and competence, in attempts to avoid feeling weak, incompetent, and rejected, especially by those we seek acceptance from. We want to be in control and strive to grasp at the things that would make us feel safe, stable, important, valuable, powerful, beautiful, and loved.

Humans are complex and creative beings with the ability to adapt in protective ways for situations. We build internal defensive systems to protect ourselves from vulnerability that manifest in relational hiding to avoid potential "dangers" to our fears, hurts, and wants. We also tend to avoid our painful feelings, thoughts, and memories through distraction, deny our legitimate hurts and needs, or reacting to the world and others. We want to avoid what we fear or what hurts and move towards what is "safe," even if it's rooted in a lie or false reality. We tend to create internal stories and narratives that justify our self protection and struggles. Does this sound familiar at all? If you're honest, it will.

This is part of my story and I think it is pretty common. Until we settle into the security of our God given identity, we will try to define ourselves and validate our worth based on what we can do and how we relate or compare to others. People hide their vulnerabilities until they grow in confidence in their identity, in emotional health, and in mature love in safe relationships. People typically are either trying to avoid pain and loss or moving towards desire and what brings them pleasure.

Authors John and Stasi Eldredge discuss the core desires of being a man or woman, uniquely masculine and uniquely feminine. They describe three primary desires that each are seeking in life, whether they know it or not. We will start with what men desire:

- A battle to fight—a cause to give himself to.

- Adventure—something that puts them to the test so they know they have what it takes in life.

- Beauty to love—to offer their strength on behalf of a woman.

Women, on the other hand, long and desire:

- To be romanced, seen, wanted, and pursued.

- To have an irreplaceable role in a great adventure.

- To be and unveil their beauty—to feel and be seen as lovely and captivating.[47]

I love how they capture these core themes. If we honestly reflect and look at the big picture, we will find some real truth here. These core areas of the soul can be bruised, deeply hurt and shut down, or pursued in inappropriate ways. But in the core of who we are, these threads and themes run deep and seek expression in our lives.

While personality types differ (some are more prone to be socially motivated, sensitive, and expressive), all personality types across all cultures need to feel and know they are important and loved, both subjectively and objectively, in both felt and practical ways. Even a compulsive melancholy personality (with a low sense of social need and little expressed needs preferring solitude, independence, and identifying as a loner), still needs and responds to love and affection. Right? It's because you were made by God to be a social and relational creature; made for love, purpose, and greatness.

---

[47] John and Stasi Eldredge, "Captivating Expanded Edition: *unveiling the mystery of a woman's soul*" © 2005, 2010, 2021

Needs Of The Soul

If we desire rest of soul, we must know that our value intrinsically comes from God and that we both are fully known and loved unconditionally, apart from our performance. We must also know our unique purpose and mission and adventure given by God, which no man or woman, angel or demon, can take away. How am I so confident of this? It's not because I simply have comforted myself in trying to make peace with myself and the world (that's impossible without utter delusion and deception). It's because it has been revealed and declared in the gospel of Jesus Christ, who demonstrated the perfect love of God. He saved us and died for us while we were still His enemy(Rom 5). It is by grace we have been saved and not by our works. But it gets better. He pours His loving Spirit into the hearts of those who believe, testifying to us that we are indeed the precious and loved Children of God! He did not leave us as orphans alone in this world. He gave us Himself to be with us, and live in us.

True security and purpose is found in the Lord, not in ourselves or circumstances. This is true in both the here and now and in the ages to come. Amen! The problem for many believers in today's hurried and over stimulating culture, is that they don't slow down enough to *BE* with God. They don't let His truth and love fill their hearts and lives in the deepest places of their needs, desires, and hurts. Most today don't even know how to do that, due to the over emphasis on "doing" more, rather than sitting at Jesus' feet and receiving His words in their hearts.

Read what my friend Katelyn wrote that speaks to the human struggle to meet the needs of the soul:

> *"Scrolling through my notes in my phone ... this was a good reminder for me :*

I can try my best to act like I don't need anyone. So that I'm not disappointed. So that I don't get hurt. I can deny the very needs inside my soul that God Himself put there. I can play it cool when things don't play out the way I wanted and just put up the mask of "I'm good, I'm chillin'."

All the while dying inside. Silently crying for a love we're too prideful to admit that we want. We have allowed shame to cover our needs and that's why they will never get met. We are embarrassed to admit that we get lonely or sad. We say to our hearts "how dare you need anyone. Don't you know you're just gonna be let down? Why would you be so stupid to admit you need and want love, attention, a sense of belonging." You can try to meet them on your own. Try to be self sufficient. Self made. But it will take you nowhere. It will bring you into a place of depression. Isolation. Insecurity. Always wondering if what is self made will be admired by others. There is no escaping this. We were made to have our needs met. It is how God designed us. To deny our needs and blanket them in shame, is to deny what the grand artist has put his finger print on. We deny divine design when we decide the needs HE created are an embarrassment."

Powerfully said right?

I used to be so insecure, constantly seeking acceptance and trying to fit a certain image. I would lie, not let myself become a burden to others, and avoid the raw vulnerability of what I really wanted. After doing this for years, I became disconnected from my heart and lost touch with myself because I was trying to be what I thought other people wanted or what would gain love and acceptance.

The dichotomy of this was that beneath my desire to please those I sought approval from, was an independent rebel who didn't care what people thought and did what he wanted. Strange mix but this is how the human heart works, especially when you are broken and don't know how to communicate in a healthy way. These are expressions of those internal defense systems we create. The rebel and the people pleasing components were a defensive system to keep people at a distance so that they wouldn't further reject or hurt me. When we live out of a place of hurt or rely on defense mechanisms built around lies, we unintentionally create the very situations we fear. This disconnects us from ourselves and others, leading to our own isolation, depression, loneliness, possible disassociation, and dehumanization. Self sabotage at its best. These systems are false refuges. That was part of my story.

It was only when I repeatedly encountered the genuine love of God at different times and in vulnerable moments that I was finally freed from the constant striving for love and the subconscious need to prove myself. I was freed from the fear of failure and rejection because I knew that I was loved and accepted in Christ— and that God, my Father, intimately knew me, wanted me, and loved me. Thank you God! This was a process that was deep and at the core of my being. God resolved it in the context of community. There, I learned to be known by others so that I could experience the love of God through people. We are broken by people but we are also healed by people, especially those in whom the love of God flows. This took years and, truthfully, there are still some places where I see I have to be very intentional, to choose to be brave, vulnerable and not hide before others and God. Freedom has been won in Christ but we must learn to stand in and continue to walk in that freedom.

One of the main reasons I share this is because we all need to encounter the love of God in a greater way for ourselves. We have to get past the superficial layers of performance and to the heart of the matter if we want to have lasting and eternal impact. We have to point people to Christ and not other false refuges and coping skills that eclipse a relationship with the Living God. If we want people to encounter the love of God through us, we have to be able to speak to the core of human desire, ambition, and difficulty. We need to learn to do this for children, teens, and adults.

A transformational leader, or aspiring one, should consider the grand scope of a person's life and story as they engage with them. This may be difficult to grasp but it is a paradigm to embrace as you listen to and lead others. This requires that we walk slowly with people.

The person or persons you interact with in any given moment stands before you with a history and backstory as well as a destiny. How shall we add value in that moment, in that season, in that God given window of time? What we do and say, or don't say, communicates and has an impact. We need to learn to walk slowly and carefully in order to be very present to the people around us. Sometimes the best thing to do is to just listen and be compassionately present. Let's make it count and sow the seeds of life, love, and truth.

The scriptures teach us to make the most of every opportunity and to be wise toward those who are outside the faith, always letting our speech be seasoned with grace. Also, knowing how we ought to answer each person, especially when it comes to the reasons we have faith in Christ (Col 4, 1 Peter 3:15). Being a "fisher of men" requires nuance and intentionality. It is more art than a science because it flows out of who you are, your relationship with God, and your knowledge of the scriptures (truth).

So, in all the ways you serve and help or aspire to help people, understand their core needs, search for significance, need for love, but also their need to be born again, forgiven, set free from oppression, and brought into relationship with Jesus Christ.

You have never met a mere mortal person. You have only met eternal beings who have an eternal destination, and one day you and everyone else will die and stand before their Maker. You have the ability to influence them and witness to Jesus Christ—to the way, the truth, and life. This must be central in your heart and vision as believers, regardless of your vocation or station in life. We have the privilege to call people back to the Lord, to speak to their heart and deepest desires that can only be satisfied in Him. We get to call people back into the glory they were made for! Consider this:

> "We are reminded of the seventeenth-century French philosopher Blaise Pascal's metaphor, that our unmet longings and unrequited desires are in fact "the miseries of a dethroned monarch." Mankind is like a king or queen in exile, and we cannot be happy until we have recovered our true state."[48]

We have the ministry and message of reconciliation to our Royal state; to become children of God! We get to love people in profound ways, to offer them the true bread and living water that truly satisfies all their needs and desires. We get to love them with the very love of God and help them encounter Him through us!

Love for God looks like love for people; The Lord's instruction to us was to love others in the way *He* has loved us. Wow! That's amazing. The scripture says that, "God is love. Whoever lives in love lives in God, and God in them... No one has seen God at any time, but if we love one another, God lives in us and His love is made complete in us."[49] This means that as we love people through the power of the Holy Spirit, with the love we have received ourselves, people experience God through us. This is so cool and makes everyday life fun! As I like to say, we get to drop love bombs on people! Ha! He has placed you in a unique situation with a unique set of abilities and talents to serve,

---

[48] Stasi Eldredge, *"Captivating: unveiling the mystery of a woman's soul"*, pg 21
[49] 1 Jn 4:12,16

express *His* love, and make an impact. The question is, what type of impact do you want to have? Are you willing to have?

Some of you reading this are well established in your vocation and career. I want to encourage you to leverage that place of influence for the cause of Christ; To live for something eternal and a greater Kingdom vision by joining the mission of Christ. But some of you may still be finding your way, in the midst of transition, and in the beginning of your journey. I want to encourage you to begin well and know how or where to best start. Some are young athletes, gifted, and passionate and want to powerfully influence your peers for the gospel. I want to spur you on and encourage you to fan that flame to use your unique creative avenue to make the Lord known. In a few chapters we'll get into this around using "what's in your hand."

Whatever platform or place of influence you have, it is first for the purposes of God to reach people and influence an industry, institution or household with the Kingdom of God; the heart and will of the Lord wants to have an expression through you to the world around you.Jesus modeled this prayer for us,"...your Kingdom come, your will be done on earth as it is in heaven."[50] You, my friend, are an agent of God's kingdom if, indeed, Christ lives in you. He wants to use you to extend His influence on the earth wherever He has called and gifted you! The earth is the lords and all its fullness.[51] That means there is no place in the world that the Lord is not interested in influencing with His will and presence. Some of us are called to be at the top of these sectors of society to help shape the culture and influence the influential, like Daniel, Joseph, or Esther. So, let's fully engage with a "yes" in our hearts to the call of God and see what Jesus will do! He's on a mission and we need to be with Him!

Are you in? Read on.

---

50 Luke 11:1-4, Matt 6:10
51 Ps 24

Pointing To Identity

Leadership and discipleship is about establishing people in the knowledge of God, helping them claim and live into and out of their Identity in Christ. We have to help them become warriors, exercising courage to overcome and claim who they really are, bravely leading and living from that place. When people know who they are and what they are called to do, they can live powerfully and make a real, eternal kingdom impact.

I encourage you to embrace the transformative principle of "being before doing. With this insight, we will not only understand the Lord's process and training in our own lives, but also know the essence of steadfast faith (the truth of what the Lord has done, who He is, and what He says about us). It will shape our ability to see what God is doing with others and how we can best serve, encourage, and coach them to come into their God given purpose and call.

God's process in the development of people is all hinged to identity—to who we are in Christ and who Christ is in us. This is what the apostle Paul prayed: that we would be strengthened with power in our inner man so that we could know the hope of God's calling, the riches of God's inheritance in us, and what the exceeding greatness of God's power is doing in the hearts of those who believe (Ephesians 1:17-22). We all live from the inside out. We must learn to understand this reality as leaders and aspiring transformational leaders to come alongside this work.

The search for meaning provides a choice to be or not to be, to hide/perform or to authentically walk in the light, to create a false identity or accept who God made us to be. We need to understand we were created with a unique purpose for both this life and the next. We are not here to simply be anything we want. We must discover who God already created us to be and fully walk in it. But again, we have a choice. Next, I want to get into the way our lives are shaped by our beliefs, choices, and responses to our experiences in life. This is a transformative truth we need to understand.

To be authentic disciples of Christ, and transformational leaders with the potential to change the world, we must settle into our God given identity and help others to do the same. Only transformational leaders can bring about transformation to those around them. This requires that we be transformed ourselves and lead from there; We lead out of who we are.

PAUSE. CAPTURE. APPLY
Prompts to help you process

1. What specific insights or concepts from this chapter resonated with you the most? Why do you think these stood out to you?

_____

_____

_____

2. How can you practically apply the principles discussed in this chapter to your daily life, relationships, or ministry? Identify at least one actionable step you can take this week.

_____

_____

_____

3. What potential challenges or barriers might you face in implementing these concepts? How can you overcome them?

_____

_____

_____

4. What are 3-5 quotes or points from this chapter that capture the essence of what it's communicating? Write them down.

_____

_____

_____

_____

5. How can you involve your family, small group, or church community in the practices and principles outlined in this chapter? What steps can you take to foster a culture of discipleship and transformation within your circle of influence?

_____

_____

_____

6. Spend a few moments in prayer, asking God for the wisdom, strength, and courage to live out the truths you've learned. Write down a commitment or a prayer that reflects your desire to grow as an authentic disciple and transformational leader to impact the world.

_____

_____

_____

CHAPTER 5

To Be or Not to Be: Being Before Doing

"Jesus came to announce to us that an identity based on success, popularity and power is a false identity-an illusion! Loudly and clearly he says: ' You are not what the world makes you; but you are children of God"

—Henri Nouwen, "Here and Now: living in the Spirit"

Ponder this: you were known by God before you were formed in your mothers womb! God saw your unformed substance, and, as the scriptures say, He wove you together in your mothers womb. You are fearfully and wonderfully made!" Ps 139. WOW!

God made you on and for a purpose in a unique time and place of history and within your family. Even the structures and traits of your DNA are by divine design. Nothing was by mistake! You are hard wired with a unique temperament, inherent potential, with particular aptitudes and abilities. Pretty cool! You are not a mistake, you're a masterpiece!

Your environment and the things that nurtured and shared your development, or lack thereof, play a part in the maturation or distortion of your unique expression in life. Plus, your upbringing is part of your sovereign story that needs to be touched by God's redemptive grace. We were all created with a divine design for unique purposes and assignments in life, but we must CHOOSE to walk in it. It doesn't just happen by itself. Integrity, honesty, authenticity, and living by faith is always a choice.

God created us with a free will to choose, a mind to think, and emotions to feel. The crazy thing is that we can choose to be what we aren't really designed to be. People do it all the time, not because they want to, but because they have been hurt, believed lies, and missed the affirmation and empowerment needed to be who God designed them to be. There is such an identity crisis in this generation. They are being systematically targeted and confused around their identity and gender, to the point that they identify with being a "furry"- or some type of animal. Though they are not stuck there, people tend to conform to the pressures, influences, labels, and expectations others place on them. People are either trying to avoid emotional or physical pain, or are pursuing some type of pleasure, desire, or aspiration. People always have reasons why they do the things they do. They are either legitimately or illegitimately trying to fill a need and desire in their hearts.

For example, if I'm passionate about singing and making music, and this is part of my calling and contribution to the world, yet my parents, siblings or teachers discourage or belittle me in those areas, I might believe their negativity means that singing and making music is bad, that I'm not good at it, or worse, associate music with fear, harm, or trauma. Consequently, this area of my life, which should be a source of joy, creativity, and fulfillment, shuts down due to these negative associations. I would then conform to this lie and abandon my musical endeavors. This would lead me to shut down the musical gifts that were hardwired into me, preventing their development.

As it would turn out, I wouldn't do what I'm called to do in the way I'm called to do it. Would I survive? Yes. Could I adapt and compensate? Yes. Would I be fully alive and expressing who God designed me to be? No. The joy and enthusiasm that loves and celebrates life would be dull and dead. Parts of my soul would be shut down, and I would probably be living and coping in depression. I would make life decisions, without consideration of these suppressed passions and forgotten joys. Life would lack fulfillment, joy, excitement, and color.

Tragic right? Yet countless people do this very thing and settle for less than the fullness they were created for. They don't express themselves authentically because they still believe a lie. Fear, rejection, hatred, and a hardened heart, to just name a few, are killers and distorters of reality. They create a false reality and produce bondage, to which the only solution is deliverance, freedom, and healing. These things affect not just personal expression and passion, but education, cognitive capacity, social ability, health, financial stability, decision making, intimacy with God and more. That was part of my story and it's the story of humanity.

When we repeatedly think and act in a particular way, our physical brain and body is affected and responds accordingly. We either align with or drift from God's design continually. We either function constricted by fear and the lies we believe, or we at the highest levels from the empowerment of love and truth. Our felt sense of being and performance in life is based on our mind and beliefs (our thoughts, convictions, imagination, and emotions). This is a really powerful truth to get.

The mind- body connection is real and must be understood. Our biology, physiology, psychology, and spirituality are all connected and all affected by everything, one another, and everyone. Brain health, gut health, your nervous system, mental health, relational health and overall health are all connected. By the grace of God you have the power to improve upon your present condition. God's refining and sanctifying process renews our minds and our bodies so that we can express the freedom He has given us. God's power and salvation is meant to touch not just our spirits and minds but also our bodies. He sanctifies us body, soul, and spirit (1 Thess 5:23) and by His stripes we were healed (Isaiah 53:5, 1 Peter 2:24). His power gives life to even our mortal flesh (Romans 12:1-2, 8:11). God's plan and will for your life involves new life and this affects your body, soul, and spirit. He wants abundance in all aspects of our lives! Praise God! More on that later.

Change can be scary and difficult because we have to navigate the mess and vulnerability of process and the unknowns. But the gospel calls us out of our past and into the truth of who we are in Christ. In the journey of transformation, becoming more like Christ, and as anyone who has dedicated themselves to making disciples understand, we often struggle to let go of familiar thoughts, ideas, and ways of doing things. From "Forget for success: walking away from outdated, counterproductive beliefs and people practices" by Eric Harvey and Steven Ventura, talk about this human tension and tendency:

" The fact is, we all carry a certain amount of counterproductive cerebral baggage that weighs us down… It holds us back.

Our loads include everything from once valid beliefs and practices that have outlived their usefulness and applicability – to miss information and misconceptions that we've accepted (and even embraced) without much examination or thought.

Why care about baggage? Because it negatively impacts us, the people we work with, the environment we work in, and the results we get. Simply stated, whatever we accept and believe determines how we behave… and how we behave determines what we achieve (or don't achieve)."[52]

---

[52] Eric Harvey and Steven Ventura, *"Forget for success: walking away from outdated, counterproductive beliefs and people practices"* (Dallas: Performance,

We have to break out of the chains that have bound us and examine the beliefs and practices that have hurt and hindered us. We want to choose to be who God created us to be and throw off the pattern of this world - the ways we have been conditioned that oppose the truth of who God created us to be. We have to be gracious and patient with ourselves and others but, my friends, It's time for stinking thinking to get the boot!

It's essential to recognize that we have the power and freedom to choose how we live how we'll invest our time, what we'll believe, and what abilities and gifts we'll harness. There is a way that flows and produces the most in our life and for the Kingdom of God. The way of wisdom and truth that leads to a fruitful and fulfilling life is by choosing to live, first through relationship and obedience to God's word, and then according to your unique, God given design.

While living in alignment with how God made us, we should also promote this in the lives of those we serve and influence. We need people to see who they really are, learn to love and embrace themselves (without comparison to others), and help them give themselves away in loving service to God and others. When we and they do this from who we are in Christ, with the power of His Spirit, we will maximize our impact, fruitfulness to the glory of God, and experience fulfillment and overflowing joy in life!

This principle is found all through the word of God. Many authors have taught this as well; such Steven Covey, used terminology such as "finding your unique voice", Jim Collins describes it in discovering greatness, and while Robert Clinton and Lance Wallneau call it living in "convergence" where your life experience, passions, giftings, abilities, etc all intersect as the central expression of your life mission and calling. They all note that many people never reach this "convergence zone" due to the lack of intentionality, discipline, and clarity.

1997), 12.

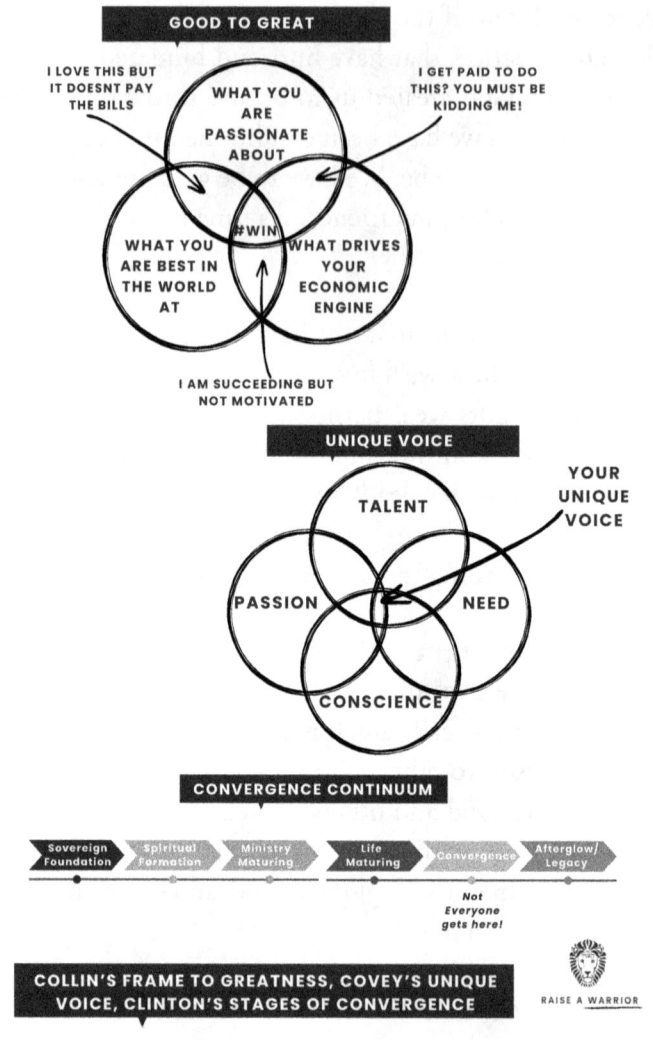

The breakthrough xp Course is designed to help you discover your purpose and craft a master plan and rule of life to move you toward and into the fullness of "convergence" and a powerful legacy.

To move into and to abide in a place of freedom, safe and loving relationships are critical to give us the space to come out of hiding that actually imprison us from being able to grow and move forward in love and truth. We need those loving relationships for ourselves and we need to provide that for those we are discipling.

So to recap, our efficiency is found in who God made us to be. Jesus' redemptive work empowers and enables us to recover the purity and original intention of God for our lives. He really does make all things new. Can I get an Amen! When it comes to serving, teaching, leading others, we need to think with this paradigm so that we can holistically lead others into a place of wholeness and healthy development. Unless we address and help others address the deeper internal systems that were constructed for survival or to avoid emotional pain, people will never be able to reach their potential. To live in abundance, personal freedom, and fulfill our God given mission, we have to get to the core of the heart and live radically from there in the safety of God's love.

To make an eternal impact as a transformational leader, it is both critical and essential to think and lead holistically. It's also important to note that it's not all on you to meet or serve all these deeper needs of people. Knowing your limitations and scope of knowledge and practice is key. We can "stay in our lane" but at least develop a collaborative network of people and services to help with these deeper things. This is also not an excuse to avoid or quickly outsource what seems "out of your scope." The Lord will put you in complicated situations in order to invite you into a place of growth or to cause you to minister in the power of His spirit to set people free; doing what no human can do. God has diversely gifted the body of Christ for this reason and so that we learn to serve and minister collaboratively with our gifts and skills. But as I was saying, having the understanding, empathy, and ability to create a safe space for people to explore and express themselves as they grow, heal, and learn is gold—and a key trait of a transformational leader.

So in getting to the core of who people are, we are drilling into the principle that *"being comes before doing"* and into the truth that *"being also precedes intimacy"*, with both God and man. Again, we have the choice to "be" or not to "be." As leaders, and as people who desire to fully and faithfully live into all God has for us, we must understand and press into these truths about identity, freedom, and growth. Without the discovery and resting in "being" the "who" we are, and the experience of being known and loved as we are, "intimacy", there is no real personal transformation, no real community and relationships, nor the ability to foster transformation in others.

To help others transform requires meaningful connection with both God and other people. Without it, we will have very limited influence to move people into God's plan. This should shape how we do life, and how we relate to those in our influence and how we think about the aims and process of discipleship. Understanding these principles empowers us to serve the eternal plan of God by participating with His Spirit to be transformed into the image and likeness of Christ who faithfully obeyed the Father, lived on mission, and changed the world.

The Identity Link & the Mind Body Connection

There is a powerful connection between our mind and our bodies. God's plan is that they are moving together in congruence, so that who we are and what we believe are lived with integrity and expressed in our lives and bodies in beautiful harmony. Our physicality operates in peace and joy and strength when we live out of the truth of our identity and unique design. Some would call this a state of "flow" or freedom in motion. When our soul is stuck in the past and operating out of old harmful patterns, movement and physical health suffers. Your brain and nervous system are functioning out of your belief systems, thoughts, and actual health. Whether we like it or not, our life is lived from the inside out. Our bodies manifest what our inner life of the mind believes. Take that in for a moment.

My martial arts instructor would always talk about how our Kata (a choreographed sequence of techniques and movements) is an expression and extension of who we are and where we are in the journey. Martial philosophers share this sentiment as well, such as Bruce Lee, when they say, that to be a true martial artist, it is to authentically and honestly fully express themselves in their practice and movement.

I love this thought and concept! It is the harmony of body, soul, and spirit moving together as one to express and reveal the truth of who we are, and ultimately the glory of God mirrored in mankind. In my primary style of martial art this concept is practiced in a kata called, "Sanchin", meaning "the three conflicts/struggles." Body, soul, and spirit are mindfully engaged to be synchronized through the movement and breath and of that movement are a demonstration of the internal qualities of heart, understanding, self control, patience, and more.

I know I have seen my own impatience and how I make decisions in life demonstrated in the timing and focus of my movements. I remember when my timing was off and a little rushed in my kata. My movement mirrored that season of my life in learning to slow down and pay closer attention to timing. I love how that works. The externals were a manifestation of my internals and became a physical witness to me of the bigger issue in my life that God was after. My level of consciousness came to a new place and I was able to add more attention to the needed area of growth in my life and in my training. (Side note for instructors, coaches, parents, educators, etc. Help your students think in this way as to foster self discovery and self awareness that leads to growth). We have to be self aware and help others be self aware lest we continually stumble from the blind spots we are unwilling to view. Examine the external "fruit" of actions and behaviors and let it lead you into the deeper internal attitudes and beliefs. In this way you can learn to shape and train both the external performance and internal beliefs that influence action.

Learning to live from the inside out speaks to the power of intention and congruence, a life lived with integrity and purpose in full transparency; Our internal beliefs and spirituality is made plain for all to see in what we say and do. Like Christ, the word is made flesh and all can see it. Truth is embodied and revealed through us; intangibles are made tangible through what we say and do.

To bring this concept and reality of the mind body connection into relation to our identity and purpose, it could be summarized as: who we really are should point to what we're really to do in life, and not the other way around. Simply doing things in life to try to define yourself is backwards. It's a different matter to discover the abilities that you already possess that become observable as you are doing things. The things we do should be a demonstration or expression of who we are. The principle is, being precedes doing. In this way, we operate from the place of rest or flow, we operate from the way God designed us fundamentally; the Master Craftsman Himself desires us to live within and out of who He made us. We function and live best according to the native design in which God created us. When the Lord created all things in the beginning of time He said, "it was very good," and He meant what He said.

The word "good" is a Hebrew word, "Tov", which means useful, beautiful, pleasant, excellent, prosperous, fertile, and functional according to design. For us, this means that to live out of how God made us is the proper order to a God glorifying, beautiful, happy, fruitful, and fulfilling life. God's created order sets the precedence and principle truth in how we ought to live and how life best works. This is wisdom, my friends. It was when sin came into the world through the disobedience incited by demonic suggestion, that shame, fear, hiding, death, and all manners of evil were loosed to distort and corrupt what was once "good." The good news is that Jesus came to redeem and restore what was lost and bring all things back to His original design.

We need to know this for our own life but also in how we parent, teach, coach, train, and influence others. We want to help people connect to the truth of who God made them to be. This is an issue of identity and is central to how we live and what we are called to. Jesus came to restore the purity of the "imago de", the image of God in us, so that we could live from and out of the rest of who God made us to be. Who God made us to be will bring Him glory when we are living and leading from that place of alignment and truth!

Jesus and The Principle of Identity

I love the precedents we see in the life of Jesus, who lived out of the power and truth of His identity as the Son of God. In fact, it was that very identity that perpetually came under attack and accusation from people and the devil himself. His claim to be God and the son of God, His very identity, is why the Jews wanted to crucify Him.

The truth of who He was is what made Him powerful and important. We see the principle of *"being before doing"* at work. Because He knew who He was He could do what He did; He knew who He was as a loved Son and He knew His unique mission in life. Therefore He could live with focus and endure the pain of the process even unto death. We need the same, to know who we are and what our purpose and mission is.

Before Jesus did any mighty work or miracle or was launched into His public ministry, He was baptized by John the Baptist, and something amazing happened. As He came out of the waters the heavens opened, the Spirit descended in the form of a dove to rest on Him and the Father from heaven spoke over Him for all to hear, "This is My beloved son in whom I'm well pleased." Wow!

This declaration of the Fathers love and affirmation rested on Jesus before He "did" anything spectacular as history records! The knowledge and security of who He was and His Belovedness before the Father empowered His life and ministry. It ought to be the same for us. Part of the plan of redemption was reconciling us to God the Father so that we would live and grow and serve out of the confidence of who God made us to be under His love and pleasure. In this way we glorify Him and we walk in the joy and pleasure of knowing Him!

Jesus' Identity empowered him to go low in service and to love well those in His care. The cool thing as well, is that Jesus knew who He was from a young age. Many others all throughout the word of God had also discerned and understood their identity and call from youth, and it informed their journey, training, and development. We need to start from the place of identity in our own lives and in the lives of those around us. This applies to our leadership, our educational path, and our approach to discipleship. We need to look at people and think as well as ask, "who is this person? How has God made him? What are they called to? What are they passionate about?....etc."

Parents, this is why the scripture call us to "train a child in the way they should go, and when they are older they will not depart from it." Proverbs 22:6

Who we are points to what we are to do and God wires us and equips us with what's needed to walk with in that calling.

Do you know who you are and what the Father says about you? Do you know what you are called to do? (I have some great resources for you to help you get clarity here. Check it out at the end of the chapter).

Both Practical and Supernatural

My story includes a journey of deep heart work, deliverance, healing, and the rewiring of my thoughts so that my broken and dysfunctional and sinful past didn't keep me bewitched, oppressed, stuck, held back by fears that stifled the expression of my God given identity and design. Can I just say, rather shout, that God is so good and He makes all things new! He redeems time and all that was lost in the years that I squandered.

My process into martial arts and performing arts has so many aspects and a written work could be done on this alone. For the purpose of this book I want to call attention to an aspect of my childhood and growing up that can serve as an example for what we're talking about around "to be or not be."

My story of how God began to heal my heart and restore His intention and design in my life was both supernatural and practical, as it really is for all of us. Let me just preface this by saying, it's important to understand that we are triune beings; body, soul, and spirit, made in the image of God. Coming alive in Christ, being born again, is a supernatural work of regeneration by the Holy Spirit of our spirit that was once dead in sin and cut off from communion with God. The Spirit of God, His divine life, gives life to our soul and our body with the participation of our faith. That participation has very practical application in the things we are called to do and practice from the heart in obedience to the word of God (Obedience to the truth from the heart is also the central aim of being and making disciples).

The Lord instructs us in how to think and behave in a way that is truly wise. It leads to beautiful fruit in what we do, our performance and interaction with others, our character, our effectiveness in the mission, and in our sense of being. There is no abundant life apart from obedience to the word and ways of God. When we walk in alignment with the truth, life prospers. It's just that simple.

The practical things the Lord would have us do are both brilliant and simply yield transformational results. I want to look at the science of some of what's happening in our brains as well, to explain some of the physiological happenings of what the scriptures teach when we are told, "Do not be conformed to the world but be transformed by the renewing of your mind."Roman 12:2

Also, I'll explain real quick why I want to look at a little bit of the science since you may be asking, "why are you telling me about this?" Well, glad you asked! Ha!.

1. Part of my story and how God unlocked my spirit, mind, and soul was through physical movement that led into a greater fulfillment of expressing my divine calling and purpose in life.

2. A holistic approach to live to the fullest ourselves and see our worship and devotion as encompassing all that we are and do—Body, Soul, Spirit.

3. Methodologies for how we instruct and influence those in our care and in our different realms of service to maximize impact. We are called to love people and make disciples, and renewing our minds is central to that. So we want to grow in understanding and harness every tool God gives us.

Holistic education equips people with both the internal and external qualities necessary to overcome and prevail in life's hardships and challenges. We also need to know how to maximize all God gave us, serve to the best of our ability, and grow to add the highest value to others as we faithfully steward our lives.

We must all know how to govern our hearts, minds, and lives both practically and supernaturally to bear fruit to the glory of God. We are not called to just survive and get by in life, we are called to thrive and reign in life through Christ! We need to know this, own this, and propagate this!

Knowing a little bit about how God created the brain to function can add more tangibility and potential motivation for the rational mind to apply divine truth. Much work has been done and discovered in the realm of neuroscience and positive psychology to accelerate personal growth and performance, learning, healing from trauma, mental health, and behavioral change. Again, some of this is just giving the practical knowledge of what the bible actually prescribes for growth in grace and godliness. Part of the problem has been this lost art of discipleship and what it means to really live an exchanged life in Christ that can lay hold of the transforming power of the gospel. We are going to look at some of the science but to be clear, the scriptures provide the truth and He has given us everything we need for life and godliness by divine power through accurate understanding of what God has given us in Christ.

Plus, sometimes people just over spiritualize things and fail to see the tangible things that can be done to make progress. Too many people play victim and let their past define them and they stay stuck. Not only does scripture and the work of the cross declare and provide freedom, science also tells us that we can literally renew our minds and be transformed, creating a new felt sense of reality. As Dr Daniel Amen says, "we are not stuck with the brains we have." Pretty amazing! This is an empowering thought for our lives and for those we are called to teach and raise up.

We all have the power and ability in the grace of God to choose life, transform the pains of the past, and refashion our reality, aka renewing of the mind according to true knowledge. One of the crazy amazing realities revealed in the word of God is that we are all called to be partakers of God's divine life and nature, being conformed to the image of Christ; we actually get to become like Him in profound ways. We were called to share in His glory and nature. Jesus was the first born among many brothers and sisters of a new creation[53]! He

---

53 Romans 8:29-30

was the forerunner and first fruits of a new creation. This is just so wild! This is the mystery of redemption and the beautiful work of being reconciled to God as heirs and co-heirs with Christ! The word of God and the sciences agree that we have the power to change and truly be renewed in our minds and lives. If we change our brains we can change our lives!

As we'll talk about later, learning and education has to be more than a transfer of Information. It must lead to transformation, morality, and real equipping for life and people's unique vocation and mission. Before we get any farther, I want to assure you where I stand. Let me just say as a foundation to education, true knowledge, and personal growth, that Christ Himself and the power of the Holy Spirit, not science and self will or self help, is at the center of it all. I believe the word of God (the Bible) is inspired, infallible, and good to fully equip us for right living and every good work in life. I believe that everything for life and godliness has been given to us by divine power through our intimate and accurate knowledge of Christ through our fellowship with the Holy Spirit (2 Tim 3:16-17, 2 Peter 1). Principally and in seed form, we see the wisdom and ways of God revealed in scripture for all the domains of life and culture.

Let me also say, we must pursue the truth in the word of God by faith with good sense and sound principles of study in the context of the community of Believers (the local Church) by the power of the Holy Spirit; No truth or revelation of scripture is subject to private interpretation and must be understood as it was intended when written by the author. There can be no sound application without proper understanding of the truth first. So it's important to not live your faith or merely interpret scripture alone and in isolation. As believers, we are called into the Family of God in a global and universal sense but also in the local family—a local church. We are all to be engaged in the community and mission of the church, being known and loved and loving others with the love of Christ, while fully serving and expressing our God given gifts in the life and gatherings of the community. We have to be discipled and disciple others in the context of the Family of God. If you are not connected to a life giving, bible believing, Holy Spirit filled, authentic church, please, get connected ASAP. An Internet church is not enough nor God's plan for His family or for you when it comes to being an actual disciple/apprentice of Jesus Christ. If you don't have an authentic church community, please reach out to me and I can help connect you or I'll plant a simple church around you (I'm serious). I understand there have been massive shifts and shakings in the Body of Christ and there are many communities that are not functioning in a New Testament wineskin nor making real disciples. So if you are not connected, please let me help you get connected. Reach out to me!

Ok, I know I just went off track a little on that so let me get back to it. For whatever reason, some people over mystify the scriptures and their application and need to see the truth in other rational or "tangible" ways to apply it. That's another reason I want to look at the science of it as well. Plus, the Lord does not see life compartmentalized as we tend to. I believe this false dichotomy must come down for us to wholly embrace our next level of growth, establishment in the faith, and teaching others holistically. Setting people free requires understanding and nuanced skills for every level of a person's being and life. It is not one dimensional or restricted to bible study and prayer alone. Our level of consciousness needs to come higher and our understanding of truth needs to become multi-dimensional, applied at every level of our person; body, soul, and spirit. Transformational leaders and good shepherds of people must approach their leadership and people development comprehensively.

So to come back around and to reinforce this tension of "being that leads to doing" and partnership of the supernatural and practical, let's look at a few scriptures here first:

- The scriptures say, "That above all things guard your heart, for from it flows all the issues of life." proverbs 4:23.

- As you see, we have a responsibility to guard our hearts. We must exercise internal government.

- "As a man thinks in his heart, so he is…"—prov 23:7

- We are told to "Set our mind (affections) on things above.." Colossians 3.

- We are told to " To rejoice always, to be anxious for nothing and to do all things by prayer making our requests known to God, with thanksgiving. And the peace of God will guard our heart and minds in Christ Jesus….and to think on what is true, noble, praiseworthy, of good report….then the God of peace will be with us" Philippians 4:1-6

- We are told to be alert and not be taken captive by fine sounding arguments and hollow philosophies that are according to the traditions of man and the elemental spiritual forces of this world rather than that of Chris. Rather we continue to walk in the truth, being firmly rooted and built up in Christ, established in the faith as we were taught, and to abounding in thanksgivingCol 2:1-8

  - Part of the whole concept of scripture teaching and the "fight of faith" is to hold fast to the truth and not be shaken, but abide in it in such a way that it transforms us and causes us to bear fruit to the glory of God. To be renewed in our minds leads to a transformed life that enables us to know, discern, and do the will of God.—Romans 12:1-2

- Trust in the LORD with all your heart, and lean not on your own understanding; in all your ways acknowledge Him, and He will make your paths straight. Be not wise in your own eyes; fear the LORD and turn away from evil.

This will bring healing to your body and refreshment to your bones."—Prov 3:5-8

- ○ The Proverbs are full of instructions to govern our heart, thoughts, words, deeds, relationships..etc to live a life that is pleasing to the Lord and that leads to blessing, peace, health, wealth, etc.

- We are instructed to meditate on the word of God day and night and to talk about it around our tables with our kids, while at home, when we are on the road, when we are going to bed and when we are getting up, to write it down and put it above our doors…etc. —Deut 6:4-9

- We are told to let what we have heard and come to believe remain in us, to abide in the truth, to let His words remain in us.—john 15, 1 John

- We are told to "take every thought captive that exalts itself against the knowledge of God…every vain imagination, argument, or idea, and make it obedient to Christ." —2 Corinthians 10

- "The mind governed by the flesh is death, but the mind governed by the Spirit is life and peace"—Romans 8:6

- ..walk by the Spirit, and you will not gratify the desires of the flesh. For the flesh desires what is contrary to the Spirit, and the Spirit what is contrary to the flesh.…Since we live by the Spirit, let us keep in step with the Spirit…Do not be deceived: God cannot be mocked. A man reaps what he sows. Whoever sows to please their flesh, from the flesh will reap destruction; whoever sows to please the Spirit, from the Spirit will reap eternal life. Let us not become weary in

- doing good, for at the proper time we will reap a harvest if we do not give up." —Galatians 5:16-17, 25, 6:7-9

- We are told to behold the glory of God with unveiled faces, looking intently as like in a mirror, and the Spirit will transform us into the same image from glory to glory, strength to strength, and faith to faith"—2 Corinthians 3:17

- We are told to not be hearers of the word alone, deceiving ourselves, but to put it into practice and be doers of the word—James 1

- The work of redemption has been completed and the dominion of sin to rule over us has been disarmed. The Lord said, Its finished....yet to "He who overcomes" will receive the reward, those who endure to the end will be saved — Rev 22, Matt 12

From these scriptures all speak to the management of our minds, the place of focus and concentration, and the subject of our meditation.

We see two things working together in tandem: the life of the mind and the life of the Spirit. The practical and the supernatural. The human will mingling and aligning with the Divine will for personal growth and development in the knowledge and nature of God. The scriptures say, "work out your salvation with fear and trembling because God is at work in us to both will and to do according to His good pleasure." — Philippians 2:12-13

We are being renewed in knowledge according to the image of the creator and learning to live in the life of the "new creation", "the new man" that accords with true righteousness and not in an image or idea of our own making. We are growing in and perfecting love for both God and man, and we do this by our faith filled choices and responses to the love and voice of God. In this way we keep in step with the Spirit of God and do what is pleasing in His sight, for this is the aim of every true believer.—Colossians 3, Rom 14:7-8

The life of our mind and the realm of thoughts is important to our growth in all of life. So let's look at a little bit of science and then I'll share some from my story.

NeuroScience & The Core Needs of Man.

The human brain operates like the central control center for all of our life functions (breathing, digestion, movement, hormones, pain and pleasure receptors, memory, storing of emotions and feelings and more).. We are body, soul, and spirit., a fully integrated whole, where each thing affects the next in an interrelated complex living system. The Lord designed everything masterfully!

Neuroscience today reveals how our brains function and how we have the capacity to form new neural pathways in our brain by learning new things and thinking differently from our normal thought patterns. These habitual ways of thinking are often developed over the years and largely shaped during our early life. A neuro pathway in brief, is a series of connected neurons that send signals from one part of the brain to another. They are like roads and highways that provide a connection of communication.

Neurons come in three main types: motor neurons that control muscles; sensory neurons that are stimulated by our senses; and interneurons that connect neurons together. These connected neurons process the information we receive. They enable us to interact, as well as experience emotions and sensations. They create and lock in our memories, enable us to learn, and form our primary ability to attach to others in a healthy way. There's a saying, " the neurons that fire together wire together." This means that when we repeatedly practice an activity, focus on a thought or engage in a particular behavior, the neurons involved strengthen their connections, creating a neural network or pathway in our brain. This network affects how we feel, the thoughts we generate , and ability to act and move with proficiency and coordination.

We already have a series of neural pathways from birth, and we are creating new ones all the time. For example, a baby develops an early neural pathway when a baby smiles, and is affirmed or rewarded by a smile in return and possibly by another warm, soothing, or loving experience like a cuddle or kiss. The same baby reasons out in his mind that if he touches something hot or sharp, it may hurt. Both are valuable learning experiences. Both build neural pathways and networks in the brain that shape our conscious and unconscious way of living, reasoning, interpreting, and interacting with our surroundings. Our lives form around our interpretation of our experiences. It's like neural programming. Many say our programming is foundationally set by 7 years old.

When we experience neglect, abuse, and trauma, neural pathways form as well that have deep impact at the core of our being. Again, we are not stuck there (though a person in that situation feel very stuck at times and may even have built amnesia walls in the brain to block out painful memories or have dissociated to create split personalities or "parts"as a protective mechanism) but it is important to understand how certain things get hardwired into our lives. Intense experiences, good or bad, go all the way down to our neurology. This programming affects our unconscious knee-jerk responses, emotions, and thought patterns.

Neural pathways are both essential and the God-created natural way we are hard wired and formed in this life; and as the example above illustrates, not all pathways may be beneficial and can become negative habits or soul orientation with conditioned responses.

To Be or Not to Be: Being Before Doing

The fact that every human being must be born again and renewed in our minds indicates that all our brains have to be retrained in the truth and love of God. Our ways and thoughts are not naturally His thoughts. When we are invited in the gospel, we become like Him in both thought and deed. Our nervous systems that hold these subconscious neural automatic responses have to be retrained by real and meaningful experiences with God and people. Even great parents and a good upbringing falls short of the Glory God has intended us to know and live. We all have believed lies and responded wrongly to people, situations, and circumstances. Those responses and beliefs formed out of these experiences that impacted us at a deep and emotional level and formed neural pathways, become locked in our body, shape our physical brain, and influence our subconscious reactions, feelings, and assumptions. They become our world view, lens, or paradigm in how we operate in life. Like a computer, it's the software or operating system that determines its primary functionality, not so much the hardware (Although that has a large part to play—the physical brain can be damaged which can cause real havoc in life and health as well. If the hardware gets damaged the software is affected too and both will need repair in specific and targeted ways).

Either way, all things must be brought to the cross of Christ, renewed in knowledge, and touched with His love and power. Repentance is where we take responsibility for our wrong responses and beliefs, break agreement with them, and renew our thinking with the truth. It's both a supernatural and natural exchange. I'm not talking about "white knuckling," trying to apply the truth in our own strength. We do have to learn to resist the old, take demonic thoughts captive and not identify with them, exercise spirit-empowered self control through faith in Christ, and stand in the truth. I'm talking about relationally exchanging with the heart of God and His victory in our hearts and mind as we behold Him with the eyes of our understanding through the Spirit (2 Cor 3:17-18). This takes faith to believe what the gospel declares is ours, intention to set aside time before God, and humility to fully receive it as a gift we can not earn. When we relationally exchange with God through faith, divine power works in us to strengthen, deliver, and transform us. Thank God! His love is stronger than death and it affects our neuro hardwiring, transforming our character at the deepest levels. We are changed by the love of God by meaningful connection to His loving kindness.

We must meditate on His nature in the fellowship and acknowledgment of the Holy Spirit. The Spirit is the One that actually transforms us and reformats our brains and neural pathways as He communicates His love and truth to us. Amazing! As He is, we are to be in this world, and it all starts with gazing into His beauty and perfection. Everything in the Kingdom of God starts with what we have first received from Him. We can only bear the fruit of the love and truth in which we are called to abide!

Discipleship must be approached and fueled with this understanding that love is at the heart of transformation. *Loving attachment to God and people are the catalyst to foster real change.*

Many believers and churches miss this piece about relational exchange in loving attachment as central to the growth and transformation of a discipleship process. According to Enlightenment thinking the formula for transformation is:

Transformation = truth + good choices + power.[54]

Truth, choice, and the power of the Holy Spirit is essential but we must offer them with love at the center. Loving, relational exchange with God through fellowship with the Holy Spirit and the people of God, are the driving agents of transformation as well as spiritual, emotional, social, and moral growth. The word of God makes this pattern plain, but we see that even modern brain science clearly indicates that transformation and character change must be anchored

---

54 Warner and Wilder, Solution of Choice, 67.

in the development of a "love bond." Love is the driving force and motivation for real change from the heart.

In the book "The Other Half of Church: Community, Brain Science, and overcoming Spiritual Stagnation" the author writes, "It is easy to believe that if our Christian communities have solid biblical teaching and doctrine (truth) and we are encouraged to apply the teaching to our lives (good choices), the Holy Spirit will enable us to understand the truth and make good choices (power). We expect this will lead to transformation. The formula looks reasonable to modern eyes, but it has a fatal flaw—it is missing the most important variable. Love, the primary mover of character, is absent. Without *"hesed"* (Hebrew word for loving attachment—italics mine), we see little transformation. I will carefully remind you, we are not suggesting that truth, choices, and power have no place in discipleship. We are restoring *"hesed"* to its central place."[55]

There is so much research here, so if you're fascinated by what I'm talking about I would encourage you to take a deep dive. Just keep scriptural truth central so you can weed through all of the psychological garbage not rooted in a biblical worldview. But the bottom line is that authentic loving attachment in Christian community is so critical to this discipleship process and something that has been lacking in the body of Christ. We are now seeing the Lord restoring across the earth the call to authentic community and authentic discipleship. God is drawing us back to the ancient paths that lead to the rest of soul and the ways of God that produce a deeper transforming work.

---

[55] Jim Wilder and Michel Hendricks, *The Other Half of Church: Community, Brain Science, and overcoming Spiritual Stagnation, Moody Publishers 820 N. LaSalle Boulevard, Chicago, IL 60610, pg. 84*

How Neural Pathways Develop

Like a physical pathway on the ground, if you keep going over the same route, a path get's worn, a routine is developed, and a habit is formed. When you are ingrained with a particular pattern or routine, it's hard to break away from it because it feels normal. When you travel a road or move in a particular pattern over and over, you could do it with your eyes closed. We tend to travel the path of least resistance or at least with what is most familiar. Things that were once created by a deliberate conscious choice, over time become an unconscious mode of existence.

Habits are the same. By always reaching for chips or a bar of chocolate when you feel low, or a drink to lessen feelings of anxiety, you are creating a pathway in the brain. This means that like your walk to the park on the trodden path, you automatically follow the same route. You're feeling down, so your brain goes along the path to the chips or chocolate bar or whatever else you have conditioned yourself to do; an association of comfort was made and this becomes the desired and preferred pathway to travel. Humans are creatures of habit and the brain is looking for routine. As believers, we want to make sure our routines for places of comfort and satisfaction are rooted in Christ and not things that ultimately enslave and hurt us. We don't want to "hewn for ourselves broken cisterns that cannot hold water", rather than turning to the Lord. He is the fountain of living water, the true bread from heaven that satisfies us. We do not want to spend our energy on what is not true Bread and what does not truly satisfy. Lord, spare us from idols and the common idolatry of our day!

The good thing is that like a real road system, the brain can be changed and adapted. This flexibility of the brain is called neuroplasticity. It enables you to change mental and physical habits that you thought were ingrained or felt too hard to stop. "Old dogs CAN learn new tricks!." The cool thing about the brain is that it can create new routes and shut off old ones, with some help and training. It's what we understand to be repentance and renewing of the mind.

So we can see that our repeated pattern of thinking and behavior digs deep pathways in the brain that triggers our conditioned responses at every level of our being (our nervous system, emotions, hormones, memories ,etc). Our lives become the product or manifestation of what we repeatedly do that's rooted in what we believe or have continually believed in our minds and hearts. Pretty wild, right?

The pattern or cycle goes like this:

- We have an experience and our response to that experience forms an initial belief.

- That belief shapes and determines our thoughts.

- Our repeated thought patterns determine our emotional responses.

- Our emotions and intuitive rationality influence the decisions and actions we take.

- The actions and decisions we make determine our results and outcomes.

- Those outcomes and results provide us with feedback which in turn reinforce our belief systems.

- The cycle continues UNLESS we introduce something new to break the cycle.

As the cycle continues without an interruption of new thought patterns, it digs deep neural pathways in our brain and body responses. When we understand this, we can intentionally introduce new thoughts and felt experiences in the grace and love of God. They begin to forge new neural pathways and literally renew our brains and minds. It's only by meditating on the truth and connecting to the love of God and others with regularity that transformation can occur. When emotion and meaning connect to new information or experiences, they begin to intersect, forming new neural networks. It changes our brain and the autonomic nervous system responses that override normal, rational thinking. This is what helps us really grow and transform.

This is a powerful truth to grasp.

Ask Yourself

So ask yourself: Do you like the fruit and results that your life is revealing and producing? If not, follow the trail and identify what you really believe and where it came from.[56] Your feelings are bridges to your beliefs in the heart. It's one thing to know something rationally in your head and it's another thing to believe in your heart.

This is where the power and reality of the gospel comes in to set us free from the influence of sin and the brokenness of our past. The Lord sets us free and makes us new. We must learn to wholly take these moments and patterns to Christ and the truth of that divine exchange. We take the unwanted, negative, ungodly thinking and corresponding behavior, and exchange it for the truth which is positive, powerful, and aligns with the will and word of God. This is part of repentance. To repent means to change your mind and to go another direction; it's taking a 180 degree turn in thought and in action. Taking new action without changing your thinking is futile and will be short lived. This is the difference between behavior modification and transformation. The former leads to striving and self effort whereas the latter leads to

---

56 Some looping thoughts, negative emotions, irrational behaviors, etc can be rooted in something misaligned in your biology or the result of nutrient deficiency, or a head trauma, or a tumor..etc and not necessarily rooted in a lie. Everything must be properly discerned and people need to be understood holistically.

rest and freedom sustained by the life of the Spirit. I want the latter, how about you?

Both neuroscience and the workings of God declare the possibilities of breaking away from what robs, distorts, or hinders our ability to live into who God created us to be.

When we are aligned with truth in loving connection to God and people, and have clarity of purpose, everything about us starts moving, thriving and flowing in a divine rhythm that empowers us in our callings.. Our sense of identity expresses itself meaningfully which results in greater impact and sense of fulfillment.

If we don't address the pains of our past we will pass them on to those we lead, especially our children. I'm sure you share my heart that we don't want to reproduce dysfunction, perpetuating our past pains and iniquitous patterns in others. We must come to peace with our past through the gospel and be transformed by the renewing of our minds.

World impacting disciples are forged by courageously facing the hurts, sins, and everything that deviates from God. This lets the power of the cross and living truth prevail in their hearts and lives. We are called to be victorious and triumphant overcomers in Christ, who chose to be just as God called us.

If you would like help journeying through some of this deep work, we have developed powerful "Encounter" weekends. They are designed to bring these deep things of the soul to the cross and truly exchange in a way that breaks you into freedom and equips you to walk it out. Through these encounters, we've helped thousands of people from all over the world find freedom and healing. We have trained leaders to implement these Encounter weekends in their communities and networks. Keep your eye out for the next one by visiting www.windhamcrossing.org/encounter or contact us about helping you implement an Encounter in your community (come experience one first). This is a great place to start. From there, developing deep and meaningful loving relationships centered in Christ is the key to transformation. Authentic biblical community where you are known and know others in the love of Christ is the context for transformation and growth. You can also schedule a Breakthrough clarity call[57] to see if working together on a one-on-one basis makes sense.

---

57 https://www.forerunnerfitness.net/schedule-a-breakthrough-strategy-session-optin

In the next chapter I'll share an aspect of my story that illustrates how a new thought pattern led me into a process of healing, growth and discovery, revealing abilities and gifting that had never before been.

PAUSE. CAPTURE. APPLY
Prompts to help you process

1. What specific insights or concepts from this chapter resonated with you the most? Why do you think these stood out to you?

_____

_____

_____

2. How can you practically apply the principles discussed in this chapter to your daily life, relationships, or ministry? Identify at least one actionable step you can take this week.

_____

_____

_____

3. What potential challenges or barriers might you face in implementing these concepts? How can you overcome them?

_____

_____

_____

4. What are 3-5 quotes or points from this chapter that capture the essence of what it's communicating? Write them down.

_____

_____

_____

_____

_____

5. How can you involve your family, small group, or church community in the practices and principles outlined in this chapter? What steps can you take to foster a culture of discipleship and transformation within your circle of influence?

_____

_____

_____

6. Spend a few moments in prayer, asking God for the wisdom, strength, and courage to live out the truths you've learned. Write down a commitment or a prayer that reflects your desire to grow as an authentic disciple and transformational leader to impact the world.

_____

_____

_____

CHAPTER 6

Crisis- martial arts, dance, education...what?

I was in a personal crisis and internal conflict because I could not reconcile what I was doing in life and ministry with what was emerging in my spirit concerning creativity, dance, martial arts, and entrepreneurship. Part of this was due to my stage in life and simple immaturity, but a major part of this false dichotomy was hinged to issues of identity. It was because areas of my life and heart had shut down and even disassociated from hurt and trauma. But God, being a God of process, had perfect timing for this leg of the journey.

I was in my early 20's and had been operating in a mode of ministry and life that hadn't made room for that type of expression. The thought of nurturing and investing time and money into the arts made no sense to me in the context of what I was doing and what I planned to do and the way I would do it. I didn't have an issue with some people being called to this, but for me, it initially felt out of place —like something that would take me away from what I perceived to be "my most holy calling" and the best use of my time. I lived with urgency and passion and was intentional to cut out anything that would rob my focus from living for eternal things, making eternal impact. At the time I couldn't see how the arts could be for me as well.

At the same time I was wrestling with this, my mind would drift into thoughts of going to school in Boston for liberal arts, dance, or expressive therapies with a focus on mental health counseling. From there, I would imagine evangelizing, making disciples, and impacting the lost and broken through the arts and wellness modalities. Then I would be struck with fear and confusion around the concept that "good ideas" are not always "God ideas" and I only wanted the perfect will of God. I fell into double-mindedness for fear of missing the will of God and getting side tracked with "petty pursuits" in regards to movement and the arts. Yet, I could not deny what was emerging inside me.

Have you ever had a situation where your heart is saying one thing and your head is saying another? Where your spirit is speaking but your rationality can't accept or translate or reconcile it? Where fear clouds your judgment and leave you in indecision?

In critical transitions in life, the birth of new understandings, and our personal evolution place us in these tensions, dichotomies, and felt paradoxes. It's a normal part of growth and transformation. It can feel even more intense when it pertains to issues that touch our sense of identity. That was this for me.

Something was shifting, changing and emerging within me. The Father was calling forth and restoring things there that were lost in my youth. He was doing it in me upon a new heart foundation that was surrendered to Jesus, oriented around His Glory and the advancement of His Kingdom purposes.

When I reflect on my story and timeline, I see the elements and patterns that have now found fuller expression and redemption in my life. In my youth, due to brokenness, poor decisions, and lack of opportunity, I didn't develop my raw talents, interests, and gifts. There were core expressions of creativity and ability that never were fully affirmed, therefore were never developed in my life. My heart lacked the permission I needed to explore, express, and take action.

Do you have any places in your life where you feel you could have been further along in life if things had been different or if you had made different decisions? I want to encourage you in these areas. God redeems time and can restore your life in the most beautiful ways, in the most perfect timing. You can trust him with your past, present, and future.

When I was 15 I hadn't really developed anything or even considered these areas of my life. Although I was very popular, athletic, and a decent student (I was actually a terrible student, more caught up in the social aspects of school caring little about learning), I had no vision and hope for my future. Truth be told, growing up I suffered terribly with hopelessness and anxiety, plagued with fear about my future. I actually have vivid memories as a 6-year- old crying to my mother, because I couldn't see myself doing or becoming anything except a homeless person. These were some of the byproducts of trauma, PTSD, and not having my father or healthy father figure in my life to impart identity and nurture confidence.

At the age of 15, something drastic and dramatic happened to me. It was my sophomore year of high school at the end of February vacation when I had a radical experience with Jesus alone in my bedroom. This moment of encounter shifted my life forever and thrust me into a whole new way of living. Father God's process of restoration in my life had begun with a single moment of exchange and encounter.

Shortly after my encounter with God, I was invited to a youth group where I met the core family of people I'm still running with them over two decades later (at the time of this writing).

"But I'm Not That Man"—

When I entered that youth group, they had just come through a significant move of the Spirit of God. They were part of a budding regional ministry being born to the whole Body of Christ to raise up the next generation called <u>Youthstorm</u>.

We held major conferences that brought together hundreds of young people and youth ministries from numerous Christian denominations. These events fostered a robust grassroots network of youth leaders coming together in hunger and friendship to see revival and awakening in New England and beyond.

We worked with local churches to help them build powerful youth ministries, bridge the gap between the generations, and raise up leaders who would be agents of transformation and renewal— in both the local church and the world. At one point, we supported nine simultaneous groups across New England weekly, with small teams going out like revivalist circuit riders of old. We were a small core group pouring our lives out, doing what seemed exponentially more than we could do as a small team. It was such an exciting season of time.

As a youth, I was traveling with these teams stirring passion for Jesus, a call to holiness, and evangelizing local towns and regions. We were helping start new groups from those who responded to the gospel. I did this all through high school and beyond. It was at this point when God activated the arts and other entrepreneurial energies in me.

As we traveled around, leading camps and conferences, we then launched a full- time residential internship program focused on discipleship (apprentice- like mentoring & training), life skills, and leadership development. This was a spiritual bootcamp with intense community living, spiritual disciplines, theological education, community service, outreach, focused mentoring, and more. It was very monastic but not in an isolating way. We were preserving and forging an expression of authentic faith and radical discipleship. I was one of the pioneering interns, right out of high school. Later, I helped oversee it. I taught classes and functioned as a key coordinator for outreach, training, and community service. I still have the joy and privilege to be one of the overseers of this internship, 20 plus years later. It now operates out of our local church and network hub in Windham, NH.[58]

In the meantime, I did what I had to do to provide for myself financially as I oriented my life around the gospel and the ministry I was doing. I did all kinds of things for work, and it helped that the leader of the ministry, Shawn, also did construction. So we were always involved in building projects, either for business or because we were working on intern and staff housing or a new office that needed renovation. Fun times and hard times, and, Oh boy, could I tell you some stories around that.

I also worked seven years as a restaurant cook after high school, during the internship, and a few years beyond. I liked it and had such cool opportunities for the gospel there. I led quite a few people to the Lord there and had such favor with my bosses. They would always give me the time off I needed for other ministry work because it made them feel like they were contributing to the work I was doing. Cool right? Staff and management would tell customers that they had a cook that would come out and pray for them. I often found myself on the floor with customers hearing issues and hurts, praying for needs, all while my manager was doing my job cooking in the kitchen. Ha! He would say, "I got this, you go do the important stuff.." This was incredible favor!

I was traveling around New England and Europe doing ministry, uniting churches and ministries, training youth and leaders in prayer,

---

[58] The Crossing Life Church Windham NH—www.windhamcrossing.org

prophecy, outreach, calling for repentance and authentic devotion to Christ. All the while, I was doing side jobs of construction, cooking and cutting people's hair to support myself. At the same time, saw such supernatural provision from different situations and people to supply my needs as I served in the ministry. And let me quickly say, I could write you a book on all the cool ways God provided both then and now.

Just for fun and to boast on Jesus, let me stir your faith and to say that when you are doing what you are supposed to do before God, His blessing and favor and provision becomes very evident and very real! When Jesus said, "seek first my Kingdom and my righteousness, and everything that the world (those who don't know me) chase after and worry about, will be given to you" (Matthew 6:33), He meant it!

As I continued to prioritize what I felt the Lord wanted me to do. He provided both finances and other material needs such as food, clothing, and cars. In high school, I had a shop teacher that would antagonize me and persecute me because of my faith. Long story short, he gave his heart to Jesus, got baptized, and became established in a local church. (He and his wife are still faithfully walking with God, serving in ministry together!!) This teacher, who was a persecutor, became a dear friend and partner in the gospel. I am forever grateful for his love and support. On his own (under God's inspiration), without me asking for anything, decided to financially support me generously every month and did so for 20 years. Not only that, but he gave me five cars over the years too! Is that crazy or what? He saw it as a partnership in the gospel, and it was.

God can turn the hearts of people to do His will, so don't fear giving yourself entirely to whatever God asks of you. He will provide in one way or the other, whether by people, by sending ravens as He did with Elijah, by the work of your own hands, or in some other creative way. God can be trusted and we can fully obey Him without worrying about the cares of this life! Amen! Do what God has called you to do and be at peace in His great love for you!

Deeper Questions

So, getting back to that season of life and the duality of ministry and odd jobs. This was when the Lord began to stir up deeper questions of identity and this stirring for arts and other life directives related to how he designed me to operate.

The Lord began to prompt and speak to my heart in a way that set into motion this transition in my life. "Josiah, who are you? What do you want to do? What do you want?" My knee jerk reaction to such questions was first, "What do you mean? I want what you want. Your will be done, not mine." But the Father would ask again, "What do you want, Josiah? I redeemed you for a unique purpose and put desires in your heart."

The Lord was trying to get me to recognize the things He had placed in my heart. Those things that hadn't found expression, had been suppressed for years but were emerging in me. He wanted me to own it, even if it didn't fully make sense to my own mind yet. As I started owning and recognizing my God given distinctives, I had to look where my time and energy was being vested. I had to determine if all the side jobs I was doing were best suited with my gifts and this growing vision and desire inside me.

There came a point where I simply had to recognize that I was not who my mentor was, though we are like hearted and liked called in so many ways. I was not Shawn and doing construction with him was not going to be for me and my future. Knowing this and owning this was the marking of a transition to start stepping into new waters more aligned with my natural abilities and to start investing in other areas. *Knowing who you are and who you are not is key and two sides of the same coin.* The process of owning my heart, acknowledging my own needs, and overcoming fears of others with vulnerable places in my heart, helped me take the action I needed to heal and grow. Those deep subconscious fears and neural nervous responses were at play at so many different levels of my soul. I thank God for the community around me and for the Spirit of the Lord that continually inspired me and urged me onward. This gave me the courage to overcome what could have easily been sabotaged by the fear that was operating in me. But praise God, that as I stepped forward, I continued to find greater freedom and expression of who God made me to be.

This is where I stepped into the river of movement (dance), martial arts, personal training, Christ- centered holistic wellness and high performance coaching. These unfolded and developed over time, but I took swift action to learn and implement. Soon I was building kingdom business and ministry initiatives, such as <u>Forerunner Fitness</u>, then later the <u>School of Warriors Arts</u>, and <u>Raise A Warrior</u> collective. The first thing I did though was start dancing and teaching hip hop at a performing arts center. When I started dancing and activating this realm of my heart and body through movement, it was amazing what happened in my soul and mind. I felt even more alive, was able to break out of unconscious cycles of perfectionism, as well as writer's block. Movement unlocked my cognitive capacity. So cool right? The mind-body-spirit connection was made profoundly real to me in this season.

Many have the chance and learning environment to explore their gifts and abilities, tailoring their educational path towards their passions from a young age. This was not my story. I had to deconstruct and revisit foundational life and identity work before I could move past the confusion and unknowing and immaturity of my potentials that were never affirmed or cultivated. That is the story for so many of us. I thank God my wife and I are chain breakers of generations of dysfunction. With God's guidance and incredible grace, we are creating something new for our kids and others that we never had, giving them a foundation to build on from the very beginning.

Let me ask you, do you know who you are and what makes you come alive? Are you clear about your strengths and weaknesses and how you are uniquely gifted? Are you invested in those areas, making room to do what you love and what you're good at in life? It's too easy to go through the motions, stay in the realm of security and comfortability, and never really be fulfilled, lacking the joy and passion for which we were created. We must answer these questions for ourselves honestly and be courageous enough to go after our God given call and passions in the way we were uniquely designed. Remember, we always have the choice to "*Be*" or not to "*Be*" who God created us to be.

Good news: I've developed a process to help you explore your identity, define your life's purpose and lifelong intentions, break into greater freedom, and craft a strategic, prayerful plan to walk according to your heavenly design. It's called the *Breakthrough XP course*. Those who purchased this book get a 75% discount if you want to check it out. Sweet deal, right? The discount is worthless unless you do the work in it and go through the process to realize the gold it will produce in and for you. It really is game changing! If you choose to get it, use this code at the check out: "**BOOKBONUS75XP**." Go to https://www.forerunnerfitness.net/breakthroughxp. If you want coaching through this process, reach out. "It's the glory of God to conceal (hide) a matter, but it's the glory of Kings to search it out"— Proverbs 25:2. You are a king or queen, a royal child of God, and the Lord is hiding, rather, holding something for you to discover! Go get it, my friend!!

I shared this part of my story for a few reasons:

1. I want you to have context and a frame of reference as you continue to read and enter into dialogue with me.

2. Because you may be in a key transition in life and want to align your life with your gifts and passions in a greater way and need permission in your heart to do so.

3. Because you need to know that God is into restoration and wants to bring forth your unique created purpose in life. He uses ALL things for good in their perfect time. We don't have to be afraid of change and loss.

4. God will move outside of our "boxes." We have to be willing to change and evolve, stepping into the unknown and new territories He leads us into. He is the Lord of our lives and we must follow.

5. God uses unconventional mediums to minister to people. He wants our areas of interest and passion and gifting to reach the world with the gospel and to bring people into spiritual maturity.

No matter where you are in life, know you were called into ministry and to make disciples. The Lord wants to use you and expand your influence. The beautiful thing is that God intends to bring alignment to every area of your life. Then, you will be serving primarily in the strength of your abilities and passions from a yielded heart before God. Even if you're in a season of life or a situation you are not particularly happy with or naturally suited for, you can trust there are people around you to reach for Christ, and there is something the Lord is looking to produce in your heart. In the right time, you will transition and move toward what is most important to you: to what eventually will be part of your life work and primary calling, assignment, and vocation. Just chose to be who God created you to be and embrace the process of growth. Be intentional to live life on purpose aligned with your purpose, and you will *live*.

After necessary healing and personal discovery of who I was and how I was uniquely gifted, I was able to embrace other dimensions and expressions of service. These not only brought me great joy and fulfillment but allowed me to reach people and institutions I would not have otherwise been able to reach. Which is the point. We are to bring the Kingdom of God wherever we go and not just expect people to come to our church services. We are to go into the world as light and salt and reach those who would never or who are resistant to come to church, and express a living Christ to them. We are called to plunder hell to populate heaven and this means learning to occupy the earth with the good news through your occupations, hobbies, and passions!

PAUSE. CAPTURE. APPLY
Prompts to help you process

1. What specific insights or concepts from this chapter resonated with you the most? Why do you think these stood out to you?

_____

_____

_____

2. How can you practically apply the principles discussed in this chapter to your daily life, relationships, or ministry? Identify at least one actionable step you can take this week.

_____

_____

_____

3. What potential challenges or barriers might you face in implementing these concepts? How can you overcome them?

_____

_____

_____

4. What are 3-5 quotes or points from this chapter that capture the essence of what it's communicating? Write them down.

_____

_____

_____

_____

_____

5. How can you involve your family, small group, or church community in the practices and principles outlined in this chapter? What steps can you take to foster a culture of discipleship and transformation within your circle of influence?

_____

_____

_____

6. Spend a few moments in prayer, asking God for the wisdom, strength, and courage to live out the truths you've learned. Write down a commitment or a prayer that reflects your desire to grow as an authentic disciple and transformational leader to impact the world.

_____

_____

_____

CHAPTER 7

Where to start: "What's in your hand"

Live into your potential, purpose, and calling—utilizing your gifts and talents.

> *"In the place God has put us he expects us to shine, to be living witnesses, to be a bright and shining light. While we are here our work is to shine for him."*
>
> – D.L. Moody[59]

So where do we start? We start with YOU. We start with what God has entrusted us with, put in us, and placed in our "hand."

It is easy to become overwhelmed in the face of all that is before us: making disciples, evangelizing the world, turning the tides in the midst of gross darkness, the church's need for reformation and innovation in our educational approach, healing for the broken-hearted, and all

---

[59] D.L. Moody, https://moodycenter.org/the-quotable-moody-d-l-moody-quotes/, accessed April 29, 2024.

the complexities that come along with that. I urge you, don't shut down with paralysis of analysis, become nearsighted, or cling to our comfortable old wineskins.

We can't afford to get stuck or stay stuck, we have to move. What's outside our control must be entrusted to God and committed to prayer (the first place to start, really). What we can control and are responsible for first is ourselves. Change starts with us!

We need to consider where we can start, where we can take the mission and what role we're to play. All change must start within us, and as many transformational leaders have said, we must "be the change you want to see in the world." We cannot be problem focused only but must be solution oriented, spending our energy on what we have the power to change and influence. Then we need to ask, what in our lives do we need to leverage to do that?

The simple but profound truth is that if we are faithful with what's in our "hand", not only will God entrust us with more, but God will also give us what's in our hearts too. There are central things we are all called to do as Believers. There are things that you are uniquely called to do within the places of your influence. So the question for us and you, as it relates to our unique assignments, starts with the same question God posed to Moses, "what's in your hand?" What is it that you have that God can use?

When God called to Moses from the burning bush and began to lay out his assignment, Moses asked, "what if they won't listen to me?" The Lord directed him toward his vocational tool, the shepherd's staff, and supernaturally empowered it. The ordinary shepherd's staff in His hand was used in an extraordinary way to release the miracles of God and lead a people out of bondage, into freedom, salvation, and eventually the promised land.[60] As Moses was shepherding his father in-law's sheep, that is what put him in proximity to the burning bush.

---

60 Exodus 4:1-5, 7:8-9, 14:13-31

Where to Start: "What's in Your Hand"

His vocation and responsibilities put him right in the path that would lead him into his purpose and calling. This is key. God meets us right where we are and will take the ordinary in your life that you commit to Him and use it supernaturally. As my friend once said, He'll take the natural things you give Him and put some *Super* on it. Ha!

We see the same principle at play with young David. He didn't know it yet but he was destined and called to be king of Israel, a shepherd of God's people. It was in the shepherding of his fathers sheep that he was sovereignly prepared to lead God's people. Not only that, David's skill with the slingshot as a shepherd was used at the opportune time to slay a giant. It freed the army of God from their intimidation, and brought about a great victory for Israel. David's love songs and ability to play music is also what brought him into proximity to His purpose when he was called upon to play music for King Saul to alleviate him of an evil spirit. Davids' music was anointed and empowered by the spirit of the Lord and it dispelled the darkness afflicting the King's mind. Pretty cool right? We can say much about the ways in which the Spirit of God empowered David in his natural skills and abilities to do all he was called to do to serve the Lord and His people. It can be the same for you.

Another great example is the young boy who offered his five loaves and two fishes to Jesus when thousands needed to eat. Jesus took it, blessed it, broke it, and then gave it to the masses. He will do the same for what's in your hand *if* you offer it to Him. God wants to use you and harness everything He has given you and made you to be.

The question is, will you offer God all that you are and have?

Pause for a moment and talk to God. Surrender to Him in a fresh way and withhold no part or aspect of your life from Him. As the scriptures invite us, in light of the mercies of God, present yourselves as a living sacrifice (Romans 12:1).

When you're ready, let's keep going.

Who Are You?

So coming back to the foundational principle, *"being precedes doing"*—we need to look at who we are, our story, what gifts we have, abilities, experiences, resources, passions, burdens… etc. We need to understand who we are, what we have in our "hand", and how we can be used for greater service to others. Whatever we have been given or whatever we have become, it is for loving and effectual service to others.

The beautiful thing is we are called to do whatever we are doing with all our might unto the Lord. When we take such a faith filled posture in our work or hobbies or responsibilities, it is met with and energized by the grace of God. His favor and presence is seen in and through what we do. That's the point, that our lives and work would reveal God and adorn the gospel, attracting those appointed to salvation.

I love Moses' prayer at the end of Psalm 90:17 and into David's Psalm 67: "May the favor and beauty of the Lord our God be upon us; establish for us the work of our hands-establish the work of our hand! May God be gracious to us and bless us; look upon us with favor Selah *so that your way may be known on earth,* your salvation among the nations." Do you see that? God's blessing upon our life, and the work of our hands is a manifestation of the ways and nature of God. The Lord wants to make Himself known through your life and in every element of your life. These are the good works that are meant to shine before men that they might see Him and give glory to God. God wants to bless the earth through your life!

Apostle Paul writes to Titus for the Church in Crete, and for all churches, that servants, in relation to their masters/employers, were to demonstrate utter faithfulness in their work, so that they could adorn the teaching of God our Savior in everything. And again to the

Where to Start: "What's in Your Hand"

Church in Ephesus, and to the Church throughout all time, servants were to work with a good attitude, as to the Lord and not to men, knowing they will receive back from the Lord.[61] Their attitude and diligence in their work was not only part of their worship, it was a visible witness to the world, and a primary means to win the respect of the "outsider," so that the gospel of God would be adorned.

Your work ethic and the quality of your work is a vehicle of ministry to others, an instrument of opportunity to the lost, a model of the faith, part of your worship before God, and a testament to the Lord Himself. Isn't that amazing? It's not business or ministry, or even business and ministry, it's business *as* ministry—"Businestry," ha!

We also need to realize that our life story, including our wounds and weaknesses, become a source of wealth and wisdom to share with others. Honestly, generously and vulnerably sharing testimony and life experiences sets others free. It also empowers them with the faith and confidence to overcome, excel, and achieve in the face of the unique challenges they'll face in life too. You really can give other people hope and encouragement when you share honestly and openly. We can use our story to give people greater insight into the heart and ways of God as well and impart the wisdom they need to succeed.

Alongside our failures, we also get to share our wins and successes that become catalysts of inspiration to others, as well as courage for them to take risks. Plus, direction and counsel to impart, and the gift of helping them truly collapse time to get ahead. We can actually help others get to where they are called to go faster. That's exciting! Our ceiling of success and progress can become the foundation on which another generation can stand. And for us, there really is no success without successors or succession. We must pass on what we have received and fully participate in the plan of God. That is to pass on not only the faith and what it means to be a disciple of Jesus Christ,

---

61 Titus 2:9-10, Eph 6:5-9

but also the knowledge, skills, and resources necessary to take what we have done in our lives, and teach others to build on it.

We need to think about legacy and works that continue beyond us. As the saying goes, Rome wasn't built in a day, and it's In this way we all collectively build and grow from generation to generation. We need to think this way and live in light of it. The baton must be properly passed on till the end of the age. We have a holy obligation and sacred charge to the next generation. This means we must be intentional to invest in them with everything we are and everything we got. This isn't just for "youth workers," it's for all of us. This is to be part of your legacy and responsibility. This is part of God's design for His Church, that "older men teach younger men; older women teach younger women."[62] We are to entrust what we have received to faithful people who will also be qualified to teach others (2 Timothy 2:2).

So where do we start in the enormity of the task laid upon us as Believers? We start right where we are and as we are in the grace of God. Life is not merely random, and the things that have happened to us, whether good or bad, can all have a redemptive purpose. Nothing is wasted. Life just doesn't happen to us, it happens for us! Who we are and what we become in the journey is not just for ourselves, it is for the Glory of God and for adding value to others. Your story, your pains and your pleasures, your wounds and your wisdom, your wins and your weaknesses, are all leveraged to bear witness to the goodness of God, the workings of His power. They are put in service for others to experience freedom, growth, healing, and development.

Are You Willing?

To say it again, the question then becomes, are you willing to open your life, be radically transparent and hospitable, vulnerable, and extravagantly generous? Are you willing to be poured out in service to

---

[62] Ps 78, Eph 5:21-6:4, Colossians 3:12-21, Titus 2

others? Are you willing to use what's in your hand? Are you willing to start small and start with the people right around you? This is the way of the warrior and an authentic disciple.

And remember, this isn't a class or something that we can punch in and punch out of if you want to have the right effect and bear quality fruit. All people, especially the younger generation need real relationships, life on life impartation, modeling, mentoring, support, time, coaching, investment, and more.

As I said before, in an age of technology and where people are drowning in information, longing for connection, they need real and loving relationships that can model and impart wisdom in how to actually live well—how to live a fruitful, fulfilling, and godly life as God intended it. Start bringing people along with you in the normal everyday things you do. Much of this is caught more than taught, it's the principle of proximity. You want to be close, reachable, and approachable in a way that shows you're there for them and open to share your heart, knowledge, and life. You don't want to professionalize this and make it impersonal.

In the grand scheme of things, we must all work together for a greater purpose, the Kingdom of God. We need to think of life as a giant collaboration to the glory of God rather than a competition for our own achievement, glory, and success. Cliche or not, it's true— Together we are better and together we achieve more, and more for the Glory of God. We need not live bound in self preservation and individualism, but within the love and grace of God that calls us to a stewardship, community, and a life of fruitfulness to the Glory of God. I want to encourage you to step over whatever hurdles may hinder you from opening up your life to others; to initiate coming alongside someone to add value to them and grow in influence for the gospel's sake.

What we have been given in life is not just for us! The very call to God's people from the beginning was to be a blessing to the nations and reveal the knowledge of God. We are blessed to be a blessing. We are called to be salt and light and fishers of men. We are called to make disciples in obedience to Christ as we go about life—our daily lives are to be a life on mission. If we claim faith in the living God, then without exception we are called to belong to and participate in the community of disciples (the Church); and reach out to the world around us with the gospel by all means possible. We are sent here as Jesus was sent and remain in the world for others sake and not ourselves. Jesus himself prayed to the Father, "as you have sent me into the world, I have sent them."—John 17:18

Are you on this mission or on a mission of your own? Do you see your ambitions and goals as connected to the greater cause and call to preach the gospel and make disciples? Do you see your vocation as a vehicle to reach people for Christ?

If not, I implore you to reconsider and go back to the drawing board. (Pick up the course I created to help you do just that, called *"The Breakthrough XP"* using this code for 75% off **"BOOKBONUS75XP"**)

CLAIM YOUR 75% OFF CODE:
"BOOKBONUS75XP"

YOUR STRATEGIC PATH TO BREAKTHROUGH, CLARITY, AND ABUNDANT LIFE!

Discover your unique God given purpose, breakthrough your barriers, craft a strategic and prayer plan with a rule of life that leads to fruitfulness and fulfillment. Leave a transformational legacy!

FORERUNNERFITNESS.NET/BREAKTHROUGHXP

FORERUNNER FITNESS

Grace For Service

Consider some of the following scriptures that speak to the truth of the gifts and graces God gave us. What God has entrusted to us was intended for use and service to others for their strengthening, and for the Glory and acknowledgement of God:

- "Offer hospitality to one another without grumbling. Each of you should use whatever gift you have received to serve others, as faithful stewards of God's manifold grace....so that in all things God may be praised through Jesus Christ. To Him be the glory and the power for ever and ever. Amen " *1 Peter 4:9-11*

  - *For stay at home parents and moms, your home is your first mission center—use it for hospitality- for welcoming people into relationships and love around a table. Sharing a meal with an outsider, stranger, the lonely, those in need, and with brothers and sisters in the Lord, was a primary way by which the gospel spread and disciples were made in the first century, It is still a primary way today. Jesus Himself was always sharing a meal and eating with the "sinners" and His disciples, so much so that He was accused of being a glutton and drunkard[63]. Hospitality is key!*

- "We have different gifts according to the grace given to each of us. If your gift is prophesying…serving…teaching.. to encourage….giving…leading…to show mercy, do it cheerfully……love must be sincere." *Romans 12:6-9*

- .".do not neglect the gift of God in you..fan it into flame … .be diligent in these matters, give yourself entirely to it, so that everyone may see your progress. Watch your life and your doctrine closely. Persevere in them, because if you do, you will save both yourself and those who hear you." "For this reason I remind you to fan into flame the gift of God, which us in you through the laying on of my hands. For the

---

[63] Luke 5:29-32, 7:33-34. I would encourage you to do a study to see all Jesus did around a meal and food and the concept of hospitality. Very powerful.

Spirit of God does not make us timid, but gives us power, love and self-discipline."- *1 Timothy 4:14-16, 2 tim 1:6-7*

- ○ We see that the use and development of Timothy's gifts and the integrity of His life was critical for his own accountability to God but also the saving influence on others.

- "Love more than tongue and word but deed and truth. If any of you have the world's material goods and see a brother in need and you close your heart to him, how can you say the love of God is in you?" The point is to love and share what you have- 1 jn 3:17-18

- "Teach those rich in this life to be rich in good works and to share with other…do not put your hope in the uncertainty of riches" 2 Tim 6

- " So Bezalel, Oholiab, and every skilled person are to carry out everything commanded by the LORD, who has given them skill and ability to know how to perform all the work of constructing the sanctuary. Then Moses summoned Bezalel, Oholiab, and every skilled person whom the LORD had gifted—everyone whose heart stirred him to come and do the work."---Exodus 36:1-2

- "All authority in heaven and earth belong to me, therefore, Go into all the world and preach the gospel to all creation. Baptize those who believe in the Name of the Father, Son, and the Holy Spirit, and teach them to obey everything I have taught you…"—Matt 28, Mark 16

- Freely you have received, so freely give- Matt 10:8

- "He gave His life to free us from every kind of sin, to cleanse us, and to make us his very own people, totally committed to doing good deeds." Titus 2:14

- One man died, therefore all died, so that the life they live they live for the will of God as a new creation and not for themselves—2 Corinthians 5

I love those scriptures! And I want you to also consider the women at the well, the man with the withered hand, the blind man from birth, or the women caught in adultery, the lepers who were healed. There are so many examples, where individuals and the community of Israel shared openly about their lives and story and the work of God, and in such a way that unlocked regions and towns to the gospel. Their testimony was part of their stewardship to multiply the workings of God's grace toward others. This starts for you with the people right around you, maybe even in your own home.

We have a stewardship and responsibility before God for which we will take account. How have we used what we have been given? How have we honored God with it and how have we added value to others? How have we multiplied what He gave us in seed form? Are we seeking to improve and build upon the gift and abilities we have? Are we pursuing mastery in an area of our skills? Can I just lovingly poke and provoke you to do so?

Consider the parable of the talents in Matthew 25:14-30

> "For it is just like a man going on a journey, who called his servants and entrusted them with his possessions. To one he gave five talents, to another two talents, and to another one talent—each according to his own ability. And he went on his journey.

WHERE TO START: "WHAT'S IN YOUR HAND"

The servant who had received the five talents went at once and put them to work and gained five more. Likewise, the one with the two talents gained two more. But the servant who had received the one talent went off, dug a hole in the ground, and hid his master's money.

After a long time the master of those servants returned to settle accounts with them. The servant who had received the five talents came and presented five more. 'Master,' he said, 'you entrusted me with five talents. See, I have gained five more.'

His master replied, 'Well done, good and faithful servant! You have been faithful with a few things; I will put you in charge of many things. Enter into the joy of your master!'

The servant who had received the two talents also came and said, 'Master, you entrusted me with two talents. See, I have gained two more.'

His master replied, 'Well done, good and faithful servant! You have been faithful with a few things; I will put you in charge of many things. Enter into the joy of your master!'

Finally, the servant who had received the one talent came and said, 'Master, I knew that you are a hard man, reaping where you have not sown and gathering where you have not scattered seed. So I was afraid and went out and hid your talent in the ground. See, you have what belongs to you.'

'You wicked, lazy servant!' replied his master. 'You knew that I reap where I have not sown and gather where I have not scattered seed. Then you should have deposited my money with the bankers, and on my return I would have received it back with interest.

Therefore take the talent from him and give it to the one who has ten talents. For everyone who has will be given more, and he will have an abundance. But the one who does not have, even what he has will be taken away from him. And throw that worthless servant into the outer darkness, where there will be weeping and gnashing of teeth."

Don't Wait To Be Perfect

Many of us are waiting to be perfect or to get it "all right" before we act and begin to use what we have been given. Don't let fear and perfectionism keep you from taking action. It's in our weaknesses that God's power is perfected and we must remember that He chose us in Christ while we were still His enemies and utterly lost. So lead now, serve now, give now, and grow as you go! And in fact, go after the deeper things in your heart that may be stopping you too, it's worth it! I want to encourage you to start with what you have and you will get more and increase over time. Do not despise the day of small beginnings nor disqualify yourself from even starting.

We can always find excuses of why we think we can't do something, or why someone else is more qualified, but the truth is the Lord put it in your heart and in your hand and you are called to be faithful. And on the other side, if it makes you come alive and it's something you both deeply enjoy and have skill in, then simply on that basis alone, you should make room and space to develop those things. So make time to put to work those graces, abilities, and activities. Because what the world needs today is people who are fully alive, who shine brightly, who do what they love, love what they do, and do it with all their

Where to Start: "What's in Your Hand"

might to the glory of God! That's what mature sons and daughters of God do, it's who they are, and how they show up in life. Remember, the frameworks that your unique place of impact and the calls to move towards "convergence" in life where your gifts, passions, and ability intersect? Go after that and align your life accordingly. You will not only be massively fulfilled you will make a massive impact.

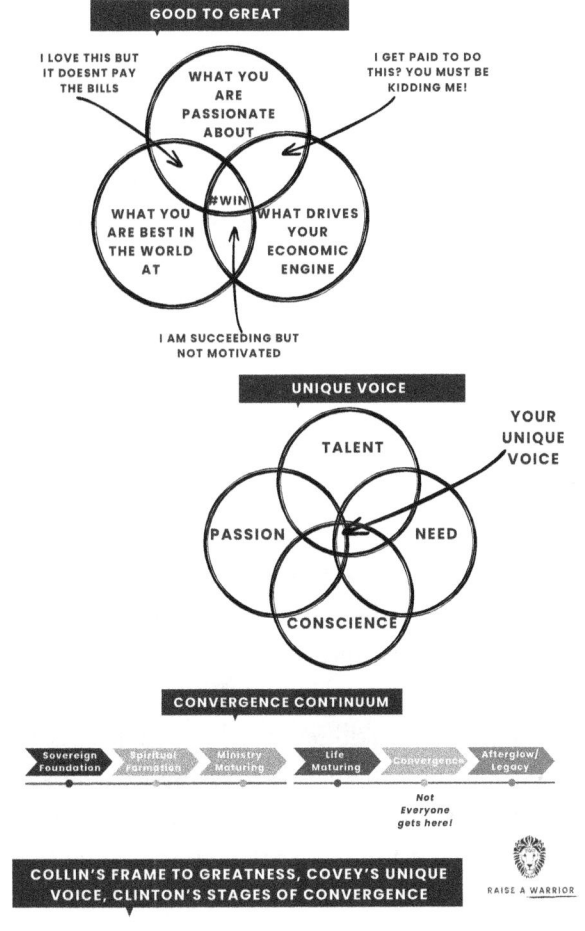

The breakthrough xp Course is designed to help you discover your purpose and craft a master plan and rule of life to move you toward and into the fullness of "convergence" and a powerful legacy.

This reminds me of a quote that I have heard from people, like John Eldradge, "the glory of God is man fully alive." Isn't that great? Redemption has to do with God making us alive again through the forgiveness of sins, the reconciliation to sonship, and the restoration of the image of God in our lives. The tarnish produced by sin and the corruption caused by the fall of man in the very beginning was removed by the work of Christ. This enables us to live and serve in the newness of the Spirit of Life in Christ Jesus.

God empowered humanity to represent Him by bearing His image, anointed by His Spirit, and created in Christ Jesus for good works that express His glory and goodness (Ephesians 2). Those works must find expression in our lives through our "Yes" to God and our willful and faith-filled partnership. Man fully alive brings glory to God!

It is a stewardship that must be chosen and not rejected or avoided, or even casually acknowledged with some periodic dabbling. We cannot be half hearted when we are called to be wholly given to God and His purpose. We are devoted burning ones, the light of the world and salt of the earth! We are called to do whatever we do with all our might unto God! Can I get an "Amen?"

From that place of gifting or skill sets, we need to leverage our ability to influence others with the love of God. You add value to other people's lives by mentoring and teaching them, passing on what you know. More importantly, you can build bridges into their heart and life through your craft and skill sets for the gospel. This is part of what becoming a skilled "fisherman" in the Kingdom looks like. People respond when they feel loved and valued and genuine interest is taken in their lives. When we add value to people and help them reach their goals, they open up. And when you are able to harness and befriend others around a common interest, vocation or personal experience, you gain access to their heart and mind. When we genuinely love people and serve them in a tangible and relevant way, not only is it invigorating and deeply satisfying, it is effective in opening doors of opportunity to share the love of Christ. *We have to use what God gave us not only as an act of worship but as a tool or vehicle of mission and ministry to others.*

Some Examples

Let's look at a few people in history and today using their areas of gifting, their story, their platform, for the gospel. Whether you're at home raising little kids, using your home as a hub of hospitality to love and serve people or whether you are a public figure with global influence, God wants to use you and all He has put in your hand. Be inspired by these examples. There are many more but we don't have time for them all.

- Gabby Douglas, Olympic gymnast and gold medalist, the first woman of color of any nationality and the first African-American gymnast in Olympic history to become the Individual All-Around Champion,"—she shares her faith and expresses to the world that she excelled and stayed focused in her Olympic events by meditating on scripture. In interviews she has expressed, "God has given me this amazing God-given talent, so I'm going to go out and glorify His name."

- Jim & Lydia O'Leary —pastors, plumber and business owners with four kids. They opened their home as a hub of love and discipleship, caring for the lost and broken. They have taken in hundreds of people in efforts to restore, heal and serve as a solution to the drug epidemic in their region. TIME magazine caught wind of what was happening and the success of the lives being healed and restored. They did a year long documentary on what was happening. The TIME journalist stayed with them and frequently visited, was personally impacted, saw the love of God in action.

Ultimately, the publication glorified Jesus and the gospel in action through this family and the local church.

- Manny Pacquiao, Filipino statesmen, born again believer, and world champion boxer, a Filipino national icon and a champion of justice for the poor of His nation.

- Tim Tebo, NFL football player, put John 3:16 under his eyes when he played and caused over 180 million searches online for "John 3:16." He's also a philanthropist and bold in his faith for Christ.

- Many networks of Christ Centered martial arts organizations and ministries such as "Fellowship of Christian Martial Artists", my school, "School of Warrior Arts" or "Black Belts for Christ", who have a vision and mission to use the martial arts as a medium of both discipleship and evangelism.

- Eric Liddell (1902-1945), whose life story was celebrated in the award-winning 1981 movie, Chariots of Fire. He was an Olympic runner and missionary to China, martyred for his faith, who famously said, "when I run I feel His pleasure." After being persecuted by religious people who didn't understand why he was running and competing rather than "going to the mission field," he replied, "I will go to China when the time is right but God also made me fast." Eric Liddell's devotion to Christ was complete, and he viewed his athletic ability as a God-given gift by which he could glorify Jesus. This opportunity came in a unique way during the Olympics.

- Billy Sunday, early 1900's Major league baseball player & evangelist. Until Billy Graham, no American evangelist preached to so many millions, or saw as many conversions—an estimated 300,000.

Where to start: "What's in your hand"

- Dr John Maxwell, leading global authority on leadership and personal development and best selling author of over 130 books! He is clear that all his principles are based out of scripture and is very open about his faith. At every certification training he presents the gospel and has an altar call. (At one of these events, I witnessed hundreds give their life to the Lord in a room of 3,500 coaches from all over the world. So powerful!) He has won over a million people to the Lord through his business and is equipping other Christian business people to do the same and learn to integrate their faith and work together. He's empowering the marketplace ministers!

- Jim Cadesel, Actor & Movie Star (played Jesus in 'Passion of Christ' and recently acted in "Sound of Freedom" about human and child trafficking,) outspoken about his faith and shaking up the industry alongside many other actors and producers. In fact, there is a movement happening in the entertainment industry right now that is shaking the powers that be. New, godly production companies are rising up to produce God glorifying movies.

- Susanna Weslea, raised 12 kids that became world changers and lovers of God. I could list thousands of women who understood the power of their God given role in the home to raise up world changers and open their homes as hubs of hospitality to love people and advance the gospel.

- Stephanie Foster and Emily Shattuck, leading <u>Dreamers Ranch, a division of Youthstorm</u>, which is regenerating the land and regenerating lives through regenerative farming, livestock and cattle programs, mentoring, entrepreneurship, outdoor adventures programs and camps, and youth leadership development. They are providing real, gospel-centered solutions in the community. Checkout <u>www.dreamersranch.org</u>

This list goes on and on of the known and unknown heroes using what God has given them for His glory. What's your story going to be and how are you going to use "what's in your hand"?

PAUSE. CAPTURE. APPLY
Prompts to help you process

1. What specific insights or concepts from this chapter resonated with you the most? Why do you think these stood out to you?

_____

_____

_____

2. How can you practically apply the principles discussed in this chapter to your daily life, relationships, or ministry? Identify at least one actionable step you can take this week.

_____

_____

_____

3. What potential challenges or barriers might you face in implementing these concepts? How can you overcome them?

_____

_____

_____

4. What are 3-5 quotes or points from this chapter that capture the essence of what it's communicating? Write them down.

_____

_____

_____

_____

_____

5. How can you involve your family, small group, or church community in the practices and principles outlined in this chapter? What steps can you take to foster a culture of discipleship and transformation within your circle of influence?

_____

_____

_____

6. Spend a few moments in prayer, asking God for the wisdom, strength, and courage to live out the truths you've learned. Write down a commitment or a prayer that reflects your desire to grow as an authentic disciple and transformational leader to impact the world.

_____

_____

_____

CHAPTER 8

Growing for the sake of the "Going"

Skill acquisition, growing in mastery, and imparting to others.

> *"I am only one, but I am one. I cannot do everything, but I can do something. What I can do, I ought to do, and what I ought to do, by the grace of God I will do."*
>
> —D. L. Moody[64]

I want to encourage you for your own sake and for those you will influence, mentor, and disciple, to become the best you can be in what you are called to do. We need to be prepared to make quality contributions to the world for the glory of God. The spirit of excellence should be a mark of the people of God, like Daniel, who do whatever they do with all their might, with integrity, care, and consistent improvement!

---

64 D.L. Moody, https://moodycenter.org/the-quotable-moody-d-l-moody-quotes/, accessed April 29, 2024.

Our good works are meant to glorify God and not be hidden from the eyes of people (although we don't do things for the eyes of people but before the eyes of people for the sake of the gospel and not for personal praise). Jesus said in Matthew 5:15-16, "Neither do people light a lamp and put it under a basket. Instead, they set it on a stand, and it gives light to everyone in the house. In the same way, let your light shine before men, that they may see your good deeds and glorify your Father in heaven."

In the spirit of seeking to do and be our best for the glory of God we always should look to "skill up" or "resource up." No one cares, including the Lord, about mediocre or half hearted work. In fact, such work would only invite correction, rebuke, and insult. We need to think along the lines of continual improvement and consistent growth. A commitment to Christ is a commitment to the pursuit of wisdom, which has to do with life long learning, continual growth, and doing whatever you do with all your might unto the Lord. Everything we do is part of our worship to God, and God forbid that we offer Him lukewarm and half hearted undeveloped talents. Christ's rebukes from the book of Revelation to the Church in Sardis and Laodicea, was just that. Their works were found to be incomplete before God and lukewarm. In Sardis, though they had a reputation of being alive they were dead. In Laodicea, they had a false perspective of their actual condition and thought they needed nothing and were fine just as they were. The Lord called them to repent with both warning and potential consequence, and incentive to overcome with the promise of reward.

We see the same thing through Apostle Paul's instruction to the Church in Colossi, "Whatever you do, work at it with all your heart, as working for the Lord, not for human masters, since you know that you will receive an inheritance from the Lord as a reward. It is the Lord Christ you are serving. Anyone who does wrong will be repaid for their wrongs, and there is no favoritism."[65]

---

[65] Colossians 3:23-25 NIV

Growing for the Sake of the "Going"

My point is, If we don't stay 'sharp' by continual practice and learning, we become dull. If we become dull, we have to expend more energy than we need to, ultimately dishonor God with our lack of stewardship, and finally, stunt the growth capacity of those we lead. We may fall short of the needed effectiveness in our skill, craft, or leadership to help them to the next level. This illustrates the "Law of the Lid."

In his classic book on leadership, "The 21 Irrefutable laws of leadership", Dr John Maxwell says that the "Law of the Lid" is your leadership ability and the lid that determines a person's level of effectiveness. The lower an individual's ability to lead, the lower the lid on his potential. The higher the individual's ability to lead, the higher the lid on his potential. For example, if your leadership capacity or skill level rates an 8, then your effectiveness can never be greater than a 7. If your leadership is only a 4, then your effectiveness will be no higher than a 3. Your leadership ability—for better or for worse—always determines your effectiveness and the potential impact of your organization, team, family, church, etc. If your skill level is at a 7, those under your leadership can only rise to a 6, unless you keep growing. You also won't attract level 7, 8, 9, 10 level people to serve with you, either (unless you keep growing). If you fail to grow, then those pressing to grow will need to shift and go elsewhere to grow or be intentionally groomed to lead in your place.

Fortunately, you can increase your capacity and skill by a commitment to growth. This is part of what it means and what is necessary to be and become a transformational leader. And let me say, doing the same thing over and over and expecting different results, is insanity! So when it comes to sharpening our skills, just practice or repetition alone doesn't lead to excellence, efficiency, or effectiveness. Deliberate practice that leads to actual improvement or progressive mastery involves things like getting a coach, challenging yourself beyond your comfort zones, developing mental representations of what success looks like, tracking your progress, and fixing your weaknesses, to name a few.

The scriptures tell us to buy wisdom, as it is the principle and chief thing. I've invested thousands of dollars and hours of my life to improve and "sharpen my ax.". I want to add real value to people and serve them at the highest level for the glory of God. Daniel in the Bible was excellent in all he did and was 10 times better than his Babylonian contemporaries. He was diligent, faithful, and supernaturally graced, as we all are in one way or another, and effective in his places of service. We can do all things through Christ who strengthens us and who has blessed us with every spiritual blessing in Christ. Amen! God wants us to excel in the things He's given us and cause us to grow in influence, favor, and meaningful service. So for God's sake, be good, rather, be great at what you do. Stretch yourself to improve, and If you're not great, no worries, it's simply your invitation to keep growing to be the best you can be and develop your potential and skills. Embrace the journey, my friend, and skill up!

10 Step Framework

Brendan Burchard, one of the world's leading personal development voices, teaches on progressive mastery and skill development in 10 steps. This is a great framework. I want to share it with you and make this interjection: the motivation for mastery and skill development at the core should be faithful stewardship before the Lord and loving desire to serve those around you. Love for God and people is what must drive us, without love we are nothing!

I have personally found this to be true; scriptures, my own experiences, and every personal development leader emphasizes that to sustain motivation and endure the necessary discipline and process of growth, you must consistently keep your core motivations and vision in the forefront. Vision gives the pain of the process its purpose. So it's important that we find ways to anchor our vision before the eyes of our heart and the eyes in our head. All studies point to the power and increased probability of achieving any goal, vision, or dream, by writing it down and looking at it regularly.

Dominican University professor Dr. Gail Matthews did a study on goal setting with 267 participants. She found that you are 42 percent more likely to achieve your goals just by writing them down. The actual statistics say that you are 42% more likely to achieve your goal if you write it down and look at it regularly.[66] For those who are super goal driven, a practice of visualizing, continual contemplation, and all consuming drive to achieve, serves you in the pains of discipline to get what you want. Right? To go after the weightier and more valuable things we want in life, we all have to endure the pain and discomfort of delayed gratification, sacrifice, and hard choices. Consider that as we talk about progressive mastery and the development of your skills, abilities, and living into your purpose. There is no way to escape the pains of process.

As you may know, change and growth can be awkward and difficult. It requires persistence and faith. Growth is a choice and an uphill journey that we have to continually choose- even daily. It's all part of the adventure you were created for, so honor the struggle and choose wisely. It's all going to be worth it!

So how do we practice this in a way that effectively moves us toward real improvement? The key to developing skills that truly stick involves a significant focus on infusing practice with emotion and meaning. This approach engages your heart and leverages your brain's capabilities for long-term retention.

If you don't care about what you're doing and you don't connect a sense of meaning and relevance, it won't stick. Remember, long term memory and retention in the brain centers around emotion and meaning. It is part of the brain's encoding process. This is really cool,

---

66 https://kitzu.org/study-highlights-strategies-for-achieving-goals/

God's designs are beautiful! This calls us into wholeheartedness, as God intends, and what it means to be mindful and powerfully present.

Other skill mastery key elements focus on socialization (engaging with others) to help you process information, and on teaching others to help you anchor what you're learning. Remember, the one who teaches learns twice. Think through this for yourself and for how you will encourage and support others in developing their skills as well.

Here's the 10 steps:

1. Start by determining a skill that you want to master.
2. Set specific and measurable stretch goals on your path to developing that skill.
3. Attach high levels of emotion and meaning to your journey and your results. (Connect why what you're doing is important—what's the bigger purpose)
4. Identify the factors critical to success and develop your strengths in those areas and fix your weaknesses with equal fervor.
5. Develop visualizations to clearly imagine what success and failure look like.
6. Schedule challenging practices developed by experts or through careful thought.
7. Measure your progress and get outside feedback.
8. Socialize your learning and efforts by practicing or competing with others.
9. Continue setting higher level goals so that you keep improving.
10. Teach others what you are learning. (He who teaches learns twice)

Now, ask yourself what skill you need to develop to serve at a higher level in life or business or your area of passion. Maybe it's a relational skill like active or empathetic listening. Maybe it's asking better questions or public speaking. Maybe it's something technical like learning a new software or process. Maybe it's learning a new style of physical training or martial skill. Whatever it is, identify it in light of where you are in life, your big picture goals, and present priorities.

Pause for a moment, and do this or if something immediately comes to your mind, write it down so you can come back to it later.

Let's keep moving.

All learning comes with feelings of unlearning and it's ok to be uncomfortable and feel awkward in the process. In fact, real growth happens outside your comfort zone, so if anything, get comfortable with being uncomfortable. As you give yourself to the process of skilling up and personal growth, honor the struggle and know that progress will be made as you take consistent action. Don't lose heart, trust the process. As competence grows so will your confidence.

I also want to encourage you to embrace the process with a sense of faith and assurance that you can do this and that you have what it takes, by the grace of God. The simple "yes, I can attitude" empowers you to learn and grow faster, see opportunities and resources that you would have been closed off if you had held to a disempowering "I can't" attitude. Your mindset or attitude, along with your confession—the words you say, are such a determining factor to whether you succeed in something or not. If you believe you can, you will. If you believe you can't, you won't. As Henry Ford said, " Whether you think you can, or you think you can't – you're right,." So embrace your next level of growth with the confidence that you have the ability to get it. If you start with this attitude of confidence, you will accelerate your ability to develop competence in your chosen practice. That competence and developed skill further fuels your confidence and sense of ability to perform in an effective way. Pretty cool right?

Let's tie this back into our call to participate in the great Commission—to go preach the gospel and make disciples. When we think about passing on the faith and leveraging our influence, we want to move people from "I want to do this but can't" to "I can do this and am actually very good at it."

Just as we learn best from a place of confidence, we want to impart that same confidence as we train people to become competent in life and areas of ability. By adding value to people's lives, fostering their confidence through skill development, loving instruction and modeling, you will grow in influence with them. This, in turn, will enable you to better minister to them with the truths of the gospel. *We build bridges to people's hearts by adding real value to their lives.*

Let's briefly talk about a key element to training people and fostering the type of confidence that is life changing.

Pressure Testing For Quality and Authenticity

When we consider sharing our knowledge and using our skills to further the mission of influencing others for Christ, it's essential to create opportunities for what's being taught to be properly tested and applied under real conditions. This verifies if the teachings can stand, but also reveals and to see what's truly been internalized and what still needs to be developed or understood.

Practice, feedback, affirmation, coaching, accountability, and correction. This is so necessary for healthy growth and development.

We see the need for appropriate testing and trials across human development and skill/knowledge disciplines:

- Plumbers have to pressure test their pipes to assess their work and must apprentice under a master plumber.

- Fighters have to compete and experience appropriate resistance against their techniques and concepts in proper progression. They need to spar to test their skills and put them to work.

- Communicators have to present and teach and write, then assess whether or not they hit the mark to their intended audience.

- People who are learning about concepts of leadership have to actually lead something.

- Programmers have to design something and launch it to test its functionality.

- Chefs and bakers have to actually cook and bake.

- Children have to be given the opportunity to succeed or fail on their own alongside your support in small things and big things as they progress in life from most other skills to problem solving. We have to let them wrestle through things and figure it out.

- And finally, sharing your faith with an unbeliever and being met with resistance, rejection, or down right insult or attack, for example, is necessary and will happen. How we respond in those and after those experiences says a lot about our faith and character.

Hopefully you get the point. Testing, trials, and qualitative assessment is important to real growth and the development of rock solid confidence and proven character.

This is the nature of progressive mastery and continual growth—build precept upon precept, simple to complex, rudimentary to mastery, all under the caring and watchful eye of someone more experienced and committed to their success. Teaching and training others is about helping people become faithful in little things so they can develop the ability to be faithful in the big things and handle more. People and healthy foundations in anything must be pressure tested to assure quality, authenticity, and the stability necessary to build upon. Only then should more complex things be introduced with proper progression. The elementary principles of anything should be mastered before trying to grasp more sophisticated concepts, truths, and skills.

Applied To The Faith

This idea relative to spiritual formation and following Jesus is really important. We can save ourselves and those we train from much frustration and time if we first focus on ensuring the foundations are solid. If we build rightly, deconstructing later in life doesn't have to be the norm leading to disillusionment. And Oh, how believers in Jesus Christ deeply need to know and live the foundations of the faith! Without it, we will only have empty religious knowledge and stay carnal and immature. Most believers could not clearly articulate the foundational and elementary principle truths of the faith, let alone demonstrate them in their life and character. This is just another indicator of the lack of proper discipleship and training. Many believers at this stage of the game, if they know the core truths of the faith, they are not living according to it. *Principles without practice are powerless and produce blinding and deceptive pride.* All the statistics and lack of community and cultural impact prove it. We really do need a reality check in the body of Christ.

That's why we need to return to the ancient paths of discipleship. A new breed and standard must be recovered and raised in our generation.

"Meat", instead of "milk", is reserved for the mature; those who have trained themselves by consistent practice of the truth to be able to think and reason biblically while living sound and wholesome lives. Sound doctrine is more than the right facts, it's freedom and a way of living born out of the conviction of the truth. There's nothing more ugly than religious hypocrisy and pride of religious knowledge void of application. I believe God is raising up a people and a generation that will close the gap between faith and works, knowing and doing, love and obedience. They are people who have submitted themselves to the process of God, yielded to His training, become authentic disciples made complete and ready for the good works He's ordained. If you've read this far, you're called to be part of the solution. You may just be one of those who have responded to His invitation. If your heart and commitment is "yes", you are part of the remnant restoring the standard of authentic faith in our generation. Praise God!

It starts with us—with you. We can only reproduce and train others to the degree of ability and faith we possess. Even more important is our heart and attitude by which we do the things we do in life. We need to live with intention and passion, never lacking in zeal and spiritual fervor as we serve the Lord in all things. The world and the next generation of believers needs to see a model of a life lived wholly for the Lord in all things. Your spirituality and faith must be expressed in your works, character, vocation, family, hobbies, etc. Your faith is not to be segmented or compartmentalized to a devotional study, private prayer time, and a church service, it's to be all-pervasive through everything. All you do is spiritual and part of your worship. Do all to the glory of God. Thus, we need to keep growing and learning and doing everything in our power, by the grace of God, to shine as a living example, continually improving in the things we do. This will help to make a way for those in our trust today and those who are to come after us.

It's powerful to see the beauty of the godly influence we can have on others. When mentoring and training people, when they truly "get it" and growth is tangible in their base of knowledge, understanding, character, and applied skills at home, at work, and in community—this is the clear sign that progress is genuinely being made.

Growth at any level should be affirmed and celebrated along the way. When people have come into their own and have the competence of a knowledge base or skill set that has been properly tested and approved, they gain confidence, and that's what we want. A good teacher imparts belief and the belief that the impossible can become possible. Jesus spoke to the nature and fruit of discipleship: that the outcome of our influence should be fully trained students who become like the teacher. There should be quality reproduction or duplication of the intended outcomes and skills necessary for the success and development of the mission or task at hand.—Luke 6:40.

Before we move into some dynamics about the call to teach others and how to do it effectively, I want to speak to the tensions and dynamics of information, memorization, and transformation. Let's discuss how they relate to the learning process, our focus on disciple-making and intent for making an eternal impact on people.

PAUSE. CAPTURE. APPLY
Prompts to help you process

1. What specific insights or concepts from this chapter resonated with you the most? Why do you think these stood out to you?

_____

_____

_____

2. How can you practically apply the principles discussed in this chapter to your daily life, relationships, or ministry? Identify at least one actionable step you can take this week.

_____

_____

_____

3. What potential challenges or barriers might you face in implementing these concepts? How can you overcome them?

_____

_____

_____

4. What are 3-5 quotes or points from this chapter that capture the essence of what it's communicating? Write them down.

_____

_____

_____

_____

_____

5. How can you involve your family, small group, or church community in the practices and principles outlined in this chapter? What steps can you take to foster a culture of discipleship and transformation within your circle of influence?

_____

_____

_____

6. Spend a few moments in prayer, asking God for the wisdom, strength, and courage to live out the truths you've learned. Write down a commitment or a prayer that reflects your desire to grow as an authentic disciple and transformational leader to impact the world.

_____

_____

_____

CHAPTER 9

What's the Goal?

Understanding the tensions of information, memorization, and transformation.

> *"Genuine spiritual knowledge lies not in wonderful and mysterious thoughts but in actual spiritual experience through union of the believer's life with truth."*
>
> — WATCHMAN NEE

How we approach the learning process and what we understand about the way we are changed at the heart level is key for our own life and those we are leading. Our curriculum (formal or informal) for growth and becoming like Christ must be comprehensive, multi-dimensional, practical, relational, and holistic. We must move toward and return to an integrated approach.

We need to holistically consider the goals, objectives and outcomes we desire from all our efforts. We must always remain aligned with the big picture so we don't get "lost in the weeds." It's crucial to remember that everything we do connects our lives, those we serve, and our very purpose of existence.

Again, we have to begin with the end in mind if we want to build a life with a deep sense of purpose, established on the unshakable and eternal rock of wisdom. We can't afford to get lost in the hustle and bustle of our lives so we fail to keep a larger vision and purpose for our lives. And this calls us to ask deeper and more foundational questions.

Without vision, people perish. They cast off restraint, wandering into unproductivity and selfishness. We must move beyond the cultural perspective of "self actualization" and towards the concept of "Christ glorification" and self transcendence. God's chief aim is for our lives to be transformed into the image of Christ; for us to be sharers of His glory as children of God, be made mature in Christ as a compatible Bride ready for His coming, and to be faithful witnesses to the ends of the earth. We are to intimately know Jesus, become like Jesus, and do the things He did. We do that not by living for ourselves but by forsaking ourselves to live for the will of God, in loving service to others for the gospel's sake.

If that sounds alien to you, I apologize and ask for forgiveness on behalf of the Church for selling you a partial and false gospel with a cheap grace void of the call and cost of discipleship.

This big picture has to be held before our heart and eyes as the canopy and driving motivation for everything we do in life. It is our primary purpose in life. Remember, your faith should not be compartmentalized from every other aspect of your life. It should inform every aspect of your life in very real and practical ways. This world as we know it, is NOT your home and your life does not belong to you. You have been bought with a price, the very blood of Jesus.

This hope of the age to come and the opportunity to give expression to it in the here and now is part of the great adventure to which we are all called. It makes the pains and perplexities of the process worth it. It's about revealing the glory and knowledge of God in all we are and do and passing on the faith to the next generation. We need to keep thinking bigger, biblically, and multi generationally (ps 78) to live a full life now and make an eternal impact. Listen to this quote by Viktor E. Frankel, in the classic book, "Man's Search for Meaning"

"By declaring that man is responsible and must actualize the potential meaning of his life, I wish to stress that the true meaning of life is to be discovered in the world rather than within man or his own psyche, as though it were a closed system. I have termed this constitutive characteristic "the self-transcendence of human existence." It denotes the fact that being human always points, and is directed, to something or someone, other than oneself--be it a meaning to fulfill or another human being to encounter. The more one forgets himself--by giving himself to a cause to serve or another person to love--the more human he is and the more he actualizes himself. What is called self-actualization is not an attainable aim at all, for the simple reason that the more one would strive for it, the more he would miss it. In other words, self-actualization is possible only as a side-effect of self-transcendence."

That "self transcendence" is really a call to know and follow Christ, to do His will and not our own.

Another thing, we can't afford to stay on the surface and suffer the perpetual pains of superficiality as an individual and as a culture. The complexity and pressures of our time and age call us both deeper and higher. We must become people that pioneer a better world, who occupy as a prophetic force of goodness and the reality of a living God until the Lord comes. This is not mere idealism, its part of the ache and hope at the core of creation. The scripture describes it as a longing to be clothed with immortality and for the age to come; a day of perfection where all things are made new, and we dwell in the perfect presence of God without corruption and evil, the home of righteousness. We should not be overly preoccupied with the Lord's coming so that we are unproductive and disengaged in this life. We are to occupy until He comes, as vice regents extending His rule and reign on earth. We are called to be agents of transformation today by expressing the God who "is" right now, through love, truth, and power." The God of the Bible is the same God yesterday, today, and forever and He will powerfully act on behalf of those who will wholly believe in Him and obey His word. The Spirit of God will move in power as He has always done for those who have said "yes" to Him.

We are called to be salt and light, devoted to the good works that bless and better people's lives now and for the age to come! You and I have a beautiful, sacred responsibility to participate in the propagation of goodness and justice, and the knowledge of God in the earth regardless of our station in life. Whether you are helping the orphan and widow, a student with learning disabilities, changing diapers and raising kids, building a hospital and creating jobs, laying hands on the sick, casting out devils, setting captives free, and preaching good news to the poor, you are called to advance the Kingdom of God.

I love what the Lord communicated through the prophet Jeremiah while the people of God were in exile for 70 years, under divine chastisement, as the people were waiting to return to the promised land, he said,

"This is what the Lord Almighty, God of Israel, says to all those I carried into exile from Jerusalem to Babylon: build houses and settle down; plant gardens and eat what they produce. Marry and have sons and daughters; find wives for your sons and give your daughters in marriage, so that they too may have sons and daughters. Increase in number there; do not decrease. Also, seek the peace and prosperity of the city to which I've carried you in the exile. Pray to the Lord for it, because if it prospers, you too will prosper."—Jeremiah 29:4-7

No matter the season or circumstances, the promise and covenant of God for His people is the same; To be blessed to be a blessing to the nations of the earth, to be fruitful and multiply, fill the earth, to rule and have dominion (Gen 12:1-3, 1:26-27). We are to seek the welfare of our cities and towns with a relevant voice and contribution to society through productive lives.

We are to be light and salt, redemptive agents of change in the earth who adorn the gospel in how we live. The pattern, order, behavior, and fruit of our lives and families should reveal God's name, ways, wisdom, and goodness. We are to be holy as He is holy! The world should be able to taste and see that God is good through us. This is our purpose as the people of God across time and culture.

Deep People

This quote by Richard J Foster helped shape my life from youth:, *"superficiality is the curse of this age and the doctrine of instant gratification is a primary spiritual problem. The great need today is not for more gifted people or talented people, but deep people."*

When I describe "deep" people, this pertains to personal transformation and the hard heart work of honest self- assessment, renewal of the mind, forgiveness, healing, reconciliation, and adopting new ways in our lives. I was stuck in many places because I was hurt, angry, avoiding life at different levels, fearful of rejection and failure, and believing lies. I couldn't even write in a notebook because, "God forbid I would mess up that blank page or someone would find what I wrote and criticize it and it reflects poorly on me, and I would look ugly or stupid or weak."

I needed something more than information or a class to change me and bring me deeper. I needed revelation and renewal. Part of the problem was that I couldn't assimilate or fully receive the things I needed when they were presented to me because I was believing lies.

Knowledge and memorization alone can deceive us to think that we actually "know" something and are living it when we're not.

I had it memorized and could repeat the truth back and even passionately teach the concepts. In reality, for the hope of personal change I needed truth to break up the foul ground of my heart and mind in a deeper way. I needed people and community for accountability and support.

The safety of God's love and trustworthy people in an authentic community is and was key to integrating knowledge and truth into the fabric of my life. Genuine repentance and transformation take intentionality and work in the grace of God. I needed to settle into the love of God, behold Him, encounter His presence, and learn to abide through consistent practice and meditation upon His truth and nature. We bear fruit in *keeping* with repentance. I had to learn to relationally exchange with the Lord as I practiced a new way of living by the grace of God. If knowledge or truth doesn't translate into wisdom, how we actually live and behave, expressed in love for God, for others, and in effective service, then we've missed it. Truth must become useful, practical and work into every aspect of our lives. Truth and education should lead us into lives pleasing to God in every respect. This takes intention and constant practice. As the writer of Ecclesiastes says and in conclusion to studying everything under the sun, " When all has been heard, the conclusion of the matter is this: fear God and keep His commands, because this is the duty for all humanity. For God will bring every act to judgment, including every hidden thing, whether good or evil."—Ecc 12:13-14.

This age of information and technology has changed the mode of our existence. Great advances have been made across all sectors of society and industry and human interaction. At the same time, in many other ways, humanity has suffered. The science and the state of global affairs, shifting economic, political, and educational realities testify to the systemic tensions and new problems that have arisen.

People have outsourced their intelligence to Siri, Alexa, Google and ChatGPT. There is so much information available. This has led people to have underdeveloped discernment and critical thinking. Many have become subject to the manipulation of slanted information and agendas. People are drowning in information, yet lacking the wisdom that leads to skillful living and joyful lives.

As I said above, people are less happy now with more available than before. They are more depressed and socially disconnected than before even though they are stuck on technology and social media grasping for connection.

You have heard it said that "knowledge is power" but this is not completely true, especially in our day. Knowledge is only *potential* power. Information alone will not change your life or give birth to solutions that better your health, family, community, church, industry. etc. If information alone could do that, we all would make some very different decisions. Would you agree? Otherwise we wouldn't find ourselves falling into these common traps: continually overeating or neglecting proper nutrition, binging on Netflix or Amazon video at the expense of sleep, failing to set healthy boundaries in toxic relationships, skipping opportunities for growth, allowing our children excessive social media and screen time, failing to pray, fast, read the scriptures, evangelize, make disciples and so on.

As the sacred scriptures say, "if we are only hearers of the word, we deceive ourselves, but if we are doers of the word, we will be blessed in what we do. Otherwise we are like someone who looks in the mirror, and after looking at himself, goes away and immediately forgets what he looks like." Paraphrased James 1:22-24

To receive the benefit of knowledge, information, and truth, we must understand, internalize, and act upon it. If I don't practice what I say I've come to understand or know, how does it serve me and how will it actually impact or change my life? It won't. Knowledge must find expression through proper application and implementation rooted in a strong conviction (faith). Memorization, though useful, is not enough.

I remember when I was trying to quit smoking. By the way, I started smoking regularly when I was like 7 years old. Crazy right? My dad first gave me something to smoke when I was still in diapers. When we had a pretty intense transition from Florida to Massachusetts. I soon found myself hanging around much older kids, smoking cigarettes and other stuff, getting into trouble at the age of seven. Long story short, I had a life changing encounter with Jesus as a young teen that shifted everything. That thrust me into a process of healing, growth, and transformation, but those stinking cigarettes were a snare that I battled for a few years.

In the process of trying and failing, over and over, to stop smoking, I grew stronger in my will to stand on the truth, I also became aware of my great need for greater faith and surrender to the truth that sets us free. I "knew" the right info and had it memorized in my mind, but I was still stuck. The reality is, breakthrough and freedom was and is a process of beholding and becoming. As we behold and meditate on the very nature and Glory of God revealed in Christ, His spirit transforms us into the same image. When our thoughts and imaginations are renewed according to the true knowledge of God, we are changed in the deepest parts of who we are, our will is strengthened, and as a result our behaviors and appetites change as well. When you marry that to accountability and transparency with others, breakthrough is near and real freedom lasts.

Knowledge alone is not enough to positively impact or transform our lives. Remember, it's only *potential* power. I had to wrestle with truth, take time to behold, and see it from different perspectives. I also had to let true and new desire rise up within me while at the same time taking repeated action to try to overcome it. It's a "both-and" situation of faith and action, beholding and doing, learning and practice, hearing and obeying, information and implementation. That's how new neural pathways were being created. I was renewing my mind and developing new structures and habits.

I remember where I was standing when my heart saw the truth in a new way and the appropriate application of the truth I had been wrestling with for a long time, clicked. In a moment of being tempted to smoke again, I stopped *trying* to overcome and I rested in the truth of the finished work of the Cross. My heart concluded and was fully persuaded that Jesus either "finished it" or He didn't. The corrupting power and problem of sin either received the death blow or it didn't. My soul learned to actually trust and rely upon this truth and walk in it. Boom! Breakthrough! I finally came to understand *by* faith, as the scriptures say, "by faith we understand…"(Hebrews 11:3). When heartfelt belief in the truth transformed the knowledge I had merely memorized and understood intellectually and activated it deep within my heart,---the true place of "knowing" and conviction—it sparked immediate change and transformation. My behavior and actions and thoughts had shifted. I no longer smoked after years of battling. Praise God!

This is the same principle truth we see with Israel who didn't enter into God's rest because of their unbelief that was the source of their disobedience. They heard the word of God, but it did not benefit them because they didn't marry that with faith. Therefore, they didn't submit to the truth but sought their own way. Faith in the truth unlocks the power contained in the truth. This is a faith that is demonstrated in the decisions and actions we take. Faith without works is dead. The faith that leads to appropriate action is where we see the *potential* power of knowledge activated and expressed! This is a very loud truth we must understand for our own hearts and lives and for those we will lead and influence![67]

---

[67] Hebrews 3:7-4:16

This faith is about knowing and a reliance upon the Lord himself and His ability to do what He has said. It is a relational exchange, rooted in the truth of God's word and nature. Many stop short of the divine encounter that frees us because they stop at the memorization of theological facts. The word of God is to lead us to the God of the word who sets us free. The Pharisees searched the scriptures thinking that eternal life was in them and failed to come to the One in whom they spoke of[68]. We must come to the Son and receive from the Son and He will set us free.

As my dear friend Steve says: The two great tragedies in the Church today are:

1) people doing good theology and stopping there, content to know about God without "knowing" Him.

2) people who think they can know God without good theology (studying the Word).

We can shepherd people into this type of breakthrough faster when we KNOW it and experience it for ourselves. But before I get too ahead of myself, let's just talk about memorization for a moment.

Memorization

When It comes to learning, memorization has a place in terms of knowledge retention, but it does not develop understanding that leads to wisdom and skillful application of knowledge that bears the fruit of a transformed life. Among both children and adults, many fail to truly learn or learn HOW to learn. Most people these days, especially in America, are not classically trained, or given the proper learning context, and have poor literacy.

---

68 John 5:39-40

For those of us who were educated in the public school system in recent decades, there's been a notable decline in literacy levels, a reduction in academic rigor, and a shift towards memorization that's aimed at passing tests or answering multiple-choice questions, rather than fostering a genuine love for learning and deep understanding. Memorization alone doesn't address character development either, though it can serve as a form of conscience on a shallow level. Memorization is a starting point and gateway to more, as it provides the raw materials for reasoning. Christians who have scripture memorized but live in contradiction illustrate that knowledge by itself falls short of what is necessary. Knowledge and memorization, though useful, is only *potential power*.

In the taxonomy of learning, science tells us that memorization is on the lowest level—it's stage 1 as an entry point—important but not the end in itself and especially when it comes to personal development. Most actually need to do more memorization to stretch their brain capacity. We can't stop here and must press on to the higher levels of learning that finally get expressed in our character, actions, and innovations.

Here's Bloom's taxonomy of educational objectives at a glance. You can see that to "remember"-is to recall facts and concepts, memorize or repeat information, is at the base of learning.[69] Unfortunately many stop here at this base level in their attempts to disciple or educate.

---

[69] "In 1956, Benjamin Bloom with collaborators Max Englehart, Edward Furst, Walter Hill, and David Krathwohl published a framework for categorizing educational goals: Taxonomy of Educational Objectives. Familiarly known as Bloom's Taxonomy, this framework has been applied by generations of K-12 teachers, college and university instructors and professors in their teaching. The framework elaborated by Bloom and his collaborators consisted of six major categories: Knowledge, Comprehension, Application, Analysis, Synthesis, and Evaluation. The categories after Knowledge were presented as "skills and abilities," with the understanding that knowledge was the necessary precondition for putting these skills and abilities into practice."—https://bloomstaxonomy.net/

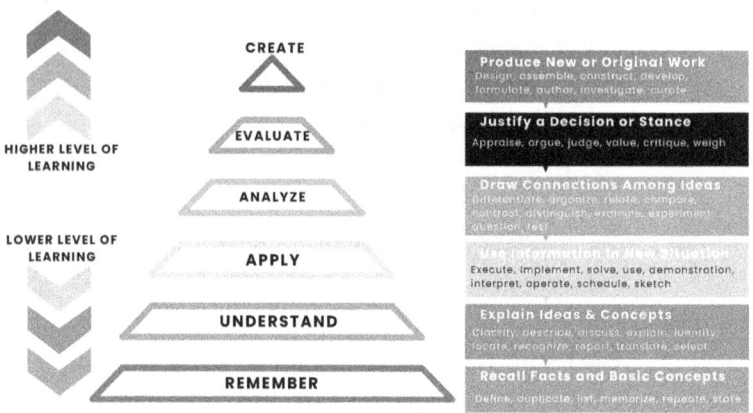

Blooms Taxonomy

When I think of dance or martial arts, where mastering a piece of choreography or a kata (a patterned sequence of movements), or even learning a sales script or any skill demanding nuance and proficiency, the role of memorization becomes evident. We need to see the moves, have them explained, demonstrated in the proper way and proper order and then broken down so that we can learn them in sequence. Similarly, we need to hear or have modeled for us the flow of conversation in a sales script. Memorization is part of the stage that holds the content or body of knowledge. I could walk through the choreography or tell you the sequence or give you the sales pitch, but that is very different from dancing the dance, performing the kata or having a sales conversation with the heart, spirit and authentic expression that makes it all come alive in a beautiful demonstration. They are worlds apart! One is hollow and one is full of life and passion. In the learning process, we all start hollow— unrefined, stupid, incompetent, and that's ok. We can laugh at ourselves, but we just can't stay there.

Anyone that has competed and been assessed by a panel of judges or who has been a judge assessing others, knows what I'm talking about. Things need to have the "spark of life," they need heart and conviction. Without it, it's hollow and will be less than the potential of that individual or team or community. Imagine loved ones going through the formalities and mechanics of a rehearsed complement they don't even mean. Or even worse, an apology without any sincerity or remorse. We would not feel connected nor would we really receive their apologies or complements in our heart. We'd probably resent it and have to press into the conversation to get to the heart of the matter. *Because we know the heart is where things matter.* Like the old saying by Mother Theresa and many others who have echoed her, "people don't care how much you know till they know how much you care."

You can say and do the "right things" because you've memorized how to do it, but it doesn't make it real yet. Is this a little intense? Are you saying "ouch....oooooo"? I think we all have gone through the motions at one point or another. We know we can't stop there if we really want to live and love and do what matters.

Plus, we can also see in this matter that people may "know" they need to forgive or be patient but they haven't done the heart work to actually become forgiving and patient people/ Two very different realities.

Memorization is not enough to produce the outcomes and goods that we really want in life when following Jesus and performing at the top of our game. Information and memorization alone only hold the potential for something greater. And it's that something greater we're after. Transformation.

Transformation

Most people think of the classic imagery of the caterpillar that transforms into a butterfly when considering the concept of transformation. The picture is a powerful image that calls out to us to continually evolve and grow as people. It points to the fact that we will experience, like the caterpillar, transitions and transformations in life that require both struggle and engagement. Life is full of perpetual transitions in a natural sense but also in a supernatural sense. God is always working in us to will and do according to His good pleasure. Hopefully we should be moving in a positive direction and becoming more like Christ— from glory to glory, strength to strength, and faith into faith. Even if your physical body decays, our faith tells us that our heart, character, and understanding, should be growing brighter, wiser, and more loving, with every passing day and through every necessary trial. We are to be becoming more and more like Him.

The butterfly and the process of metamorphosis reminds us about upgrading and not downgrading in life, about moving into a superior way of operating and living. It is about forward progress and moving from one plane of existence into a better one. Apostle Paul says it this way in 2 Corinthians 3:18, 4:16-18, " *And we all with unveiled faces contemplate the Lord's glory, are being transformed into his image with ever increasing glory, which comes from the Lord who is the spirit.... Therefore we do not lose heart. Though outwardly we are wasting away, yet inwardly we are being renewed day by day. For our light and momentary troubles are achieving for us an eternal glory that far outweighs them all. So we fix our eyes not on what is seen, but on what is unseen, since what is seen is temporary, but what is unseen is eternal."*

In a world where information and distractions bombard us incessantly, it's crucial to learn—and teach others—to quiet themselves, focus deeply, and embrace what truly matters for life, faith, health, relationships, and vocation. It takes Intentional focus and discipline to sift through the abundance of data, avoid distraction, and apply it meaningfully. We must slow down to speed up, moving past information, into implementation and practice for genuine transformation. We are so conditioned for instant gratification and just want everything now. People have a hard time with the process and anything that takes time or effort. My friends, real growth takes time. Character is forged over years of faithful service and submission to God. There's no shortcuts.

Maturing from a "childlike" state in thought, word, and deed, into adulthood involves understanding God's plan, ways and character and incorporating His truth consistently and habitually into our lives through faith and relationship - i.e. practice that is married to the faith that trusts God's Spirit to change us as we both meditate on and obey His word, no matter the cost.

Transformation is a process and we must wholly submit to the process to be changed. This applies to areas of the soul, character development, discipling others, sharing your story and evangelizing. It is the same for natural things. Skills and abilities grow and mature for someone when they are in constant use alongside reflective development aiming to improve effectiveness and efficiency. People become seasoned and nuanced in their abilities and have a command and mastery in their skill sets through constant use through time and testing. What might start off awkward, hard, and unknown becomes easy and effortless as the process of patient practice and reflective learning takes its course. The struggle is real but perseverance produces the product of new found ability, capacity, and power.

If we endeavor to advance in a skill or ability, we would do well to also adopt a baseline confidence and belief that we actually have the ability to grow and learn. Many believe that they can't and remain stuck in life in different areas. The heart and mind posture that believes they can grow and learn is a key to actual learning and growth. Starting with confidence or a self efficacy rooted in Christ, accelerates gains in competence. When we step out to learn or grow into a new thing or a new way of operating, the simple faith that believes it has the capacity to do so, has already won half the battle. We learn faster when we believe we can.

To Live a Life of Love

Transformation is the continual goal that empowers our ability to live a life of love and service. Christian maturity is the perfecting of love and holiness.

In making disciples or influencing others, maintaining focus in this principle is crucial. Otherwise, our methods may deviate from the path and fail to achieve our desired outcomes, including those most valued by the scriptures. Perfecting love and holiness must remain a core "why" to the things we do, because the "why" always empowers the "what" and the "how."

If what we're doing isn't fostering transformation and challenging people to the next level of growth in godliness, we have a problem. We are called to become like Jesus, be conformed to His image, and let our faith be expressed in love and service to others. Knowledge puffs up but love builds up. This should be our aim in all things, to love as

He loves and to perfect holiness in the fear of the Lord (1 Corinthians 8:1, 2 Corinthians 7:1).

In the words of Apostle Paul, " Brothers and sisters, I do not consider myself yet to have taken hold of it. But one thing I do: forgetting what is behind and straining towards what is ahead, I press on towards the goal, to win the prize, for which God has called me heavenward in Christ Jesus. All of us, then who are mature, should take such a view of things. And if on some point you think differently, that too God will make clear to you. Only let us live up to what we have already attained. Join together in following my example, brothers and sisters, and just as you have us as a model, keep your eyes on those who live as we do."—Philippians 3:13-17

We see a call to continual growth. To change any attitudes that forsake familiarity, mediocracy, and whatever would cause us to stay camped out at one level, to only plateau and eventually become dull.

Have we become dull and too easily satisfied? Are we in fiery pursuit of the Lord and greater levels of transformation in our life? Are we spurring others on to do the same from the heart? Good question. Maybe pause for a moment and consider.

This was the Lord's command: to love one another as He has loved us and to walk as He walked, to "be imitators of God and live a life of Love, just as Christ loved us and gave himself up for us as a fragrant offering and sacrifice to God."—Ephesians 5:1-2. He was clear when He said, "there is no greater love than this that a man lay down his life for a friend"—(John 15) That's exactly what He did for us. He didn't just go to the cross in one final act of love for us in obedience to the Father, but He also lived a life of love and selflessness. He demonstrated moral purity and sacrificial service as a way of life. Then He then said that He was the way, the truth, and the life, as it relates to knowing the Father and eternal life.

He showed us how to live and has given us the grace to live it. This should inform our aims in training others and in keeping the big picture vision and goals before those we lead and influence: His motivation in His suffering and obedience to the will of God as He lived into His purpose was twofold. He loved and desired to please the Father, and He loved us.

We know that Christ was fully God and fully man. To love us well and rightly represent the Father, Jesus knew He had to perfectly represent and embody the truth. If He had been a coward and compromised in life, failing to be the warrior He needed to be, then salvation for all humanity could never have been purchased. The value of Christ's sacrifice was hinged upon His sinless life as a man. His obedience resulted in our justification and reconciliation. Love for the Father and for us was a driving motivation in His commitment to truth, and so shall it be for us. We ought to love one another as He has loved us. Love is the motivation that drives change, growth and obedience to truth.

Jesus Himself prayed and revealed this part of His heart in John 17:19 when He said, *"... I sanctify myself for my brethrens sake, that they too may be sanctified (set apart for God)."* The apostles and writers of the New Testament express the same thing in affirming to the Church that "they have sanctified themselves in obedience to the truth, *in sincere love of the Brethren*, now continue to love one another deeply from the heart." 1 Peter 1:22

What's my point? Information or memorizing alone won't produce transformation and conformity to the image of Christ. Nor will it be sufficient for satisfying our purpose as people. The meaning and significance of our life can only be found in Christ, by giving our lives away in obedience to Christ, and in love for others. What matters is authentic faith moving through love. This manifests in what we feel, think, say, and do. It's costly action and internal restraint. It is not just good ideas and concepts void of substance or application. As the scripture says, we cannot just love in word and tongue but also in deed and truth.[70] It is by this that men will know that we are His disciples, that we love one another.[71]

The Bible describes Solomon as the wisest man in history. He said, "Now all things have been heard: here is the conclusion of the matter: fear God and keep His commandments, for this is the duty of all mankind. For God will bring every deed into judgment, including every hidden thing, whether it is good or evil."(Ecc 12:13-14) Jesus said, "if you want to save your life, you will lose it, but if you give your life away, for my sake and the gospel you'll find it." He calls us out of ourselves, into a hope and faith filled life that transcends ourselves. Thus we become useful in His hands for a purpose and works far greater than we can ask, think, or imagine! When we pursue a life that loves others with the very love of God as demonstrated in Christ, we cannot help but be transformed. To love others requires that we lay aside all selfish ambition and prefer each other over ourselves in humility and sincerity.

In all the ways we lead, we must keep in tension the goal of transformation by writing on people's hearts with the love of God but also the necessary elements in place for people to internalize truth themselves, not just memorize it. Truth must be embodied, lived out, and expressed in relationships. To make disciples, influence people with eternal truth, help people become authentic, it's vital that what they learn, how they learn, and why they learn, all foster a deep intimacy with God that results in the obedience born from faith. Out of friendship with God should grow godly character, practical skills, and wise living, all actively serving the greater community.

"Now the goal of our instruction is love that comes from a pure heart, a good conscience, and a sincere faith. Some have deviated from these and turned aside to fruitless discussion. They want to be teachers of

---

[70] 1 John 3:18
[71] John 13:35

the law, although they don't understand what they are saying or what they are insisting on."- 1 Tim 1:5-7

Thinking through your own learning journey. What's that been like and how does it compare to what I'm talking about?

Do you see the difference between knowing and doing? Knowledge that puffs up versus the experiential knowledge that leads to love for others that builds up? Memorization versus understanding? Comprehension versus demonstrated ability? Knowledge versus love and character?

PAUSE. CAPTURE. APPLY
Prompts to help you process

1. What specific insights or concepts from this chapter resonated with you the most? Why do you think these stood out to you?

_____

_____

_____

2. How can you practically apply the principles discussed in this chapter to your daily life, relationships, or ministry? Identify at least one actionable step you can take this week.

_____

_____

_____

3. What potential challenges or barriers might you face in implementing these concepts? How can you overcome them?

_____

_____

_____

4. What are 3-5 quotes or points from this chapter that capture the essence of what it's communicating? Write them down.

_____

_____

_____

_____

_____

5. How can you involve your family, small group, or church community in the practices and principles outlined in this chapter? What steps can you take to foster a culture of discipleship and transformation within your circle of influence?

_____

_____

_____

6. Spend a few moments in prayer, asking God for the wisdom, strength, and courage to live out the truths you've learned. Write down a commitment or a prayer that reflects your desire to grow as an authentic disciple and transformational leader to impact the world.

_____

_____

_____

WHAT'S THE GOAL?

FREE VIDEO SUMMARY'S

WANT VIDEO SUMMARY'S OF EACH CHAPTER & MORE?

Transformational Tools & Resources

Think about this **FREE** resources as a training process and master class loaded with value and discussion prompts for your people and your own reflection.

ARISEANDRETURN.COM

CHAPTER 10

Teaching isn't for me or is it?

The Call to teach, equip, & make impact—how we do it effectively.

> *"Education is the most powerful weapon which you can use to change the world"*
> —Nelson Mandela.

> *"The mediocre teacher tells. The good teacher explains. The superior teacher demonstrates. The great teacher inspires."*
> —William Authur Ward

In my younger years, I struggled in school due to several factors (a turbulent home life, the subject's lack of relevance to my life, the lack of accommodation for my learning style). School was not for me. It's ironic that today I'm passionate about holistic learning and transformative education.

Amid the social distractions that often overshadowed true learning, I found inspiration in the adults who engaged with me at school, in sports, during after-school programs, camps, and other activities. The teachers who stood out formed real connections, expressed genuine interest in my life, sincerely affirmed me, challenged me to reach my potential , and engaged with me at my level. These folks made me feel seen and loved and provoked, even inspired me to be more and do more. Plus, they loved what they did and it was seen and felt in the way they taught.

Science today affirms the power of these meaningful connections as the greatest contributing factor to sustained motivation, resilience, and higher performance. We have to capture the heart if we really want to train the mind and impact a life. Educating the mind alone without capturing the heart will not lead to the transformation and influence we've talked about. Without the experience of love, roots will not take hold in the heart and fruit will not be born in the outworking of life. Like the parable of the sower, the seeds of truth we seek to sow will either be snatched up by the enemy, be short lived, choked out and not retained, or best of all, take root in the soil of the soul and bear much fruit.

It was after my heart encountered the love and reality of Jesus that hunger to learn exploded in me. I was 15 years old and had never read a book. I cheated my way through school and did the same book report on the same book for years in a row. That's hysterical and sad at the same time. It's crazy that I got away with it, and I'm definitely laughing as I write this. But when I gave my heart to the Lord, I started reading all the time. It began with pouring over the scriptures for hours at a time, reading, praying, and weeping over what was impacting my heart. Then I started writing and journaling and reading other books. I started listening to older, wiser people than me, imitating what I saw as good and godly. I was like a sponge, hungry to grow in wisdom and understanding.

Imitation is a function of discipleship. It multiplies learning. As Andrew Meltzoff, American Psychologist who identified and named social learning said, "it is faster than individual discovery and safer than learning by trial and error." I didn't know this at the time but I was picking it up and seeing the results. My mind, heart, language, decisions—everything began to change in an incredible way. It all accelerated as I immersed myself. I later discovered that "learning" and "input" are in my top five Strength Finders™ qualities. I actually have a huge, multi-faceted ability to learn, and I can take in large amounts of content and assimilate it. Ha! Where was this in my younger years, right? It was there but dwarfed alongside some other problems that hindered my growth and educational experience in school such as:

- The learning environment was not multidimensional or engaging.

- The style of teaching was pretty narrow and didn't appeal to various learning styles including mine.

- The outcomes or goals of the educational approach missed other competencies and intelligences I was expressing—it was too stuck in a box and not individualized.

- I lacked interest in the topics.

- There was a lack of relationships from many teachers and there was not a peer group motivated or interested in learning (though there was available the "SkillsUSA" group focused on career readiness skills).

- My personal brokenness and family life stress.

- And the lack of correlation of things being taught to the bigger purpose of "why" in life, their relation to other subjects and domains in life, personal purpose and identity, or a compelling vision for life was not communicated or imparted.

- And probably other things as well.

But when those components were put in place, BOOM! The dormant seeds of grace; potential and learning capacity sprung to life and began to bear fruit.

I attended a vocational high school where we did both academics and focused on learning a trade. I loved the dynamics and it was in high school that I met the Lord and had a restored love of learning. If I was more mature then, I would have taken more advantage of the training available there. But, my priorities then were more about impacting souls for Jesus than learning plumbing. Ha! But that framework of being prepared for life with practical skills and a work ethic to engage in a competitive world, was great. Though imperfect, not truly holistic and having limited personal connections with staff (minus a few stars who did impact my heart), there are many great things about vocational trade schools. I'm sharing this for a reason, stick with me. As we'll get into, there are other things to consider when using our places of influence to disciple and educate others.

Out of high school, I pioneered an internship with the ministry Youthstorm, as I shared before. This was an intensive learning and growth environment with rigorous academics alongside multiple other components. That matrix of holistic education in the context of vision, clear purpose, community, and mission, became the green house for transformed lives. It created diverse opportunities and skill acquisition of all types.

The scriptural and historical Hebraic roots of education suggest that all elements of education happen in the context of family and community with an apprenticeship (on the job) training model. The process of learning and doing while on a shared mission framed by a cohesive worldview is powerful. This is a biblical approach to discipleship, which is truly an educational process (not merely academic though it includes a mastery of a body of knowledge). I urge the Body of Christ to return to this approach if we aspire to raise a generation who can positively change the world for the glory of Jesus Christ. Discipleship is more than a bible class or biblical knowledge!

Jesus modeled this type of training of His twelve disciples, Paul modeled this with Timothy, Titus and others, giving them clear instruction to teach others to do the same (2 Tim 2:2). I believe church communities need to reform by adopting comprehensive education models that integrate the church, the home, the family, the workplace like:

- Train and educate members of all ages in skills that enhance their personal and professional lives.

- Equip them to actively contribute to their communities and industries in meaningful ways.

- Encourage and develop full participation in the mission of the Great Commission and disciple-making, fueled by authentic love and devotion to God.

This comprehensive approach actually fleshes out the great commission; to make disciples who love God and love others and teach others who do the same. There is much to discuss concerning educational models and the historical roots of educational traditions, so we'll save it for another time. But I want to invite us into the call to teach intentionally, effectively, and holistically. This is for you and for me.

The great commission and the "how to" of making disciples must be important to us. The imperatives of "going, baptizing into community (the Name of God), and teaching" are primary parts of that road map we must consistently walk. If you love the Lord and desire to follow Him, this is your call to participate. So let's engage in the journey and mission of changing the world by sharing the gospel and making disciples. You are called to tell, teach, and to raise kingdom warriors!

To be most effective in passing on the faith, one of our main jobs should be to identify and train more leaders, not just to have "followers" or people we're leading. We have to think about multiplication, spiritual reproduction and delegation. This is the only way to truly have a multiplying and fruitful work that will last beyond us for generations. We want to make disciples who know how to make disciples and train leaders who can also reproduce and multiply other disciple makers.

We need to continually train others in a reproducible way and then teach them to do the same. We must frame the concept of being fruitful and multiplying with the idea that teaching and leadership is a function of equipping and activating others to do the work, rather than making them dependent on the "expert." We want to be a people who empower others. It's the same for parenting. Part of our job is to ensure our children are not just our followers or "mini me's," co-dependably leaning on us or living with us till they're 35 years old. We are to equip our kids and bring them into maturity as their own unique person. To be capable and responsible adults who can lead, raise and train their own households, and change the world. We need to think in a multigenerational way. We need to live for more than ourselves and consider how what we do can outlast us. It's about legacy, moving toward a biblical design for our roles as a teacher, leader, parent, or influencer.

Many people, parents, and churches lack an intentional, ordered, strategic, and relational development process. I'm inviting you to consider such an intentional plan for your life, family, and ministry. Like parenting, discipleship must be purposeful or we will miss the mark. People have outsourced their responsibility to teach others because they lack the knowledge or skills to teach or just haven't seen it as a priority. So many are just caught in the tyranny of the urgent, stuck in the weeds and have lost sight of the bigger picture. People tend to be reactive in life rather than proactive to architect what they want and how they will get there. This must change and we are all being called up higher.

We All Teach

We all teach and are all called to teach in one way or the other. Actually, we are always teaching through the life we live, whether we like it or not (plus, this is the first and most important part of the equation—teaching through personal example. We must live lives worthy of being reproduced). I want to encourage you that there is a more powerful and adventurous way to live as well, *by teaching with intention.* Take up the challenge of reproducing other disciples and disciple makers. An essential part of being a transformational leader is to multiply ourselves and reproduce other leaders who can do the same. You are called to be a disciple and to make disciples who can likewise make disciples.

Eternal impact comes through obedience to God's design and plan. That plan hasn't changed and won't change till the end of the age. For us, that means we are to:

- Rightly respond to the gospel in faith and repentance from our old lives, and be filled and clothed with power from on high to be His witnesses. (Acts 1:8)

- Be productive in life, to be fruitful and multiply. (Gen 1:28)

- Go into all the earth and make disciples of all nations. (Matt 28)

- Entrust what we have received to faithful men who are qualified to teach others. (2 Tim 2:2)

- Set an example for the Believer in speech, in conduct, in love, in faith, and in purity..(1 Tim 4:11)

- Do the work of an evangelist.(2 Tim 4:5)

- Preach the word; being prepared in season and out of season; correcting, rebuking and encouraging- with great patience and careful instruction. (2 Tim 4:2)

- All while taking heed to our own life, doctrine and gifting, persevering in them, because if we do, we will save both ourselves and our hearers. (1 Tim 4:11-16)

Simply put, we *love God* with all our hearts, soul, mind, and strength, *love others* as He has loved us, and be intentional to make disciples who multiply.

We can have confidence that He is with us and will empower us to carry out the plan He's given us. It will bear fruit! Why? Because He said so! Thus, we must give ourselves in the obedience of walking out the great commission by teaching with intention. Preoccupation with secondary and lesser things is too easy of a temptation in our day.

We must focus!

Be Fruitful and Multiply

The "Creation Mandate" tells us that God blesses humanity and bestows purpose and mission upon us from the very beginning— "To be fruitful and multiply, fill the earth and subdue it."[72] We are image bearers, made in the likeness of God. We were created to create and be productive, blessing the earth and revealing God's Glory and goodness. Part of this passage is obviously about filling the earth with godly offspring. But take note, teaching others is part of the mandate that makes it possible to be fruitful and multiply. We sow the seeds of truth as faithful stewards, passing on what God entrusted for its growth and propagation. The pattern of reproducing after our own kind is the nature of the created order. It's what we see Christ do as

---

[72] Genesis 1:28

the "seed" that fell to the ground in order to produce a righteous crop patterned after His own likeness.[73]

We are to follow suit by teaching with intention and laying our lives down for others. Discipleship is spiritual reproduction—where others are taught to wholeheartedly follow and become like Jesus.

If we fail to sow and give what we have been given, we fall short of our purpose in life. Should we fail to share the gospel and the teachings of Christ alongside our unique identity, knowledge, skills and resources, we will be profoundly startled when we face God and recount how we utilized what was given to us. All that we are is part of our stewardship before the throne of God and the chief duty of man is to fear God and obey His commands (Ecc 12). It is more blessed to give than to receive. In that spirit, we are to give, impart and sow everything we possess into the lives of those around us. We *must* teach and woe to us if we don't.

This principle of stewardship is key for every Christian, authentic disciple, and leader. Like the parable of the talents, if you don't multiply or use what you do have, it will be taken from you. But if you put to use what has been given to you, more will be entrusted to you and your influence will grow. Your growth and expansion is how God extends His Kingdom. This Kingdom expansion through your life is part of God's plan.

I'm sure you want to be faithful to the Lord and grow in your stewardship, right? If not, examine the reasons why you don't, repent and renew your mind. If you're overwhelmed with your present level of responsibility, that's okay. Be faithful with what you have, do well with it, and in the right time, you'll be ready for what else the Lord has for you. *Side note: do you have someone in your life who is mentoring you or discipling you? Ask them to help you discern what needs to shift in your life and where you need to focus to be more firmly established. If you don't*

---

[73] John 12:24

have someone close or someone to whom you are accountable, pause and ask Jesus to show you your next step in obedience. Then obey. After that, prayerfully consider bringing people into your inner circle.

We are called and empowered to be fruitful for God. Fruitfulness validates that we're actually disciples truly following Him and abiding in His love. To bear fruit and be productive in the grace of God at work in us is a hallmark of authentic discipleship and a demonstration of a living and healthy faith. Fruit is the manifestation of abiding, it's the byproduct. Fruit is about the nature of God being produced in us—a growing in character and holiness. Fruit is about obedience to His commands to love and serve others. Fruit employs our divine gifts to serve and build up the Body of Christ. Fruit is good works. Fruit manifests as laboring for the lost to be saved and making disciples. It is about growing in genuine intimacy, love, and devotion toward God.

In John 15:5-8 (HCSB) it says, "I am the vine, you are the branches. The one who remains in Me and I in him produces much fruit, because you can do nothing without Me. If anyone does not remain in Me, he is thrown aside like a branch and he withers. They gather them, throw them into the fire and they are burned. If you remain in Me and My words remain in you, ask whatever you want and it will be done for you. *My Father is glorified by this: that you produce much fruit and prove to be My disciples.*»

Romans 7:4 (HCSB) says, "Therefore, my brothers, you also were put to death in relation to the law through the crucified body of the Messiah, so that you may belong to another — to Him who was raised from the dead — that we may *bear fruit for God."*

Friends, we have work to do and teaching with intention is part of our application to make disciples, raise up the next generation, and help others become active disciples along the way. If you think you have no time to do so, there is some reorientation to be done in your heart, understanding, and life, if you are going to follow Jesus for real.

Passing On The Faith

Some are comfortable mentoring and teaching vocational skills to others but not so comfortable to pass on the teachings of Christ. For others, it is easy to share the faith in bible study and spiritual matters, but difficult to help people with things like life skills. The good news is that we can combine both approaches, make disciples and carry out the call to teach others. We make disciples *as we go* and *wherever we go*, we just need to be intentional about it.

As we do that, we bring our disciples into the faith within the life and community of Believers. The community becomes the context for ongoing discipleship and shared mission. Just as we need to progress past mere Bible study with church members, we should also consider how we can assist them in other aspects of their lives, enabling them to fully live out their faith and thrive. Discipleship is about learning, obeying, and sharing truth with others, inviting them to join in the adventure of following Jesus. *The biblical model of teaching is not so much a transfer of academic information as it is apprenticing and modeling in a context of relationship and service.* The faith encompasses all aspects of our lives and we need to embrace it as such. So keep your eyes open to those around you who are hungry to learn and grow and bring them into deeper, intentional relationships. Start a small group or cohort given to growth and get started.

You are called to make disciples by TEACHING them to OBEY everything the Lord has commanded, and HOW to do this effectively is our wrestle. Passing on the faith to others is a critical responsibility of the believer and the Church at large. This doesn't just happen at a Sunday school or in a church building. This passing on of the faith is paramount and a biblical priority for every believer in Jesus Christ. Pause for a sec and say to yourself, "he's talking to me."

Passing on the faith must be an intentional investment we make over and over as we are going about life, in every aspect of our life. I can't stress it enough because there is such a disconnect from what people KNOW and DO. *Passing on the faith is not a transfer of knowledge alone. It's a training in obedience to the word of God that leads to spiritual maturity in Christ. This takes serious and focused work.* I hope you are getting the point because I'm making it over and over and over.

When we think about how we equip people with life or vocational skills, as a bridge for the gospel, we need to consider what it means to effectively pass on the faith. If this is a biblical command, then we need to be able to do this well. We might assume that parents would intentionally impart the faith to their children, but the statistics are staggering, revealing that this has not been happening effectively. Something is not right in the way people have understood the word, ways, and nature of God. Time for change, my friends! For a quick reminder, one million youth are leaving the faith every year! This is a wake up call to the Church and to Christian families. This must change and I do believe the tides will turn. In His mercy, God will and is answering the prayers of His people for His own name's sake, to send both a profound revival among His people and an awakening across our generation. It will spread across the land, ushering in a massive influx of young people into the Kingdom of God. I'm personally seeing it in pockets but it will be global and widespread, and soon. Get ready! So, we have to get focused and intentional about passing on a living faith and learn to do it well.

We are exhorted to contend earnestly to pass on the Apostolic faith that was passed on to us (Jude). This is no light thing or afterthought, but central to our lives. In our day and age, we must be awakened to the hour we live and the need to hold fast to sound doctrine. We live in a time where good has been called evil and evil has been called good. We must recover the truth in the scriptures and disciple those God has put in our trust. We need to consider how to lay solid foundations in people's lives to know the truth and live into it skillfully. Just having a bunch of theological facts without the accompanying heart, wisdom, and lifestyle will not foster the faith we are seeking. Truth must be embodied in well ordered lives. Our teaching must lead to the obedience of the faith out of sincere love for Jesus and others, from right motivations, expressed through love in wholesome relationships and service, not just the intellectual acknowledgment of the truth. Faith without works is dead and in fact, is no faith at all, or at best an incomplete faith. We are called to teach people to OBEY everything the Lord has commanded and continue until we all come to spiritual maturity—which is conformity to the very nature of God—Jesus Christ. We are to be as He is!

"Those that claim to know Him or live in Him must walk as Jesus walked....This is how love is made complete among us so that we will have confidence in the day of judgment: In this world we are like Jesus."[74] For Apostle Paul who modeled for us, we see the aim that harnessed his energy and ambition around discipleship and establishing a community in the faith. *"We proclaim Him, warning and teaching everyone with all wisdom, so that we may present everyone mature in Christ. I labor for this, striving with His strength that works powerfully in me."*[75] This doesn't happen in a lecture alone or in a classroom, but in everyday life with serious focus and energy.

Discipleship is spiritual shepherding that has a parental element, fostering not only internal heart attitudes but also external habits directing people towards godliness and the fruit of the Spirit, toward a conformity to the nature and likeness of Christ in all things. Our efforts and engagement with others are a cooperative effort with the Holy Spirit moving through us and in the hearts of those we are serving for the gospel's sake. It truly is a partnership of God and man through love, truth, and power.

---

74 1 john 2:6, 4:17
75 Colossians 1:28-29 (HCSB)

Starting at Home

When it comes to our children and our homes, we want to prepare our kids and the next generation for the future world and to do our part to move the world forward to a better place. Thus we must train and equip, laboring to lay solid life foundations which include a deep sense of purpose, godly character, and the capabilities to make a difference. "Train up a child in the way he should go, even when he is old he will not depart from it." Prov 22:6. Our homes should be a place of safety, love, and belonging but also a place of mission, purpose, and intentional training.

Dr. George Barna had it right when he said, "We can confidently predict what the future of the world will look like by carefully studying the way children are raised today." Passing on the faith starts at home.

The household is the context for discipleship. Fathers are charged to oversee the process of education and training in the Lord without exasperating them (Ephesians 6:4). Parents must be intentional to teach their children at every level of their life and provide the environment, opportunities, and relationships that help them properly grow. To stop the mass exodus from the faith, we need to pray and trust God first to do only what He can do. We must also forsake passivity and engage raising up our kids with grace and truth. We cannot abdicate our responsibility and utterly outsource our kids' training and education. As Mother Theresa said, "If you want to change the world, go home and love your family."

What does that look like for you right now at this stage of your life? How can you intentionally engage in a greater way to lead, love, and train your kids and grandkids in the ways of the Lord, unto the works they are called?

If our commission from the Lord is to make disciples of all nations, it must start in our homes, local churches, and local communities.

And again, our focus is on raising authentic disciples that become transformational agents of God's Kingdom, not just people who simply survive and live spiritually mediocre lives, coexisting in society. Starting at home means we raise fiery, devoted sons and daughters of God. Those who destroy the works of darkness in the power of the Holy Spirit, releasing life and justice and the goodness of God in the earth through prayer, love, and practical service. We must resist and rebel against the status quo that leaves our youth to the way of the word, entertainment, and laziness with no responsibility.

We must lead the way.

We must train others to be ones who know God and have the skillful wisdom to provide real solutions, while keeping the gospel central in all our efforts for the salvation of souls.

We need to understand that good citizenship, seeking the welfare of the city itself and not just the salvation of souls is actually an expression of the gospel. The good news of Christ and His redemptive work has greater utility than just the forgiveness of our sins. *The utility of redemption empowers good works that not only reveal His light and truth but also blesses the earth in practical ways.*

God rebuilds desolations, ruined cities, and redeems lands as well as people and families. He beautifies and restores dignity according to His original design for all things, and He uses us to do it. In fact, as God redeems hearts, people come alive and become far more productive in life. They become inspired to see the Kingdom of heaven on the earth and expressed in every sector of society. God fills the earth with His glory through renewed people who abound in fruitful work that bless the earth. Wow, God is good! This is what we see in Isaiah 61 and what we are called to do, starting at home in the raising up of our Kids. They are part of the solution and have much to contribute to the world today. Surely they will inherit the world of tomorrow, so we need to engage and train them now. We need to call them higher and into this vision.

We are called to be salt and light, a city set on a hill, a powerful people, a Church victorious through faith that the gates of hell cannot not prevail against! Come on, say, "AMEN!" We cannot be silent.

Call them Higher

One of the reasons a million youth are leaving the Church in America a year right now is they are not finding true belonging and purpose. They are not being called into both authentic relationships in community or a community that is on mission. People want to be known, loved, feel significant, and be given to a cause worth living and dying for. People need to see the beauty and worth of Jesus Christ Himself and see it expressed in the lives of those around them who profess the faith. From there, the context and process of development needs to be established so that they can come into biblical maturity—this is discipleship. Kids don't need to be just entertained, they need to be equipped and called higher.

So much of the lack we see can be attributed to the fact that so many don't call youth into greater expectations, often opting to enable rather than empower them.

We don't challenge them enough nor call upon their energies and potential to do hard things and great things for God, their families, friends, society, and themselves. They can do it if we call them to task with the right support and coaching.

Read this quote by Douglas Wilson, *"As we bring up our children, we should descend to their level in one sense (humility) in order to lead them to our level (maturity). This is not the same as descending to their level (immaturity) in order to lead them to our level (pride). He must be servants to our children; you must not cater to them. One of the central problems with bringing up children in our day is the constant temptation to underestimate their capacities. We teach them profane irreverent little ditties, not psalms and hymns. We give them moralistic little stories, not biblical doctrine and ethics. We expect them to act as though they have no brains or souls until they have graduated from college. We aim at nothing, and we hit it every time."*[76] This must change!

In our churches, "Youth ministry needs to be re-engineered to be gospel-advancing and disciple-multiplying,……It is not about meetings but about the mission. Young people are longing for a cause that matters. So they need to be equipped and youth leaders *(and parents)* need to be equipped to equip them."[77]

Youth and adults alike need to see the gospel for real and authentic faith lived out in devotion, family, and mission. For people to become real disciples, mission oriented, and capable of withstanding today's pressures, they must personally encounter and experience Jesus' loving, powerful presence… That's what happened to me alone in my bedroom when I was 15. One real encounter with God radically altered my life forever and changed its trajectory.

His love and truth is transformative. When people encounter Him and connect to a loving authentic community of Believers who can come alongside and truly disciple them, then we will see a generational renewal and the rebuilding of what has been long devastated. We'll see beautiful people prepared for the Lord; people in whom the Lord is actually glorified and who are doing His works on the earth.

We can engage and set the stage for God to do a great work in and among us.

---

76 Douglas Wilson, "Standing on the Promises: a handbook of Biblical Childrearing."—pg 15
77 https://www.Christianpost.com/news/report-projects-35-million-youth-to-leave-Christianity-by-2050-greg-stier-responds.html

If you are feeling overwhelmed right now or like this is burdensome, pause and breathe. You may have missed something in your understanding and in your experience with the grace of God. This would be a great opportunity to press into God and ask for insight and fresh encounters with His heart for you. The commandments of the Lord are not burdensome! The task is overwhelming but His grace is sufficient.

When we are serving, teaching and working from the place of love and from the grace of being loved by God, there's rest of soul. The same rest that God promised those who believe, is what we must learn to live out of and operate from— both rest and intimacy with God. Serving this way is not burdensome. It's not something we are doing in our own strength or as an additional part of our lives or something we need to "add" into our lives. It is part of the very purpose of our lives and lived out by the strength of His might at work in us who believe—we can do nothing apart from Him. This is the rest of faith. He causes us to bear fruit and provides the divine energy to serve, to grow, and to love.[78] We must learn to live by faith, trust in the power of God's grace that works in us who believe, and become productive in the truth. Resurrection life is on the inside of you!!!

Start With The End in Mind

The things I'm saying are not just hype and rhetoric without action steps. Understanding the big picture must intersect with real truth and practicality. We need to think long term and generationally in our education, training and parenting approach, both at home and in the classroom/Dojo/training hall/studio/workplace/church. I love to encourage, as scripture does and as many success practices do, to *think with the end in mind.*

---

78 1 john 5:1-5, John 15:3-13

We need to think strategically and reverse engineer how we will reach our desired outcomes, vision, and intentions.

If a new student comes into my martial art school who wants to be a black belt, he or she must reach certain competencies and standards that must first be met. There is an intentional process that incrementally develops what's needed for students to arrive at their intended goals with the accompanying competencies. We have to instruct, train, and coach with the end and outcomes in mind. Curriculum cannot be fragmented from subject to subject or skill to skill. It must be a unified vehicle where everything fits together and understanding is fostered where the student sees how things relate to each other. Otherwise, they master nothing and fall short of true comprehension and competency—lacking wisdom. When students spar, they're putting their skills to the test and looking to get everything they have learned to work for them effectively. If they can't put all the pieces together effectively, they haven't really learned yet. If the instructor hasn't provided the appropriate opportunities and training experiences to help them make it work, or the curriculum has failed in either its design or execution. The same is true with faith, academics, healthy relationships, business or life skills. *We need a wisdom based approach that is holistic and comprehensive, rooted in a biblical worldview, that equips people to live and prosper in all aspects of life.*

I helped found and launch a K-12 private Christian school called, The Crossing Life Academy, in Windham NH, situated on a 100 acre farm, as a ministry of the Crossing Life Church. When we began dreaming together, fleshing out the vision we had to start with the end in mind. Part of that was coming up with a graduate outcome. We defined and articulated what a graduate would look like in terms of character, understanding, skills, and competency, etc. Every grade and year and the overall process of development worked towards that end, outcome, and bigger picture. It's strategic and intentional.

To effectively fulfill our call to teach. We must begin with the end in mind. I want to encourage you to do this for your students, clients, teams, and children. Go back to the drawing board because it is worth it! Think about this for your life as well. In fact, do that first. Starting with your own life, think about your goals, responsibilities, and aspirations. How are you going to show up and be the best you can be, reaching your potential? How are you going to achieve your goals? Start with the end in mind and plan backwards. What skills will you need to develop? What knowledge will you need to know? What people or resources will you need to connect with? What key milestones and tasks will need to be done? What type of character and habits will you need to achieve your goals and keep progressing? And so on.

Answering some of these questions and mapping out a prayerful and strategic plan is a game changer for your life and those you lead and influence. God blesses the plans of the diligent. Moses said it right when it comes to living intentionally, wisely, and in the fear of the Lord. He says, "Teach us to number our days so that we might gain a heart of wisdom" (Ps 90). To live with wisdom is to live skillfully with the *end in mind*. We should seek to live this way and teach others to do the same.

Pick up the "Breakthrough XP course" to help and use the discount code **"BOOKBONUS75XP"**.

CLAIM YOUR 75% OFF CODE:
"BOOKBONUS75XP"

YOUR STRATEGIC PATH TO BREAKTHROUGH, CLARITY, AND ABUNDANT LIFE!

Transformational Tools & Resources

Discover your unique God given purpose, breakthrough your barriers, craft a strategic and prayer plan with a rule of life that leads to fruitfulness and fulfillment. Leave a transformational legacy!

FORERUNNERFITNESS.NET/BREAKTHROUGHXP

Quick recap: the call to teach and to do it effectively:

- Teach by example

- Teach intentionally

- Teach the faith in and through all things you do.

- Be intentional to reproduce yourself and train other leaders.

- Think strategically with the end in mind to govern your process of education or in the design of your curriculum.

    - Think of designing curriculum even in informal settings—it's the nature of purposeful discipleship and ordered learning.

- Think long term and generationally—legacy

- Think equipping, empowering, and activating so that others can stand on their own as capable and responsible people. Help people learn and then obey/practice.

Reproducible Frameworks

I want you to think about your areas of ability, skill, or vocation, as a key outlet to mentor and minister to others. It's your "fishing net" to win and influence souls for the Kingdom of God. The mission of the gospel harnesses every aspect of our lives if you let it. Plus, it's essential, fulfilling and beautiful to influence people by teaching real skills and abilities that enhance their lives, thereby fostering their competence and confidence. It's the way God designed it.

This teaching framework has proven effective and reproducible. It is seen in the apprenticeship type model of discipleship and education Jesus demonstrates with His twelve. We also see it with Apostle Paul with Timothy, Titus, and others. When we want to effectively pass something on, train leaders, and reproduce a skill or ability, try this framework:

- "I do it, you watch.—we talk
- I do it, you do it with me.—we talk
- You do it, I do it with you.—we talk
- You do it, I watch.—we talk
- You do it, another person watches to learn—we talk
- And the process continues...."

Another simple way of saying this is: *I do it, We do it, You do it.* This can happen in a short period of time in learning micro skills, and it can take a longer time, years if need be, depending on what is being learned. The beauty of this is real time learning in the context of the mission or job at hand. Things are being modeled, experience is being gained, coaching is happening, and lessons and wisdom are taught.

So much good stuff and relational exchange happens within this framework, it's transformative and instills the type of confidence that grows alongside the development of real competence. This type of reproduction can create exponential growth and impact if we integrate it in everything we do while teaching others to do the same. This is the way discipleship happens and a basic framework for how we engage others in learning to follow Jesus too.

He who teaches learns twice. When we teach what we know it further establishes that truth, concept, or skill within us. And as teachers/

educators/parents, we can never stop learning and growing ourselves. As the saying goes, "He who dares to teach must never cease to be a student."

One of the components of learning effectively requires that we teach others what we know or are learning as well. Cool right? This has been proven in so many studies and observed in practice over the centuries. Truth gets internalized within our hearts and encoded into our brains (neuroscience explains this) when we write things down, put them into our own words, and give personal expression and application to them in ways in our lives and when we share with others. We need to do this and teach others to do the same.

So when you are learning something, find someone asap and teach them or tell them about it. Not only are you enriching someone else's life when sharing your findings and insights, you are forging greater retention and understanding in you of what you've learned as well. When you teach and disciple others, help them make it a practice to teach or share with others what they are learning sooner than later. They have to be talking about it, thinking about it, and practicing it. When they do, It will accelerate the learning process and reinforce the idea and need to be passing onto others what they have received. The saying goes: learn it, live it, lead it, or as some have framed it, teach others to: *learn* it, *obey* it, and *share* it with others.

Robert Clinton, shares in his book, "Making of a leader," one of his guiding principles for life and ministry concerning being grounded in truth and what it takes to really learn something, is that *"Deeper impression (happens) with personal expression."* I have personally found this to be true as well. When someone really understands something, they have thought it through critically and are able to put it in their own words and relate it to many other things in life as they can 'see it' at play conceptually and principally. Teaching others facilitates that personal process and helps us take complex things and practice making them simple. Teaching others also helps us take simple things and understand their implications to the other domains of life, and that's what we want. To personally stay sharp and grow, it necessitates that we express and teach others what we know. "Win win" right?

Effective teaching also harnesses the power of simple to complex frameworks to communicate truth, methodologies, processes, and practices in visual ways. The more we can create a model that becomes easier to comprehend the better when it comes to informing, instructing, and reproducing. My friends at Kingdom Builders Academy call it "boxing your brilliance." It's about organizing your intellectual property, proprietary process, or expert system.

I have found framework thinking extremely helpful to organize my own thoughts and life, my business, and my strategy in creating holistic training processes for others. There are so many ways to communicate this, including: shapes, acronyms, flow charts, narrative and allegory, or milestones. You can be as creative and unique as you want. The point is that your frameworks are supposed to help you teach and produce your desired outcomes and solutions in others and provide a clear path of development. When people can see the path or plan, understand the process, identify where they are, and what's next, it fuels their engagement. I'd like to share more with you on this, so be sure to sign up for the **FREE Video summary and resources at - AriseandReturn.com.**

Succession = Success

As the saying goes, "there is no success without a successor or succession plan." The test of our leadership is about what happens after we're gone. This is the law of legacy. We should want to live in such a way that builds a life and life work that outlasts us. Living with the end in mind is the essence to intentional living and critical to making a real impact. Being a transformational leader means living for more than ourselves and thinking and operating in a sustainable, long term way.

Remember when I said that we fall short of our purpose and function in life if we fail to reproduce or give away what we have received? Well, when it comes to being effective and thinking generationally we must learn from the master Himself, Jesus Christ and some of His Apostles, namely Paul.

Paul was called a wise master builder and was given the stewardship to lay a trustworthy foundation for the administration of God's house and purpose upon which others could build. The early church passed on what they had received strategically, intentionally, and relationally, and we are to do the same. They multiplied and reproduced the word and work they were called to by training others who could also train others; they made disciples. We see plainly Paul's instruction to his son in the faith, Timothy, *"And the things you have heard me say in the presence of many witnesses, entrust to reliable people who will also be qualified to teach others."* 2 Tim 2:2. Also, a key mission of Jesus was to mentor those entrusted to Him by the Father, equipping them to fulfill God's ongoing plan following His ascension to heaven. It's incredible to think that by focusing on a few, Jesus was able to ensure the lasting nature of His mission. To go big, think small, to go far, go deep with the few. Maybe it could be said that the new big is small. It's the compound effect. Modern day marketers understand this as well. To distinguish themselves in their industry, they look for "blue waters" (less crowded market segments) to carve out their own micro niche. Massive impact and targeted impact happens as a result of their focus. If they want massive impact, they have to narrow their focus and go deep with the demographic they are passionate about serving. Mission success is hinged on dialing in. It's the same when it comes to the call to make disciples and train leaders.

When our Church community with a global vision was making some strategic shifts years ago, we had a theme of the season of pruning. It was, " Establish local to Impact global" or something like "Act local, think global." That's a crazy thought huh? We need to think in a more focused way to make a larger impact. Quality investment in the few will produce qualitative results and have exponential quantitative impact as well. The truth and wisdom about "less being more" shouts to us here. People are doing so many things but not really accomplishing the main thing God has commanded. Let's get focused on understanding God's plan to change the world and execute on it. We will find that the wisdom of God often gets expressed in simplicity. Less is more. Simplification leads to multiplication.

> " We will not make disciples through methods of mass production that attempt shortcuts to maturity. Robert Coleman clarifies the challenge: "One must decide where he wants his ministry to count – in the momentary applause of popular recognition or the reproduction of his life in a few chosen men who carry on his work after he is gone." The irony is that focusing on a few takes a longer range view by multiplying the number of *disciples* and *therefore expands* a church's leadership base."[79]

This type of focused investment expands both local and global church's leadership bases. It concurrently grows the leaders of your organization, team, community, or family. Quality investment like this creates community and organizational health alongside generational stability and longevity. So focus on the right people and the right things.

Giants of the faith who have now passed into glory like Billy Graham and Bill Bright, said some shocking things about the impact of their ministry around the globe. They both said that if they could go back and do things again, they'd invest themselves into 8 to 12 men in contrast to the large crusades.

---

[79] Greg Ogden, " *Discipleship essentials: a guide to building your life in Christ.*", (Intervarsity press, Downers Grove, IL. 2007), pg 21.

The following quote was by Billy Graham in 1965 and is still prophetic in our day, aligning with much of what I'm talking about:

"Multitudes of Christians within the church are moving toward the point where they may reject the institution that we call the church. They are beginning to turn to more simplified forms of worship. They are hungry for a personal and vital experience with Jesus Christ. They want a heartwarming personal faith. Unless the church quickly recovers its authoritative Biblical message, we may witness the spectacle of millions of Christians going outside the institutional church to find spiritual food."—Quoted in World Aflame, pp. 79-80.

Here is another priceless quote by Graham:

"I think one of the first things I would do would be to get a small group of eight or ten or twelve men around me that would meet a few hours a week and pay the price. It would cost them something in time and effort. I would share with them everything I have, over a period of years. Then I would actually have twelve ministers among the laymen who in turn could take eight or ten or twelve more and teach them. I know one or two churches that are doing that, and it is revolutionizing the church. Christ, I think, set the pattern. He spent most of his time with twelve men. He didn't spend it with a great crowd. In fact, every time he had a great crowd it seems to me that there weren't too many results. The great results, it seems to me, came in his personal interview and in the time he spent with the twelve."[80]

At the age of 70 Graham said in an interview that in reflection upon his life and in what he would do differently, *"I wish I had traveled less and spent more time at home as our children were growing up."*[81] This is key in understanding the different life domains and the priority relationships that have the greatest return for our investments. *Being*

---

80 Quoted in Billy Graham Speaks: The Evangelical World Prospect, Christianity Today, vol.3, no.1, p.5, Oct.13, 1958.
81 https://billygraham.org/story/billy-grahams-my-answer-reflecting-back/

present to disciple your kids is a Kingdom assignment and one of the greatest works and contributions we can make to both the church and the world.

The apostle Paul was referring to was spiritual multiplication in his second letter to Timothy. "You must teach others those things you and many others have heard me speak about," he said. "Teach these great truths to trustworthy men who will, in turn, pass them on to others." We need to think long-term and generationally when it comes to how we are making disciples.

In His book, "The Making of a Disciple," Keith Phillips looks at the numeric difference between one person per day coming to Christ and one person per year being disciples to maturity (you could double and triple these numbers too if they were launched sooner to reproduce other disciples who would in turn do the same).- CATCH THE VISION OF THIS AND START INVESTING YOUR LIFE NOW IN THE FEW GOD HAS PUT IN YOUR INFLUENCE:

YEAR	EVANGELIST (addition)	DISCIPLER (multiplication)
1	365	2
2	730	4
3	1,095	8
4	1,460	16
5	1,825	32
6	2,190	64
7	2,555	128
8	2,920	256
9	3,285	512
10	3,650	1,024
11	4,015	2,048
12	4,380	4,096

13	4,745	8,192
14	5,110	16,384
15	5,475	32,768
16	5,840	65,536

As each of us develops a personal strategy, God can use us to play a critical and essential role in helping to fulfill the Great Commission and impact the world with the gospel.

Gut Check

Who are you intentionally investing in? Do you have a successor in view or a succession plan for your life, family, ministry, business? Are you thinking about multiplying yourself? Are your eyes open to those around you? Are you looking for those you are to mentor and raise up? Do you have a plan to develop them?

Remember, leaders must raise up other leaders or be leading in such a way that equips and activates those in their influence or oversight. A student is not greater than his master, but when the apprentice is fully trained, he will be like his master. We should look to fully train people by passing on what we are, what we know, and the faith to be lived. Like Paul said, "follow me as I follow Christ....I have left you a pattern to follow, " is the correct approach as we earnestly seek to live our own lives with integrity and authenticity before God. (Luke 6:40, Matt 10:25, 1 Cor 11:1, Phil 3:17, 2 Tim 1:13)

It all boils down to this simple equation:

YOUR SUCCESSION PLAN + ACTION = VISION/GOAL—A DREAM & SENTIMENTALITY

VS

YOUR SUCCESSION VISION/GOAL + PLAN + COSTLY ACTION = REALITY & FULFILLMENT

When we consider who to be investing in in a *deeper* way, look for **FAT** people: **HOT** people and people of **Faith** who are also aligned with your values and mission. Just as it was with Christ, he may have chosen the unlikely, the unworthy and the most ordinary and even the foolish in the eyes of the world. But He saw their potential and raised them up. Nonetheless, choose wisely. Your time is precious and limited. You have to be strategic about who you are investing in in a deeper way. Remember Christ loved all, taught many, but only *trained a few*. Discern and look for your *few who will continue to pass on and multiply the deposit.*

- **FAITHFUL.** Do they demonstrate consistency and commitment to Christ? Are they already serving faithfully in ministry in some capacity?

- **AVAILABLE.** Do they have the time and space needed to go to the next level of commitment and service? They may be faithful and teachable but not available due to other commitments for that season of their life. Availability is key for meaningful investment and development.

- **TEACHABLE.** Are they open to receiving coaching and correction? Are they humble or defensive? Are they willing to be a team player, be accountable, to change and learn new things? Can they respect and submit to authority? Do they seek the Lord and reflect upon their ways as to learn and grow?

Or

- **HONEST.** Someone who speaks the truth and lives authentically, even when it's difficult.

- **OPEN.** See teachable above.

- **TRANSPARENT.** Someone who is vulnerable and willing to share their struggles, thoughts, and experiences without pretense.

Or

- **FAITHFUL.** See above

- **AVAILABLE.** See Above

- **INITIATIVE.** Are they eager to grow, hungry to learn, and self motivated? Do they seem responsible?

- **TEACHABLE.** See above

- **HEALTHY.** Do they demonstrate enough emotional and relational health and stability to begin to build leadership and ministry responsibility with them? Or do they need more foundations in the gospel, pastoral counsel, or deeper therapy? Do they have the capacity to receive corrections and challenges without offense? Do they work well with others and have the capacity to build relationships? Do they seem to have the capacity to be others focused, lift people up, and lead with care and confidence?

Jesus, the master teacher

Jesus, the Master Teacher and example of all, made disciples/apprentices and transformed the world both then and now. We must look at the pattern/strategy He modeled and instructed His followers to perpetuate. Let's examine Jesus' basic pattern of discipleship.

First, we need to understand that *discipleship is a relational influence process of purposeful development and equipping.*

The word disciple in Greek is *"matheteuo,"* which is to become a pupil, to enroll as a scholar and learner.

Webster expands the meaning of discipleship as follows:

1. A learner; a scholar; one who receives or professes to receive instruction from another…

2. A follower; an adherent to the doctrines of another. Hence the constant attendants of Christ were called His disciples; and hence all Christians are called His disciples, as they profess to learn and receive His doctrines and precepts.

A word closely aligned with disciple and discipleship is discipline.

- ***Discipline—as a noun*** is defined around the thought of education; instruction; cultivation and improvement in a field of study; training that corrects, molds, or perfects the mental faculties or moral character, and the control gained by enforcing obedience to the system of rules.

Discipline—as a verb was to instruct or educate; to inform the mind; to prepare by instructing in correct principles and habits; as, discipline youth for a profession or for future usefulness.

I love this: to be taught and disciplined in a particular way of life for future usefulness in the truth and mission. We see that Jesus taught through relationship as He called the disciples to be *with Him first, then to do the works of ministry.* From there, His instruction took shape in many forms:

- He taught by example in all He did. (Life, character, devotion, and works)

- He taught by instruction, parables, and metaphor.

- He taught through correction and rebuke.

- He taught through posing questions and dialog.

- He taught at formal times and informal times along the way (in the synagogues, on the mount of Olives, and in real time along the way in the context on ministry and around the table).

- He taught by sharing responsibility and delegating authority in shared mission and service.

- He taught personally to individuals, to small groups, large gatherings, and to the masses. *He loved all, taught many, trained a few.*

- and He taught with authority with demonstrations of the Spirit's power.

A disciple was with Jesus all day, every day, and was given to know Him, become like Him, and do the things He did. So it is with modern day disciples. Our aim is to be with Jesus, be conformed to His image, and be His faithful witnesses by doing the things He did in the power of the Holy Spirit.

We can come alongside others with this intention, to help them grow in knowing Jesus, following Jesus, becoming like Jesus, and do the things He did. As active disciples, we must live authentic lives worthy of the gospel, and embody and model what we seek to see reproduced. As I previously said, look for the hungry ones who are **F.A.T.**—faithful, available, and teachable (willing to learn and apply the truth).

We now see how Jesus discipled. His disciples, on the other hand, were to follow and learn in such a way as to become like their Rabbi (Jesus) and do as He did in the way He would do it.

If we seek to disciple another in the way of Christ and seek to be discipled ourselves by another, we should learn to *follow and serve as unto Christ, sound and godly people and teach others to follow us as we follow Christ.* This is really hard for people to grasp without disqualifying themselves. Many feel they have to be "perfect" before they step out. Yes, you are called to live a life worthy of the gospel, worthy of the calling, but that doesn't mean you have to get it all "right" and be perfect before you start. This requires humility and transparency as we all press on to the upward call of God in Christ. You can pass on what you do know and not pretend that you have it all.

If you stay centered in the tension and relational sandwich of what I'll call the *discipleship matrix,* you'll stay in a safe and accountable space to grow and learn as you lead and teach others. As you invest in others, you yourself are being discipled by someone more mature than you. So there is someone you receive from and someone you pour into. You also need to run alongside peers who are pursuing Christ with pure hearts, where you are all provoking each other to love and to do good works with mutual accountability. The final part of the matrix has to do with looking outward and missionally toward those who do not know Christ. We should always be engaged in intentional prayer for them while cultivating relationships and opportunities to love, serve, and share with them. The tension of evangelism and discipleship is closely related with those you are actively nurturing to come to the faith and yield their life to Jesus. We would do well to always live in the tension of the matrix for maximum growth while teaching others to do the same.

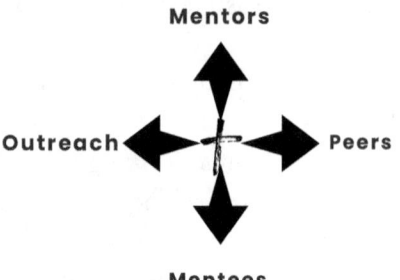

4 DIMENSIONS OF A DISCIPLES MAXTRIX

Spiritual health and accelerated growth comes when we live in the tension of this matrix.

- We are being mentored by those more mature than us and voluntarily placing ourselves under their authority and influence.
- We are running along side peers who are also pursuing Jesus, seeking to grow, and exercising mutual accountability - iron sharpens iron.
- We are investing in those younger in the faith than us and passing on what we have received in the safety of the body of Christ and mature believers.
- We are reaching out to the lost and keeping missional fervor in prayer and action.

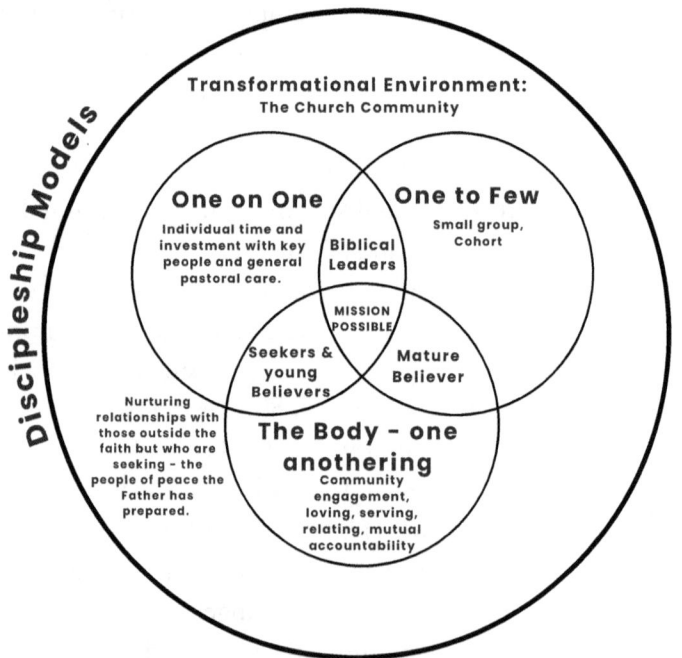

Discipleship Matrix & Models

The person being discipled should:

1. Submit to a mentor/teacher (as unto Christ) who teaches them how to follow Jesus- in a context of community and relational accountability.

2. Learn Jesus' words and teachings. They must study the scriptures and be established in the gospel truth, the New Testament teachings, and the full testimony of scripture (Genesis to Revelation).

3. Learn Jesus' way of ministry and mission. What and how He did the things He did: His mission, methods, models, and practices in the power of the Holy Spirit as directed by the Father (Jesus did what He saw the Father doing and we must learn to do the same. We must learn to follow the leadership of the Holy Spirit—this is *the way*).

4. Learn to imitate Jesus' life and character—be transformed into His likeness through the fellowship of the Holy Spirit and the practice of truth. This includes relational and social skills.

5. Actively be sharing the gospel, their testimony - "fish for men", save souls, and make them disciples. At the same time, also finding and teaching other existing believers to faithfully follow Jesus and become disciple makers. Disciples must reproduce the process of bringing people into spiritual maturity and healthy productivity in the Kingdom of God— "go do unto others what was done for you."

Dr Paul Jehle writes, "As one can readily see, discipleship is quite comprehensive, and to be a disciple of Jesus, one must enroll as a full-time scholar and student in His school! It is the only Biblical context for education as well! We must cease thinking that education is merely the transfer of knowledge, even if it has a Christian viewpoint.

Educational discipleship is taking a group of youth and disciplining them for future usefulness in the kingdom of God. Discipleship comprehends educational instruction, but it is much broader than that.

Practically, it must take place in a joint concert between parents and teachers, as we have stated numerous times. It involves every area of life; spiritual, social and physical. This is the kind of instruction received by the disciples and it is why they could turn the world upside down after they graduated, (see Acts 17:7)!"[82]

Discipleship is multi dimensional and leads to transformation at every level of life. I can't state enough that we have to keep in mind the goal of transformation and maturity; Christ being formed in people, sincere and consistent obedience to the truth and teachings of Christ, and faithfulness to the good works they are uniquely called to do in life. That is the aim we are to labor toward (Colossians 1:28-29, Ep 2:10, Titus 2). This is a paradigm that bears down in our practice and methodology and affects how we actually flesh this thing out. One dimensional discipleship is so much easier and cleaner, though not as fruitful. What I'm talking about is messy, hard and requires deep involvement in the lives of those we're discipling.

I have heard this said so many times: a good teacher will let you *see* into their life, but a great teacher will let you *into* their life to become part of it. We really need to understand discipleship and transformational leadership requires authentic relationships that go deep. They are far beyond the transfer of knowledge and require loving care, friendship, transparency, and accountability in the context of the mission of the gospel and Church. *Biblical discipleship is about the family of God walking together on mission from around the table of fellowship and love.*

These guys were friends and family and committed to lay down their lives for one another in love, as modeled for them in Christ! No greater

---

[82] "Go ye Therefore vo 1" pg 352 Dr Paul Jehle

love than this, that a man lay down his life for his friends. That's what Jesus said and what He did (John 15:10-17).

The kingdom of God is about a divine family on mission that is self perpetuating through the ages by intentional discipleship at every level of life. Jesus Called the disciples to *Himself first, to be with Him,* and then to preach, cast out devils, heal the sick, and more, in a shared mission (Mark 3:14). Jesus called His disciples both brothers and friends, and together they changed the world. There was imitation through obedience and impartation of grace with instruction and delegation from the context of intimate friendship. Let's follow His lead!

But first things first, pause for a moment. *Will you choose to step into this place and call to teach? Will you be intentional to pass on what you know and pass on the faith? Will you embrace the great commission? Will you reproduce yourself, make disciples, and teach them to do the same?* Start praying now about those you are to invest in (just as Jesus did with fasting and prayer).

If you feel lost and like you need to be discipled first, start praying about who you need to be accountable to and mentored by. Are you submitted somewhere and accountable to someone to grow? You can't answer, "Jesus." God called you into the Church family and into healthy submission and relationship to godly leaders and brothers and sisters in the Lord.

Take a little bit of time before reading on and write down your thoughts. Self assess and invite the Holy Spirit to speak to your heart.

Are you living in the tension of the discipleship matrix? What's missing? What needs more attention? Where do you need to be more consistent?

PAUSE. CAPTURE. APPLY
Prompts to help you process

1. What specific insights or concepts from this chapter resonated with you the most? Why do you think these stood out to you?

_____

_____

_____

2. How can you practically apply the principles discussed in this chapter to your daily life, relationships, or ministry? Identify at least one actionable step you can take this week.

_____

_____

_____

3. What potential challenges or barriers might you face in implementing these concepts? How can you overcome them?

_____

_____

_____

4. What are 3-5 quotes or points from this chapter that capture the essence of what it's communicating? Write them down.

_____

_____

_____

_____

_____

5. How can you involve your family, small group, or church community in the practices and principles outlined in this chapter? What steps can you take to foster a culture of discipleship and transformation within your circle of influence?

_____

_____

_____

6. Spend a few moments in prayer, asking God for the wisdom, strength, and courage to live out the truths you've learned. Write down a commitment or a prayer that reflects your desire to grow as an authentic disciple and transformational leader to impact the world.

_____

_____

_____

CHAPTER 11

Make Impact, Leverage Influence

"You have one business on earth – to save souls."
— JOHN WESLEY

"Only one life, 'twill soon be past; only what's done for Christ will last."
— C.T. STUDD

"If you want to reach the people that no one is reaching, you have to do things that no one is doing."
— CRAIG GROESCHEL

We have more information, biblical teaching, scholarly work, apps, devotionals, podcasts, studies,.etc. available to us than ever before. Yet so many still remain in spiritual infancy and adolescence. Why? I believe one of the reasons has to do with HOW, WHERE, WHAT people are being taught.

The art of discipleship has been lost and must be rediscovered. I believe this is also happening and starting to sweep the globe. Many are seeing that the old wineskins and the way they have approached the call to discipleship and their paradigm of the role and purpose of the Church has proven insufficient. People are waking up to God's original intention for the Church Family- to the Church *as* family. Though there has always been a remnant, forerunners who have held fast to the way of Christ and the Apostles seen in the early Church, the majority, however, have suffered the divides of "clergy/laity/professional minister" syndrome, taking an overly formal, impersonal approach or overly informal lax approach without structure, strategy, or clear goals. Many have also focused on knowledge and self discipline alone, stuck in their unquestioned traditions. This has rendered the church superficial, immature, unhealed, lacking a culture of renewal and revival, and ineffectual to impact culture with the power of the gospel in many ways.

Plus, with all the teaching available, statistics still say that 80% of believers today have NEVER LED SOMEONE TO CHRIST! This is a problem and reveals a great disconnect from what we "know" versus how we actually live. There's a difference between good theology and good theological praxis (practice).

And here's part of the problem, many believers don't really "know" the scriptures. If the word was alive in them and they had understanding in the heart, it would change how they actually live. True internal belief leads to external behaviors. Another way to say it is that our paradigms produce our practices. If we really believe something then we are really going to live it (*this is what James was saying— faith without works is dead*[83]) or we are just straight up rebelling against the truth.

As it is written, there are " ....people who suppress the truth by practicing unrighteousness, even though what may be known about God is plain to them, because God has made it plain to them. The

---

[83] James 2:14-26

wrath of God is being revealed against such people...." (Romans 1:18-19 paraphrased).

So because many believers don't "know" the scriptures, they don't live the scriptures. Many believers don't understand what God thinks or really requires of them, so they don't live to produce kingdom impact on others nor foster their own growth and maturity. So many are not truly known in community, lack deep authentic relationships, or are not even connected to biblical community. Furthermore, many believers are not actively serving the Body of Christ with their gifts and abilities. They are merely spectating, acting like consumers or have compartmentalized their faith into a religious box of attending services without engaging in the mission of winning souls and making disciples. This is a problem. At large, many altogether lack the experiential love and knowledge of God. They know *about* Him but don't *KNOW* Him.

Don't get me wrong, God still uses the Church in her present state and releases some good through her. Thank God for mercy and grace! However, there is so much divine purpose for us to engage with, should we choose to intentionally pursue spiritual maturity, become strong in Him, and carry out our calling. This involves discipling others, preaching the gospel, and readying the earth for the Lord's return. We need to get clear and focused to become the men and women of God He has called us to be. We must return to Him and His ways!

We need to think biblically, not according to the patterns, wisdom, and traditions of this world. The powers of our reasoning must be sanctified so that we can know and discern the will of God. We are transformed by the Spirit through our obedience to the truth out of sincere love for God and others. But, if we cannot understand the truth first then it's obviously hard to apply it. Jesus prayed in John 17:17, *"sanctify them by your truth, your word is truth.."*

So first things need to be first. We have to *experientially know* the truth and help believers do the same. Jesus said, "If you hold to my teaching, you really are my disciples. Then you will know the truth, and the truth will set you free."[84]. Jesus often demonstrated something and then explained it or He taught something then demonstrated it. This pattern of "telling" us and showing us the truth, is what washes us and renews us in our understanding of reality. And "We know that the Son of God has come and has given us *understanding*, so that we may know Him who is true."

To help people come into God's full intention for them, we have to help them break out of their present paradigms and see the truth that can set them free.

I have found two primary ways we come to know the truth, the living word, with understanding:

1. We encounter God in a relational, experiential, and supernatural way. This imparts a living knowledge and understanding that changes us at our core and bears fruit in our lives. This can happen through personal encounters with the Holy Spirit, a dream, to moments of divine discipline, to some other form, person, or circumstance that brings about light and revelation in our life. From that seed of truth born out of an experience, the Lord begins our journey of growth. This process aims to firmly establish that truth in our lifestyle, with further depth, biblical truth and understanding, and character development.

2. We engage in a discovery process as truth and revelation unfold. Learning, study, and experiences lead us into understanding and clear thinking. Truth discovered, understood and prayerfully practiced will lead us to an encounter with the God of truth. He rewards those who diligently seek Him (Heb 11:6). Much

---

84 John 8:31-32

like what we see described in Proverbs 2: the prayerful pursuit of wisdom, knowledge, understanding, and insight, will lead us to the discovery of the knowledge of God. I believe this is talking about far more than an academic knowledge of God. It refers to an experiential intimate knowledge or "knowing" of who He is. This "knowing" of God is like how Adam "knew" Eve. Not in a sexual way, but in describing personal and relational experience of union. This is what He wants for us and what we must strive to attain - in fact, to learn to abide in. By His doing we are already *in* Him and He *in* us. We are being renewed in our understanding to perceive and "*know*" what is ALREADY ours in Him.

In both cases, the Spirit of Truth is leading us into all truth so that we can think rightly and order our lives around the word and will of God. Once we see the truth, we then have the choice whether to wholly believe it and rely upon it or not. If we believe the truth and lay hold of it by faith, we experience the power of truth. And so the opposite is true as well, to hear the truth without marrying faith and obedience to it will profit the heart nothing[85]. Belief in the truth, from the heart, is key. But if the mind is not fortified and fully persuaded as well, the seed sown in the heart through encounter can be robbed and choked out. To internalize truth from a cognitive level to a deep seated conviction (aka biblical faith) it will also require clear and critical thinking.

Critical Thinking

Critical thinking is essential for not only for internalizing truth, but living out the truth with wisdom, the process of growing in maturity, and helping those we teach to truly love learning as well. The skill of critical thinking is essential. Thinking is hard work and a lot of people don't do it these days. As I said before, people have outsourced

---

85 Hebrews 4:2-

their intelligence to technology, and have been conditioned for instant gratification. If people can't get an answer right away they tend to move on or just ask google or ChatGPT. Students have been given simple fill in the blanks and multiple choice and have not been appropriately challenged to actually learn, research, think for themselves, reflect, express in their own words, or apply knowledge skillfully. In fact, people in the majority have not been taught HOW to learn or how to think at all. We must turn the tide in our circles of influence and take the necessary time to teach and go deep.

Cultivating critical thinking and reasoning skills means you no longer accept things at face value or fall prey to eloquent but empty persuasive speeches that lack substance and are not rooted in truth. With critical thinking, you begin to probe into the reasons behind the current state of affairs and can identify the underlying principles. By studying people in life and in history who saw something wrong in the world and had the courage to do things differently in their personal lives or organization, or the courage to lead a family, church, community, or nation towards a needed new direction. We find that they did so from a foundation of critical thinking, discernment, and deep conviction. This enabled them to challenge the status quo and create breakthroughs, needed insights, conviction, and inspired action.

As many times before in history, we need such character, courage, and the tenacity to take action and speak up. It starts with encounter and the kind of instruction that wakes us up, makes us hungry for God's will to be done in our lives, families, and communities. When we can stir the type of reasoning skills that breeds awakening and understanding in people, it helps us and empowers those were influencing to think clearly and biblically in such a way where they realize they can make a difference too. In fact, we are called to do it. Every believer is meant to live and take action born out of burning conviction. Making impact and leveraging our places of influence requires that we help people internalize truth, think clearly and biblically, so that they can know the truth that sets them free and empowers them to impact the world around them. Sound reasoning skills yielded to the spirit of God, in a prayer approach, can foster life changing revelation and application of the truth. People perish without true knowledge, but an encounter with God—through experience or study—brings understanding, making transformation possible.

Listen to this quote by Martin Luther King, "**The function of education is to teach one to think intensively and to think critically. Intelligence plus character – that is the goal of true education**"

Education and transformative teaching should lead to the formation of character, convictions, meaningful action, and a life prepared for living out its purpose.

But the big question for so many is HOW do we do that? How do we see that kind of result? How do we train and help people to think critically, clearly, biblically, strategically? How do we get people to put in the time and work to really grow?

We'll discuss these factors in upcoming chapters but in a nutshell, *it starts with you.* You are the first factor (outside the inspiration of the Holy spirit). Your living example, your commitment to Christ, His Kingdom, His word, His Church, His mission. When the heart is in the right place and we have clear biblical thinking and biblical literacy, then the mechanics, methodologies, and strategy flow from there with greater effect. Mastery and establishment in truth will allow us to use whatever means is needed to serve those were leading in whatever ways are most effective for them.

A Living Example

My community has been devoted to making disciples and have had multiple expressions in doing so over the years. When it comes to helping believers understand actual biblical reasoning to guide their discernment and decision making in life, it takes work and personal investment. Sermons alone won't do it. Transformation requires that the word of God gets down into the rationality and logic of a person, so that they can learn to think like Christ with a renewed mind. This requires a lot of teaching, discussion, personal meditation, prayer, wrestling with truth, correction, and consistent application in life. But the teacher must be there first in some capacity as a mature believer to guide and shepherd the process. If the teacher/mentor is not there, it's the blind leading the blind. The quality or present maturity of the one teaching truly affects the learning process. *Thus why training leaders, and your continual personal growth, is so critical to the welfare for those you lead.*

At our church, we lead people in an ordered process through the scriptures in small group socratic discussions. We emphasize applying the truths discovered alongside active engagement in the life of the community. These small "First Principles" cohorts literally reshaped our community years ago. They gave greater stability in truth to the church, providing common language and one mindedness, and are a key pathway to firmly establishing people in the faith. But the way each small group is led makes it or breaks it. Although we train the cohort leaders, there have still been gaps in the way some lead that fail to produce the desired outcomes and design of the process. We have needed several fresh starts to ensure the correct approach. This is because people are so deeply entrenched in education models that don't spur action, transformation, and real life change. It takes time to help people unlearn and relearn at a paradigm level. You think people "get it" at first, but in time it is seen that they don't or only partially. But so goes the nature of messy discipleship.

We consistently are seeking to train and disciple our leaders better so that they can be effective catalysts for change and shepherds after God's own heart. As we all should be.

Without application to the truths discovered through these studies and conversations, we aren't really serving people. Biblical knowledge alone without obedience to it leads to religious deception and a life lacking the power of truth. Transformation comes by the grace of God flowing through our faith and obedience to the truth out of sincere love. So when we see people go through a two year process in these groups and still have real paradigm gaps, lacking the fruit of a changed life, we look at the leader first.

We had a funny, not funny, situation where one of the communities favorite cohort leaders was leaving out the most important and difficult part of the process. I wonder if that was why they were the favorite. Ha! They led a great discussion, got everyone participating, but never had people design personal applications for the truths discovered nor ever followed up about living the truths. This was the most important part!

If the leaders are thinking soundly in truth, asking the right questions, challenging appropriately, making relational connections, and holding people accountable to apply the learnings, things would be different in many cases. From the student side, growth is a journey. It takes time and everybody is unique and personally responsible for their own growth and response to the word of God. Even Jesus had fallout, people didn't understand His teaching, and the Father had rebellion in heaven. So there are definitely cases when the leaders have done things well and people still fail to grow and they give up. The saying, "There are no bad students, only bad teachers" is only partially true. The Lord himself regularly said, "if you have ears to hear…." And described four universal responses to the word of God. The soil of the soul is rooted in personal repentance and choice—the will of man.

My point is, our influence on others starts with our own hearts, lives, understanding, and capacity to lead others. We need to learn it, live it, then lead it, if we're going to "leave" it as a kingdom legacy and seed in the hearts of those we lead. The teacher is the textbook, a living example of what's to be imparted. We lead first by example.

We teach what we know but we reproduce who we are! We need to pursue mastery in our areas of expertise but, first and foremost, in the core truths and principles of scripture. When we are firmly established in the first principles of the faith we can apply God's truth to every area of life, and live with true wisdom. The message is embodied in our lives for our children and students to see and experience. Nothing is more powerful than our example.

"No matter what we teach or what we tell or how many books there are on the shelves, we teach the most by what we are in ourselves"—unknown

When it comes to communicating the Gospel, spiritual truth, and biblical principles, if we know it and understand it, there will be fluency and skillful ability to creatively communicate and contextualize the truth for those your speaking with, whether saved or unsaved, mature or immature. Skillful fishers of men and discipleship practitioners require this fluidity and mastery of truth to serve people and work for their progress in the faith. One of the greatest joys of sharing Jesus with people is relating who He is and what He has done and still does in ways and metaphors people understand and can receive. It's disarming. I love taking peoples present skillsets, circumstances, vocations or interests and leveraging that as a metaphor to relate the gospel or biblical truths. It's a game changer and builds bridges to meaningful conversations and creates real impact. More on that soon

Skills and Approaches

I know some amazing people who are highly proficient but are not great at conveying information in a way that people will get it. And then there are those who have the knowledge and the ability to teach it, but lack the patience to walk with people where they are in the journey nor the wisdom to honor their discovery process when they don't immediately comprehend.

Learning to teach is important but teaching occurs through many methods or expressions. I think that every teaching method has its place when used in the appropriate context. Some examples include: traditional classroom instruction, counseling people to process their past, through coaching people into their next level of growth and performance, or facilitating a small group study or lecturing with an interactive presentation. It's one thing to lecture or preach and unfold key points of information of truth to your intended audience in an engaging way. It's another thing entirely to foster deep dialogue through well crafted questions, hold the space, and engage people in a dynamic process of discovering truth for themselves. Transformational leaders should develop and use both skill sets when necessary.

Different learning approaches require different skill sets. To really get into the hearts and minds of people, you have to enter into real conversations, ask hard questions, be willing to challenge people, and help them learn to express what they really think and believe (We'll talk a little more specifically about the Socratic method later). In the same way we must have fluency and mastery in truth as to be able to skillfully win people to the Lord and help people grow in their faith, we need to be able to help those we are discipling to do and become the same. If transformation is the goal, we must become specialists in facilitating metamorphosis through how we teach. As stated before, it starts with you!

Love

When we think about the *teacher being the textbook,* we need to establish love and relationship as the basis for teaching and discipleship. Parents, teachers, instructors, Pastors, must be mentally and emotionally present with those they teach; they must be lovingly engaged so that their heart is felt and experienced by the student or mentee. This does not mean an over-familiarity void of healthy boundaries where the leader is "trauma dumping," for example, and airing all their struggles in attempts to relate. But it still stands that true discipleship is deeply relational, not superficial, cold, and impersonal. Plus, anything done without love is nothing before God, incomplete in His sight, and won't endure the fire of His judgment. WOW! Love never fails.

Remember, Jesus taught his disciples in this relational environment and it's what He intends for the Church. He called them to Himself to be with Him and He loved them with the very love of God. He enjoyed them in the process of growth, even in their weakness and lack of understanding. His acceptance and commitment to them was felt while the space was held for them to struggle, learn, and grow. *We are to do the same toward one another.*

The disciples also deeply loved and respected Christ in return. The nature of that relationship with Him and each other was the draw that bore weight upon their hearts to keep changing and growing. It was only amplified when the Holy Spirit came to live within them to empower the process of transformation.

Some of the greatest issues we see in culture stem from the absence of a loving parent, authority figure, and community relationships. As Mother Theresa said, "People don't care how much you know until they know how much you care." Now read these powerful words written by Viktor E. Frankle, in his classic work, "Man's Search for Meaning": *"For the first time in my life I saw the truth as it is set into song by so many poets, proclaimed as the final wisdom by so many thinkers. The truth—that Love is the ultimate and highest goal to which man can aspire. Then I grasped the meaning of the greatest secret that human poetry and human thought and belief have to impart: The salvation of man is through love and in love."*

Love never fails, as the scriptures say. The truth spoken in love is transformative and the way we truly build people up and strengthen their lives. As said earlier, information alone is not enough to cause real growth. But information energized by the Spirit and expressed through our love will cause that growth, even when correction or rebuke is necessary. A life giving rebuke imparts wisdom and the blows that hurt cleanse away evil[86]. Either way, loving instruction becomes a catalyst for transformation and imparts life.

Remember when we talked about the science of the brain? Loving attachment and the experience of joy is critical for the development of character and spiritual formation. Through loving attachment a life can thrive in joy, peace, healthy relationships, and more. Love actually causes changes in our brain that then changes us fundamentally at our core. We grow and learn best through love. In fact, we obey the Lord because we love Him, and without love it is much harder to obey, learn, or grow. Because we are secure in His love for us and ours for Him, we can also endure His chastisement that leads to holiness as we are trained by it.[87] Love is the fuel of grace, growth, and true enjoyment.

In my own life, I want to obey God and do what is pleasing in His sight, because I deeply love Him! In hardship, affliction and suffering, I still yield my heart to Him in hope and out of great love and tenderness. I respond in love because He has saved me and poured His love into my heart by the Holy Spirit. Though He slays me or chastises me I still bless Him and thank Him because I know that He is good and His intention is good. Plus, where else can I go, He has the words of eternal life. In my younger years in the Lord I was more prone to complain and resist and rationalize where the Lord was disciplining me or requiring obedience where I was afraid. His faithfulness and tenderness and perfect fatherhood continually won me over. As I'v always like to say, "He killed me with kindness". I have learned to die

---

86 Proverbs 20:30, 29:15
87 Heb 12:4-11, proverbs 3:12, 1 Peter 1:6-9

and surrender and let God transform me by learning to receive His goodness and love over my life. I was prone to be self critical and self condemning, but He is not that way. His love is as strong as death and more jealous than the grave. His love is the economy of the soul that continually transforms us and is ever so generous and abundant.

Consider how your love for someone drives you to grow and change.

For example, I want to love my wife well in selfless and sacrificial ways, as Christ loved the Church, and lay my life down for her. But it is because I love her with affection and passion too. My desire is for her. I also desire to love her well and have a positive influence on her heart as we learn to walk together as one for the glory of God. But my ability to do that requires that I continue to die, change, and grow in the love of God, that we might also truly live. It's love that drives me and motivates me to do so. You can see that growth and learning is most energized by the motivation of love and meaningful connection to God and people/[88] When we care and people matter to us, we do whatever it takes to grow to serve and love them better. Remember that *Hesed*—loving attachment, is the single most important factor to change and growth at a deep level of the soul. God's plan and design is perfect: *Wholly love God, love yourself as He has loved you, then love others in the way He has loved you.* When we love others with the love we have received, love has and is being perfected in you. As love is perfected among us He is seen through us.

---

[88] One of the driving forces of holiness is not only love for God but love for other people. Sin in all forms, violates love and hinders relationships, it breaks the fellowship of believers and hinders growth in godliness. Our usefulness to one another is hinged to us walking in obedience to the truth, otherwise the waters get muddied by selfish ambition. In first Peter 1:21 It talks about how we have purified our hearts in obedience to the truth from the heart out of sincere love for the brethren… and we see that Jesus Himself says, " I sanctify myself, for my brethren sake" in John 17. Jesus knew that if he had compromised and yielded to sin in his humanity, he wouldn't of been able to accomplish the father's mission and save his brothers (humanity) from the power of sin. Love was the motivation for obedience to the father, and for the salvation of all who believe.

And yes, I also obey God out of reverential fear in the knowledge that He is both my Lord and my God. I know that I will stand before Him, and be judged for my life in the end. Love, in the realm of affection and felt connection, empowers the change process. Remember, God is coming back for a bridal people who have holy longing and love for Him.[89] This deep affection and love fuels the sacrificial element of our allegiance and obedience to God. We follow Him wherever He leads because He's God but also because He is good and we both want Him and love Him. "If one were to give all the wealth of one's house for love, it would be utterly despised" - Song 8:7

The more we employ a holistic approach and leverage our influence through loving well, while also addressing the whole person in spiritual formation, the better off we will be in our call to teach and disciple others. Open your heart, your lives, your homes, and see the impact it will have on others. This was Apostle Paul's appeal to his churches when he shared how dear the church was to his heart. He not only shared the gospel with them but his very life:

" …even though as apostles of Christ, we could've asserted our authority. Instead, we were like young children among you. Just as a nursing mother cares for her children, so we cared for you. Because we loved you so much, we were delighted to share with you not only the gospel of God but our lives as well. Surely you remember, brothers and sisters, our toil and hardship; we work night and day in order not to be a burden to any of you while we preached the gospel of God to you. You are witnesses, and so is God, of how holy, righteous, and blameless we were among you who believed. For you know that we dealt with each of you as a father deals with his own children, encouraging, comforting, and urging you to live lives worthy of God, who calls you into His kingdom and glory."—1 Thessalonians 2:6-12

---

89 2 Timothy 4:8, 1 Peter 1:8, 2 Peter 3:11-12, Revelation 22:17

The heart, example, and appeal of love maximized their impact and influence for the glory of God. The kingdom of God is manifested as family level love and affection for all people, and especially toward those who believe.

Vision

People's personal vision and ambitions point to a place in their lives that can be leveraged for positive influence and impact. Beyond our words, if we embody the qualities or behaviors we hope to inspire in those we lead, they will want to imitate us or learn from us to become and do what they desire. And as I said, imitation is an incredible way to accelerate learning. If someone wants to imitate you or model what they want after you, then you have already gained access to their mind and heart. This means you have the power to challenge and impart to them in profound ways and call them into their potential.

The vision, model, and the potential your life exemplifies serve as the fuel for the hard work of growth and learning for those wanting to imitate you. Your life should be a visual aid that inspires others onward and upward. The principle at play is: We reproduce who we are and not what we "teach." We should aspire to say like Apostle Paul, "follow me as I follow Christ" by living lives worthy of the gospel. Paul taught not only by words and instruction but through the pattern and example of his life. Discipleship that effectively leads to people becoming more like Jesus in everything they do directly correlates to our relationship with them. The vision we embody and hold out before them is the measure of influence we have with them.

The inspiration that leads to transformation comes from the proximity of our relationship and the powerful example we set. "Better than a thousand days of diligent study is one day with a great teacher." People just need to be able to see what following Christ looks like authentically in the midst of real life. Mature believers model the faith. Concepts, ideas, and theology have to be seen in reality and worked out in relationships and service. Reading the scripture that says "count trials as pure joy" is one thing. It becomes real when you see someone you're walking with actually giving thanks and worshiping God through severe trials. We call people higher by actually operating in faith and modeling the way of God's kingdom.

This relational context for discipleship is at the heart of anything that matters in the Kingdom of God. Everything is relational and the Kingdom is about family—His Family. We see the deep love and relationship Jesus had with His disciples. He called them friends and brothers and sacrificially gave Himself up for them in love. He radically redefined leadership and family. He told John to consider Mary to be his mother and John her son as He hung on the cross. We see the type of relational closeness Jesus had with the disciples in examples like John resting his head on Jesus' chest, reclining at the diner table. And of course, in terms of proximity, they did everything together everyday. Life was modeled for the disciples in the mundane and the spectacular.

We see Paul describe his relationship with Timothy, who was apprenticing under him, as a true son in the faith, remembering his tears when they departed. It was evident that the affection of Christ and a deep relational connection existed between them. We see that when Paul was leaving the elders in Ephesus in Acts 20, that they all hugged and wept. We see many more examples throughout the scriptures describing the relational context of discipleship that had deep affection and godly bonds of love in Christ. This needs to be rediscovered in a real way. The world will know we are His disciples by how we love one another (John 13:35).

It's this kind of love and relational connection that activates our whole brain and accelerates personal transformation. Love and meaningful relationships are the first and foremost "HOW" in making impact and authentic disciples. We have to be intentional. We also see that

Christ called leaders in humble servanthood, accessibility, relationship, and through personal example. That was radically different than the hierarchical, relationally detached way of the world.

Growing in influence starts with you, your development, your conduct, and your relationships. You lead by example. If you're a parent, you know that your kids typically follow your example and follow your lead especially when they are young. If you're a leader of a team, organization, community, or business, the same goes for you.

It's our example and leadership capacity that determines the culture and standard of operations and performance of our people. But position alone does not ensure people will follow you, receive from you, be open to learn from you, or give you their best under your leadership.

How we lead and relate to others casts the vision and provides the picture and inspiration for others to follow. So be the message.

Building Bridges

The law of buy-in says that people buy into the leader before they buy into the vision or work. If people know you, like you, and trust you, they will follow your lead! We want to be the kind of leader who inspires them, and calls them into their potential. Leaders who model for them at some level who and what they aspire to be and are called to be.

There are those in your circle of influence that you may not have a deeper connection with yet. Ask yourself, *"How do we begin to build bridges with people? How can we be close enough to model or share what they may desire or aspire to be, know, or do? How do we create and cultivate opportunities for connection and the gospel?*

When we consider our role in the great commission and using our platform of influence to reach people for the gospel, we need to think about living with a sense of mission that translates into seeing opportunities to respond in love every day.

We build bridges through hospitality of heart and practices that create space for connection and meaningful conversations.

I want to differentiate between two general types and models of evangelism and disciple making: one for the stranger and one for the people you already know. Both could be referred to as your "neighbor" in terms of our call to "love our neighbor as ourselves."[90], But, for the sake of a visual, I'll use the biblical model relative to our realms of influence ."... to be My witnesses in Jerusalem, Judea, Samaria, and to the ends of the Earth" from Acts 1:8.

The stranger in this context is the person you do not know. He or she may be around you in the context of daily life, (ie the homeless person on the street corner, the lady in the grocery store, or your waiter at the restaurant).

You don't see these people frequently nor are they always in your direct relational influence except for the moments you see or run into them. This could also be considered to be divine appointments: when you help them, pray or share the gospel or a "word of knowledge" with them, or just serve someone, making an initial connection. It's the evangelism that is more random and spontaneous and integrated as part of your life. We need to be open and have eyes to see these opportunities and seize these moments when they come. Truly the harvest is plentiful and all around us all the time. We should be looking for opportunities to share the love of God and the good news with those around us. The stranger in these cases can also become a friend, potentially someone who transitions into your more regular

---

90 Matthew 22:37-40, Mark 12:30-31, Galatians 5:14, James 2:8, Leviticus 19, Romans 13:10, Luke 10:25-37, Matt 5:38-48

influence. This would depend on how they respond to you and your continued efforts to build relationships.

For simplicity sake, we'll also put in this bucket the focused evangelistic campaigns where teams go into an area specifically to go share the gospel with people who are there, but not necessarily in your relational sphere of influence.

The other bucket is those connected to you in your places of regular influence. This is your home, kids, family, extended family, friends, neighbors, co-workers, business partners, or people you see regularly at your gym, bank, school, local store, church, etc. These people can be targeted in a focused and strategic way. You can intentionally cultivate opportunities to serve them, love them, connect deeper, and share your testimony, life, and gospel. These people, for the sake of the conversation, will be those in your "Jerusalem and Judea" whereas the stranger would be in your "Samaria and ends of the earth." This is a fluid concept just for you to think through.

The point in either case, for the stranger or those more connected, is to build bridges to deepen connection, add value through love and service, for either invitation to the gospel or deeper growth in Christ.

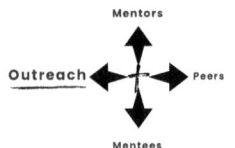

THE 4TH DIMENSION OF A DISCIPLES MAXTRIX - MISSIONAL OUTREACH

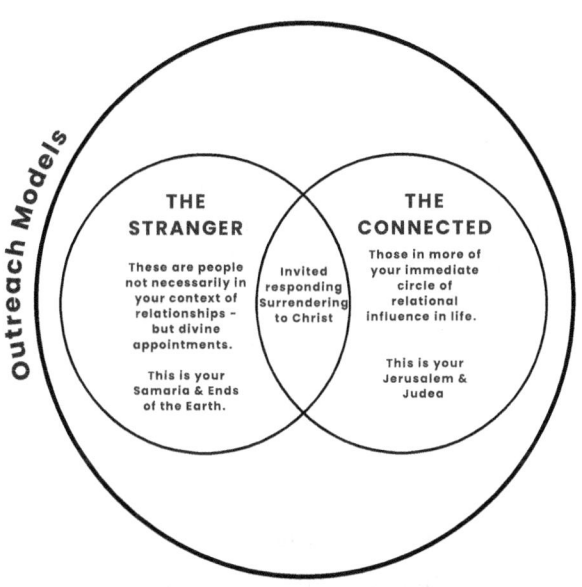

Outreach Models

THE STRANGER

These are people not necessarily in your context of relationships – but divine appointments.

This is your Samaria & Ends of the Earth.

Invited responding Surrendering to Christ

THE CONNECTED

Those in more of your immediate circle of relational influence in life.

This is your Jerusalem & Judea

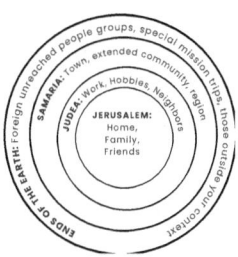

Outreach Models – THE STRANGER & CONNECTED

Here's a few thoughts that are by no means comprehensive:

First, be intentional to sincerely pray for those you want to influence and for new open doors for the gospel. This shifts your heart and mind towards people and God just may reveal key insights to help unlock a way to pray more specifically for them, encourage them, or how to specifically serve them. Plus, prayer is the first place of partnership with God in His mission to reach the world and advance His will on the earth. Start with prayer, continue with prayer, end in prayer. Pray always.

A great exercise I encourage believers to do is to create a list of those in their circle they want to influence for the gospel and who need salvation in Christ. Sometimes, people focus on three to five people they are really going to "press in " for. Other times, like the evangelist of old, DL Moody, they have a list of 100 people whom they regularly contend for in prayer. Cool note about Moody, 96 of the people on his list came to faith and were saved while he was alive. The remaining 4 came to faith at his funeral![91] The point is, get INTENTIONAL, and see what God will do!

As we pray, we keep our eyes open to those the Father has prepared who are open to us and spiritually curious. We need eyes to see what the Father is doing and learn to partner with Him in it. Remember, no one comes to Christ unless the father has prepared them.

Second, when it comes to influencing people around you we have to build rapport. Rapport opens the door. In order to gain access to people's heart and life they need to feel safe and have a measure of assurance that they can trust you. There are different levels of rapport that bear increasing measures of influence in people's lives, such as respect due to a position or particular accomplishments. But, there is something deeper and more impactful that we should look to develop

---

91 Accessed 6/10/24— https://www.eauk.org/news-and-views/praying-come-to-know-christ

toward the stranger and those our regular place of influence. We have to learn to *connect,* which requires a little bit of social intelligence and good communication.

People are social beings no matter their personality type. They want to be loved, enjoyed, seen, valued, respected, appreciated, etc. A good working knowledge of the complexity of people's personalities will help you know what people value, the type of communication they need, and how they best connect with others. *For any leader and aspiring transformational leader this is a MUST in order to lead well.* But it's also really important for all believers to grow here so that they can become effective "fishers of men." This knowledge enables conversations seasoned with grace, knowing how to speak to those outside the faith. People hate feeling pressured and the sense of agenda behind conversation or interaction. The saying goes, everybody communicates but not everyone connects. The concept and practice we need to get a hold of is *connection.* That's where the magic happens whether I'm talking to the stranger in the grocery store for the first time or going to the person I work with every day. We must cultivate sensitivity here and grow in social IQ so that people will open their hearts and lives to us.

Basic connection and rapport may start with common ground, such as common interests, or expertise that establish authority and respect (especially when people are coming to you for help or for a service), or shared values, But going deeper, we have to learn to relate and speak to people wherever they are and to who they are with unconditional positive regard. Simply, we have to actually love people. When we do, people feel that and open up, eventually.

Respect builds a bridge to relationship and relationship reaches the heart. People must feel that we are for them, like them, and have a genuine interest in them. Us humans are prone to quickly judge others, relate out of our own biases, not listen well, and are self absorbed. Those types of things hamper connection and harm people's ability to receive from you. Love believes the best about others, prefers them over ourselves, and sees them through the eyes of Jesus Christ, the eyes of love. Therefore, it's important to listen well and observe people with thoughtful reflection, before we respond with purpose and love. As the scripture says, our speech is to be seasoned with grace.[92]

Connection starts with eye contact, a smile, and *listening*. When we put those things into practice, we help people feel and know that we have seen them and heard them. When we practice things like reflecting back to them what they have said, asking meaningful questions, it can really open things up. We should be curious about people and ask them about their lives, not assume. That's a great place to start before moving on to interject our thoughts, insights and story.

It's a precious thing to be invited to speak into someone's life or work. Let's treat it with such honor and make quality relational investments. Every interaction we have with someone can move them closer or farther away from receiving from us, so let's be wise and handle it with great care.

When building connection, we must be authentic. Relate to people from your own life's experiences, while not monologuing or using too much "Christianeeze." People have to be able to relate to and understand what we are saying who are not in the Christian subculture. Language, tonality, and the pace in which we speak matter when connecting and building bridges to deeper relationships. Another powerful thing is the willingness to share your own failures and weaknesses. Honesty and vulnerability about our lives break walls down from the typical stereotype of "religious Christians" who appear self-righteous. It's good to pepper your relational interactions with good humor too, and remember to use people's names when talking to them.

This may seem like a no-brainer to you, but I have found many to be lacking in these basic relational skills.

---

92 Colossians 4:6

Third, it's so important to have an overarching attitude and pervasive practice of honor, respect, and the valuing of others with sincerity. It is good practice to learn to become a person who can encourage and make specific but sincere affirmations about people and what you appreciate about them. Recognizing people and their efforts and expressing that to them is a big deal. More relationships have been broken and stay broken for failure to practice this alone. Treat and make people feel special, seen, and important, because they are. Not everyone is good at this, but you can learn to be. It's a skill that can be developed, that's rooted in love. It truly builds social currency and is one of those power keys to actually unlock and build relationships, create opportunity, and make room for greater influence. And I'm not talking about flattery. Sincere compliments and verbalizing appreciation absolutely lifts peoples spirits and deeply encourages them. Expressing value and honor towards others is part of the language of love. It will open doors of influence. Little things, for instance, like a hand written note go a long way in building bridges, rapport, and community with people.

I belong to a martial arts group where I have seen that the little things really do matter. The times where I've genuinely encouraged others and helped people celebrate the small wins have had a big impact on their hearts and created space for more meaningful interaction. One thing builds on the next. Our love expressed in listening and affirmation creates a felt sense of safety and trust, and that's what we want. Our interactions with people ideally should be life-giving and sowing positive effects. From there we have their heart and ear to share our story and how Jesus changed our lives and can do the same for them.

Scriptures say that we are the fragrance of life to those being saved and the fragrance of death to those who are perishing.[93] Sometimes our kindness, love and good behavior stir up hate or resentment in others and invite insults. Persecution and resistance to love and truth is to be

---

93 2 Corinthians 2:16

expected. Don't be moved by it. Keep loving people and overcome evil by doing good. If you're persecuted for Christ's sake, you're blessed and considered worthy to suffer for His name's sake. Plus, scripture says that when we are persecuted for His name's sake, that the spirit of glory and of God rests on us.[94] Pretty sweet!

Some will love you and others will hate you, but nonetheless keep loving, sharing, and building bridges looking for those the Father is drawing to Himself. You love, honor, and do good to all, but look for the "people of peace"[95] who are receptive, hospitable, favorable toward you, and prepared by the Father.

The bottom line is that our life should shine and be contagious, attractive, and provoking desire and hunger in others to know God. *Those who don't know God but know us, should eventually want to know God because they know us.*

I am the only dojo owner in the association with a faith based, Christ centered school. This blatant expression of my faith alone has created conversation and reactions to say the least. But I will say, by the grace of God, I have gained access and rapport in many ways leading to numerous opportunities to speak into the lives of fellow students, senior leaders, families, and other community leaders. I've had incredible gospel conversations and meaningful times of prayer with people on the dojo floor. I have often been trusted with deeply personal and confidential matters of people's lives. Because they feel I'm "the real deal," they trust me and will receive from me. Their idea of what it means to love God and be a Christian gets redefined or at least is seen in a new way. I'm not saying that to puff myself up in any way but to just give an example. We should all aim and desire to represent the Lord and what He is like to those who are without God and may have a bad taste in their mouth due to prior experiences

---

[94] 1 Peter 2:12-20, 3:8-17, 4:14, Phillipians 1:29, Romans 12:21, Acts 5:41 and many more scriptures
[95] Matthew 10:11-15, Luke 10:2-12

with Christians and religion. We need to give people a good and right picture of God.

In a quick observation from my experience and from what aligns with the instruction of scripture, we see a couple things at play in how we can build social rapport and cultural currency. I'll focus on the things TO DO instead of what NOT to do:

- Be a person of character and integrity—be authentic and unashamed of your faith.

- Be others focused and serve them; honor and prefer them over yourself. Jesus took the lowest position and washed people's feet, so should we. Look for the little things to help lighten other peoples load in life. No task should be beneath you, keep serving. "The son of man didn't come to be served but to serve and give His life as a ransom for many." Mark 10:45

- Ask questions, take genuine interest in others lives and stories, and listen well.

- Look people in the eyes and smile. Give people a firm and affectionate handshake. Some people like hugs as part of a greeting, so be sensitive to that. Some cultures appreciate kisses on the cheek too. Know what is appropriate.

- Be affirming and look for ways to sincerely encourage the good in people and the good they have done or are doing. Help people recognize the bright spots in life and celebrate them in small ways. Empathize with their weaknesses and normalize their struggle while pointing to hope and the potential of redemption.

- Respect people's boundaries and ask permission to speak into their life or situation. Speak the truth in love and don't back away from saying the hard things. Just do it with gentleness and respect. Be peaceable and know when to back off. Arguing is futile and useless.

- Be excellent at your craft and skill set, set an example, work hard, and add value to others. Your gift will make a way. Work ethic and competence go a long way in the eyes of the unbeliever. It wins their respect and also provides a great example for those young in faith.

- Be warm, welcoming, authentic, and hospitable.

- Be generous, joyful, grateful, and sincere. Kindness is a weapon of grace that earns favor with people. Smile ridiculously.

- Be brave, take risks, and go the extra mile for people for the Lord's sake. Be sacrificial and inconvenienced to serve and help people.

- Be humble, work hard, and communicate clearly with respect and gentleness.

- Be succinct and avoid rambling when it comes to sharing your faith or story. Be aware of how much you share and what people are ready to handle or absorb. If they start checking out, switch it up and engage them.

- Listen carefully, empathize, and be very present with people. Be slow and intentional to respond.

Our life and conduct should shine and be distinguished from the world. The scriptures are so clear about living respectable lives, being careful how we speak to and behave towards those outside the faith.

They call us to be careful to maintain the good works that adorn the gospel. We must learn to *cultivate* and *create* opportunities and *take* the opportunity to share the faith and love of God with others. Sometimes it's quick and immediate and many times it's slow and earned through sacrificial commitment and patience. You have to be committed to the long game and consistent in your prayers, love, and witness. Tilling the ground, sowing seed, waiting and watering patiently, and reaping the harvest is a continual process. You may enter people's story at harvest time and it just takes a word or invitation and, boom! Or you may be standing in the gap for hardened, lost souls. You may need to till the ground for years before they are even ready to have a gospel conversation where seed can sink in. Either way, we have to be intentional to build these bridges and do the work.

Living authentically before God and loving people well, valuing people and adding value to them, builds bridges. That allows us to be able to teach others, share what is good, and make a real impact. Becoming skilled fishers of men requires that we learn to cultivate opportunities and break down walls of resistance for the gospel to be shared.

Many believers don't make space in their schedule to be around the lost for intentional influence for the gospel sake. Ask yourself, when did you last invite someone who doesn't know Jesus over for a meal to get to know them and intentionally start building a bridge for the gospel's sake? Maybe it's not dinner or lunch but what about out to do something recreational with missional intention?

We must make space to be with, love, and reach those who are without Christ. The same could be said for those who believe but desperately need discipleship and brought into closer relationships and a development process.

The acronym "BLESS" can help us use this simple process of cultivating and sharing the love and message of Jesus with others. Dave and John Furgeson wrote a book called "BLESS: 5 Everyday Ways to Love your

Neighbor and Change the World" that dives into these topics. Great little read:

B- Begin with prayer: pray for the people at your work, in your families, in your recreational circles, who don't know Jesus. Ask the Lord how you can bless them. Get a heart for the people around you and believe God to move on their hearts. Remember, no one can come to the revelation of the Son without the father ready-ing and preparing their hearts. We help till the ground and co-labor with God first through prayer.

L- Listen: pay attention to their story. Ask questions, and look for both evidence of God at work in their lives and opportunities to add value to them. Understand how they think and what they value—relate to them and learn to speak their language. People will be more open to hear from you when they feel heard and not judged and given space to process. When people feel heard they feel known and loved. When people feel loved, the door is opened. At the same time of looking for evidence of what the Father might be doing with them be listening to the voice of the Holy Spirit for key insights and directives. He knows best.

E- Eat together: invite them out to lunch or coffee. Continue building a relationship, and learning more about their personal story and circumstances. Jesus was a friend of sinners and knew how to love and enjoy people even in their weaknesses and sins, without condoning or affirming their sin. As you eat with people they should feel your love, acceptance, and enjoyment of them, not criticism and mere toleration. As you spend time with people you grow in love and compassion for them, and as you love them, you grow in influence with them.

S- Serve & Sow: be attentive to opportunities. You can serve them at work, at play, and in life. Consider how you can leverage your time, talent, or treasure to bless them in some way. Maybe you know people that can help or meet a specific need they have and be willing to connect with them when it's appropriate. The point is to actually do something to add value and help. You can also look to pray with them for physical needs and see the power of God heal them. God's demonstrated goodness in touching their body will open a door to share the good news. People need to know that God is a living God and acts and intervenes right now in life. The gospel is more than just the forgiveness of sins and a future hope, it is a living reality of eternal life and salvation now. The kingdom is not mere talk, its power.

S- Share Christ & your story: once you build a relationship and trust, look for opportunities to share how Jesus has changed your life and offer the same hope to them. As we get to share the gospel we can also be listening to the Holy Spirit to give us insight in how we could further minister to them in the moment and create a space and opportunity for them to encounter the presence and power of God.

From there, we build on that influence and draw them into deeper relationships and connection, where we can have greater impact.

Keep in Focus

When we talk about the goal of "transformation", the way we are defining it is more than becoming something different in a general sense or the "true and best version of you " as the world may define it. People can transform themselves into whatever they want for all kinds of reasons. In fact, they may find themselves doing or becoming the very opposite of what God may have intended for them *(remember, "to be or not to be" from earlier on?)* And worse, though well intended, it is dangerous for a deluded self help and self empowerment movement to be promoting life transformation without Christ. Positive outcomes apart from Christ can be very deceptive and lead to a self righteousness that robs people's perception of their need for the gospel. It is kind of a scary thought but it's the truth.

Only those who have been born again by the Spirit of God, come to know Jesus Christ, and do the will of the Father will enter the Kingdom of heaven. It was for that reason Christ died, that we would be reconciled back to God and no longer live for ourselves but for the will of Him. Transformation is about becoming like Christ and is the result of submission and obedience to God.

We need to help others know God, discern His will for their lives, and obey Him faithfully. Discipleship is about obedience and conformity to the word and ways of Christ. It's in fact, helping others learn to yield to the life of Christ on the inside of them, allowing Him to live through them. As said before, what benefit is it to gain the whole world but lose your soul and stand before Him in the end or when we die to find Him say, "You did a bunch of things but depart from me, I never knew you."

We don't want to find ourselves or those we have the opportunity to lead into the faith saying "Lord, lord...did I not....in your Name do...." And He say, "Not everyone who says 'lord, lord' will enter the Kingdom of heaven, only those who do the will of my Father will enter. I don't know you, depart from me ... .the things you did were un authorized ." We must be vigilant and beware of pseudo spirituality, dead religion that's coated with Christian language, and straight up humanism. We must lead people to Christ and help them bring every area of their lives under His lordship. He is the only way to eternal life.

This is one reason I'm serious about responsibly using our influence for the Kingdom of God. We need to realize we have a part to play in helping prepare people to stand before God and take account of their lives. Wow...take that in for a moment! This is part of why I'm even writing this book.

The question is, *will you leverage your influence to make an eternal impact? Will you work at building rapport and cultivating opportunities for the gospel sake?*

Souls are to be won to Christ and the gospel of the Kingdom must be preached to every tribe, tongue, and nation before the Lord can return. We have a great work to do in our generation. I believe the Spirit of the Lord is inviting us in a fresh way to make ourselves ready for greater use! We are called to be intentional and proactive about this. This missional focus to build bridges to influence the hearts of people for the gospel's sake is central to our calling and identity as disciples of Jesus Christ.

When those people have responded to us and the gospel, the job is not done. We are called to continually nurture and follow through. The next step is water baptism and an active life as a new disciple enjoined to the Church and the mission of Christ. Yes, "some sow, some water, some reap, and God brings the increase." I'm talking about those we're connected to and in our regular rhythm of influence. With them, we must go deeper, partnering with the Holy Spirit and the Church to see these new believers firmly established in the faith, moving along the journey to maturity and fullness in Christ.

The great commission is to go and preach the gospel to all creation and make disciples of all nations, baptizing those who believe in the Name of the Father, Son, and Holy Spirit, and teaching them to obey everything the Lord commanded.[96] Once people are baptized the next phase of development is crucial. People are not delivered from the dominion of darkness and brought into the Kingdom of God, out of the waters of baptism, only to be brought into the seats of a Sunday service to become passive spectators in a religious show. No, they are to become active disciples who, out of love for God, embrace the journey of spiritual formation and transformation into the image of Christ.

---

96 Matthew 28:18-20, Mark 16:15-20

A whole new way of living and understanding must be learned and practiced. This journey touches every aspect of life, it's comprehensive, it's holistic. In the next chapter, we will look at some of the dynamics around our learning approaches and models in holistic education. We will consider how it relates to the goal of discipleship and what it means to restore the ancient paths of authentic discipleship to impact the world.

PAUSE. CAPTURE. APPLY
Prompts to help you process

1. What specific insights or concepts from this chapter resonated with you the most? Why do you think these stood out to you?

_____

_____

_____

2. How can you practically apply the principles discussed in this chapter to your daily life, relationships, or ministry? Identify at least one actionable step you can take this week.

_____

_____

_____

3. What potential challenges or barriers might you face in implementing these concepts? How can you overcome them?

_____

_____

_____

4. What are 3-5 quotes or points from this chapter that capture the essence of what it's communicating? Write them down.

_____

_____

_____

_____

_____

5. How can you involve your family, small group, or church community in the practices and principles outlined in this chapter? What steps can you take to foster a culture of discipleship and transformation within your circle of influence?

_____

_____

_____

6. Spend a few moments in prayer, asking God for the wisdom, strength, and courage to live out the truths you've learned. Write down a commitment or a prayer that reflects your desire to grow as an authentic disciple and transformational leader to impact the world.

_____

_____

_____

CHAPTER 12

Holistic Education & Making disciples

A call to reform our learning approach

> *"If Christ is indeed Lord, He must be Lord of all of life- in spiritual matters of course, but just as much across the whole spectrum of life, including intellectual matters and the areas of culture, law, and government."*
>
> —Francis Schaeffer, "The Great Evangelical Disaster."

> *"it's easier to put a man on Mars than it is the change the school systems."*
>
> —Elon Musk

In this section, I will weave in between the concepts of holistic education and disciple making in different realms from both general educational approaches in relation to basic discipleship practices. I'm talking about a paradigm and culture shift to frame our approach to learning, people development, and spiritual formation.

In many cases, general education and the call of discipleship intimately interact and relate. This particularly applies when working with young people in the primary and secondary school years (K4- college). But whether working with kids, youth, or adults, it's important to understand that education, spiritual formation, growth, and the call to discipleship begin as early as the womb and continues through every stage of life until death. In fact, it will even continue into eternity as we forever grow in the knowledge of God and rule and reign with Him in the ages to come. We never stop learning and growing. Wild thought, right? So keep in mind as you read that I'm referring to all ages.

This call to holistic education and discipleship is for all of us. If we're going to shift culture and paradigms to more effectively produce the biblical outcomes of people who live and act like Jesus, and have the capacity and know how to influence culture, then it must start with leaders and those in positions of influence. Leadership and headship create culture, and culture trumps strategy every time.

The Church has an educational mission in preaching the gospel, making disciples of nations, and passing on the faith to the next generation. We get to help educate the world with the values, ways, and culture of the Kingdom of God. If not us, then who? The knowledge of God must be modeled and taught with clarity and relevance if it's to become a transformative agent in our world. This will help bring about the obedience of faith and expand the culture of the Kingdom of God in our communities and neighborhoods. *The Church, the home, and the school can dynamically integrate to restore firm foundations, ancient paths, and create cultural beachheads of gospel advancement in local communities. We can systemically reshape the lives and minds of families, leaders, and the next generation. This takes reform, intention, and hard work in the grace of God.*

*M*assive reform in education, our learning approach, and the Church itself, is part of that answer. The hour is urgent and the call to arise is at hand. In gross darkness, the Church must arise as a redemptive agent to bless the earth with goodness. We must do our part in discipling families and the next generation through holistic and Christ-centered education.

Rethink The Wineskin

Have you ever heard the adage "measure twice, cut once?" I think it's important to stop and think again and give consideration to what and why we are doing these things. To build a church, community, team, or life truly committed to and effective at discipleship, we should reevaluate every assumption about what it means to be a Christian or authentic disciple. We must apply the lens of the Scriptures, and especially Jesus' methods for doing discipleship and church. Even secular studies see the wisdom and strategy of Christ and His Apostles, namely Paul, regarding complex networks and strategy that literally shifted culture and changed the world.

We are thinking too small if our aim is anything less than to change the world for the Glory of God. Our job description is *heaven on earth until He comes*. We need to be willing to make radical shifts if we want the impact and fruit that is proportionate to the invitation in scripture. New Testament Christianity is unstoppable and shakes and shapes everything! We live in unprecedented times and the people of God need unprecedented responses as He does unprecedented things on the earth.

The Lord is calling all of us to reconsider our ways and return to Him and His word with all our hearts as we lean into the new thing He is doing on the earth. He always releases "new wineskins for the new wine." But, are we ready and willing to shift? Are we willing to reconsider the lens and paradigms by which we assess and know things? Many of us operate under traditions and teachings that were passed down through the generations, without critically evaluating whether they actually align with the scriptures and the ways of God. These traditional methods worked for us in the past because they were commonly accepted by many leaders.

That's the dangers of old wineskins and paradigms, they keep us confined to the old because they are comfortable and useful. Most people are afraid to move beyond the safety of the constructs they have been given or created. Those who have reassessed their assumptions and traditions, have either deconstructed them and become disillusioned without properly rebuilding according to truth. They have stayed stuck for fears of change and making waves, or they have jumped onto the newest fad without returning to the source with due diligence.

We need to return to the word of God with fresh eyes and let it speak for itself and not be entrapped by traditions taught as though they are the commands of God. We need a *bible revival*, as it was in King Josiahs day[97]. The restoration of prophetic and apostolic foundations will lead us back to the ancient paths of the good way, the way of Christ. The ways of the Lord produce good fruit—the kind of fruit that transforms lives and communities. It is evident there's a great disconnect with the prevailing immature, carnal, and superficial church. It lacks the substance to be the transformational agent she is called to be. Therefore, we see a major wake up call to the Body of Christ. It's an invitation to a spiritual revolution, reform, and ultimately a great call to return to the way of the Lord. We must look to the rock from which we were hewn and cry out for a spirit of wisdom and revelation to illuminate the eyes of our understanding.

We need to think differently about how we are training, educating, and making disciples. Many churches have been conveying doctrinal facts and creeds alone without expecting a commitment to discipleship and

---

[97] 2 Kings 22-23, 2 Chronicles 35

transformation of life. Instead, we need to have a mind and mission for mastery, excellence, conformity to His nature, and working wisdom for those we lead.

The ambition and experience of spiritual formation should be embraced with enthusiasm. It should be fueled by the joy of knowing Christ, and the love of learning in a missional community. For too long, people just crammed knowledge into their heads only for it to be soon forgotten, their lives left unchanged, character untouched. We need to slow down and return to quality, depth, obedience, the aims of transformation: intimacy with God, and the stewardship of human potential.

Rediscovering the lost art of discipleship is about helping people walk with Jesus and be conformed to His image by beholding and sharing in His very nature and glory. It's amazing! This relational journey should be experienced from a context of friendship and intimacy with God, as His precious child, and with our brothers and sisters in the Lord - fellowship. This is not dry, academic, and linear. It's glorious and messy, full of suffering and joy. It requires immersion, authentic relationships, and time.

Scripture instructs us to "discipline ourselves in godliness"[98] and to "add to our faith virtue...unto brotherly kindness and love."[99] This is contemplative and monastic, centered on the heart first. It leads to our total transformation into the likeness of Jesus while growing in the intimate knowledge of Him. I'm not talking about isolation or becoming a hermit, but rather an orientation of the soul that cultivates self examination, an awareness of God, and dynamic exchange with Him—a beholding Him in our Spirit, in community, that leads to transformation.

---

98 1 Timothy 4:7-8
99 2 Peter 1

Spiritual formation and the call into the fullness of God in Christ, encompasses all of life, utilizes all things. It anchors into the centrality of learning to be with God, abide in God, ordering our lives according to the word of God, and doing all things unto God. Our faith and spirituality is not compartmentalized. Consequently, throughout our endeavors, learning and application, we focus with faith, knowing we are stewarding our lives in the fear of the Lord and laboring to be useful in His hands. Yet, there is rest in Him and we learn to live and labor within the rhythms of His abiding grace. I want you to sense the passion and intentionality of what I'm saying about this kind of pursuit and way of life.

This is a little different from what many people have thought or experienced in terms of discipleship or Christian education. Most educational institutions, Christian practices and approaches fail to keep the bigger picture in mind. They certainly fall short of keeping the vision and values before the minds and hearts of learners. This goes back to the need to grow in our leadership capacity. Solid visionary leadership and administration can bring cohesion and flow, creating a culture that can walk the tensions without compromising one aspect for another. However, it is common for academics and training to disconnect from acknowledging God and the missional advancement of His kingdom in and through us.

We have to bridge the gap!

As talked about before, memorization will not produce what God is after in us. We cannot afford to settle for anything less than the fullness that God has ordained. We need to be rooted and grounded in truth, built up in it, and able to harness the powers of biblical reasoning and discernment. Through this, the will of God can be known amidst much cultural confusion and lived out in the power and grace of God.

In the complexity of culture and society and in an ever increasing technological age, we must ground the next generation to think biblically and also contextually in order to apply truth with relevance. There is a critical need for people who possess both the inner qualities and outward competence to live differently than society, who can also help solve the problems of our day and innovate solutions to the glory of God. We need a new breed of disciples who are clear headed, anchored in Christian community and a biblical worldview, competent, obedient to truth, and burning with the fire of the gospel to change the world.

This is why the Church, the home, and the school should integrate in a dynamic way to train, educate, and disciple families and the next generation. There are many methods and models that can be used, but the local church can serve as a hub of training, education, and holistic discipleship to help turn the tides in our generation and raise up people who can impact the world.

Our curriculum paradigms need to be reformed to produce a different quality of person—a different kind of messenger. They should be able to flourish in the day they live, utilizing their giftedness to add real value in their workplace and influence. Training and education should foster deep love for God and others; a transformation of character that leads to godliness, contentment of soul, well ordered lives, and the ability to make a positive impact for the gospel wherever they are.

Seems to be a tall order, but, nonetheless, the call.

This requires an approach that is markedly different from what most people are familiar with or have experienced. People have to unlearn so much in order to come out from the confines of old paradigms to embrace the new. The concepts I'm expressing might be difficult, if not impossible, to fully grasp or implement within the typical framework of a conventional compartmentalized Western paradigm of education, community life, and discipleship.

This is directly connected to how we think of the Church and our past experience of it.

This type of authentic community with such integration and intention in training, education, and discipleship is uncommon. There is not only deep historical precedent for this, but it is also part of the new thing God is doing and restoring on the earth with His people. You can start now.

He's calling us back to the ancient paths and into the new thing He's doing on the earth.

I love the scriptures that talk about, "the scribe instructed in the kingdom of heaven who takes both old and new out of his treasury to give light and understanding to his household."—Matt 13, and Jeremiah 6:16, "stand at the crossroads and cry out for the ancient paths, the good way that leads to the rest of soul.."

I propose that we innovate by blending the time-honored wisdom traditions of the past with modern technology and science, crafting new models and wineskins to train, educate, and empower the next generation. Learning communities and environments should foster and engage a love of learning (the pursuit of wisdom) grounded in a sound and comprehensive biblical worldview. This will forge godly character, healthy relationships and social skills, problem solving, and the discovery and development of talents, gifts, and passions which can be harnessed to enrich communities and change the world.

One of the distinctives of our local church training model is the placement of the presence of God at the center of community life and spiritual formation. There is a shared sense of hosting and stewarding the presence of God and prayerful devotion. Intentional discipleship starts, is sustained by, and ends with a spirit of worship and adoration, delighting in His presence. If our education and training isn't producing a people who KNOW the Lord and burn to make Him known, we're missing it. If this sense of loving devotion is missing from the essence of our process and approach to spiritual formation, we need to realign and recenter on Him. The heart of first love devotion must be first fueling good works and service.

"We remember before our God and Father your work produced by faith, your labor prompted by love, and your endurance inspired by hope in our Lord Jesus Christ." - *1 Thessalonians 1:3*

Regardless of our strategies and approaches, He must be preeminent in all we do. We behold the Lord, we delight ourselves in Him, we become and are becoming like Him, we do all things in Him unto Him, and for Him. We preach *His* word and advance *His* mission, to give Him *His* reward, so that others would come and behold *Him,* know *Him,* become like *Him. Training, education and discipleship that doesn't lead to the joyful engagement of the first commandment and the great commission, is off track.*

It is time to reform the local church into authentic learning communities that honor the call and commission to make disciples of all people, bringing them to maturity in Christ. The cultivation of authentic discipleship in a local community is a glorious witness to the watching world. Partnership of the home, the church, and the schooling of our people, from youth to adults, must be forged together to shine and impact our communities. Jeff Reid says, "Our home base witness must be genuine, overflowing from lives that are deeply entwined in a loving, unified community, which provides a context for the people of the community to see an undistorted picture of Christ as they encounter His claims."

We need to create immersive experiences that are truly interactive, personal, and transformational when it comes to training, coaching, and educating. We need a holistic approach. Remember, It's more than passing along information. It's about impartation, transformation, and skill development that fosters whole life formation and wholeness, to the glory of God. We want learning and growth environments that give opportunities for true engagement, connection, and personal expression, spaces that are guided by an overall sense of cohesive purpose and mission. *Discipleship and Christian education has to be an experience and obedience based process that leads to intimacy with God and conformity to His nature.*

If the goal is about following Him (Christ), intimately knowing Him, and becoming like Him, just "knowing" things about Him is not enough. To love Him is to obey Him and to obey Him is to practice the truth. To practice the truth manifests in righteousness, peace, and joy in the Holy Spirit. It is the practice of light—of all that is good, right, and true demonstrated in love for God and others.[100] We need to exercise faith-filled, heartfelt, and obedience-based practice in order to reach our desired outcomes.

David Sunde said well, " The Church needs right belief (Orthodoxy), but the Church also needs right practice (Orthopraxy). Knowledge alone, without mission, incarnation, or *(notably)* spiritual reproduction is not effective for God's work in the world, much less in Christian hearts."[101]

Harnessing Technology

Students and teachers alike need to be brought into the joy, strength, and energy of learning and serving with a greater sense of purpose and mission. People need to know why what they are learning or doing is important; education done with vision and intention around something they love and believe in is transformative, fruitful, and fun. The truth is, people will go deep and work hard for what they love, believe in, and are interested in.

---

100 Romans 14:17, Ephesians 5:9, Galatians 5:6, 22-26
101 David Sunde, "*Small-Batch Disciple Making: a rhythm for training the few to reach the many*", Navpress 2024, pg110-111

We need to work with that.

Having the right vision for learning and effectively communicating it will inspire hearts and minds. It will call forth focus and concentration for learning that produces real growth and discovery. Lord help us do this!

We should also harness modern methods and tools that foster and engage the whole person and various learning styles. Not only do we need vision and purpose, but also the right frameworks to effectively serve those in our trust. The rapid advancement of technology offers numerous possibilities that should be utilized where appropriate, while remaining sensitive to its liabilities of technology, especially in the formative years of children. The need for human connection is crucial and must be guarded. But in the same breath, we should understand that we are in a digital age and must embrace a digitally native generation that is changing the landscape of industries, education, economy, and the world itself.

For example, the concept of immersive learning theory and experiences is emerging on a global scale. Traditional classroom based learning techniques largely rely on auditory and written learning styles. Whether in an educational or work related training space, this has significant and widely recognized limitations. Every learner is unique in how they process and retain information. Providing engaging and interactive content offers a more inclusive and accessible learning experience. This is especially true for those that are predisposed to a visual and kinesthetic style of learning. Plus, people are hungry to press the bounds of what's possible and are seeking immersive experiences that engage all of their senses. If we can use that for good, it's my belief that we should.

Immersive learning is a hugely effective way for many learners to develop their knowledge, passion, and skills. New skills and techniques can be learned, viewed and perfected using augmented reality, artificial, digitally created content and environments that accurately replicate real life scenarios. Learners aren't simply passive spectators; they get to be active participants who directly influence outcomes. This is pretty wild and where things are moving in this generation and the next. Innovation is accelerating and is not slowing down anytime soon.

Consider things like virtual reality (VR) based learning that can provide a risk-free, safe space where learning can be repeated, customized, and success can be accurately measured. Think about flying a jet, preparing for skydiving, disarming a bomb, or architecting a bridge. In these scenarios, they use simulation before doing the real thing. It's practice-based learning where the sky is the limit. Students using VR can manipulate virtual objects, conduct virtual experiments, or solve interactive puzzles and more. And with AI integrations, personalized and adaptive learning only accelerates learning and engagement. It helps people learn 2.5 times faster than standard programs. This approach helps develop critical thinking skills, problem-solving abilities, and a deeper understanding of complex concepts. Plus, it's just fun!

Imagine teaching kids science, math, language, art, history, bible lessons, and more, with interactive and immersive games that also get their body moving while developing gross and fine motor skills too. Cool right? Also, social -emotional learning through play and fun has a great impact on kids and adults alike. We just have to get out of our boxes and inject the learning journey and discipleship process with fun and adventure that engages all of our senses.

With VR education and things like interactive projectors, students can visit historical sites, explore the depths of the ocean, travel to different countries, or even journey into space— from the comfort of home or in a gym, or a classroom at church, without breaking the bank.

We see malls, dentists, museums, amusement parks, arcades, special needs learning centers, airports, play places, restaurants, thousands of schools, learning apps, and more, integrating these technologies for both entertainment and education. The Church should be intentional to engage some of this and create these spaces and experiences as well, especially for the next generation.

We should not fear nor shy away from it, but should embrace aspects of this as a creative way to both reach people and develop those in our influence. The world is doing a great job at it and targeting our kids. We should also be pioneering and forerunning this, not lagging behind, to be able to keep a younger generation in meaningful connection to the faith and the community of believers. No, not by games and gimmicks, but by authenticity, relationships, passion, mission, and the power and love of God, while also harnessing creative means of development and Christ-centered education.

When we consider rethinking the wineskin, engaging creative ways of learning, training, and discipleship will help pull all the domains of life together in the context of community. Kids, youth, and young adults should be able to associate the Church as a place of belonging, relevance, fun, purpose, truth, etc.—a place they *want* to be, not a place they need to take a break from in order to have fun, focus on "real life," and learn the things that enable their lives to flourish.

So concerning technology, some people are enthusiastic about it, while some utterly reject it along with many technological advancements. We can balance the best of both worlds. It's simply important to know that this is the world we live in today and it's only accelerating. There's entire VR educational systems harnessing a classical educational approach that are producing quality outcomes with live teachers and students from around the globe.[102] I'm all for the old school analog approach—good old pen and paper. It's best for brain development and learning, but I hope you hear my heart about utilizing technological

---

[102] Optima Academy online based out of Naples FL, is using virtual reality and online learning platforms as a primary base of learning. Www.optimaacademy.online

advancements for good without becoming overly dependent upon them. Apostle Paul knew how to harness the things at his disposal in his day: his Roman citizenship, use of cultural poets on Mars Hill, eating with gentiles, debating with Jews, his vocational tool of tent making and so on. He was clear about "becoming all things to all men that he might win some."[103] If Paul was here today, I'm pretty sure he would harness the technologies useful for the mission to reach souls, connect with his churches, and have crucial conversations with his leaders across the world.

If you're open to this, getting to know the different types of technologies is the first crucial step for educators looking to embrace immersive experiences. If what I'm talking about is foreign to you, I would encourage you to do a little research.

However, actual experiential and project based learning opportunities, alongside loving mature believers such as farms, outreaches, team building, entrepreneurial projects and more, where concepts can be tested and real life encountered, *is key and should be the first option.*

Real people and *real* situations are better in most cases than technology-based learning, but there are benefits to technology that should be applied where appropriate.

In matters of faith, (prayer, sound doctrine, meditating on scripture, evangelism, leading bible studies, planting churches, and using spiritual gifts), you just have to get out there and do it to grow and learn. Then again, technology could be utilized here as well. People from all over the world can learn from each other and interact in things like Zoom rooms, chats, or other online private communities. I've personally led online groups of people from all over the world for bible study, classes, coaching, prayer, spiritual gift training, leadership and team development, and more. I prefer to stay deeply connected in personal settings with people for life on life training and discipleship,

---

[103] 1 Corinthians 9:19-23, Acts 17

but we have the capacity to continue to influence in a profound way through technology as well.

We need to have wisdom and discernment, holding fast to both the ancient paths and wisdom traditions as well as modern technologies and science to grow into where we need to be. The ways of the Lord do not change. The methods and mechanisms He uses to develop His people adapt for the unique time and season in which His people live.

We need to continue to evolve and effectively interface with the world we live in, while staying anchored to the Eternal Rock.

Experiential Learning

Consider and remember how Jesus taught and the type of learning environment He provided. It was immersive, experiential and definitely holistic.

You know as well as I know that information about something versus experiencing something, are worlds apart. The two dynamics can work together. But if I had to choose just one, I would want to experience the thing I'm trying to learn over just reading or hearing about it. I want to do more than read or listen, I need to see it, feel it, do it, experience it. The good thing is that often we can do both *(learn about it and experience it)*, and as leaders, we should seek to provide these opportunities for those we are teaching. Learning and doing, learning *by* doing. One experience is worth thousands of words on a page evaluated. Experience is transformational and a core source of true knowledge. *A leader's responsibility is to create a context or provide opportunity for experiences to happen.*

I mentioned Bloom's taxonomy of learning earlier. It classifies memorization as the base form of learning that progresses upward to understanding, applying, analyzing, evaluating, to creating. The process points to the internalization of truth or concepts. This happens through process, deep thought, practice, and more, typically harnessing forms and learning styles. When thinking about holistic education and connecting our learning to real life, we need to consider experiential learning as part of the "how" and "way" we learn.

So many forms of discipleship are academic alone, focused on the right knowledge without ongoing follow up, a relational context, evaluation, and outlets for application. *People are too quick to want to check the box of discipleship and fail to realize that it is ongoing, messy, and relational.*

Experiential learning and situational learning is about *learning by doing* in the actual context of what's being taught. This is more than listening to a lecture about something or how to do something, it's where the students learn through the experience of actually doing the task or project. The environment itself and learning experience is a key component we need to consider and, as I said, the responsibility for leaders to provide.

The four dimensions of psychologist David Kolb's Experiential Learning Taxonomy is a useful framework. It can help accelerate education, making it immersive and engaging, leading to internalization, wisdom, understanding, and personal impact. We learn things in the experience we would not learn otherwise or in other ways of learning alone (i.e. reading or listening to a lecture in isolation from the context or task).

Experience engages many aspects of who we are and our forms of learning and intelligence (visual, audio, kinesthetic, relational, intuition..etc). Combined with reflection and a continual process of application with new insights from our previous evaluated experience, it's powerful and accelerates learning.

Actual competency is developed when we are practicing and doing the things we are trying to learn. For example, we can teach people the nuances of prayer, fasting and discerning the voice of the Holy Spirit. But it is something that must be personally practiced and experienced to know, learn, and grow.

One of the discipleship tools I created called **"The *Core H.O.T (Habits of Transformation): Essential Practices of Authentic Discipleship,*"**[104] takes this approach through seven essential practices and has been very powerful in shaping people's lives and understanding. More curriculums and tools need to take this habit and practice based approach to learning and growth. Reach out if you'd like to get a hold of the *Core H.O.T workbook* as a discipleship tool.

Experiential learning can integrate various facets of equipping and personal development in the discipleship process too. Its the nature of apprenticeship:

- Modeling -(experience) character, conviction, grit, methods, application, nuance, presence etc.

- Teaching - (academic truth and information) concepts, academic, thinking, theory, truth, principles, etc.

- Training - (actual practice) habits, techniques, skills, practice, behaviors, conduct etc.

- Encouraging, Correcting, & Coaching - (affirmation) asking good questions, support, feedback, accountability, exhortation etc.

---

[104] This is meant to be rolled out in a small group experience where there is accountability, coaching, peer relationships, and over all socialized learning. You can pick up a copy here: www.raiseawarrior.com or coming soon on Amazon—See the graphic at the end of this book.

In brief, Kolb's taxonomy and learning theory is a cycle and he defines it as, "the process whereby knowledge is created through the transformation of experience." Consider these follow up questions we can ask ourselves or those that we are leading to foster transformative learning. Here it is:

1. Concrete Experience. Try something out and use your senses and feelings to see what happens.

    a. What did you do and what were the things you were actually doing?

2. Reflective Observation. Reflect on the experience.

    a. What went well? What was challenging? What surprised you?

3. Abstract Conceptualization. Compare and contrast the experience you had with existing knowledge. Did something change in your conceptualization of the topic based on the experience? Then try to come up with new hypotheses or questions based on your new knowledge.

    b. What lessons were learned? What new insights gained?

4. Active Experimentation. Come up with a new experiential or experience to test new hypotheses or explore new questions that arose during the cycle.

    c. How can you use those lessons to improve in future experience?

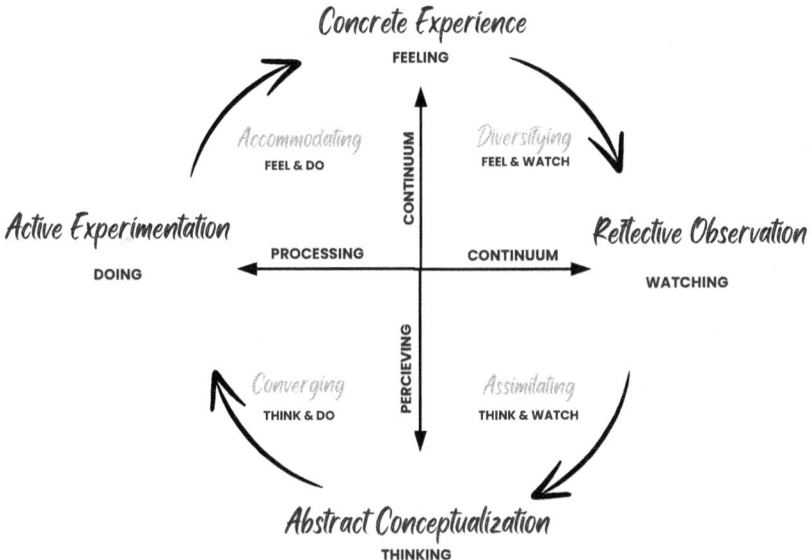

Experiential Learning - Kolb's Taxonomy

I recommend integrating this learning model with the succession framework I shared earlier and effectively passing something on, it's powerful. Our second-year interns compile monthly reflective reports on their ministry oversight areas. They use these questions as a framework to derive insights and plan future actions. In the military, they call it an "After Action Report" (AAR). The process of some rigorous analysis and meaningful reflection really does strengthen overall comprehension, readiness, and effectiveness.

It's the same with habit formation in people's lives. They need to take time to reflect on their experience of trying to practice something new, then let it help them continue to make data informed and outcome based decisions on what is working and not working. They need a system of feedback, measuring progress, and implementing lessons learned.

John Maxwell once said, "Experience is not our greatest teacher, evaluated experience is."

Here's a quick reminder of the other framework mentioned earlier:

- "I do it, you watch.—we talk

- I do it, you do it with me.—we talk

- You do it, I do it with you.—we talk

- You do it, I watch.—we talk

- You do it, another person watches to learn—we talk

- And the process continues…."

Read the reflections from some thought leaders, online educators, and human development entrepreneurs who are committed to experience oriented learning. These folks are focused on getting people results and understand that engagement from their clients/customers/students is key to getting real results. They are always looking for ways to better engage and keep their people engaged in the process that leads to breakthroughs, growth, and transformation.—According to Marisa Murgatroyd, Founder of "Live Your Message" and Creator of the "Experience Product Masterclass,"

> "A shift has been happening that the online business world has been slow to adopt.
>
> It's a shift that I've been shouting from the rooftops for years and something that completely transformed my business for the better…
>
> Experiences OVER information.
>
> And in 2023 *(and beyond)*, your customers will crave experience above all else (even above your price point!). So it's time to make the shift to creating experiences tailored to your customers… experiences that get them to take action and transform their lives in a meaningful way."

"Experience tailored to the customer" is very much like what we need in holistic education and discipleship. People are unique with different needs and callings. There are many factors for each stage of people's development and life circumstances that have to be taken into account if we want them truly engaged in a way that leads to transformation. Like parenting your kids, you love them all the same, they're all part of one household led underneath the same values and principles, but your training, discipline and engagement with each child is unique and custom, based on their personalities, motivations, gifts, unique struggles, etc.

When it comes to discipleship, many people are looking for fast and scaling approaches or a quick curriculum, 12-week program, or class. But quality and authentic discipleship is NOT that way. It is *ongoing, messy, and relational. If the goal is spiritual maturity in Christ, duplication too fast will lack the root system of character to sustain health and longevity. Without mature believers actively involved in shepherding these rapidly growing disciples, within a network of small groups or micro churches, there is a real risk of failure. People will fall away from the faith, be very unbalanced in the practice of their faith, and or eventually disconnect from the community altogether.*

Enjoying the Journey, Forming Habits

«*More important than the curriculum is the question of the methods of teaching and the spirit in which the teaching is given*» —Bertrand Russell (2014). "On Education", p.181, Routledge.

Neuroscience, positive psychology, behavior change and similar things harness the power of the brain, gamification, and dopamine triggers for the pleasure reward experience to fuel the consistent action necessary for change to happen. This reinforces the habits and practices that lead to growth, learning, and transformation.

The process of growth is difficult by itself, so well designed pathways that keep people focused, self initiating, and energized to keep moving forward should be deeply considered. We can enjoy the journey and create enjoyable systems of growth for our lives and those we serve. Discipline doesn't have to be drudgery. Many of us need to learn how. Number one, we trust the Holy Spirit to produce desire and love for God and growth in our hearts. But we should learn to create and curate educational processes that trigger students' and our own motivations and interests. Without vision we perish and cast off restraint. This will help them (and us) keep going and keep implementing the things that are moving life, growth, and education forward. We need to know what makes us tick and harness that. It's not always a matter of just being lazy and needing to work or try harder; people need to learn to work smarter. We live in an age of distraction, so implementing what triggers desire and enthusiasm to fuel discipline is a good thing that should be leveraged. Discipline can become a delight when we stay connected to purpose and mission. But O *we have to learn how to trigger people's internal motivations with vision, challenge, and opportunities.*

We can all agree that consistency and discipline are needed for anything valuable in life, especially when it comes to growth, learning, and obedience to God. Being consistent and disciplined is hinged to our relationship with those we are teaching and to the sense of connection with others on the journey. Remember, meaningful relationships are key to life and key to produce change in our life. When people are learning and growing together, having fun and struggling together, a special bond of friendship is made. That fellowship and shared bond gives oil and joy to the journey and motivation for growth. Shared experienced and positive peer pressure is so powerful. But there are things that can be done to enhance the process as well. So how can we best impart and stimulate desire to cultivate such habits of the soul for learning and growth?

Sometimes it's just a simple reflective question, pointing people towards the Lord and giving room for the Holy Spirit to speak. Sometimes it's reminding people why they are doing this in the first place so they reconnect to their vision and purpose. Sometimes its a firm challenge, and other times, it's a matter of clarity on their next steps, or it may be identifying a reward and incentive for some desired outcome. But here's the thing, like all habit formation, it takes consistency. You may say, "of course." But the real question for many struggling or trying to help someone is, "how do I become consistent?" Or "how do we help them become consistent?" This is where we can grow in our own lives and as discipleship practitioners.

For one, we need to stay connected deep enough to people in the journey and operate in a framework that allows for follow up and followthrough. You may just call this relational accountability, but so many fall through the gaps here in the context of the local church.

Secondly, it's safe to say that most people want to be consistent (unless they are ambivalent for reasons which may provide valuable information for dialogue, and coaching). But they desire to be consistent to reach their goals and grow. But how?

One powerful approach I found in effectively creating change is mapping out a clear path forward in how to do or become the "thing" through the *GSPA* process and *reverse engineering*.

- G is for goals
- S is for skills
- P is for practices, and
- A is for actions

Together, these things create a system and process of continuous growth. Goals alone are not useful except to set a direction. How to get there and actually achieve the goal becomes the holistic process for change. We help by creating a pathway and system in collaboration *with them* by identifying first, a specific goal. Every goal has corresponding skills that need to be developed to reach that goal. We help students think through the skills that would need to be developed in order to reach their goal. Every skill has associated practices to develop that skill that increase the possibility of reaching their goal. In every core practice for skill development, a specific action or behavior is needed, the thing they're actually going to commit to do daily. We help them make their selection and identify the right action they are *ready, willing, and able* to do with executable confidence. They need to feel good about being able to take action on what they've decided for it to be successful. People need small wins and need to learn to embrace small progress and not try to be perfect and learn all the skills at once. Many people really struggle with the "all or nothing mentality" and have a hard time with a growth mindset that embraces small incremental changes.

Lack of clarity of *how to* make changes is where most people stumble in conjunction with lack of support and accountability. But once we do that, results come and progress is made. Small wins matter. Another helpful dynamic that triggers motivation and fosters real change is to choose a cue or trigger to remind them to do their intended action. Next, choose or plan a *meaningful* reward or positive association with that practice to anchor the desired behavior in their life until it becomes part of their normal routine. Some people may know this as the "habit loop."

Said another way, in terms of making change easier, James Clear, in his popular book, *Atomic Habits.*[105] talks about four laws of behavior change that are a simple set of rules we can use to build better habits. They are (1) make it obvious, (2) make it attractive, (3) make it easy, and (4) make it satisfying."

- Make it OBVIOUS: Don't hide the books you need to read or the fruit you want to eat, display them to remind yourself to form new habits.

- Make it ATTRACTIVE: Read the books you like to read, and it'll encourage you to read more.

- Make it EASY: If you want to eat more fruit, eat the fruits that are easy to eat.

---

105 James clear, "*Atomic Habits: An easy & proven way to build good habits and break bad ones.*" Random house business publishing, 2018

- Make it SATISFYING: If you are satisfied, you will want more.

If we apply this to all good habits, and do the opposite for bad habits(make them invisible, unattractive, difficult and unsatisfying), we will make progress faster and possible.

See the image below illustrating the GSPA and habit loop—This is about creating a clear path to win.

Holistic Education & Making disciples

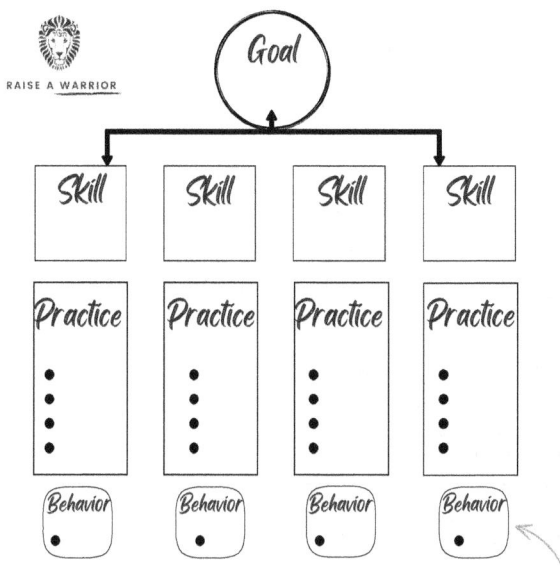

Identify 1 behavior to daily practice with in a key skill that supports the big picture goal - Its about daily progress NOT perfection

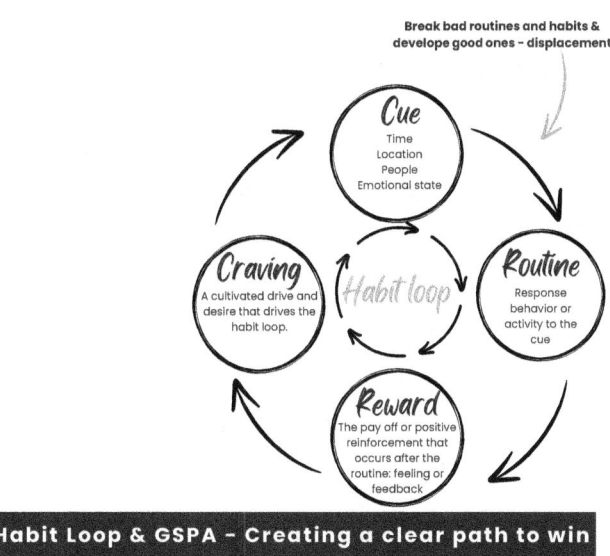

Break bad routines and habits & develope good ones - displacement

Habit Loop & GSPA - Creating a clear path to win

Change that lasts requires small incremental improvements that are built into a way of life- a rule of life. We have to think and practice in a way that is sustainable. Helping people adapt and think on a continuum, so that they can prioritize and make good decisions to move their life forward, will keep them from getting stuck and feeling powerless. Breaking goals down into skills, practices, and actions they can do daily, is very empowering. At the end of the day if people can focus on the one thing that is meaningful and going to move them forward, that is the thing we want to help them do and celebrate.

I do this with folks adjusting their health and wellness habits and with people looking to develop a devotional life in God too. Consistency is about what we regularly do. It's what we regularly do that determines where we go and what we will become in life. *The key is to make the practices as small and manageable as possible to achieve success.* Whenever possible, help people learn how to make it fun.

Every action has a result. By helping people gain self-awareness and guiding them through the change process—reflecting on the effects and outcomes of their decisions and behaviors—we can accelerate breakthroughs, progress, and transformation. The habit loop is like a feedback loop that we need to key into. If the feedback or outcomes from our actions doesn't move us toward where we want to go, then we need to adjust and try again and again. Sometimes it's micro adjustments and other times it's macro adjustments, but nonetheless, we have to be intentional to keep progressing and learning.

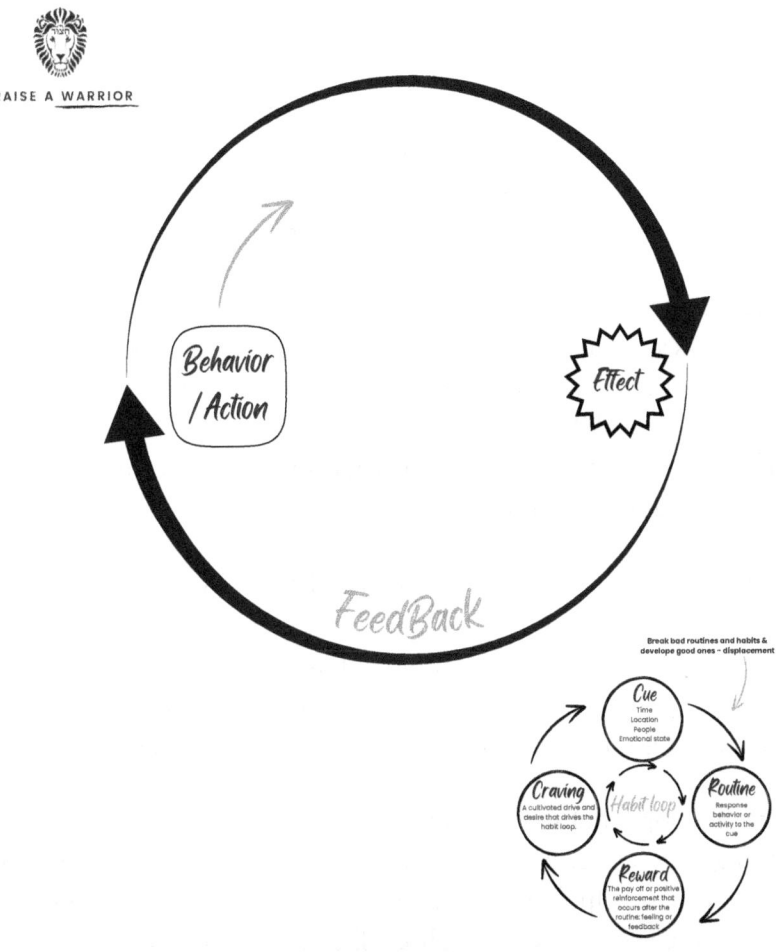

key for making outcome based decisions and growing in self awareness so that intentional growth and improvement happens as part of their life and process.

- Mentors, pastors, parents, and coaches can provide feedback and reflective dialog.
- And mentee, student, child..etc can use this as an internal system.

Feedback Loop

Capacity grows and momentum builds when people can see some progress and have victory in the small practices they've chosen. Those "wins" are fuel to keep going and trigger motivation. Enough conscious practice eventually develops unconscious habits and routines that feel effortless and lead to lasting change. A new norm is created. The things that were once seemingly impossible or difficult to do become effortlessly embraced, and part of a new way of life. As the saying goes, "a journey of 1,000 miles starts with a single step."

In learning to even take that "single step" on the journey, we may personally experience and will need to help encourage people through the experience of feeling awkward. As we start small in forming new habits and skills, transforming principles in to skillful practice, awkward growth is normal growth. All learning of new things can feel weird and vulnerable and unknown.

As you practice and use things like the GSPA process, we pass through phases of comprehension and competence and progress into proficiency and mastery, if we keep with it. That's one reason why it's so important to stick with the process, embrace discipline, and learn to make it enjoyable. If you give up you don't get the reward.

As we develop a holistic and strategic approach to education and the learning experience, it's crucial to incorporate key touch points and practices that: help foster engagement, make the journey enjoyable, encourage perseverance through challenges, facilitate discovery, and develop necessary skills and capabilities forged through the repetition, practice, and study.

Some have described these phases of progression in competence and ability as: *unconscious incompetence, conscious incompetence, conscious competence, and unconscious competence:*

- ***Unconscious Incompetence****:* We don't know what we don't know. We do not understand or know how to do something.

We are unaware of the skill itself and unable to perform it. We don't even recognize that the deficit is nonexistent. We are blind and don't know we are blind.

- ***Conscious incompetence:*** We recognize and value the new skill we want to learn but are incapable of doing it. We begin trying to learn but its messy, hard, awkward, and uncoordinated. Its a normal part of the process of learning something new. We are blind and we know we are blind, but we are trying to see.

- ***Conscious Competence:*** We understand and know how to perform the new thing. However, doing the thing may necessitate breaking it down into steps and still requires intense concentration. We can see and are growing in our scope of perception, but are still consciously aware of the effort it takes to keep our eyes open to be aware of our surroundings.

- ***Unconscious Competence:*** We have had so much practice with the thing that it has become "second nature" and can be performed easily and effortlessly, even while executing other tasks. We may be able to teach it to others too. We see and perceive our surroundings and are able to take action on other things based on the subconscious analysis of our perception. We could teach others about situational awareness, perceived threats, opportunities, and exit plans in any given situation. We were blind but now we see.

The Lord's intention for all of us, regardless of the struggle and trials we face, is to learn to walk in the joy that is inexpressible and full of glory (1 Peter 1:6-9, 4:12-13). Joy is strength and transmutes our trials. Embracing necessary hardship is part of a victorious paradigm that rests in the intention of God to use all things for our good, development, and growth. Such faith and assurance is key to abiding in a state of joy and peace throughout the awkward process of learning.

The struggle of growth, and every circumstance of our life can and should become a cause of rejoicing and what the Bible calls pure joy (James 1). We can have God's Joy that is deeply rooted in both His nature and the hope of what He is producing in us. We are the children of God, loved and accepted, holy and chosen, and yet continually growing in grace and the knowledge of God. In our weakness He still delights in us, and we are loved apart from our performance, praise God! So we can learn and fail and stumble and not get it right, and rest assured that God still rejoices over us and is committed to our growth. This is not a heavy burden. In him there is no condemnation! I say this because the majority of people partner with the accuser and are overly critical of themselves and self condemning. The good news and joy of the gospel MUST FRAME OUR LEARNING APPROACH.

In our journey of sanctification in this age, God is producing in us, in and through all things, the glory of His Son and eternal reward. Hope does not disappoint when it's anchored in the truth of God's nature and intention for our lives.

We can enjoy the journey and rest assured that we are in Christ becoming like Christ. As we develop holistic pathways of growth and development, in partnership with the Spirit of God, we can be intentional to infuse the road of habit formation with joy, reward, and celebration of progress.

Curiosity

Repetition is the mother of mastery but it is also the father of boredom. Thus we need to curate creative ways to reinforce lessons or create a space to stir intellectual curiosity and personal discovery. Self-discovered truth is what is actually transformational. Both personal experience and studies show that when people realize something themselves, it's a game changer and it sticks forever. This is true in learning and discipleship, just as it is true in evangelism and winning the lost. People need to be invested and personally own the truth for it to be transformative. In the same way, studies reveal that learning in a meaningful context is far superior to learning things that are just theoretical and disconnected from what is being taught. Learning must stay relevantly connected to the life, mission, and vision of the student. This tells us something important that we need to keep in mind to fuel curiosity and growth; A focus on purpose and vision is essential as we teach and as we learn. As discussed previously, in regards to functions of leadership, we always need to be reconnected to the "why" of what we are learning.

Research shows that when people simply learn with the goal of doing well on a test, their learning is superficial and quickly forgotten. The bigger picture is lost and true learning hasn't happened. So we have to keep the heart and goal of learning in mind if we want to be effective. We can cultivate opportunities and environments for the flame of intelligence (revelation) to be ignited and a culture of growth that is enthusiastic and celebrated, where learning and progress is both affirmed and desired.

"You can teach a student a lesson for a day; but if you can teach him to learn by creating curiosity, he will continue the learning process as long as he lives." ~ Clay P. Bedford

And that's what we want, curiosity and personal interest is a driver for learning and growth for all ages. Let's not squash that in our lives and in our kids nor in the lives of those we influence. We need to honor people's journey of discovery and respect their unique learning styles while encouraging them to align their learning habits with their strengths and intelligence.

People have to be engaged in the process of learning or it won't stick and true learning won't happen. Passive listening to lectures alone and theory without practice becomes irrelevant and doesn't touch the lives of the learner. It would be like trying to become a disciple of Christ without a commitment to obedience to His commands and ways. It just doesn't work.

How do you need to rethink your wineskin of learning, teaching, and training?

In the next chapter will talk about the integration and anchor of a biblical worldview as essential to produce the outcomes we are called to bear in the grace and knowledge of God.

PAUSE. CAPTURE. APPLY
Prompts to help you process

1. What specific insights or concepts from this chapter resonated with you the most? Why do you think these stood out to you?

_____

_____

_____

2. How can you practically apply the principles discussed in this chapter to your daily life, relationships, or ministry? Identify at least one actionable step you can take this week.

_____

_____

_____

3. What potential challenges or barriers might you face in implementing these concepts? How can you overcome them?

_____

_____

_____

4. What are 3-5 quotes or points from this chapter that capture the essence of what it's communicating? Write them down.

_____

_____

_____

_____

_____

5. How can you involve your family, small group, or church community in the practices and principles outlined in this chapter? What steps can you take to foster a culture of discipleship and transformation within your circle of influence?

_____

_____

_____

6. Spend a few moments in prayer, asking God for the wisdom, strength, and courage to live out the truths you've learned. Write down a commitment or a prayer that reflects your desire to grow as an authentic disciple and transformational leader to impact the world.

_____

_____

_____

CHAPTER 13

Curriculums of Transformation

"The aim of Christian education is not to produce learned men, but to produce saints."

— A.W. TOZER

"The goal of discipleship is not to inform but to transform."

— DALLAS WILLARD

Anchoring Holistic Education To A Biblical Worldview

Noah Webster (1758 – 1843), a lexicographer and a language reformer, is often called the Father of American Scholarship and Education. In his lifetime he was also a lawyer, schoolmaster, author, newspaper editor and an outspoken politician. The man knew 26 languages! He famously said, "Education is useless without the Bible. The Bible was America's basic text book in all fields. God's Word, contained in the Bible, has furnished all necessary rules to direct our conduct.... Education in a nation will propagate the religion of that nation. In America, the foundational religion was Christianity. And it was sown in the hearts of Americans through the home and private and public schools for centuries. Our liberty, growth, and prosperity was the result of a Biblical philosophy of life. Our continued freedom and success is dependent on our educating the youth of America in the principles of Christianity."[106]

What an amazing quote!

The main thing has to stay the main thing. We have to keep the big picture continually before us. Our training and educational aims must be unto the first and greatest commandment: to love the Lord with all that we are. Added to that should be obedience to Christ to love others in the way He has loved us, and to the great commission to make disciples. Otherwise, we are out of alignment and doing a disservice to those we are leading. All things must start from and be shaped around being disciples of Christ who are radical and authentic in devotion to Him. Disciples live for God's will and not their own. They're oriented around growing in the intimate and experiential knowledge of God, with an emphasis on being conformed to His image. Sound education and authentic discipleship focuses on obedience to the truth, and to Christ, and bearing the fruit of the Spirit.

Education that leads to eternal fruit, will be balanced and produce the desired outcomes through knowing goals(knowledge), being goals (character), and doing goals (skills & abilities). Anything eternal starts from this, and if we are not leading others into this place of relationship with God and obedience to Him first as a primary motivation, we are missing it. As Apostle Paul said, " we make it or aim to present every person complete in Christ " Col 1:28.

Our curriculum is the vehicle to get us there.

In general education, we must seek the Kingdom of God first and His righteousness, then everything else comes out of this. This is

---

[106] https://webstersdictionary1828.com/Quotes

not allocated to just a religious realm. The dichotomy of secular and sacred does not exist, for the earth is the Lord's and everything in it. Academic rudimentary disciplines apart from a biblical worldview are an injustice, leading to the perpetuation of isolated, irrelevant faith that does not impact the world. We must break away from the compartmentalization of life and faith that has kept us in spiritual immaturity and impotency. The people have been lied to when it comes to understanding the role of the faith and the scriptures in founding a just and free society. The body of Christ should have a voice in culture as she is the pillar and foundation of the truth. The people of God are called to be the prophetic conscious of the nation as well as in their local communities. We are called to go into all the *world*, that is the greek word "Kosmos"—κόσμος, ου, ὁ- for world systems, worldly affairs, the world order.[107] We are to influence the world's systems and institutions with the word and ways of God, and to raise up believers, who like Daniel and others, excel in their craft and glorify God through their vocations.[108] Win souls and bless the world.

If maturity in Christ is the goal, we have to design an integrated curriculum and approach that considers the tapestry of life in all its roles and stages. In this way we will develop healthy people and avoid the trappings that are so prevalent in culture. Remember, *maturity in Christ demonstrates godliness in our character, dependence on Christ, and skillful living according to the word of God that gets expressed in love for God and others in well ordered lives with a missional fervor to impact the world.*

The very call to maturity speaks of the nature of progression and development. We don't get born again and then suddenly arrive into

---

107 Mark 16:15, Strong's Concordance—2889 kósmos (literally, "something ordered") – properly, an "ordered system" (like the universe, creation); the world.
108 People may categorize the spheres of cultural influence in different ways but here are some major players to consider: Church/Religion, Business, Education, Media, Government, Family & Social affairs, Sports and Entertainment, Medical… where are you called to influence?l

a place of maturity. We continually grow and blossom in the grace and knowledge of God at every level. We grow from glory to glory, strength to strength, faith to faith (2 Cor 3:18.)[109] As we consistently apply ourselves to the truth in a relational context with God and others, we are transformed by the renewing of our mind.

Peter Scazzerio says it this way, "An emotionally healthy disciple slows down to be *with* Jesus, goes beneath the surface of their life to be deeply transformed *by* Jesus, and offers their life as a gift to the world *for* Jesus.

An emotionally healthy disciple rejects busyness and hurry to reorient their entire life around their personal relationship with Jesus, developing rhythms, setting limits, and following Him wherever He leads. At the same time, they intentionally open the depths of their interior life—their history, disorientations, areas of brokenness, and their relationships—to be changed by Jesus. They are deeply aware that everything they have and all they are is a gift. So they carry a profound awareness of stewarding their talents as a gift to bless the world for Jesus."[110]

Just as there is a natural progression in our biological age, so there are also progressions in our spiritual age. The two (spiritual & biological maturity) are not the same but could correlate in many cases if we start well in our homes with our kids with intentional discipleship. But the great tragedy of people 30 years in the Lord who still act and think like spiritual infants is unacceptable and must stop.

---

109 2 Peter 1, Mark 4:26-33 -We see the nature of growth in the Kingdom of God that starts small and progresses. We have to add to our faith virtue, grit and perseverance, knowledge, brotherly kindness, and ultimately love. In reference to grain the lord illustrates the progression: the seed, stalk, head, then the full kernel head.
110 Peter Scazzero, "Emotionally healthy discipleship : moving from shallow Christianity to deep transformation." Grand Rapids : Zondervan, 2021. Pg 26

Biblical discipleship with curated curriculum and holistic methods is part of that solution.

The call to evangelism and discipleship goes far beyond just sharing the gospel message, saying a prayer, winning a convert, and doing a 12-week class to teach basic doctrine. Teaching doctrinal truth and teaching for obedience are two worlds apart. We need to design our discipleship curricula in alignment with the stages of development and maturity in a spiritual and natural sense. The scriptures and early church history attests to the fact that there are first principles to the faith to be learned, understood, and lived into before moving onto more advanced concepts and truths. We should respond to this and establish learning paths in the proper order alongside the natural, developmental, and biblical learning trajectory. Milk before meat. It's an important factor to healthy growth and solid foundations.

As a martial arts instructor, it would be wrong to apply black belt thinking and maturity to a white belt (beginner) and expect them to get advanced concepts and be able to demonstrate advanced competencies. In the same way, it would be foolish to be frustrated with a new Christian who is immature, unrefined, and clearly not grasping all that Christ has made available to them or requires of them. It would be wrong to teach new believers things like Christ's eternal priesthood according to the order of Melchizedek. They don't necessarily need to know that *yet*. They need to obey foundational truths first, such as forgiving others, loving their enemies, rejoicing always, and forsaking sexual immorality. As the scripture says, as newborn babies they need to long for the "pure milk" of the word that they would grow in respect to salvation.[111] Meat is for the mature; those well practiced and developed in the foundational truths of the word.

---

111 1 Peter 2:2, Hebrews 5:12-14

There is a time, place and procedure for everything under heaven. We need to think strategically and purposefully in this way. It's wisdom. The right things, in the right way, and in the right order. This is how we build a house that lasts. *Yes, discipleship and teachable moments happen along the way and in every day of our lives through all kinds of things, and of which we should be sensitive to leverage. But in collaboration and in an overall strategy to build a solid foundation for the believer, the elementary principles of Christ should be taught, studied, and practiced first.*

Curriculums that transform start with the end in mind, and understand the necessity of firm foundations. It's the elementary principles of Christ that shape our worldview and give us a baseline of biblical discernment and thinking by which we can go on to know the will of God in any given situation and bear fruit in it.

Traditions of Wisdom

Now, let's look at the wisdom traditions of the past in relation to our holistic education approach. They understood and identified the essential things that needed to be learned at each stage of life. These wisdom traditions look at the full scope of a person's life and have been used for centuries, guiding for instance, the practices of the Jewish people.

Due to the breakdown of family, Western individualism, and many other things, we have sabotaged the harmony, connectedness, and rhythm of life that the ancients had passed down. Western over-compartmentalization and drive to achieve has made the soul sick and confused the mind from attaining wisdom. People are too busy to be still, reflect, and listen for the voice of the Holy Spirit. People just don't know how to do life anymore and it's only more difficult due to technology.

The Jewish people built their education strategies from the developmental frameworks and stages of life articulated throughout the wisdom literature of scripture and the Talmud, completed around 400 AD, in "sayings of the fathers" and their concepts of the "ages of man." In his book, "The Seasons of a Man's Life," Daniel Levinson unearths three ancient life development examples from three wisdom traditions: Greek, Chinese, and Hebrew.[112]

---

112 Daniel J. Levinson, The Seasons of a Man's Life (New York: Ballantine Books, 1978), excerpts from pp. 324–326.

Greek Tradition	Chinese Tradition	Hebrew Tradition
In the 7th century B.C., Solon, a Greek poet and lawmaker, set forth a life development example built around a model of ten stages, each seven years in length. 0–7 A boy at first is the man; unripe; then he casts his teeth; milk-teeth befitting the child he sheds in his seventh year. 7–14 Then to his seven years God adding another seven, signs of approaching manhood show in the bud.	Confucius, writing about 500 B.C., identifies six stages in the life-development process that match very closely with contemporary life-span research. The Master said, at 15 I set my heart upon learning. At 30, I had planted my feet firmly upon the ground. At 40, I no longer suffered from perplexities. At 50, I knew what were the biddings of heaven.	From the Talmud, finalized around 400 A.D., in "The Sayings of the Fathers," it talks of "the ages of man." 5 years is the age for reading (Scripture); 10 for Misnah (the laws); 13 for the Commandments (Bar Mitzvah, moral responsibility); 15 for Gemara (Talmudic discussions; abstract reasoning); 18 for Hupa (wedding canopy);

14–21 Still, in the third of the sevens his limbs are growing; his chin touched with a fleecy down, the bloom of the cheek gone. 21–28 Now, in the fourth of the sevens ripen to greatest completeness the powers of the man, and his worth becomes plain to see. 28–35 In the fifth he bethinks him that this is the season for court-ing, bethinks him that sons will preserve and continue his line. 35–42 Now in the sixth his mind, ever open to virtue, broadens, and never inspires him to profitless deeds.	At 60, I heard them with docile ear. At 70, I could follow the dictates of my own heart; for what I desired no longer overstepped the boundaries of right.	20 for seeking a livelihood (pursuing an occupation); 30 for attaining full strength ("Koah"); 40 for understanding; 50 for giving counsel; 60 for becoming an elder (wisdom, old age); 70 for white hair; 80 for Gevurah (new, special strength of age); 90 for being bent under the weight of the years; 100 for being as if already dead and passed away from the world

42–56 Seven times seven, and eight; the tongue and the mind for fourteen years together are now at their best. 56–63 Still in the ninth is he able, but never so nimble in speech and in wit as he was in the days of his prime. 63–70 Who to the tenth has attained, and has lived to complete it, has come to the time to depart on the ebb-tide of Death.		

More contemporary voices like Steven Covey, Robert Clinton, John Elderage, and many more speak to the stages of life cycle development, the typical psychological questions being answered, and behavioral transitions in particular stages of life. These key development patterns give great insight into how one might design curriculum and pathways of discipleship.

The wisdom traditions and literature, such as the book of Proverbs, were a way to unpack an ordered worldview. They outlined sound foundations laid from youth in the fear of the Lord, the love of God, morality, work ethic, people skills, and more.

The main Hebrew word for wisdom is "chokmah." This literally means skill in living. Some commentaries connect it to a picture of a prophet up upon a mountain peering into the heavens, discerning the movements of God and coming to understand how to regulate his life in light of that. This is a picture of all aspects of life coming into alignment with the revealed will of God: Decision making, lifelong learning, character, life planning, family life, work, health, community life, finances, education, etc. All of life must be lived in a way that pleases and glorifies God. This is part of what it means to "seek first the Kingdom of God and His righteousness….and everything else will be given to you." (Matthew 6:33 paraphrased).

Wisdom traditions embraced life in seasons and rhythms that gave life balance and harmony rooted in community and family life. Take for instance the Jewish feast days that the Lord had commanded, the weekly sabbath, and the jubilee years. They contributed to a way of life that fosters rest, worship, productivity, abundance, community welfare, and a missional witness to the wisdom and ways of God. I'm not saying we are obligated to keep the Jewish feasts, but I am saying they point to a pattern and rhythm of life that cultivated spiritual vibrancy, health, wealth, and multigenerational continuity.

In considering discipleship as a multidimensional and holistic approach to lifelong development, we recognize four core and interrelated parts that continually evolve. They must be taught, coached, and nurtured for the Christian to reach maturity:

- Individual core identity, character, knowledge, and work ethic

- Family roles and values

- Their role in the church and local community

- Their role, call, and contribution to the Global community (world)

    - It's important to note that people need to be able to see what they do in life is connected to the bigger picture of humanity and the fabric of society

Where I live, we work with all our leaders, interns and youth to create personal development plans, what I call *"Legacy Battle Plans"* that include these four core elements. It's part of the pathway of growth and discipleship in our community. As leaders, we always review these plans with them as we assess where they are, present focus in life, and what they feel is next. Our holistic approach aims at maturity as we help them customize and design their own personal curriculum of growth and development.

The Breakthrough course I mentioned earlier walks you through this powerful process to come up with a comprehensive, prayerful life strategy of discerning and living into your God given purpose. Make sure to pick it up with your 75% discount with this code **"BOOKBONUS75XP"** at https://www.forerunnerfitness.net/breakthroughxp or by using the QR code below.

CLAIM YOUR 75% OFF CODE:

"BOOKBONUS75XP"

YOUR STRATEGIC PATH TO BREAKTHROUGH, CLARITY, AND ABUNDANT LIFE!

Discover your unique God given purpose, breakthrough your barriers, craft a strategic and prayer plan with a rule of life that leads to fruitfulness and fulfillment. Leave a transformational legacy!

FORERUNNERFITNESS.NET/BREAKTHROUGHXP

FORERUNNER FITNESS

Most churches don't have an intentional discipleship process to train their people, but there is a major global shift moving towards discipleship training. At the time of this writing, I've been working with a network of leaders around New England to help churches start embracing discipleship in a more biblical and effective way. This is a must if we are serious about obeying the Lord to finish the task of the great commission. Becoming effective fishers of men and discipleship practitioners is imperative. As we talked about earlier, this requires a paradigm and culture shift in the life of the church.

The Church

When we consider the state of the church and its role to change the world by making disciples, we see approaches and methodologies that are not producing the fruit of authentic followers of Christ. One of the main problems is that the goal and desired outcome has not been properly defined nor the corresponding way to "get there."

You may say, "the goal is simple—know Jesus, become like Him, and make Him known….bring heaven to earth." But many stop there without thinking through those implications and the deeper, practical work around it. Concepts and catchy statements don't translate into effective practice for many. Daily, weekly, monthly, and yearly life rhythms and habits have to shift.

The path for training and equipping is hinged upon the main goal or central vision. If there is no clarity of terms or goals, and how it should look, then energy is spent on random ministry activities and programs that are not focused on the primary things. A mark not defined is a mark missed. The lack of Christian maturity and community impact validates that what churches are trying to implement, the tools they are using, or *how* they are using them, are ineffective and must shift.

Part of the core issue is that the paradigms that undergird and fuel the practices are not compatible and cause the strategy and implementation of tools to be shallow and short lived. Why and *how* we do things matter.

We have to begin with the end in mind. Our plan, curriculum, or path to get to where we want to go is critical for lasting fruit. That's why we must take a holistic approach and integrate knowing goals (knowledge), being goals (character), and doing goals (skills and abilities) that are situated within the life and mission of the church. We need to think about creating a context, a laboratory if you will, for the sake of experiential, practice, and project-based learning. Mentoring and apprenticeships are so valuable where there is hands-on learning and opportunities for application. Youth, young adults and even those who need to rebuild their lives and learn life skills they were never taught need these opportunities. The church and local community is a massive resource we need to engage while having people deeply connected in supportive and shepherding type relationships.

Making disciples considers all the domains of life that need to be nurtured, trained, and brought into God's purpose and plan for that individual or family. Plus, the Church is a family which means, as we have shared, that this thing called discipleship is a relational process, not a mechanical production. It requires a lot of customization as we walk with people and households to get established in the faith, stable in life, and come to maturity in Christ. Moreover, it's essential that we rely on the Holy Spirit, trusting on His power and presence, to encounter people and do only what He can do in their hearts and lives. That's the secret sauce. We can have a great process but without the power of God, we can only go so far. We have to continually welcome and acknowledge the Holy Spirit and the dynamic operations of His grace.

We can either have an overarching strategic and intentional process, reliant on the Spirit's work that is moving people along a path to maturity, with necessary assessment along the way. Or we can choose cookie cutter programs, plug in tools, and fragmented curriculums, which will only produce short lived or superficial results at best.

Consider this framework as a principle-based approach you can customize for your life and those you intend to disciple, from your children to your leadership team.[113] This framework can be applied to every level of maturity when done in the right spirit in a relational approach.

---

[113] Adaptation is necessary for little children in the learning process, but application of knowing, being, and doing goals still apply. Knowing what children need to be learning at each developmental stage is important to building solid foundations spiritually, emotionally, socially, intellectually, and physically.

CURRICULUMS OF TRANSFORMATION

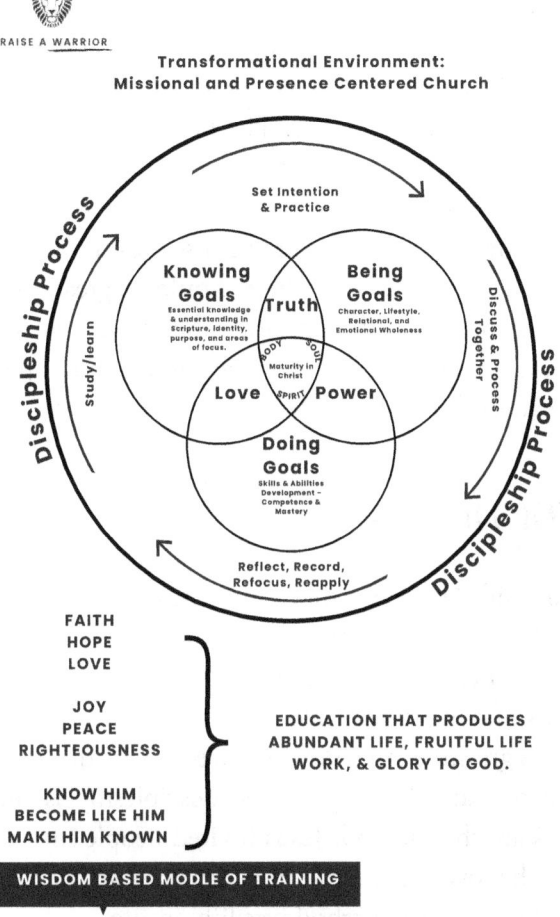

The Western church has outsourced their theological education, neglecting to train up competent leaders within their own communities in the context of the needs of the local church. Discipleship has been reduced to a class, SOAP bible studies, and attending services. Those zealous people who have a passion for the mission and deeper formation rarely see an outlet for training in their local context and get shipped out to a parachurch organization or seminary for training. This shouldn't be! *The first place of training should be the local church.* We need to get back to biblical discipleship and the models we see with Paul and Timothy, Christ and His disciples, and the pattern of the early Church as seen in Acts 2:40-47. *Local churches should be disciple-making and church multiplying missional communities and serve as a greenhouse for training, transformation, and the sending of laborers into the harvest to plant new works.* The relational environment of the church should be such that hearts are burning hot with passion for Jesus. It should be where the power of the Holy Spirit is manifested in the gifts of the Spirit through active disciples serving in their God given graces and capacities. And there should be great joy there in the fellowship of knowing God alongside other believers. Abundant life really is abundant and is a felt experience of life and hope even in the pains and deaths of growth.

Method Of The Master

Jim Putnam said, "I believe that most Christians have divorced the teachings of Jesus from the methods of Jesus, and yet they expect the results of Jesus." I think his methods are just as divine as his teachings. He showed us that the fundamental methodology in making disciples is relationships grounded in truth and love. Jesus is the greatest disciple maker in history, and his way works. Discipleship is the emphasis. Relationships are the method. Jesus invited people into relationships with himself; he loved them and in the process showed them how to follow God. His primary method was life-on-life.

The method Jesus used with his disciples was the same method that the Old Testament advocated for parents to disciple their children. Deuteronomy 6:5–9 states it succinctly: "You shall love the LORD your God with all your heart and with all your soul and with all your might. And these words that I command you today shall be in your heart. You shall teach them diligently to your children, and shall talk of them when you sit in your house, and when you walk by the way, and when you lie down, and when you rise. You shall bind them as a sign on your hand, and they shall be as frontlets between your eyes.

You shall write them on the doorposts of your house and on your gates" (ESV). Parents were to equip their children to love and obey God. The method was relationship ("when you sit in your house," "when you walk by the way," and "when you lie down"). And the whole process was discipleship, or in today's language, apprenticeship. It is spiritual parenting."[114]

So you can see that this call to raise up the next generation is critical. This paradigm of discipleship should permeate our existence as believers and define the culture of our church communities. It should touch how we raise our kids, how we reach the world around us in our everyday lives, and how we prioritize our time. It should drive our understanding of effective ministry in the life of the church.

The book "DiscipleShift" describes the problem and present context of many church cultures. It outlines four broad stroke models of church they see at play. Each one by itself is incomplete to meet God's design for the Church as it relates to discipleship:

- The educational approach- with a methodology of classroom and lecture to establish people in biblical truth.

- The attractional model- with outreach and entertainment as a method to win the lost.

- The missional model- with community involvement, social justice, and service oriented outreach.

- The organic "house" model with a methodology of fellowship and relationship focus, of " doing life together."

The author goes on to say,

---

[114] DiscipleShift, pg 32-33

"None are intrinsically wrong, and leaders of each model can use proof texts to create biblical reasons for what they do. Plus, there are pockets of effectiveness in each model — even tremendous effectiveness for a period of time. But there are also tremendous challenges with each. Again, we must ask if any of these models are truly succeeding. Are people being transformed from spiritual immaturity to maturity, and are they following Jesus in regular, lasting, and effective ways? The answer, according to the statistics we referred to earlier, is sometimes yes and sometimes no. But mostly, unfortunately, no. The common element in the four categories of churches is that the models are incomplete. The focus and the methodologies are improperly placed, in such a way that there are missing components that leave the church one-dimensional, when it was meant to be complete. That only causes problems in the long run. That's what we're aiming to shift."

The book continues, "What's the solution, then? If the purpose of a church is not primarily to transfer information, if it's not primarily to attract people, if it's not primarily to serve our communities, and if it's not primarily to encourage fellowship, why then does the church exist? All four functions are important components of a church, but none should be the main focus of a church — not as Jesus defined it, anyway. So what is the main focus of the church supposed to be?

A solution emerges when a church shifts its focus to biblical discipleship using the methodology of relational environments…..but notice those two key words again in relation to what we're espousing, and keep the ideas in mind so you can begin to chew on them.

- Focus = biblical discipleship

- Methodology = relational environments

We believe that discipleship should be the core focus for the church. And we believe that the relational model Jesus utilized is the timeless and best methodology for discipleship. The "relational discipleship model" embraces all aspects of the main four categories, yet it espouses something different as the one driving focus. This model doesn't measure success by how many people come to a church, how much money is given, or even how many converts are made. These things are worth measuring, but they're always secondary.

The model we advocate measures success by how many people are being loved and led into the way of Jesus, are coming to Christ and following him. It measures how many people are being transformed into Christ's likeness and are pursuing his kingdom mission. It values and measures how many are actually becoming disciples who can make disciples."

Boom! I think that's pretty good right?

God designed the Church in such a way to accomplish His purpose, divinely charged by His very Presence; for He is in all and through all and with us till the end of the age. He has given us people and practices endowed with divine power for His purpose. Ephesians 4 talks about equipping graces given to the church to train the people of God for works of service so that the Body could serve each other, minister deep healing and truth, be built up, and come into the unity of the faith in the knowledge of the Son of God, so that together we could be brought into the full measure and stature of Christ, unto a mature man. And that's the point, our approach and methodologies must be holistic and comprehensive to bring about maturity in Christ. *That is the goal of all education: to know Him, become like Him, and faithfully make Him known wherever we are and in whatever we are doing.* Our unique skills and abilities were intended for service in the church and in culture. It's worth noting that the local church provides the most conducive environment for them to be nurtured and developed through apprenticeships and loving relationships. As we build up the Body of Christ with this type of discipleship, we must maintain the missional focus of impacting the world with the gospel. We are called to use all that we have to the Glory of God to serve and bless the Family of God as well as the rest of humanity. Our vocational and skill development is key for adorning the gospel in culture, and our responsibility to be a faithful steward of the gift and talents we possess before God.

Every believer is responsible to participate in the "one-anothering" of discipleship as they spur each other on to love and good works. And we must remain accountable to live according to the faith by speaking the truth in love to each other. Older men and older women, mature in the faith, are instructed to teach the younger how to live well according to the faith. And also, how to order their households and walk out their roles as husband, wife, father and mother, according to Christ's design (sadly this has become a rarity in our day and age). Ephesians 4 gifted leaders are to equip and release the people to better serve each other with the divine graces entrusted to them. Appointed elders are responsible for further overseeing the welfare of the house of God and seeing to it that the community remains within the faith manifested in ordered lives according to the teachings of Christ.

Christ has the perfect and eternal blueprint for His Church to blossom into maturity and fullness, we need only to recover His divine design revealed in scripture. The Church is the very household of God Himself and the pillar and foundation of the truth. His instructions in how we are to conduct ourselves and relate to each other is His plan to make known His wisdom and ways to the world. As we live according to His design, we will embody a redeemed society of people living in the freedom and power of God . We should model eternal life, a life lived in fellowship with God and each other in perfect love. All will see the continual witness of the reality of transformation taking place in the lives of its people. In this way, our lives and good works will shine before all men to see His goodness (1 Timothy 3:14-15).

Disciple Making Churches

"The primary mission of the church, and therefore, of all the churches is to proclaim the gospel of Christ and gather believers into local churches where they can be built up in the faith and made effective in service; thus new congregations are to be planted throughout the world."[115]

For over four decades, the mission community has been grappling with this issue of making real disciples, planting churches that reproduce disciples, and so on. This is the crying need in our time for the Body of Christ, especially in America. I'm hopeful and see people responding and reforming their ways to move toward a biblical design in accomplishing God's mission on the earth and what it means to be a real follower of Jesus Christ. Yet it remains true that overall in developed nations, the work of making real disciples and impacting culture with the Kingdom of God is lacking.

Even with significant visitations of the Spirit where people are being renewed in hope, and faith, and the love of God, most don't have a framework to establish their experience in truth. They lack the paradigm and infrastructure of organic missional living and a united missional community seems to be all together lacking or shallow in its expression. I have found all over the absolute void and deficiency of biblical community (with healthy authority), I see this as one of the primary issues that causes the lack of fruit in disciple making. The context of biblical community (the local Church) for training and disciple making is essential to the overall plan and mission success. Without the proper wineskin or infrastructure of a New Testament type, our sincere ambition to obey the great commission and sustain cultures of revival that contain the power for cultural impact and glorify God, are undermined. The right wineskin and biblical design for the Church holds the wine. O, let us return!

---

115 David Hesselgrave, "The Heart of the Christina Mission" from Planting Churches Cross Culturally: North America and Beyond. 2000 baker, Grand Rapids

We need the right paradigm:

- The right context of Church community as family, healthy leadership, and supportive relationships

- The contextually right process and pipeline to train and establish people and multiply leaders

- The holistic approach with a knowing, being, and doing focus with appropriate accountability, discipline, and follow up systems that are relational and organic

- The right tools and resources

Making converts and disciples are two different things. It is critical to understand that making disciples is not just an individualistic pursuit but a community responsibility. The great commission was given to the Church, not just individuals, though the individual actively participates in the practice and call to make disciples. Western individualism has not helped our interpretation of scripture, the call to biblical community, and the practice of the great commission. The mandate to "go and make disciples" was entrusted to the Church, to the *Ekklesia* - the ruling Body of called out ones. Against her the gates of hell will not prevail.[116] We need to remember that the majority of all the New Testament letters were written to church communities and leaders of communities. The teachings, and traditions passed on from the Lord and the Apostles are understood best in a community context, lived out together.

---

116 Matthew 16:18

CURRICULUMS OF TRANSFORMATION

GO INTO ALL
THE WORLD.....

**THE GREAT COMMISSION WAS GIVEN
TO CHURCH & EVERY BELIEVER**

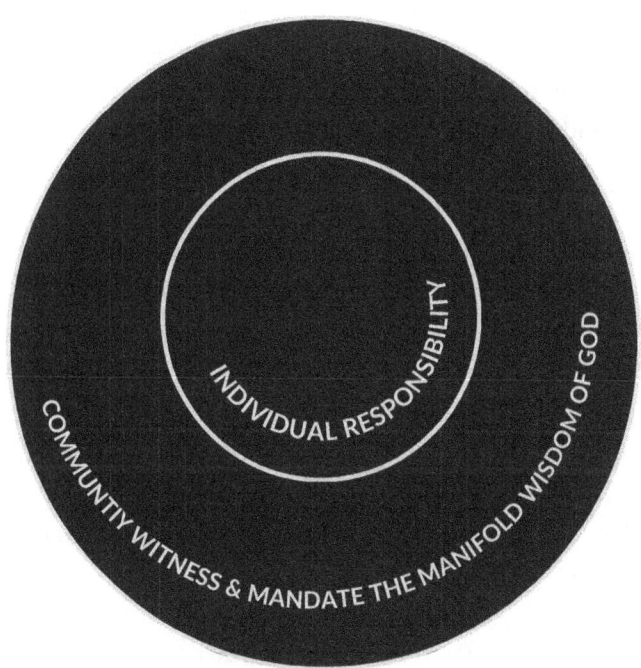

Outreach Models – THE GREAT COMMISSION

The great commission is the church, made up of disciples, practicing *the way* of discipleship in community, collectively and individually proclaiming the good news and reproducing other families of disciples. In other words, the church plants churches, who continue the imperative of making disciples. It's not just an individual pursuit, although it may start with one person. Ultimately we birth and shape a community of believers, a spiritual family of active disciples, fitted together in Christ for a Kingdom purpose that's hardwired to multiply and reproduce.

The Church, which is greater than one person, provides the context for the individual and the household to grow into God's purpose and plan in relation to others. The Church is a family of families and God's central concern in this age. As believers relate to each other in community, they learn to love and be loved with the love they have received in Christ. The community relationships influence and shape individual lives, families, and even other communities through modeling, serving, and the multiplication of Christ centered communities. These communities, families and individuals are rooted and grounded in the gospel, embodying the teachings and mission of Christ which is at the heart of a unified church. This reveals God's eternal plan in Christ to the watching world and spiritual powers in heavenly places.[117]

God's design is that people, individually or within a natural family, are part of the Church. The Church, as God's family, also supports and strengthens the natural family. What is learned within each context flows into each other, and together they shine as a witness of Christ and His ways. They reinforce one another and together grow with the increase that comes from God.

---

[117] Ephesians 3:1-12,21, 25, 4:13, 5:27—Jesus is coming back for His Church—His Bride—the one new man: one Body of believers made up of Jew and Gentile that God would be glorified in and by the Church. The Church is the broader context for the call to discipleship. There is a tension between the community and individual responsibility of sharing the gospel, making disciples, baptizing, and teaching to obey everything Christ taught.

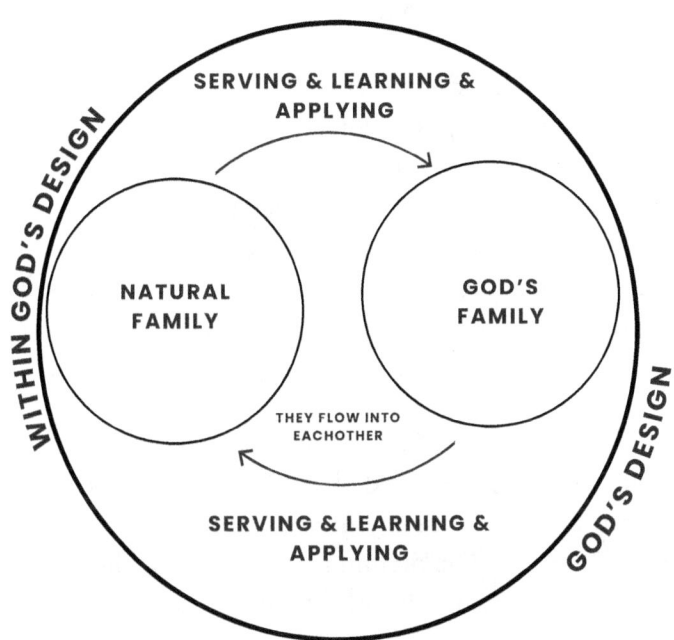

NATURAL & CHURCH FAMILY INTEGRATION

Many today try to belittle the need and value of the Church, because of her imperfections and misuses of power. They isolate their practice of faith to just their own household or loosely held sporadic times of fellowship with other believers. God's design and plan for the Church is fuller than that. The Church is needed in order to answer the call to authentic discipleship and spiritual maturity for both the individual and the Body of Christ as a whole. Jesus will come back to Earth for a Church, not one person or one family, but His Family.

Even discipleship practitioners have "left" the Church today for small group discipleship in rejection of the models and traditions they've experienced. The hunger for something real and effective is good. Fresh expressions of small groups of believers getting together to study the bible, pray, and be accountable is great, but incomplete. Many of these disciple-making movements are doing great things. However, they are missing key elements of the divine design of the Church that are necessary to press into the fullness of what God has called us to.

God is serious about his Church and our role in it. So much so that I want you to understand that God's family takes precedence over natural family. "Who's my mother, brother, sister?" Jesus asked (Matthew 12:46-50). The premium He placed on allegiance to Him and His church supersedes that of the natural family when it comes to following Him and obeying the Father. That doesn't mean we neglect our family or dishonor them or don't provide for them. In fact, we love and honor them better, as it demonstrates our faith and obedience to His word.

If you just knee jerked and said, "No way, that's wrong! This guy is cultish or crazy,!" hold on and let me explain briefly.

Jesus, as a Jew under the law, honored His parents as paramount and in perfect righteousness. So when His family, especially His mother, was outside wanting to speak to Him, you would think anything would have been done to make that happen. But Jesus was making a point, which He also makes in many other places, that is at the heart of His teaching in regards to consecration, salvation, and allegiance to Him and the Father over all.

"Someone told Him, "Look, Your mother and brothers are standing outside, wanting to speak to You." But Jesus replied, "Who is My mother, and who are My brothers?" Pointing to His disciples, He said, "Here are My mother and My brothers. For whoever does the will of My Father in heaven is My brother and sister and mother." (Matthew 12:47-50)

"Do not assume that I have come to bring peace to the earth; I have not come to bring peace, but a sword. For I have come to turn

> 'a man against his father,
>
> a daughter against her mother,
>
> a daughter-in-law against her mother-in-law.
>
> A man's enemies will be the members
>
> of his own household.'

Anyone who loves his father or mother more than Me is not worthy of Me; anyone who loves his son or daughter more than Me is not worthy of Me; and anyone who does not take up his cross and follow Me is not worthy of Me. Whoever finds his life will lose it, and whoever loses his life for My sake will find it." Matthew 10:34-39)

"I have come to ignite a fire on the earth, and how I wish it were already kindled! But I have a baptism to undergo, and how distressed I am until it is accomplished!

Do you think that I have come to bring peace to the earth? No, I tell you, but division. From now on, five in one household will be divided, three against two and two against three. They will be divided, father against son and son against father, mother against daughter and daughter against mother, mother-in-law against daughter-in-law and daughter-in-law against mother-in-law." (Luke 12:49-51)

There is much more scripture about this in both the Old and New Testaments that speak to the realms of priority, commitment to truth, and the holiness of the congregation to be maintained. In the New Testament we are commanded to love our enemies and not judge those outside the faith, yet we are told not to even eat or fellowship with someone who claims to be a "brother in the Lord" but is unrepentant, and living out of step with Christ's teaching. (2 Thess 3:6-15, 1 Cor 5:9-13) Of course the heart is always reconciliation, forgiveness, and restoration for the repentant, but my point here is about the seriousness of God toward His Church and her witness in the Earth. The Church bears His name and that's why judgment must start in the house of God first. (1 Peter 4:17)

In the Old Testament, do you remember the radical things the faithful had to do even to their own family to maintain purity as a community before the Lord? From parents stoning their own kids, to the Levites and others having to wield the sword against their own family because they chose idolatry over the lord, and more.[118] It's a crazy thought and boy, am I grateful to live under a covenant of grace!

Hopefully you see the point: The Church community is greater than and not isolated to our biological believing families. Our families are part of and called to be integrated into the life of the local church. Together we walk out the great commission and great commandment.

The purity and design of the Church is to collectively witness to the gospel and glory of God as the pillar and foundation of truth. The

---

118 Exodus 32:15-35, Deuteronomy 21:18-21

Individual and family are within that context participating personally and collectively in the call to evangelism and discipleship in their "Jerusalem, Judea, Samaria, ends of the Earth."

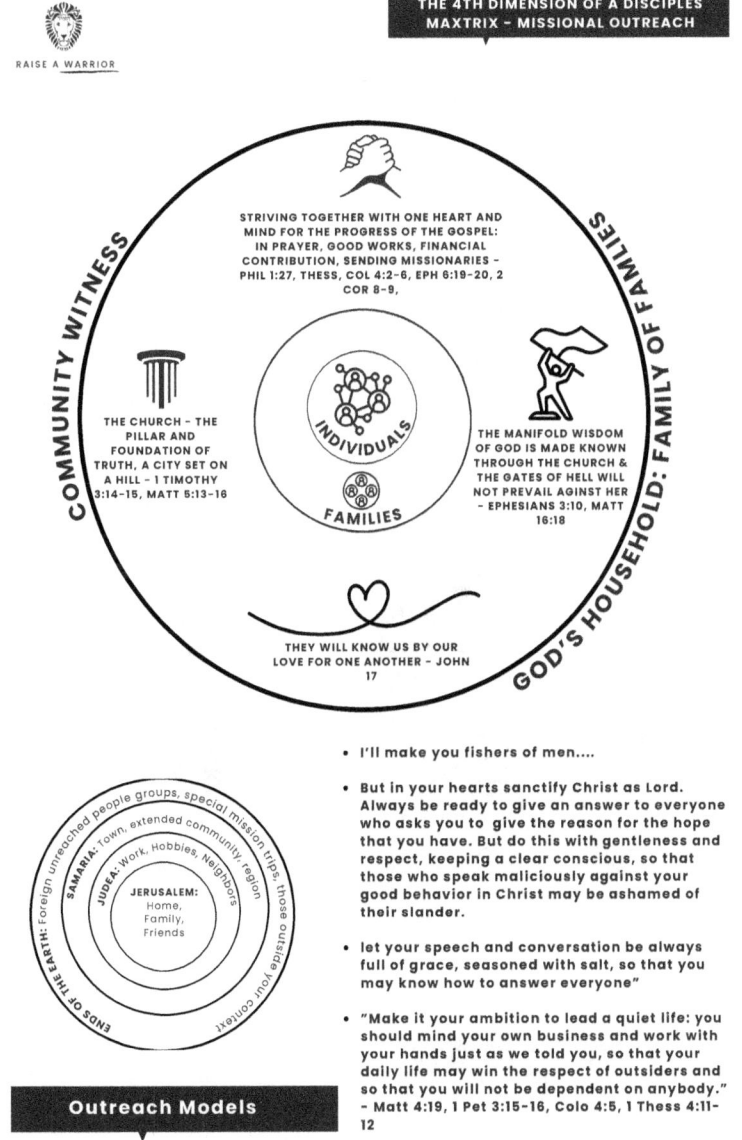

- I'll make you fishers of men....

- But in your hearts sanctify Christ as Lord. Always be ready to give an answer to everyone who asks you to give the reason for the hope that you have. But do this with gentleness and respect, keeping a clear conscious, so that those who speak maliciously against your good behavior in Christ may be ashamed of their slander.

- let your speech and conversation be always full of grace, seasoned with salt, so that you may know how to answer everyone"

- "Make it your ambition to lead a quiet life: you should mind your own business and work with your hands just as we told you, so that your daily life may win the respect of outsiders and so that you will not be dependent on anybody."
  - Matt 4:19, 1 Pet 3:15-16, Colo 4:5, 1 Thess 4:11-12

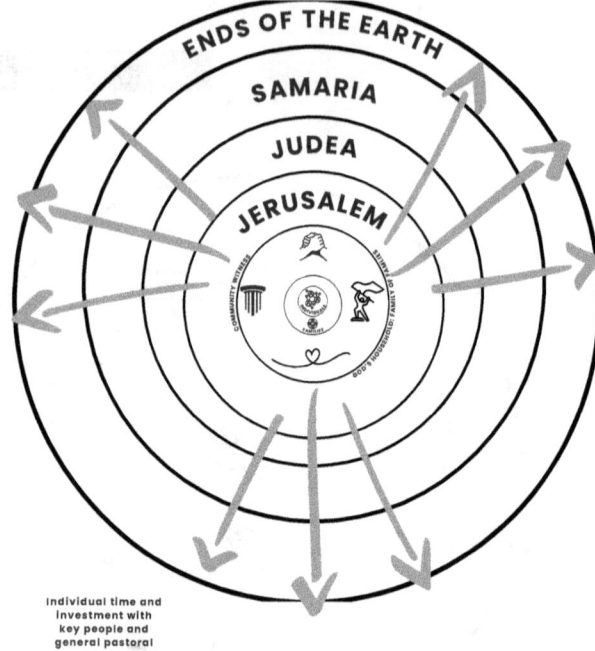

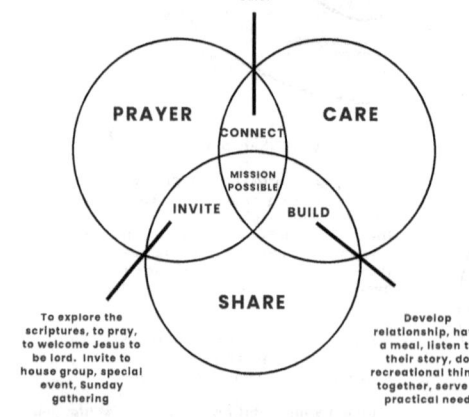

CURRICULUMS OF TRANSFORMATION

THE 4TH DIMENSION OF A DISCIPLES MAXTRIX - MISSIONAL OUTREACH

- I'll make you fishers of men....

- But in your hearts sanctify Christ as Lord. Always be ready to give an answer to everyone who asks you to give the reason for the hope that you have. But do this with gentleness and respect, keeping a clear conscious, so that those who speak maliciously against your good behavior in Christ may be ashamed of their slander.

- let your speech and conversation be always full of grace, seasoned with salt, so that you may know how to answer everyone"

- "Make it your ambition to lead a quiet life: you should mind your own business and work with your hands just as we told you, so that your daily life may win the respect of outsiders and so that you will not be dependent on anybody." - Matt 4:19, 1 Pet 3:15-16, Colo 4:5, 1 Thess 4:11-12

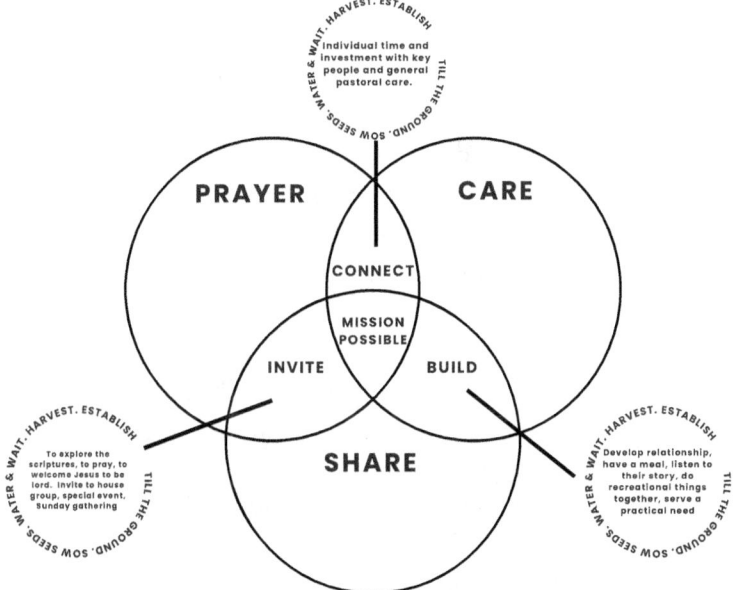

Outreach Models

Ideally, when communities are planted and established with a culture of authentic discipleship, people are transformed into the image of Christ and come into full spiritual, emotional, relational, and missional maturity. As people are saved and added into the Family of God to grow, mature, and continue in the mission of gospel advancement, we see the Church begin to bring reformational change and redemptive influence in culture. Nations, cities, and communities come under the influence of the Kingdom of God. It's more than what an individual can do in just one on one discipleship, though one on one is part of the whole package.

Disciple making churches are committed to people coming into maturity in Christ and the expansion of the Kingdom through the world. God wants His kids to grow up in Him and He wants His family to grow and increase in number—He came to seek and save the lost and shepherd His people. Churches, leaders, and believers who carry God's heart will hold these things central in their hearts and priorities:

- The growth and maturity of the Church in love and the knowledge of God unto the full stature of Christ

- The preaching of the gospel and winning the lost

- The multiplication of churches throughout the world

Consider the findings of this report that looked into U.S. discipleship making churches and scaled five categories of disciple making. The findings speak to the great need to rise up into what God has called us to as His people—To make disciples—to pass on the faith regardless of our station in life because this is central to our purpose and mission in life.

First, of those interviewed in this study, it is important to recognize that people and leaders had a disconnect of their definitions of terms and their actual practices. I believe the redefining or recovering of terms is a significant happening in this time of history as well. The Lord seems to be bringing people back to the roots of the way of Christ and His Apostles. He is unearthing the scriptural truths of the early church that led to the spontaneous expansion of the gospel and turned the world upside down. Biblical truth is being re-discovered and captivating a new generation and a people serious about the gospel and the mission of Christ to make disciples. We are in days of revival and restoration in the midst of gross darkness, but oh, how far we have fallen!

Check this out:

"Human beings sometimes see things as truth not because they're actually true, but for other reasons – because we so badly want them to be true, because others perceive them as true, because we're taught those things are desirable, etc. When pastors are asked about disciple making, many report lots of effort and a high priority, but then they're often not able to report any tangible results…or even a method of measuring results. Either there's significant disciple making activity going on that's ineffective, or the reality is that there's far less activity going on than many pastors want to admit to others or even to themselves.

It may also be that a significant part of the problem is definitions. Exactly what is disciple making? What is discipleship? What activities comprise either one? Prior to being asked any questions about disciple making in this study, pastors were given a very specific definition:

People intentionally enter into relationships to help others follow Jesus, become more like Jesus, and join the mission of Jesus. Disciple making includes the whole process from conversion through maturation and multiplication, which is making disciples who in turn make other disciples.

The definition stresses intentionality, building relationships for the purpose of disciple making, conversion, maturation, and multi-generational multiplication. Yet despite the definition, it can be easy for pastors to slip mentally back into whatever definition they are used to using in their own context."[119]

My friends, we are fighting to turn the tide and forge a new paradigm, returning to ancient paths, the way of Christ and the Apostles. I hope you are gaining greater clarity and that, as a people, we can come out of the fog of vague ambiguities, giving ourselves with focused energy to the work of making disciples. *Seasons have changed, and it's time to engage in the spiritual revolution of restoration and reform our ways.*

God's plan has always been that the Church will transform the world. We need to get back to His plan and stop outsourcing the responsibility to train our people because we feel disqualified or unable. God has called you, along with the church community, to make and multiply followers of Jesus who burn with fiery love for Him with vision to change the world. The Lord will build His Church and the gates of hell will not prevail against it.

This can start small and simple, but must be intentional. The kingdom of God is like a small piece of leaven that grows and grows and eventually permeates everything—*"of the increase of His government and peace there will be no end."* Individuals, families, small groups, and churches committed to making and multiplying disciples will change the world around them. Just get started.

Craft Your Plan and Process

Designing a transformational pathway of growth allows a church to shift the culture of their community to focus on discipling people

---

[119] Disciple Making Study – Discipleship.org, Exponential and Grey Matter Research – March 2020

deeply, authentically, and strategically. There must be an intentional plan that provides the structures for organic and authentic encounters with God's presence and truth. Kingdom life requires a wineskin that fosters continual growth and *the way of life* scripture invites us into.

I will share a few models of discipleship pathways, but my desire is that you would contextualize these processes and pipelines for yourself. First, identify what you may already be doing so that you can understand the process and identify where you are in it. Then, determine your next steps. If you're a pastor or leader and have an existing pathway, ask yourself if it's working well, if it could be refined or innovated or how you can more clearly communicate its vision and purpose to your people. And finally, if you don't have an intentional process, may this help you consider crafting one. Your process must produce the outcomes of transformed lives who know God, love God, are becoming more like God, doing the things He does in a multiplying way. *We are after holistic outcomes of holiness to the Lord, body, soul, spirit and readiness for works of service: The head (knowledge and a sound mind), the heart (character, attitude, emotional wholeness), the hands (works, skills, abilities), the feet (habits, lifestyle).*

As I have mentioned, our community has an ecosystem of expressions that serve as the matrix of evangelism and discipleship. Every person and aspect plays a role, yet certain core elements permeate the rhythm of community life, notably a culture of Spirit led prayer, worship, and authenticity. Our spiritual DNA is felt and imparted in all our expressions of ministry, small groups, outreach, and personal mentoring.

Here's an example of our community-based, intentional process at the time of this writing[120]. Our process and "right of passage" for children,

---

[120] Core principles of development remain the same but we are sensitive as a leadership team and community to discern the present needs of the people and community over all and make adjustments and changes accordingly. The Spirit is the Lord, and we follow His lead for His people. The pipeline/process has fluidity and we make tweaks and customizations as we need. There is a tension between a community wide process and focus

youth, and adults is slightly different but includes some of the same elements as we live in community together as families.

Our approach isn't strictly linear and various elements overlap. People find their way into our community through diverse entry points, have different backgrounds and understanding of the gospel, and span a broad range of ages, abilities, interests and gifting. But once connected with our community the goal is to engage them in our process. For instance, we encourage all new members to attend Encounter weekends (mentioned previously in this book). They are a key catalytic and transformational event that is a must in our body. The weekends introduce people to the power of the gospel, key kingdom paradigms, and the DNA of our community. People may already be part of a life group or Holiness Club or in Sunday school before they participate in an Encounter weekend or they may be introduced to the community for the first time through an Encounter weekend. Nonetheless, an Encounter weekend is essential to our process of discipleship and establishment in the faith:

---

for a season and individual needs and development. We have to navigate those waters with grace, discernment, and wisdom.

CURRICULUMS OF TRANSFORMATION

 Specialized classes + processes for healing, discipleship, and ministry focuses.

PHASE ONE
THE GOSPEL
- Sunday School
  (Christian foundations)
- Redemptive History
  (The meta narrative of Scripture - the story the bible is telling)
- Life Groups
  (key of community)
- Encounters
  (Freedom, Healing, deliverance, Confession, Repentance, Vision)
- First Loved
- Baptism

PHASE TWO
TEACHINGS + CHURCH
- First Principles
- Gospel Series
- Serve on a Team
- Internship (optional - 2 years)

PHASE THREE
LEADERSHIP
- Antioch School
- Leadership Focus Groups
  (Apprenticeships)
- Leading & Co-leading a Life Group

CROSSING LIFE CHURCH– Discipleship Pathway

The basic thought behind the order of the phases has to do with maturity, what we call "establishment" in the faith, where people clearly know the core truths of the faith and where there is demonstrated fruit in their life and relationships. People are living the truth in a dynamic way. This is more than "knowledge" though it includes a core body of knowledge. Progression through the phases is based on qualitative and holistic assessment to determine where people really are. This is far different than checking the boxes of going through a class. We consider their understanding of the faith, their character and attitudes, their relationships and interactions with others in their family and the community, their skill sets expressed in love and humility, their season of life, and their overall growth.

Apostle Paul served as a master builder and architect in God's house, ensuring the house was built to last. He was entrusted with the stewardship of revealing God's plan for His Church. He was given the divine blueprint showing how it was to be ordered to adorn the gospel in every respect as the pillar and foundation of the truth. Paul wrote a third of the New Testament and as we see, there is a progression in his focus in his early, middle, and late letters written to churches and his key leaders. His early letters emphasized the gospel message and the appropriate response to it as a foundation. The middle letters focused on the grand vision of the Church, the teachings of Christ, and the call to walk together in unity, love, and one mindedness for the progress of the gospel. HIs later letters to his sons in the faith outlined how to carry out the work, train and appoint leaders, be faithful to their own calling, and further address what was lacking in the churches. He charged them to guard the deposit of sound teaching and entrust it to other faithful people.

So our big picture framework and establishing process is biblically ordered and strategically planned, drawing from the apostolic model of Paul's divine administration. This Includes the gospel with its implications, the teachings of Christ and the Apostles on how the Church ought to live out truth and unity unto maturity and fullness in Christ, leadership development for the stability of the Church, and the multiplication and furtherance of the gospel.

To assess and discern people's positions in the continuum of spiritual maturity, we function through the progressions we see in both the natural and spiritual life development phases:

- Preconception/dead in their sins
- Born again and infancy in Christ
- Child
- Adolescent
- Young adult
- Adult
- Parent

Each phase of growth needs specific things and has typical earmarks of growth and key transitions. We should know where we personally stand in these phases and where the people we influence stand, so that we can serve and relate to them appropriately. We don't want to relate to a "young adult" like a "child", or treat an "infant" in Christ like a "parent" in the faith or worse still, treat a "dead" person (an unbeliever and seeker) as a responsible disciple of Christ and impose the same standard of judgment on them. That would be wrong and counterproductive to winning them over to Christ.

The image below demonstrates the stages of faith and spiritual maturity. There is much to learn and understand about these various stages that help us better walk out the practice of discipleship, community, and evangelism. Stay connected with us and keep an eye out for articles, workshops, courses, or other resources about it.

STAGES OF FAITH & MATURITY

Infant	*Young Child*	*Adolecent*	*Young man*	*Adult*	*Wise man/Father*
NEPIOS Strong's #3516	PAIDION Strong's #3813	TEKNON Strong's #5451	NEANISKOS Strong's #3495	HUIOS Strong's #5207	SOPHOS & PATER Strong's #4680, 3962
Life changing awareness of God and Intro to new relationships, ways, and habits.	Discipleship & Learning to connect to God, others, and their identity and purpose in Christ.	The Active Life- Serving and engaging in community life.	Journey Inward & apprenticing

Growing strong in faith, overcoming the evil one | Journey outward - maturely leading and serving

TELEIOS Strong's #5046 Complete, Morally perfect, Mature, Finished | Transformed into Love. Spiritually discerning and skillful. One who imparts life & is committed to it. |

1 COR 3:1, 13:10-11, 1 JOHN 2:12-15, 1 PETER 2:1, 2 PETER 3:18, HEB 5:13-14, MATT 23:34, JAMES 3:13

Curriculums of Transformation

I can't stress to you enough about the value of context for effective and fruitful discipleship. With all the areas of growth that we need as a church community, because we are far from "perfect" and have tons to refine and improve, and because discipleship and people development is messy, it's our relational and devotional culture and context that proves to be powerful and life changing. When you look at our discipleship pathway, part of the powerful dynamic is that it is situated within a loving authentic community on a shared mission that's also oriented around the presence of God in day and night worship and prayer.[121] The culture of prayer, intercession, and Spirit led worship and praise, fuels it all. This process and right of passage has proved truly transformative for individuals, households, and our community at large.

---

[121] Christ Himself is at the center of all we do, as it truly is for the Church of Jesus Christ, but as one of the expressions that's anchored in the heart of the life and activity of our community is day and night worship and prayer, 24/7. We have larger worship and prayer gatherings throughout the week but in every hour of the day and night we have sustained prayer and devotion as a community by people taking 1 to 2 hour shifts of prayer, scripture reading and meditation, and ministry to God in worship and praise. We are hosting His presence and placing God's people before Him to Behold Him. We are changed in His presence.

THE WAY OF CHRIST AND HIS APOSTLES

PROCESS OF ESTABLISHING STRONG CHURCHES →

PAUL'S EARLY LETTERS	PAUL'S MIDDLE LETTERS	PAUL'S LATE LETTERS
Strong in the Gospel	Strong in the mission/vision of the Church	Strong mature Housholds and leaders

BILD - Process of Establishing Churches

[122]

---

[122] Image adapted from BILD Resources.

Taking the time to lay proper foundations in the gospel is so important and something we have found that believers of all denominational backgrounds have not experienced. We must go back to the basics and think about mastery and depth before moving on to "meat.".My experience leading small cohorts of people from other churches or in our church who came from other churches has illustrated the need for foundational education. People who were elders and leaders in their previous communities had some serious gaps in their understanding of the faith and their intimacy with God. This then translated into how they were ordering their lives and the substance of their devotional life in the word and prayer.

People's positions, titles or previous experience is not an exemption from the requirement to be firmly rooted in the faith. *Longevity in church is not the same as spiritual maturity. It's easy to use jargon and catch phrases and coast along using your skills and talents while still seriously lacking a sound understanding. This manifests in types of barrenness and immaturities in life.* We should always circle back with people to look at the foundations of their understanding and life in God without making assumptions or false judgments. You'd be surprised. I do the same when coaching and training people in wellness, nutrition, martial arts, fitness, etc. We have to always go back to the foundation and build from there.

The problem we find in the church is that people just don't have framework to work through. Thus why we must design a transformative pathway of discipleship that brings people from conversion and spiritual infancy all the way to maturity and adulthood in Christ. The wisdom traditions and particularly the Jews, had a discipleship pathway to bring boys and girls into adulthood in life and the faith through the scriptures, community, family, and tradition. We need to think the same way.

Similarly, we should apply this to leadership development. The 17-year journey of Timothy with Paul progressed from a young man commended by the churches (Acts 16), to an apprenticeship in a shared mission on a team, to Timothy himself becoming a master craftsman, developing teams himself and fully entrusted with the work. *We need a framework for such faithful development.*

As the saying goes, "to go fast, go slow." In order to build well we need to go slow and go deep with quality investment in people. Proper development and training takes time and intention. When we do this, we will see more accelerated and exponential growth with lasting impact- a multiplying effect. Solid leaders and effective ministers are needed now more than ever. The world's brokenness and trauma is crying out for the people of God to arise in the grace of God to release healing, deliverance, comfort, and freedom.

Church planters, disciple makers and those wanting to live as God intended as an authentic disciple, need a path and curriculum of development. Some level of customization will be necessary for each person, based on their unique gift mixes, character development needs, relational dynamics and other factors that require nuance and discernment. But using a structured process and path helps you build well, be intentional about growth, and prepare for multiplication. When someone is evidencing a call from God, growth and consistency, and a desire to lead and establish a new work, what's your next steps? How are you going to onboard them to the next place and prepare them to launch? What's to be included? What do they need to know and learn? What competencies must be developed? Things to consider right?

Here's an example of the SEND Networks Multiplication pipeline:

Curriculums of Transformation

RAISE A WARRIOR

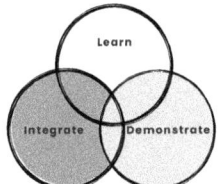

DISCOVER
Help every member identify their calling.

LEVEL 1: LIVING ON MISSION
- Spiritual Formation
- Bible Fluency
- Spiritual Design
- Evangelism
- Relationships
- Understanding the Church
- Servant Leadership

DEVELOPE
Equip every member with tools to serve.

LEVEL 2: DISCIPLE MAKING
- Self Awareness
- Communication & Team Work
- Understanding Context
- Spiritual Readiness
- Making Disciples
- Multiplying Leaders
- Church Planting
- Making a Difference

DEPLOY
Send every member on mission.

LEVEL 3: CHRUCH PLANTING
- Emotional Health
- Confirming their Calling
- Family Dynamics
- Church Planting Models & Stratgies
- Support
- And more...

SEND Network: Multiplying Pipleline

The book "Emotionally Healthy Discipleship" by Peter Scazzero emphasizes the importance of having a plan for deep transformation. It introduced many people to the concept of assessing both spiritual and emotional maturity.

Concerning creating a church culture that deeply changes lives, he circles back to a key question, "What are the beneath-the-surface failures that undermine deep discipleship and keep people from becoming spiritually mature?" He addresses four failures:

- Failure 1: We tolerate emotional immaturity

- Failure 2: We choose to do for God rather than be with God

- Failure 3: We ignore the treasures of church history

- Failure 4: We define success wrongly

He goes on to say, "We must address these failures in our own lives first, then in our equipping of others, and finally, in creating healthy, biblical communities that provide a context for serious discipleship. To do so effectively, we need a transformative discipleship pathway."

Curriculums of Transformation

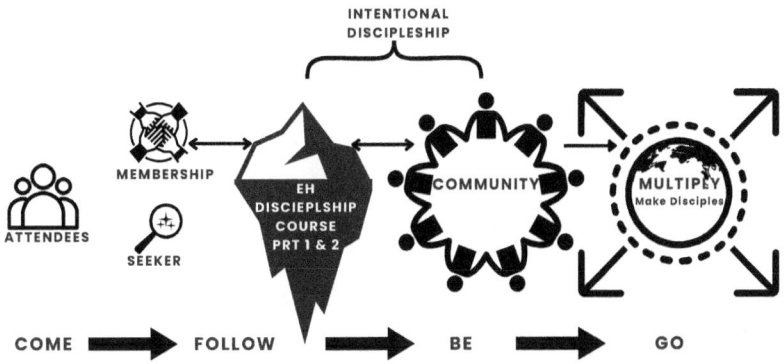

Peter Scazzero - Disciplship Pathway
"Emotionally healthy Discipslship"

Notice the progression. Most people begin their discipleship journey as "attenders" who participate in a church or community. If they are seekers, often there is a seeker-targeted course or other one-on-one opportunities to explore faith in Jesus. The long-term goal is to help people experience deep change within the context of community life so they can progress to the final circle on the right—to multiply by making disciples, thus impacting the world as Jesus commanded (Matthew 28:18–20). Deep change is what Emotionally Healthy Discipleship (EHD) is all about. In Part 2, he goes on to talk about seven marks of a biblical discipleship that deeply transforms lives. I love that one of his first and main points is so much of what I have written about and what I have lived around, " being before doing." As I shared some of my own story in earlier chapters, the deep work of identity and being with God was so central to the deep work of healing in my life. His seven marks of discipleship were:

- Be Before You Do

- Follow the Crucified—not the "Americanized"—Jesus

- Embrace God's Gift of Limits

- Discover the Treasures Hidden in Grief and Loss

- Make Love the Measure of Spiritual Maturity

- Break the Power of the Past

- Lead out of Weakness and Vulnerability

I also love that he illustrated and continued to point out that "each of these marks fall within this larger biblical framework of community, including life-on-life discipling relationships, small groups, and serving."[123]

I see a lot of overlap of Scazarro's model in how we function as a community and what we advocate and provide space for in our discipleship process.

Here's yet another example of an intentional process of development from a different global church network that gives a framework for properly discipling and caring for God's people, particularly those experiencing or coming out of very difficult circumstances. They suggest a "Pastoral Taxonomy" to help approach the care and development of people and families on a faith level, life skill level, and ongoing education/life work level.

People need an intentional and holistic plan and the church has a primary responsibility in providing it as shepherds and overseers of souls. We will take account for how we've cared for the flock of God (If you are a leader in a church, please read that again and slowly). The church should not be so quick to outsource the care of their people to "professionals." When needed, we should learn to properly partner with special assistance organizations while remaining actively engaged in the shepherding process. I could tell you horror stories of some of the foolish counsel given by "professionals" that have shipwrecked people's faith, encouraged pseudo spiritual practices, and destroyed marriages. I'm not saying people in the church haven't done damage as well, because they have. Thus, we need all the more the type of training and development I've been talking about. But my point is: the care of the Flock of God is a divine trust given to appointed spiritual shepherds who will take account to God for how they oversaw and cared for His people (I had to say it again). They need to be deeply engaged to know the state of their flock, and be wary of a "professional model" of care that operates outside the word

---

[123] Peter Scazzero, "Emotionally healthy discipleship : moving from shallow Christianity to deep transformation." Grand Rapids : Zondervan, 2021. Pg 24-25

of God and the involvement of spiritual overseers who are deeply connected to the person and process. I understand that I just made a big statement and there are tons of implications which we cannot get into right now. Take the point that the church needs a well thought out, strategic, and biblical plan to ground people in the faith that produces the fruit of transformed productive lives and families that reveal the Glory and wisdom of God to the watching world. The gospel and teachings of Christ provide the answer. The need is for skillful ministers and disciples of Christ who can holistically shepherd people into the freedom Christ purchased (body, soul, and spirit). Last time I checked, the blood of Jesus, the word of God, and the power of the Holy Spirit have not lost their potency and power!

Curriculums of Transformation

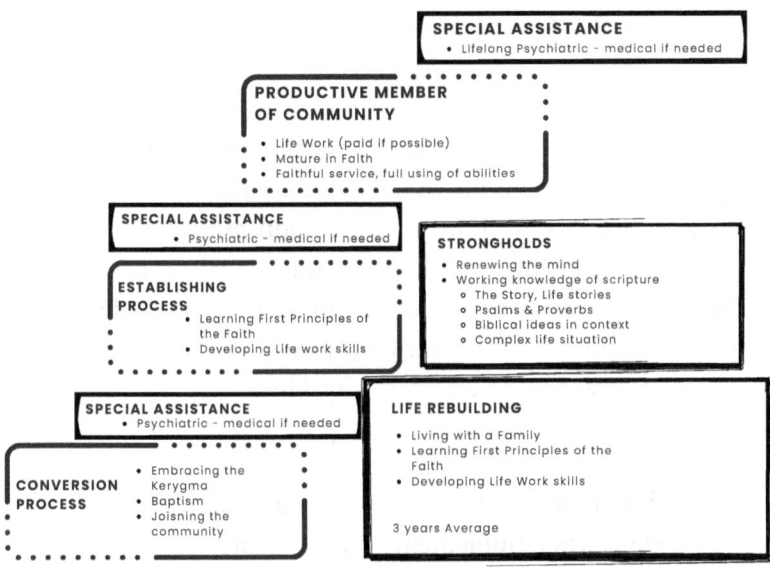

BILD: Pastoral Care Taxonomy

---

124 Jeff Reed with Randy Beckett and Nancy Reed, "Shepherding and Counseling Manuel: A Training Manual for Shepherding and Counseling in the Tradition of Pastoral Care", 2019. 2400 Oakwood Road. Ames, IA 50014

Before a final example of one of our leadership development tracks, I want you to see a "Both-And Integrated Approach" model that can combine the rapid multiplication focus of DMM/DBS (Discipleship Making Movements & Discover Bible Study Method's) with the depth and maturity goals of traditional and holistic discipleship approaches. This hybrid strategy seeks to leverage the strengths of both methodologies while addressing their respective weaknesses. As I've mentioned before, different methods are needed for different times, situations, and the people involved.

Many in the DMM/DBS practice think the other approaches take too long and are too centralized and typically have never seen more traditional models foster genuine application and obedience based discipleship that multiplies, while other traditional models question the depth, actual transformation, and maturity within the DMM/DBS approach. Both models have their own strengths and challenges in fostering spiritual growth and maturity. Go figure. We are working with people. It's always messy if its going to be real.

Nonetheless, I have found the wisdom of God in the tensions of "Both And" applications when implemented well. In brief explanation of an integrated approach:

1. **Multiplication and Maturity:**

Combines the speed of DMM with the depth of traditional discipleship. It acknowledges the urgency of spreading the gospel while fostering robust spiritual growth over time. For example:

- Small Groups Within Larger Network

    - Form relational, obedience-oriented small groups for discipleship and accountability. These groups remain dynamic and capable of multiplying. (As I will share more on later).

- Connect groups to a centralized church or network to provide theological depth, pastoral care, and resources for holistic growth. Pair emerging leaders with mature mentors who guide them in both practical ministry and personal character development.

- Encourage these leaders to immediately disciple others using DBS methods while receiving deeper training themselves.

- Balancing Multiplication and Depth with Assessment

  - Evaluate success by measuring both quantitative growth (e.g., new disciples, groups formed, souls baptized) and qualitative depth (e.g., spiritual maturity, overcoming sin and life controlling issues, leadership and relational skills, marital health).

  - Use tools like discipleship assessments or spiritual formation inventories to track progress in both areas. BILD (Biblical Institute of Leadership Development) has some great tools that virtually take the scriptures and organize them in a way to assess personal and ministry growth.

- Community Impact and Cultural Engagement

  - Encourage disciples to integrate faith into daily life, impacting their communities socially and spiritually.

  - Promote holistic outreach initiatives (e.g., addressing social justice, education, healthcare, entertainment and recreation, etc) that reflect the gospel's transformative power.

2. **Dual Emphasis on Leadership and Leadership Development:**

While disciples are encouraged to lead quickly (a strength of DMM), they also receive ongoing support and mentoring to ensure leadership maturity. In a New Testament wineskin a plurality of elders shepherds the community or a cluster of small house churches, as well as Ephesians 4 gifted ministers that are training and equipping people and leaders for the works of service, that are circulating and deeply involved locally, regionally, nationally, or internationally, based on their scope (metron) of influence and call. There are many ways this can happen to help bring stability and strength to the growing community and work of discipleship:

- Introduce a rhythm of leadership workshops or retreats focused on relationship, growing in servant leadership together, character development, shepherding skills and coaching, and strategic planning.

- Equip leaders with tools for contextual evangelism and disciple-making while fostering long-term ministry resilience.

3. Holistic Growth:

Incorporates a balance of obedience-based discipleship (DBS) with structured theological and character development programs. For example, combine discovery methods and structured learning.

- DBS for Immediate engagement: Begin with Discovery Bible Studies to encourage new believers to engage directly with Scripture and apply it in their lives. Use questions like, "What does this teach about God?" and "What should we do in response?"

- Structured Growth Tracks: Gradually introduce doctrinal teaching through structured materials, classes, and deeper discipleship processes (e.g., first principle series, modern catechisms, workshops, internships, systematic theology,) to deepen understanding and growth.

By integrating these practices, the hybrid approach seeks to create disciples who are both deeply rooted in their faith and equipped to multiply their impact broadly and sustainably.

Example of Voices Advocating for Integrated Models:

1. Jim Putman in *Real-Life Discipleship* emphasizes relational discipleship with a balance of rapid reproduction and deeper spiritual formation.

2. Mike Breen in *Building a Discipling Culture* argues for creating a culture where discipleship and leadership development occur simultaneously.

3. Neil Cole, a proponent of organic church growth, advocates for integration between multiplication movements and structured equipping for sustained growth.

ASPECT	DMM/DBS APPROACH	TRADITIONAL DISCIPLESHIP APPROACH	INTEGRATED DISCIPLESHIP APPROACH
FOCUS	Rapid multiplication who make disciples.	Holistic development of individuals toward spiritual maturity, prioritizing depth over speed	Both multiplication and maturity: creating disciples who grow deep and multiply broadly over time.
METHODOLOGY	Discovery Bible study (DBS) focuses on obedience-based learning through self discovery.	Structured teaching with an emphasis on doctrine and systematic theology	Combines DBS for rapid multiplication with structural teaching with a obedience-based approach for long-term growth and deeper theological understanding
ROLE OF THE DISCIPLE	Disciples lead and facilitate early in their faith journey.	Disciples are trained extensively before leading, ensuring preparedness.	Disciples are empowered to lead quickly but receive ongoing mentorship and training to grow in maturity and leadership.
COMMUNITY STRUCTURE	Small rapidly multiplying groups meeting informally in homes or communities	Larger, centralized congregations with formal structures and designated leadership.	Small groups for relational connection & Discipleship, supported by larger church or network for Theological depth & holistic development.
SCRIPTURAL ENGAGEMENT	Focuses on direct participative engagement with Scripture, encouraging obedience and application.	Relies on mediated learning through sermons and teachings, often guided by leaders.	Encourages personal discovery in community dialog while incorporating doctrinal teaching and broader Biblical literacy over time.
GROWTH MEASUREMENT	Success measured by the number of new groups and disciples formed within short timeframes.	Success measured by individual spiritual growth, doctrinal understanding, and long-term faithfulness.	Success measured by both multiplication (new disciples) and holistic growth (spiritual maturity, leadership readiness, and cultural impact).

Here's a final example of one of our leadership development tracks that takes 3 to 5 years to complete, while being active in the life of the church, doing the work of ministry and serving the people of God. One of our values is life long learning and continual growth as an expression of the pursuit of wisdom. The process and call to the word of God and its diligent study and practice, is not as a mere academic discipline, but passionate devotion and faithful stewardship before God. As you'll see, this model includes knowing goals, being goals, and doing goals with integrated assessment and competencies. This is fleshed out in real relationship, along with the wisdom based training model.

HOUSE CHURCH LEADER (A 4-Year Training Program)

Character Development	Ministry Skills	Theological Soundness	Life Preparation
Encounter	Sunday (reach out, establish)	*First Principles*	1. Secure solid commitment from spouse and family
Journey/Journey Leader Training (if needed)	Help lead to Lead LIFE Group	*Redemptive History* or *The Story*	2. Gradually adjust life to make room for the responsibilities of a house church leader
Life N⁹ (Produces PDP, Personal Development Plan)	Outreach (Hospitality)	BILD Leadership Series*	3. Work on any area of managing your household, any relationships in the church and any aspects of community reputation that need improvement (1 Tim 3:1-7, Titus 1:5-9)
	Teams (Serve on Sunday team)	1. Acts	
Character of a Leader Course	Teaching *First Principles*	2. Pauline Epistles	
	Teaching *Redemptive History* or *the Story*	3. Leaders	
Read "Leadership in the Church" document and understand its Expectations	Skill Building Workshops:	4. Shepherding	4. Financial Peace University (FPU)
	1. Essentials	5. Essentials	
	2. Socratic Discussions	6. Interpreting the Word	
	3. Portfolios/Mentoring	*Or consolidated Leadership Course	
	4. Prayer Ministry Training	Complete Ministry Philosophy paper and a	
	5. Conflict Resolution	Kerygma/Didache paper	

Goals:	Goals:	Goals:	Process of Selection
1. Understand the Gospel and receive healing in matters of identity and the soul (mind, will, emotions) through the work of Christ	1. Gain Experience in hospitality, leading, and shepherding	1. Gain a solid philosophy of ministry	1. Desire to be a house church leader
			2. Elders affirm his desire to become a house church leader
2. Work on Character traits that need improvement	2. Gain greater wisdom and skill in living (didache.) "The wise are to become wiser."	2. Develop and ability to handle sound doctrine I Tim 5:17	3. Commit to the full training process while doing the ministry of a house church leader
3. Develop a solid and balanced life plan		3. Gain a clear sense of his or her biblical role and responsibility	4. Be commended before the church at the start and finish of the process

ULTIMATE GOAL: To become fully qualified house church leader with three or more years of experience and already adjusted to the role. This includes a developing a genuine conviction for lifelong learning and growth. (See list of yearly continuing education options after this tack is complete.)

CROSSING LIFE CHURCH: House Church Leader Example

THIS IS NOT ACADEMIA OR JUMPING THROUGH HOOPS. IT'S AUTHENTIC DISCIPLES WHOLEHEARTEDLY RUNNING THE RACE IN A MANNER WORTHY OF THE GOSPEL OUT OF BURNING LOVE FOR JESUS AND THE GLORY OF THE FATHER! LABORERS STUDYING TO SHOW THEMSELVES APPROVED AND RIGHTLY HANDLING THE WORD OF GOD.

THE HEART SHOULD BE THAT OF SINCERE LOVERS PURSUING THE ONE THEIR SOUL LOVES AND CITIZENS OF HEAVEN PREPARING THEMSELVES TO INHERIT IMMORTALITY AND FULLY LIVE IN THE KINGDOM OF GOD THROUGH THE GOSPEL.

This is the way of diligent pursuit and our humble attempt to restore ancient paths of authentic discipleship and raise up a new breed of believers who can glorify God and impact the world. We continually revisit this and make adaptations and customizations for what is needed in times and seasons for our people.

CURRICULUMS OF TRANSFORMATION

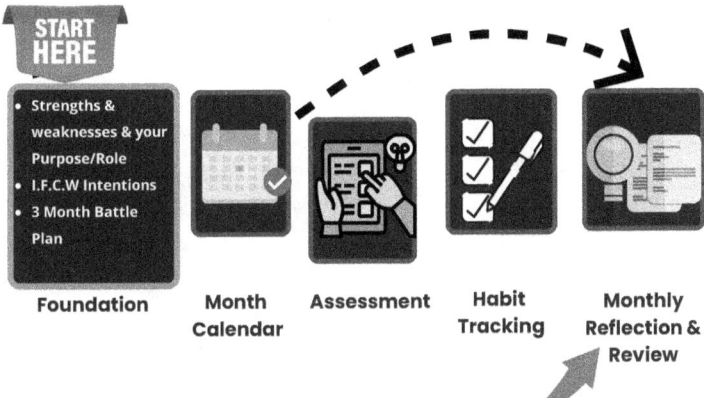

SUCCESS MAP

START HERE

- Strengths & weaknesses & your Purpose/Role
- I.F.C.W Intentions
- 3 Month Battle Plan

Foundation — **Month Calendar** — **Assessment** — **Habit Tracking** — **Monthly Reflection & Review**

TURN IN MONTHLY: Competencies for courses will also be turned in as you work through the leadership curriculum.

STAY CLOSE TO THE FIRE

Consistent growth comes as we are consistent. More than half the battle is to "show up" regularly and be open in your communication and transparent in your process. Let's honor the struggle and put in the work of growth!

The format and design of this workbook is as follows and repeats each month for 3 months. At the start of the 4th month some of the foundational tools will need to be re worked if appropriate such as the "90 Day Battle plan" and a refining and assessing of your I.F.C.W. Intentions.

Crossing Life Church Leadership Blue print

Arise and Return

RAISE A WARRIOR

KNOWING GOALS

- Gain a solid philosophy of ministry.
- Hold the faith with a clear conscience and rightly handle sound doctrine..
- Gain a clear sense of his or her biblical identity, role, & responsibility.

BEING GOALS

- Understand the Gospel and recieve healing in matters of identity and the soul (mind, will, emotions).
- Greater skill in living the faith with demonstrated fruit of the spirit (didache)
- Relationships are peaceable and loving free from wrath and unforgivness.
- Family is biblically ordered and lived out in love and respect.
- Be an example of the believers in the way you live and devote yourself to the word, prayer, and using/developing your gifts, 1 Tim 4:1

DOING GOALS

- Gain experience in serving
- Greater skill in living (didache)
- Effectively lead a team of people.
- Motivate with vision
- Solves problems
- Continually resolve conflict
- Effective Evangelism and gospel presentation
- Effectively train other disciples and leaders.

CURRICULUM

COURSE

PERSONAL DEVELOPMENT PLAN(PDP)

REDEMPTIVE HISTORY

FP- SERIES 1-3 & TEACHING FP

ACTS, PAULINE, ESSENTIALS ACCELERATED

CHARACTER, PERSPECTIVES

SHEPHARDING

ENCYCLICALS 1-7

MINISTRY PHILOSOPHY PAPER

KERYGMA & DIDACHE PAPER

*REFER TO THE LEADERSHIP DEVELOPMENT TRACK FOR YOUR SPECIFIC COURSES.
*COMPLETION OF COMPETENCIES FOR EACH COURSE IS NECISSARY FOR THE COURSE TO BE "DONE".

Crossing Life Church Leadership Blue print

CURRICULUMS OF TRANSFORMATION

RAISE A WARRIOR

**Transformational Environment:
Missional and Presence Centered Church**

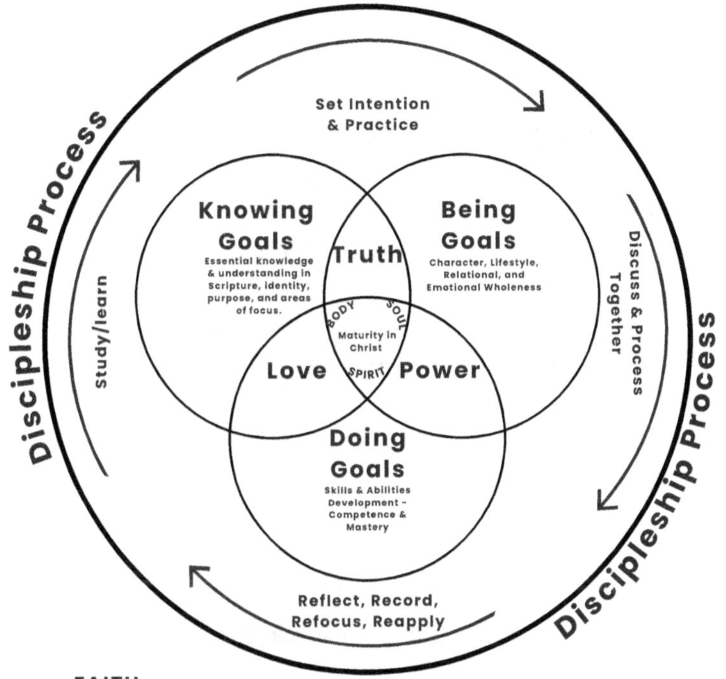

Discipleship Process

Set Intention & Practice

Study/learn

Discuss & Process Together

Knowing Goals
Essential knowledge & understanding in Scripture, identity, purpose, and areas of focus.

Truth

Being Goals
Character, Lifestyle, Relational, and Emotional Wholeness

BODY · SOUL

Maturity in Christ

Love · SPIRIT · Power

Doing Goals
Skills & Abilities Development – Competence & Mastery

Reflect, Record, Refocus, Reapply

Discipleship Process

FAITH
HOPE
LOVE

JOY
PEACE
RIGHTEOUSNESS

KNOW HIM
BECOME LIKE HIM
MAKE HIM KNOWN

} **EDUCATION THAT PRODUCES ABUNDANT LIFE, FRUITFUL LIFE WORK, & GLORY TO GOD.**

WISDOM BASED MODLE OF TRAINING

Some Questions to Consider for Pastoral Leaders and their Team:

- Define terms with your team and craft a transformational curriculum: What is a disciple? What does it mean to be discipled? What should that entail? What are the goals and outcomes? How should you assess growth and progress? How are we going to do this as a church? What's the plan and strategy? And so on..

- What does the curriculum include? What are the teaching methods to be used? What experiences are needed?

- Could you design a visual framework to communicate your process of development?

- What needs to change in your understanding and paradigms?

- What needs to change in your heart? Your church community?

- What activities and ministries need to be reshaped or pruned?

- Who are your leaders that you can train/disciple and prepare to disciple others and turn into disciple makers?

PAUSE. CAPTURE. APPLY
Prompts to help you process

1. What specific insights or concepts from this chapter resonated with you the most? Why do you think these stood out to you?

_____

_____

_____

2. How can you practically apply the principles discussed in this chapter to your daily life, relationships, or ministry? Identify at least one actionable step you can take this week.

_____

_____

_____

3. What potential challenges or barriers might you face in implementing these concepts? How can you overcome them?

_____

_____

_____

4. What are 3-5 quotes or points from this chapter that capture the essence of what it's communicating? Write them down.

_____

_____

_____

_____

5. How can you involve your family, small group, or church community in the practices and principles outlined in this chapter? What steps can you take to foster a culture of discipleship and transformation within your circle of influence?

_____

_____

_____

6. Spend a few moments in prayer, asking God for the wisdom, strength, and courage to live out the truths you've learned. Write down a commitment or a prayer that reflects your desire to grow as an authentic disciple and transformational leader to impact the world.

_____

_____

_____

CHAPTER 14

Creating transformational environments—a leaders responsibility

"There's a world of difference between insisting on someone's doing something and establishing an atmosphere in which that person can grow into wanting to do it"

—Mister Rogers

"You cannot make people learn. You can only provide the right conditions for learning to happen."

— Vince Gowmon

"The work of education is divided between the teacher and the environment."

— Maria Montessori

A transformational environment is a greenhouse that provides the atmosphere for life to flourish. Regardless of your realm of influence and oversight, you are responsible to steward the environment of not just your heart and mind but the contexts and people you oversee and influence. As leaders, we must ensure the environment contains the necessary elements for clarity, healing, connection, joy, growth, and transformation.

We are all leaders in some capacity, but for those entrusted with leadership and oversight of others, we have to understand that the environment created, which consists of both mission and culture, is our responsibility. When we create a culture of discipleship in our lives, homes, small groups, community, and in all things, the environment drives the experience. Leadership is about keeping the mission front and center and aligning the community, culture, and environment with that mission as a reinforcing agent. If the environment and culture contradicts or undermines the mission, leadership has not done its job. "Leaders are God's catalysts and caretakers of mission and its culture…..Leaders exist to establish, embed, and continuously true up mission and culture. A mission without a culture is like a car without wheels – it may be a great car, but it's unable to fulfill its purpose. On the other hand, culture without a mission is a whimsy, and it will drift with circumstances and crises instead of holding to purpose. But mission and culture are dependent on the stewardship of leaders to keep them focused and operating."[125]

Regardless of our station in life, we must always keep in view the primary mission of the gospel to impact and transform hearts. Beneath the surface of administrative duties, technical guidance, or therapeutic and coaching techniques, there should be a deep commitment to dismantling obstacles to growth, unlocking people's potential, and reaching their heart for the gospel's sake. The environment will either help this happen or hinder it.

---

[125] Dennis Allen, "*The Disciple Dilemma: Rethinking and reforming how the church does discipleship*", Morgan James publishing, 2022. Pg 240

We want people to encounter God and His goodness and understand that He cares about every aspect of their lives. So the aim of growth and transformation in a holistic way must be kept in focus in all our efforts to influence others. The common saying "keeping in our lane" compartmentalizes our responsibility to share and impart the faith can keep us nearsighted, limiting our potential to influence people at deeper levels. Loving and serving people well means considering the whole person and fostering an environment that nurtures the whole person and moves them forward in the plan and purposes of God. Remember, you are a priest of God, have direct access to the Lord, and have been commissioned to share Christ with others.

It's not "someone else's job," it's yours.

We can coach, educate, and train people to achieve world class proficiency in their craft and vocation, but it's equally important to help them develop in matters of character and faith, while keeping the broader aspects of their lives in view. If we gain the whole world or help others gain the whole world but they lose their soul and never come to know Christ in a real way, fully participating in His mission, what good have we really done? To only focus on helping people secure their hopes for this life alone is nearsighted and earthbound. As Apostle Paul said, "if we have hoped in Christ for only this life, we are of all people most to be pitied."[126]

It takes focus and intention to live on mission and to be a leader who fosters and promotes the kind of transformation called for by the scriptures. We have to help people consider eternity and look up. Calling people to know God intimately, to obey His will and live for another age, and to fulfill His purpose for their lives while pressing on to maturity in Christ, is the work of leaders. We have to keep this in focus in all our endeavors as central to our sole ambition, *to know Him and make Him known.*

---

126 1 Corinthians 15:19

In all cases, let us hold in tension the responsibility to avoid too narrow a focus in teaching or training that we fail to really leverage our influence for eternal matters. We can do both. We can create world class immersive educational, wellness, and training experiences to pass on our knowledge, skill, craft, or ability, and we can also be intentional to share the faith, biblical principles, and love of God. These immersive transformational environments are essential to address the whole person for lasting results. Many doctors and psychologists agree that the spiritual and social components of people's lives are one of the most important elements to their overall wellbeing and productivity in life. *This is where the Church should be shining all the more with redemptive solutions by creating environments and processes that heal and transform.*

Believers and the Church should be forerunners of people development, healing, education, the arts, and many other realms. We have access to the very presence and mind of God for all things. *We have the divine advantage of divine intelligence and the Holy Spirit's power for real solutions.* This is why we must all increase in the grace of God so that we can serve at the highest levels to set people free, release goodness and justice in the earth, and advance industries to bless humanity and make a way for the knowledge of God to fill the earth. *The environments, cultures, and structures we create need to be able to foster and facilitate the revelation of God, dynamic growth, and transformation of life. This is the leader's responsibility.*

Boundaries & Responsibilities

Let's start with the reminder that the real, lasting transformation is a matter of the heart and is the work of the Holy Spirit. Leaders have a responsibility and a "burden" to carry, but only to a certain extent. The people we serve also have a responsibility to grant full access to the work of God in their lives. We have to do our part but we cannot make people's choices for them and we cannot do what only

God can do. There's rest and freedom in that. We even see apostle Paul appealing to the Corinthian church to open their hearts to him because they were being restricted by their own affections (2 Corin 6:11-13).

When we talk about lasting transformation in people's lives versus behavior modification, we are talking about changes that are made from the inside out—from the heart. For example, let's use someone's health journey and people who want to lose weight and undergo a physical transformation. If they don't renew their thinking and mindsets and really embrace internal transformation, their external results won't last.[127] I've seen it over and over as a trainer and coach. But when issues of identity and new mindsets are adopted, where there is repentance and renewed thinking, the skills and habits created last and the external results stick. The inner game is the hardest. The will of the person must come into alignment with the Lord and the truth, that's where breakthrough happens. People have to internally align in what they believe to be truth and own it so that it becomes the driving conviction for action. That's faith in action.

The principal remains the same when we think about wanting to impact culture. If we have external reforms without internal transformation by the power of the gospel, nothing will last. The external structures help create a container but the real answer lies in the change of heart. That's where the primary focus must be while we seek to create environments that reinforce that mission and aim.

As those who want influence others for Christ, we have to understand our own boundaries, limitations, and responsibilities. Otherwise, we'll just get frustrated with the people we are trying to serve, love, and lead. *First we need to settle in our own souls that we are powerless to*

---

[127] External results that are gained in healthy and natural ways that leads to real wellness of life that gets expressed in joy, peace, confidence, contentment, soundness of mind, healthy relationship to food and self image ect versus surgeries and unnatural attempts to physical change.

transform someone in and of ourselves. Let that settle into your thoughts for a moment. We must relinquish control and the misuse of power so that we can actually serve the process of transformation by simply providing the context, opportunities, conversations, and structures for it to happen.

There is a real measure of rest of soul in knowing this. *You can not change people, but you can be a positive influence and catalyst for change to happen.* People must learn to make sincere and faith filled choices themselves for their own life before God. *Our job as leaders is to help provide the right context and to point people into the right context even though we ourselves may be a conduit of change and formation in their lives.*

A leader is a co-laborer in the Lord's field, and one of our responsibilities is to provide the right environment for healthy growth to happen. God provides the grace of illumination and transformation, but we help provide the right ingredients and remove the obstacles that would choke out the growth of the seed of the kingdom. This is what leadership and governance is about, setting the right parameters and standards for freedom and life to flourish (we also can help clear and prepare the way in prayer, too. In fact, we can do nothing until we have prayed and prepared a way through intercession).

With clear expectations communicated and the necessary authority to help enforce or protect the environment, an atmosphere conducive for growth will flourish and as a result people, households, and communities will be changed. But the truth is that the Lord is the one who brings the 'increase' and growth within the hearts of people as they believe and apply themselves to the truth and love of God. We may plant or sow, water or plow, but it is the Lord who does the work by His Spirit, even if He is using us as the ones to write on people's hearts. Although we have a responsibility as stewards to dispense what the Lord has entrusted us with by His grace, yet He does the work. He has given us the ministry of the Spirit in order to minister to others with great effect.

The big picture of eternal work in discipling and winning people to the Lord has to do with our partnership and cooperation with the Spirit of God. We get to see what He is already doing and partner with Him in letting Him move through us to touch the world around us, for we are ambassadors of Christ! He wants to move and speak through us to touch the world.

We just have to be willing and open and unhindered by our fears and false constraints.

Every work of God is born of God and sustained by God, for *"It's not by might nor by power, but by my Spirit, Says the Lord"* (Zach 4:6). We must learn to live, lead, and minister out of the power of His might. We see the partnership of our labor of love and the Spirit's work in what Paul said, "We write on the tablets of people's hearts by the Spirit of God."[128] Part of God's design for how we grow in His grace is by receiving the grace that flows through each other as we serve one another in the ways God has enabled. Remember, it is by what each joint supplies and by their effective working that the body of Christ is held together, nourished, and built up into maturity and fullness in Christ.[129]

So let us love others in the way we can and let ourselves be loved too. Through the love of God, which never fails, we are all changed.

Part of the boundaries for those of us deeply engaged in helping others with the deeper areas of their hearts and lives, is that we do not draw people to ourselves but to the Lord Himself who is the ultimate provider of their needs. He is their God and their source, not us. We are not to foster codependency but empower people to stand on their own feet in Christ—rooted and grounded and built up in Him. We point people to Him and not ourselves even though we may provide a model or example for them to follow. We help people

---

128 2 Corinthians 3:3
129 Ephesians 4:11-16, 1 Peter 4:7-11

know Jesus, become like Jesus, and help them effectively serve in the mission of Jesus from within the fellowship of the Body of Christ and not from isolation. When we are discipling people and they are drawn into greater levels of discipleship, *it should never lead to isolation and a drawing to ourselves as a source,* but healthy connection and relationships within the broader context of the church.

In the context of the Church, the classroom, business and so on, we have seen people cross the appropriate lines of those they are trying to help and serve, intentionally and unintentionally, and it leads to forms of abuse, dysfunction, and immorality. We must be above reproach and lead with integrity in the fear of the Lord and maintain appropriate relational boundaries while exercising spiritual discernment and putting in place the accountability structures needed to safeguard all peoples involved.

The work of transformation can be messy and we need to think soberly around the frailty of people, the need to keep watch over our own hearts, and be mindful of the schemes of the devil that would love to usurp, defile, and disrupt God's plan for people's healing, growth, and development in truth. Time and time again we have seen those well intentioned people fall into a trap simply by not honoring boundaries, and all kinds of damage is done to those involved while also bringing reproach upon the Church and the faith. And woe to those who have used their positions of influence with ill intent for their own corrupted desires and caused others to stumble and be ensnared! They have put Christ to open shame.

Quality Soil Equals Quality Returns

Let's make no mistake about it, the context and quality of the *environmental* "soil" determines the amount and quality of the fruit that can be born in people's lives. The environment we create or steward can either make or break people, liberate them or oppress them, accelerate them or hinder them. Remember the parable of the sower? Four different types of soils determine different outcomes, and even in the good soil, some bore 30 fold, 60 fold, or 100 fold fruit.

For context, the soil in the parable is about the hearer's heart, mind and their response to the word spoken, this speaks to the recipient's responsibility. For leaders who have influence over the playing fields of life, hear what I'm saying in context of providing the right conditions to maximize growth. The reality is that people are still free agents who choose how they will respond to what's been provided. This is a whole point in and of itself that *the learners must have the onus put on them to take responsibility for their learning.*

You can have the perfect context and powerful content, and people will still miss the richness of what was provided and available. Remember the garden of Eden with Adam and Eve? In perfection they chose to believe a lie and chose to disobey. Remember Judas? He was in the inner circle of Jesus with everything he needed in a perfect environment to grow and learn but he did not choose wisely. He had not broken up the fallow ground of his heart and allowed the seeds of truth to be sown among the thorns in his soul and truth got choked out.[130]

We all have different environments we oversee or influence, from whole communities or companies, teams, households, or our personal relationships. We hold a space of interaction with dynamics, nuance, unique culture, and expectations both spoken and unspoken that we need to recognize and understand. These spaces, relational webs, and infrastructures, hold the potential and possibility for something truly amazing. But it's how we relate to it that will determine whether we can tap that potential and extract it to its fullest or not.

These spaces or environments provide avenues to infuse the heart and ways of the Kingdom of God at every level. There we can

---

[130] Jeremiah 4:3

intentionally nurture opportunities for the gospel and growth in the faith. It's important to say again that this is for EVERY BELIEVER IN CHRIST. This is the mission of the Church in whom you belong if Christ lives in you—we are to change the world and prepare for the Lords coming by being an authentic disciple who is about the Father's business of making disciples and bearing witness to His name.

So I want to encourage you to be excellent in the things you are called to do. Leverage your influence to create an environment that cultivates connection and quality conversations so you can get to the heart of the matter. If it is within your power to organize experiences and routines (things like family habits, relationship expectations, accountability structures, company cultures and practices, department policy, athletic ministries, creative programming, and youth ministries), then let them be formed in such a way that propagates Kingdom culture and biblical values with relational environments in which intentional gospel sharing can happen and deep discipleship can take place. That's gold!

If we make space for the presence of the Lord and loving connection with people in the environments we steward, we'll watch the miracles happen and be amazed by the working of God's grace. So go for it, the Lord is with you, and the truth is, it is your responsibility and mission to do so!

Jesus did not lose one that was entrusted to Him, minus the son destined to destruction. As a good shepherd, He knew how to keep those in His care and we should aspire to do and be the same. God forbid the people in our trust perish on our watch. Lord, give us the wisdom and diligence to lead in such a way!

Side note: God's design for His people revealed in the scriptures give us the plan and administration for such an environment. God has ordered His family perfectly to produce the desired outcome of biblical maturity—the fullness of Christ. Nothing has changed and we have to go back and rediscover, or discover for the first time, the ancient paths, the way of Christ and His Apostles revealed in the New Testament and in early Church history.

We need to pour over the scriptures and lay hold of truth, rather, let the truth lay hold of us. Transformational environments hold Christ Himself at the center. They make space for the Lord's presence and open vulnerable accountable relationships that walk together in shared mission. If we order our lives and work according to God's design, we will bear fruit that remains to the glory of God.

Without the right ingredients, we will not get the desired outcomes we want of authentic disciples with fiery hearts and the capacity to change the world. The right ingredients produce the right results. Without the correct amount of ingredients (challenge, accountability, loving support, genuine relationships with feedback, coaching, and mentoring), we won't create the right type of environment to produce world-changing spiritual warriors and pioneers.

The Law of Environment

The Law of Environment, one of John Maxwell's 15 laws of growth, states that growth thrives in conducive surroundings. To experience personal growth and promote it for others, we must change our environment to support our growth goals, and the formation of growth goals for those who have none. *Most people don't have a plan to grow, and as aspiring transformational leaders, we want to help people develop a plan and act on that plan successfully.*

So what are some of the elements of a growth environment and how will you know when you're in a fertile personal growth environment? For one, you'll feel encouraged and motivated. You may be challenged and it can be hard, but you are reminded of your potential and constantly pushed to fulfill it in a growth environment.

Do you feel that way where you are? Do the people you're leading or influencing feel that way? If you're not sure, take some time to get some honest feedback from them.

Consider some of these elements of a growth oriented environment:

- You're surrounded by others who are more mature than you or ahead of you. You must always be learning.

- You're continually challenged and having to overcome obstacles

- You have opportunities and responsibilities that give you context and room to grow.

- Your focus is forward though you reflect, heal, and learn from your past experiences (successes and failures)

- The atmosphere is affirming of your call, strengths, and potential

- You are out of your comfort zone and stay brutally honest and transparent

- There's excitement because you're connected to purpose, vision, passion

- Failure is not your enemy but your friend for growth and learning

- Others are growing with you—there is a real sense of community

- People are seeking continual improvement

- Growth is modeled for you and expected of you with relational accountability

A growth environment created by healthy leaders promotes and releases an atmosphere of freedom, breakthrough, and acceleration. I can tell you hundreds of stories of people who were stunted, plateaued, and unfulfilled. Yet, when they transitioned into a growth environment, explosive growth happened in almost every area of life.

Those people and families entered into personal revival and renewal (emotionally, intellectually, relationally, physically, financially, spiritually), as the result of the right environment that provided the right ingredients for breakthrough and progress to happen. This is real folks!

Don't you want to be able to create an environment that brings people into greater freedom, joy, confidence, clarity, purpose, growth and more? If you have read this far, I'm sure it's a "YES"!

Let's remember, it is the Holy Spirit that powers these structures that bring transformation. God's ways work even when unbelievers put them into play. When community organizations, businesses or people operate by or practice biblical values, they will thrive and do well. Many secular organizations operate by the "golden rule" of doing unto others what they would want done to themselves, They have amazing HR departments, working cultures, and customer service. They aren't necessarily run by Christians but they recognize the power of Christian or biblical values for treating people well.

On another note, let me repeat again and caution, the wrong environment and structures can suppress or restrict people's growth and the liberty of the Spirit. Like Jesus taught and what we see principally, you can't put new wine in old wineskins or they could both be lost. This is pretty important. *The structures and environment we create matter to the type of transformation and growth we produce.*

And It starts in our hearts and minds first. Remember, the teacher is the textbook and we reproduce who we are, not just what we teach. If we are not growth oriented and exercising diligent and faithful leadership, those under our influence will suffer for it. But, when we grow and improve those around us benefit. Even with the right structures and elements in place, but the wrong motives and an unsurrendered heart, the people under your leadership will not bear the desired fruit. *It's a spiritual reality, the heart and faith of the leader matters.* But when you have both working together, Boom!

Let's talk about a few practical components that help create these structures and greenhouses of growth.

Things to Consider to Creating Transformational Environments:

One more time: transformative environments play a crucial role in setting the stage for meaningful learning, personal growth, and high performance. As referenced before, our holistic models for education, training, and discipleship, are stronger with *immersive experiences that are truly interactive, relational, and transformational.* For incredible results, we must create learning and growth environments that give opportunities for true engagement, connection, personal reflection and expression connected to a sense of purpose. Students, teachers, and parents alike should be immersed in an educational journey that has clear purpose, focused objectives, and shared beliefs, where they are in connected relationships that foster growth. The environment sets the stage.

To make a lasting impact, education and development should be tied to a sense of unique purpose, calling, and life direction. When we understand that life is a journey of people discovering, expressing, and serving through who they uniquely are, then we see the value of a relationships-based education framework that helps people discover who they are and what they are called to do. The value becomes greater when we are actually equipping them to do what they are called to do and grow into who they are called to be. In settings like martial arts schools or sports teams, the training and development process could and should still possess elements that tie the principles of their practice back to real life, character formation, and the broader context and domains of their lives. The curriculum (an ordered process to achieve particular outcomes), community, and coaching that is created should strategically foster transformation and the betterment of their lives. We have to develop the whole person—body, soul, and spirit. Keep in mind the tension of knowing goals, being goals, and doing goals that contribute to holistic personal formation.

For example, my martial arts instructor in an Okinawan art called Uechi Ryu, is Grandmaster (10 degree Black belt) Mr Buzz Durkin. He's a precious man that has a powerful legacy of changing lives through the martial arts and serving people at a high level. He's an icon in the traditional martial arts world and regularly a keynote speaker to martial art school workshops and business seminars. He and his team have created an atmosphere that leads to incredible retention rates and student longevity. Generations of families train there and a large group of master ranking black belts who have stayed with him for 20 to 50 years. At the time of writing this, I have been there for 18 years. It's like a sign and wonder in the martial art community, and in any organization for that matter. In March 2024, we celebrated his 50 years of teaching the martial arts (1974-2024).

People always ask why students stay so long, especially since he only offers traditional martial arts (instead of what many do by providing as many options or martial and fitness disciplines as possible to foster student retention). What he says is simple and profound and an example of what I'm talking about. He is not just teaching karate. *He is teaching people first and the values and virtues that transcend technical practice.* He uses the martial arts as a complete discipline of body, soul, and spirit for student success and promotes high personal standards.

People don't stick around that long nor financially invest just for a work out and self defense instruction. Their lives, health, and relationships are better as the result of their training and the community experience on the Dojo floor. The training itself, combined with the personal interactions with other students and instructors, work together to create the space of growth and change. The culture and environment is pretty great and possesses the elements that make the magic. He always says the Dojo experience is more like a church than a business- it's a family.

As a fellow martial arts instructor, I learned from him years ago (and what I continue to see in practice in his Dojo), that every class should include the following:

1. Something physical -for fitness and health

2. A sense of accomplishment with a personal touch of progress

3. Something meaningful, philosophical, a theoretical point or concept

4. Something practical and useful in terms of self defense

5. A sense of completion. Class as a whole should have a identifiable theme or goal that includes a wrap up review or summary

He also was one of the voices who continually reinforces the concept that the leader is responsible for creating the right environment for growth to happen. The point I'm emphasizing is that when we aim to train, educate, and develop people, we must consider the entirety of their lives. The environments we create have the highest potential for deeper impact if we engage people holistically—physically, emotionally, socially, intellectually, spiritually and completely.

Ok, so let's keep going.

Steven Covey in the book, "The 8th habit" addresses the nature of the whole person when it comes to finding your place in life and thriving. He talks about these intelligences as they relate to people finding their unique voice or their place of significance and impact:

- Physical Intelligence (PQ) which needs to be developed into discipline

- Mental Intelligence (IQ) which needs to be developed into a vision

- Emotional intelligence (EQ) which needs to be developed into a focused place of passion

- Spiritual Intelligence (SQ) which needs to be developed and steered by conscience

These elements should be considered in our educational approach for academia and overall discipleship. Mr. Covey is just saying in another way what I shared earlier about the four core domains of life that create a strategic life plan (Legacy battle plan). Specifically, Covey's framework speaks to helping the individual dial in their unique identity, voice, and place of impact. When discipling, considering who they uniquely are (remember being before doing), should be the fountainhead of our approach, in tandem with the first principles of Christ. As leaders and influencers, we must use our places of impact for these fundamental causes in the kingdom. For we are in Christ, to become like Christ, and uniquely created in Him for pre-ordained good works. It's for these purposes that we live and seek to serve and train others. Mark Twain said, "The two most important days in your life are the day you are born and the day you find out why." As leaders we get to help people discover their why and purpose and help them live into it. Amazing!

The environments we create should go beyond traditional classrooms or mere lectures. To see transformative growth, we must incorporate elements that foster curiosity, exploration, collaboration, creativity, and true learning into our spaces.

So let's assume that we are taking a holistic approach in everything, addressing the whole person in whatever context we find ourselves in as described above. And as we move forward, let's consider these other important elements of transformative environments and some practical ideas for their implementation. Let's assume in light of everything we've talked about that authentic and trusting relationships are being built and have infused the hearts and essence of everything we do. We know those type of relationships of meaningful connection are the bedrock and prime movers of influence and transformation.

The following elements are not comprehensive or ultimately conclusive to transformative environments but definitely critical components.

1. The Presence of Visionary Leadership

John Maxwell says, " if your actions inspire people to dream more, learn more, do more, and become more, then you are a transformational leader."[131]

As we talked about in the beginning of the book, leadership is critical. People need to SEE the vision and be spurred on to more than simply external goal achievement but ongoing growth and personal mastery. Transformational environments require visionary and transformational leaders who can model and articulate a compelling and inspiring vision. Leaders of all kinds, including parents, should communicate a clear sense of purpose, direction, and values that resonate with the learners. The vision itself serves as a guiding light and framework that aligns all efforts toward a common goal and inspires individuals to reach

---

[131] John C Maxwell, *"Leadershift: The 11 essential changes every leader must embrace"*, HarperCollins Leadership 2019, pg 215

their full potential. That vision must be consistently communicated and reinforced in a way that is meaningful. Without it, things become stale and stagnant, and the joy of the journey gets lost. Continual inspiration and direction needs to be offered in what we model and in what we are saying. We need passion and enthusiasm to infuse the atmosphere. Painting the right picture in the minds and hearts of the people you're leading says a thousand things and becomes the underlying engine driving their process. Remember, "people perish for a lack of vision….and where there is no revelation, people cast off restraint." (Proverbs 29:18)

We talked about this previously so I won't elaborate much, but it's important to state that the visionary aspect of leadership is what many leaders lack. This is the challenge of all leadership: to inspire and hold the vision before the hearts and minds of those they lead. Truth must be alive in the heart of the leader and expressed and imparted with clarity and conviction to those they are leading on a regular basis.

When people get into the grind and the hard work or get lost in the mundane of repetition, this is exactly when the presence of visionary leadership is required to energize the heart and mind of people to persevere with fresh meaning, focus, and conviction. People need to see the "why" we are doing what we were doing to help them endure the pains of the process. Vision is the breath and anchor to keep people centered, refreshed, and disciplined.

Practical Idea:

- Craft a clear vision statement that distills the core values and mission of the educational environment into a concise and compelling narrative. This statement serves as a North Star or compass, guiding decision-making and setting the tone for the transformative journey.

- Integrate regular check-ins. Know where people are at, where they are struggling, and reconnect them to why they are doing what they are doing. If they don't know why they started in the first place it's a great time to take them through an exercise I call, *7 levels deep*. It will help them get down to their core motivations.

- Be intentional to inspire and cast vision at every meeting, gathering and relational touch point. Lead by example and with conviction while holding in tension the needs, wants, and struggles of your people. Try to create a clear picture in their hearts and minds of the value and importance of what they are doing.

2. Teacher as Facilitator, Guide, Mentor, Coach, Shepherd that Integrates the Faith with Accountability:

It starts with you as a leader. The teacher creates the culture of what is felt and experienced. An environment of love, safety, honesty, and openness is key where people are free to learn and fail and ask questions. A fear based culture and perfectionism quenches creativity, internal growth, and the formation of healthy relationships. Encourage teachers to shift from being knowledge providers only to facilitators of learning undergirded with a nurturing, parental type care, fostering genuine relationships and positive regard. They should maintain proper authority and discipline while imparting the pleasure of learning and growth.. Like coaching, your job is not to give the answers, but to facilitate the space for raising a person's or group's awareness so that they can discover their own solutions, make their own decisions, and take radical responsibility for their growth and development.

Like any good leader, you also want to provide support and resources for those you are serving so they can succeed at the task or objectives at hand. Not everyone has developed resourcefulness yet, and they need guidance to cultivate this skill. However, in your role as a mentor, guide, or shepherd, you can offer that support or, at the very least, pose the right questions to aid them in figuring out what they need to move forward. People will feel loved and secure to do what needs to be done when they know they will have what they need to get the job done. When people don't feel supported in that way they check out. Good questions to ask people is, "Is there anything you need from me that I can help you with or get for you to make your work easier? How can I support you right now? What is the next practical step that you need to take to move you in the right direction?"

If you're an overseer of teachers, coaches, pastors, parents, etc, train them in this way. Provide support with professional development that equips teachers with innovative teaching strategies, this core paradigm and its accompanying skills.

The other component is Integrating the faith by weaving spiritual and biblical principles into the educational fabric of whatever you're doing. This integration provides a foundation for moral reasoning and a sense of purpose in the learning journey. People so often over compartmentalize things and don't know how to make the connections in their education or life experiences to their faith and biblical truth. As people called to make disciples this is our primary task. We need to help people learn to see God in and through all things, learn to perceive His ways and works. This at times requires the ability to think abstractly, parabolically, and metaphorically.

In some settings your focus is the faith itself, and if you are the leader, parent, or mentor, the shift is in *how* you are teaching and helping people learn. Lecture may not be the way to go as previously described, or at least not lecture alone. Things like Socratic discussion and experiential or project/service based learning is the way for them to gain experiential knowledge. Then you can process, debrief, ask questions, coach them in real time, and so on. Part of this equation is also providing the right tools, opportunities, and curriculum to foster transformation. As I have suggested before, integrating "Know" goals, "Be" goals, and "Do" goals, keeps it holistic and should be considered when you are implementing a curriculum or any type of formal or informal training and Discipleship.

When it comes to shepherding people as well, one thing to consider for transformational environments is the issue of appropriate discipline. In today's culture there is overemphasis on positive reinforcement and not appropriate consequence. The ways of the Lord are superior to modern science and pop fads that study the frailty of man. Plus, today's science in positive psychology, neuroscience, and high performance are starting to identify what actually leads to authentic change, confidence, and resilience, and it is not what many people today have been doing since the self esteem movement of the 80-90's. *It has to do with embracing reality, self awareness, and hard work.* The scripture says that godly sorrow leads to repentance and so does God's kindness. There is a tension that must be discerned and navigated to know what is right for the moment and context. In the same way, obedience from the heart, which often requires discipline and correction, keeps us in alignment, doing the right things from the right heart motivation (accountability to a divine requirement) that grants us confidence before God (1 John).

Formative and corrective discipline is absolutely necessary but should always be motivated by and done in love. The law of reaping and sowing is real. Consequences for our attitudes, words, and actions must be held in the context of development and training. God rewards the faithful and takes from the faithless. This "everyone's a winner and everyone gets a trophy" culture is not the Kingdom way. It is not actually helpful, but rather misguided good intentions that lead to delusion and perpetual immaturity. Training people in proper discipline by teaching sowing and reaping and stewardship are part of reality and preparing people for real life and for eternity.

Creating Transformational Environments

We serve people well when we create an environment where people can receive appropriate feedback and constructive criticism. This provides the opportunity to think of themselves soberly, and rightly, and not in some sort of delusion. If we want people who have true character, competence, and confidence, we need to understand that confidence is built upon experience and realistic understanding of their capabilities and the grace of God. People need to see themselves rightly, and feedback, assessment, and discipline are necessary for that to happen.

Practical idea:

- Create learning contracts that identify outcomes, goals, deadlines, along with the character traits necessary for development. Contracts should also include agreed upon consequences and rewards for accomplishment or failure.

- Integrate assessments around character, knowledge, skill sets and competencies that are first rooted in the standards of God's word. Then add what is unique to the field of discipline or practice.

- Encourage risk-taking: Create an environment where students feel comfortable taking risks and trying new things. Celebrate effort and resilience rather than just the end results.

- In group setting, expectations, rules of engagement, and standards of behavior should be outlined with clarity on the consequences for non-adherence. When I have led cohorts for all ages (in church, online coaching groups, my martial arts school, and in other contexts), I have asked people to leave or sit out due to continued disregard for the conduct standards. This was done with care. I suggested courses of action for their ongoing growth and an open door to re-engage when they were ready. People have also been affirmed and acknowledged for doing what is right and used as examples of what is good and right. Reenforcing and rewarding the values and behaviors that you want to see is key to creating and sustaining the culture you want.

- Teachers should also learn to ask more reflective questions to help students process their actions, thought processes, and answers.

3. Flexibility, Adaptability, Modification in the Learning Spaces, our Approach, and in our Hearts:

There are times when strict adherence to things like schedules, approaches, and projects is necessary, but recognizing the people's diverse needs calls for a tailored approach[132]. The scriptures even teach that wisdom from above is pure, peaceable, and able to be reasoned with—it embodies a relational flexibility that allows harmony among different parts and does not overly burden people. The Lord walks with us where we are at and we should do the same for others. Plus, fostering genuine resilience for embracing growth and transformation is more about coaching people in various internal and external skills to tackle challenges effectively. The ability for people to persevere in learning, performing, or overcoming difficulty hinges on people's ability to see and utilize multiple options to achieve the goal. This requires a flexible approach that honors people's space and process.

One way to address this is to design learning spaces that are adaptable and conducive to different types of learning styles and activities. Include areas or opportunities for group collaboration, quiet reflection, hands-on projects, and technology integration. Give people options and freedoms within the necessary boundaries. This concept can be applied across all kinds of domains in life.

---

[132] Unique needs require leaders and instructors to exercise intelligent individuation and provide flexibility, modifications, and accommodations.

Flexibility is a practice of peace and true servanthood. This get's at our heart and character and calls us to the next level. We have to relinquish control to do things "our way" inorder to meet people where they are. It's a practice of patience and love to help others learn and discover at their own pace.

The Lord is a good shepherd who walks with us where we are. He does not exasperate us; rather He is a consistent encouraging force empowering us to change, grow, and overcome. He is not overly rigid even though He asks for all of us. Those who say "yes" to Him and are committed actually find that His yoke is easy and His burden is light. For He accepts and walks with us where we are to allow us to grow, learn, and become like Him. He is SLOW to anger, rich in mercy, and full of hope for every person. We need to emulate Him in walking with people who have said "yes" and accommodate their needs the best we can while providing the appropriate challenges.

Practical Idea:

- Take time to really understand who you're working with, their present capabilities and capacities, and their needs. Find out what has worked and not worked for them in the past . Assessments are great for this.

- Set up flexible seating arrangements or options so that students can choose their preferred learning environment based on the task at hand.

- Give people three levels of difficulty (easy, moderate, difficult; slow, medium, fast) on a task, movement, path of growth, approach, etc., and let them choose the level that matches their desire or ability.

- Learn to ask great questions to facilitate personal reflection, evaluation, and discovery.

- Use technology and AI powered learning platforms to help people:
    - Streamline administrative tasks
    - Customize learning experiences and lesson plans
    - Facilitate self paced learning
    - Employ adaptable assessments

  AI can be harnessed in a powerful way.

- Give people space and encourage them to research and pray before making a decision or fully concluding on a matter. Help them make space in their heart, thoughts, and decisions for the Lord.

4. Empowering Pedagogy: A Student-Centered Approach:

"Student centered" in the way I'm defining it does not mean that the student or child drives the agenda. Depending on the age, context, and overall goals, empowering the learner to take an active role in their education can be a driving factor and accelerate their learning speed. They focus better on their areas of interest, desire, and passion. If we can capture their interest and help them clarify their goals they will buy in and invest themselves fully. This eliminates the need for constant status checks and cheerleading to maintain motivation and successfully complete the necessary work. To foster a love for lifelong learning, we need to tap into their currency and they need a voice in the process. Self-directed learning breeds ownership and responsibility. When we leverage our role as a parent/teacher/shepherd/mentor, we can also help address and bring awareness to the other areas of needed growth when they may be prone to not "see it" or want to look or spend energy on their weaknesses. In the context of their interest and passion, we can help them see how other seemingly unrelated or less interesting subjects may actually impact their areas of passion. It's an indirect way to keep a holistic approach that balances the student centered and teacher led approach.[133]

An empowering pedagogy still requires intentional leadership to exercise healthy and appropriate authority without becoming passive. Like parenting as prescribed in scripture, parents and specifically fathers, are instructed to train their children in the ways of the Lord. They are to do it without provoking them to anger or embittering them so that they don't become discouraged (Colossians 3:20-21). We are to train our kids in the way *they* should go, so that when they are older they would not depart from it. This is an art of respect, discernment, and sensitivity towards our kids' unique purpose; This type of skillful instruction should lead to the deep reception of the faith and obedience to the truth.

In a student centered approach, we have to give them a sense of control and awareness about their own readiness, willingness, and ability to successfully reach their goals. Empowering people to overcome the barriers hindering their progress by making achievable and actionable steps helps them get there. Working with people where they are at and honoring their will and choices in the process is key. People wont go where they are not ready or willing to. We must still provide the necessary or appropriate level of challenge when people are stuck or unwilling. We need to properly discern the best approach. This is where the paradigm of teacher as a shepherd is more appropriate, especially regarding matters of the faith and obedience to the truth.

When we are student centered, we work with their unique learning styles and preferences. Growth and change can be hard as it is so we

---

[133] There are two different philosophies in tension here that can be united in the right approach. A teacher, mentor, Shephard, authority..etc can still lead and oversee the whole training and development process and overall guide the student/learner into the needed competencies while still providing the space for the student to have a voice and develop a sense of control and ownership in the learning process by providing choices and options.

want to remove unnecessary resistance and obstacles where possible. We have to choose our battles and not try to force square pegs in a round hole. Let's work with their God given hard wiring and learning aptitudes.

In "Do Hard Things " by Steve Magness, he references a scientific study on 200 basketball players and their coaches on performance and mental toughness. He notes that the main takeaway is that players and teams that were led by these coaches, created an environment of trust, humility, inclusion, and service. These coaches were player and team centered and taught the skill sets necessary to handle the pressure of the game and life. They created space and flexibility to help the players learn things like adaptability to act under discomfort with an array of approaches.

Problem-solving skills and autonomy are so important to build true confidence. That confidence and self efficacy is transformational and what we want for the people we are leading, teaching, and influencing.

Practical Idea:

- Encourage goal-setting, self-assessment, and reflection. Provide choices and autonomy within the learning process.

- Implement project-based learning, where students engage in hands-on projects that align with their passions and interests. Encourage collaboration and teamwork. Similarly, encourage group discussions, debates, and peer-to-peer teaching. This teaches character and social skills as well.

- Foster a culture of reflection among both students and educators. Encourage them to think critically about their learning or teaching experiences and how they can improve.

- Harness the power of technology and AI tools to customize the process and experience.

- Try Inquiry-Based Learning, where you can design learning experiences that prompt students to ask questions, investigate, and discover answers on their own.

- Support students in conducting research, experiments, and developing problem-solving skills. Giving opportunity for autonomy with the right support and coaching is really empowering and fosters better performance.

5. Fun, Celebration, and Pre performance Warm Ups: Changing your State with Something Physical & Musical to Foster Joy and Eengagement!

In the spirit of the mind- body- spirit connection we have to engage all aspects of who we are to maximize learning and growth. God made us to be fully engaged with our body, soul, and spirit. When we try to live and learn in a compartmentalized way we handicap ourselves. Plus, in the scope of life we want to create an environment of joy, hope, and the affirmation of progress. A whole generation is burdened by perfectionism and need to learn how to celebrate progress, and accept themselves in the journey. We can help this through the art of celebration and play.

Everything stays fresher and more enjoyable when we can keep it fun and learn to give thanks at all times—and most importantly in the struggles and pains of the process. Believers are to be the most joyful people on earth, sustained by a living hope and the love of God. His Joy is our strength and the good news of the gospel should undergird our attitude and approach to learning, process, and training. Growth can be hard and long. Therefore it needs to be framed and oiled with joy. Plus, if you're working with youth and kids, you HAVE TO HAVE FUN and play! The truth is, adults NEED this too.

There is a saying that says, "all learning is state dependent." How you presently feel in your body and your mood affect your ability to engage and retain information. It's important to learn to manage what you can control and shift your mindset and energy towards a positive place before trying to engage in productive learning and skill development. People need to loosen up and get into a joyful and restful state of being. Stress, fear, and cortisol are killers to learning, growth, and retention.

Breath work, exercise or movement, hydration, nutrition, vocal activation, laughter, play, and music, can shift your present state and activate your ability to engage. Japanese culture has communal exercise each morning, to foster health and longevity as well as prepare people to serve and learn at their highest levels. It's a way of life and it has become a cultural environment. We can learn from this.

At the Christian school we started, we kick off our morning routine with some free play then stretching and light exercise to activate the body and the brain of the students and faculty. Then we have a short dance and praise party! We also work with the families in their homes. This helps with the order and environment for wellbeing and growth too, down to the things like nutrition, meal planning, and routine. We understand that our diets and sleep schedules affect our energy, mood, and behavior. We dont force anything on people but we are intentional to engage the conversation. This is part of locking arms with the families to help them grow and to raise up their children as authentic disciples.

When we think about a transformational environment within the ecosystem of a community, we need to consider all the elements to maximize the potential of growth and the likelihood of reaching our goals. It's similar to a sports team where coaches work with parents to ensure each player can excel by connecting their home and social lives, connecting their home life and other activities to their performance on the field (sleep, nutrition, hydration, managing stress, social relationships and more).

Music activates some of the broadest and most diverse networks of the brain. Multiple studies based on brain scans show that the brain actively responds when hearing music. This makes total sense since our God is a singing God, who spoke the world into existence, and upholds all things by the power of His word! If you search the scriptures, you'll see the commands to make music to the Lord. We were wired to make music and be moved by music!

Our own experience shows us the benefits of hearing and making music. But check this out for a moment. It's obvious that music activates our hearing (the auditory cortex in the temporal lobes close to your ears), but that's just the beginning. The parts of the brain involved in emotion are not only activated during emotional music, they are also synchronized. Music also activates a variety of memory regions and may increase neurogenesis in the hippocampus of your brain. This allows production of new neurons and improves memory. Not only does music pull up memories and emotions, it helps create and lock in memory and emotions to new information or experiences.

Basically, music enhances learning especially when it's the type of music that promotes a sense of joy and pleasure. Joy and celebration is so important to the environment of the soul, life of community, and for transformation.

And, interestingly, music activates the motor system. In fact, scientists theorize that it is the activation of the brain's motor system that allows us to pick out the beat of the music even before we start tapping our foot to it! That's cool! That's also why we can develop coordination and muscle memory faster as we practice with music. This stuff excites me!

Andrew E. Budson, MD, writing for the Harvard Health Publishing, reports on a survey on music and brain health conducted by AARP. It reveals some interesting findings about the impact of music on cognitive and emotional well-being. He notes that this wasn't necessarily findings by a medical study, but the findings are still useful:

- Music listeners had higher scores for mental well-being and slightly reduced levels of anxiety and depression compared to people overall.

- Of survey respondents who currently go to musical performances, 69% rated their brain health as "excellent" or "very good," compared to 58% for those who went in the past and 52% for those who never attended.

- Of those who reported often being exposed to music as a child, 68% rated their ability to learn new things as "excellent" or "very good," compared to 50% of those who were not exposed to music.

- Active musical engagement, including those over age 50, was associated with higher rates of happiness and good cognitive function.

- Adults with no early music exposure but who currently engage in some music appreciation show above average mental well-being scores.[134]

Andrew goes on to say, "So just how does music promote well-being, enhance learning, stimulate cognitive function, improve quality of life, and even induce happiness? The answer is, because music can activate almost all brain regions and networks, it can help to keep a myriad of brain pathways and networks strong, including those networks that

---

134 https://www.health.harvard.edu/blog/
why-is-music-good-for-the-brain-2020100721062

are involved in well-being, learning, cognitive function, quality of life, and happiness. In fact, there is only one other situation in which you can activate so many brain networks all at once, and that is when you participate in social activities."

So cool, right?

This goes well with designing a celebratory atmosphere for learning and growing. It underscores the key role of praise and worship to help foster transformation. Inner healing, renewing the mind, internalizing truth, memorizing information and more, is accelerated when we engage our entire being and include music. Even biblical meditation involves singing the truth, our prayers, and praise. Apostle Paul said, "sing in the spirit and sing with your understanding." (1 Corinthians 14:15)

On a sober note, it's critical to recognize the profound impact of music in our lives. It has intentionally been used to mold values, beliefs and harmful ideologies, impacting a whole generation.

Practical ideas:

- Take time to express gratitude and thankfulness as a group or as an individual. Be vocal and be sincere about it.

- Express appreciation and affirmation of people's efforts and work. It will energize their hearts and give them a sense of internal reward and renewed energy to continue on with excellence.

- Create milestones and anticipated celebration times to refresh, reset, and recognize work, progress, and achievements. Things like exhibitions, presentations, or showcases where students can display their work and achievements are fun.

Plus, they invite parents and the wider community to celebrate student accomplishments too.

- Share a special meal together and have some social connection outside of the grind of the work or learning. This helps make it fun and keeps people motivated in the shared sense of mission and community—real fellowship is the camaraderie and the glue that holds it together.

- Start your day together with a stretch, breathing, and move your bodies to some fun and positive music. Have a mini dance party and release jubilant praise to God! Oxygenate your brain and body before engaging in reading, study, or administrative tasks. Attack the day with joy and confidence.

- Create patterned interruptions throughout the day with movement, stretching, singing, and uplifting or calming music to refocus and re-energize. You'll find a fresh sense of focus, productivity, and creativity as a result. At home, I call it a praise break. We stop what we're doing and just give praise to God with our voice, dancing and clapping for one to three minutes. Spontaneity is needed in life.

- Educate on the power of music and how it correlates to our brain, body and performance. Create exercises and opportunities to study, learn, or practice in conjunction with music. In study halls or other focused work times, you could lightly play classical music that enhances the brain's functions. There's so many options to explore the use of music to enhance focus, learning, and growth. And the same goes with exercise. It is the standalone and highest marker that engages better cognitive performance, mood enhancement, and overall well-being.

6. Ambiance and Aesthetics

An emerging science in the last decade highlights the importance of atmospheres that leverage and use colors, light, space and decor to enhance emotion, speed healing, and foster inspiration.

When we look at modern productivity hacks, a major component is shaping your environment to help you focus. Your surroundings can either help or hurt when it comes to achieving your desired outcomes and sustaining motivation. So depending on your goals, shaping the atmosphere to communicate your anticipated outcomes is an essential ingredient to the success and joy of your mission. The disposition of the soul and brain that experiences joy and pleasure, enhances learning and puts you at peace. It even allows you neurologically to develop and grow faster. We would do well to consider the findings of neuroscience to accelerate learning, growth, healing, and personal transformation.

God is a God of color and creativity, and has given us a world of beauty to cause us to be filled with wonder, Joy, and instruction in the knowledge of God. Day to day prophesies concerning the knowledge of God, and night to night reveals knowledge… creation reveals God's eternal attributes and divine power (Rom 1, Ps 19). The environment and ambience of the world has provided the canvas and backdrop for our exploration, learning, healing, and growth. We were made to behold beauty and come to the knowledge and worship of God as a result.

I forget who said this: wonder rather than reason is the true source of learning. Likewise, we should give our best effort to craft our learning experiences and environments to foster the sense of wonder. We were created to create, and should exercise that ability to produce environments of beauty and spaces for people to encounter God, love the process of learning, or ease and accelerate the journey of healing.

Your ambience is part of shaping your culture and reinforcing your values as a family, community, or brand. So go have fun adorning!

Practical ideas:

- Think through the sense you want people to have in your environment or space, and align your color schemes and decor accordingly. This also will require you to look at how certain colors psychologically affect us.

- Add the appropriate music or sounds into your setting.

- Find the areas you can start small in to add in some color or decor to enliven your environment. Add inspirational quotes or pictures that speak to your values and mission.

- Encourage your people to connect with the places that nourish their souls

7. faith, the power of God, and prayer

Regardless of your environment or situation, cultivating an awareness of God needs to be central to our lives as a personal practice. We must also exercise this with intention in the environments we create, oversee, or engage. His peace and presence can be perceived and is one of the greatest gifts we possess as both a guarantee of all that is to come and His present reality. He is God with us. Jesus said, My peace I leave with you, a peace the world cannot give.[135] Believers and unbelievers can sense His peace when He's taking up residence in our homes, facilities, works space, and in our very lives. We are to be carriers of His peace as we practice the art of abiding in the Lord.

We want to be intentional to pray and invite the Lord's presence and Kingdom to come, and His will to be done right where we are. His

---

135 John 14:27

Creating Transformational Environments

blessing and grace crowning the environment is the difference maker. Truth is, the single most distinguishing factor of God's people is His actual presence among us. We don't serve a dead God or a mere idea or philosophy. We serve the living God, the One true God, who dwells among His people and who brings us from glory to glory, strength to strength, and faith into faith, by the power of His Spirit. He is the transforming agent of a transformational environment. Part of the good news is that the structures and frameworks we create can be infused with the grace and power of God.

Hearts shift when they experience God and where there is an atmosphere of expectation and belief. Faith puts a draw on the grace of God and invites the Lord's kindness and power to manifest.

Looking for opportunities to pray with people is not only an act that communicates love and care, it also serves as a conduit for God to act in a powerful way in conjunction with our faith. No matter what we pray for, God is glorified. When we pray in the name of Jesus, and He answers, a seed of the gospel is sown into the hearts of those who bore witness, received prayer, or heard about it through the testimony. I have seen many miracles on the dojo floor, in my training studio, in restaurants (including the one I worked at), parks, grocery stores, my home, friends houses, airplanes, .etc. Wherever you are, you can bring the kingdom and power of God through faith filled prayers and by the simple reality of your heart overflowing with grace. As carriers of His presence, and as we grow in our friendship and intimacy with God we also grow in our ability and capacity to both host His presence and release it. When we step into our identity and call to be transformational agents of change, we can serve the world around us at a higher level. Faith is bold and unashamed and often spelt as RISK. We must step out and offer the greatest gift we have- Him!

Plus, there is an element of spiritual warfare that is very real. We wrestle not with flesh and blood but with spiritual powers and rulers in heavenly places that seek to blind the minds of the unbeliever from seeing the light of the gospel. When we wield our spiritual weapons in the grace of God, starting with faith filled prayer and the declaration of His word, we open the space and atmosphere to the light of God's presence and truth. It's then that the Spirit of God enables Christ to be seen with the eyes of the heart. Then the Kingdom of heaven breaks in with the needed provision, wisdom, freedom, healing, breakthrough, etc. People's minds can come out of the fog and dullness to the truth and their lives can be changed as a result. We possess the keys to freedom—the gospel truth and the Spirit of God.

We want to create an atmosphere of light where growth is unrestricted. Then, people within our influence can experience acceleration, conviction, and breakthrough. For this reality to prevail in our relationships and the environments we create, we have to go back to the truth about who we are and how we live. Are we walking in the light and walking in truth? Are we a people of prayer looking with expectation for the power of God to do what we cannot? Are we staying vigilant on our watch and taking advantage of the opportunities that are before us?

Take a moment to consider these questions. We don't want to just profess to know the living God, and yet just leverage the best techniques and tactics of modern science but ignore the reality of His presence. No my friends, we are children of the living God, who have been given the grace and power of God through His spirit. Let's be unashamed of the gospel, and make the most of every opportunity to see His kingdom manifest in our midst.

For the sake of time, I'll just briefly mention a few other elements to consider for a transformational environment and some components for learning:

1. **Cultivate Creativity and Innovation:**

    1. Provide opportunities for artistic expression, such as visual arts, music, drama, and creative writing.

    2. Organize innovation challenges or hackathons where students can develop solutions to real problems.

2. **Community Engagement:**

    1. Establish partnerships with local organizations and community members to provide students with real-world experiences.

    2. Organize field trips and service-learning projects that connect learning to community needs.

The Early Church & Eternal Pattern

In a final note in regards to transformative environments, I want to point out the broad framework but biblical pattern for the core elements that we see in the habitus of the early church that fostered not only the growth of authentic disciples, but the spontaneous expansion of the gospel throughout the earth. This is what we want.

The body of Christ is to be ordered to contain these elements, practices, and experiences, while being rooted in authentic community life. These things can vary in form. We see that the church had all things in common and they sincerely devoted themselves to prayer, fellowship, breaking of bread, and the apostles teaching, as they met from house to house and in the temple daily (Acts 2:40-47). There was great joy and simplicity of heart as they delighted in God and one another. The power of God was evident among them, they had a sense of awe, they cared for one another, and they continually praised God. They continued in the way of life they had learned when they walked with Jesus. As a result, not only were they growing, it says that the Lord added to their number daily. What was happening among them and through them was visible, evident and magnetic to those around them. The favor of God rested on them as they lived in the pattern entrusted to them.

These regular rhythms and sacred practices are foundational to an environment of growth and transformation. They are part of the divine blueprint scripture has given us as the people of God. The cradle of transformation is found in this context of a Christ-centered Family given to the regular practice of truth in the joyful fellowship of the Holy Spirit. As we grow to understand the nature of the faith, we see there are other micro habits practiced throughout history. They were understood for a life anchored in the spirit such as meditation, silence, solitude, fasting, singing, celebration, etc.

Are these elements and practices finding real expression in your life and community? I want to encourage you to study the book of Acts and see the essence and keys that are there. Even just take chapters 1-4 and meditate on them.

Without diving deeper and laying out the specific roles of every relational role (father, husband, wife, mother, children, servants, older man, older women, young man, deacons, elders, prophets, pastors), the administration of the church was laid out as a divine blueprint. It provided a foundation for how the church was to order herself and behave in their homes and in the community. Those relational structures and roles are the foundation and context by which we are transformed and on which life is built.

Other tactics in pursuit of creating a transformational environment without the most basic and primary framework described in scripture is vanity and like trying to build a house on sand. First things must be first.

Let's pause for a moment to take stock of our lives and consider the "house" we are building and be sure its foundation is on the rock. Are our lives ordered according to the scriptures?

From a solid biblical base, let's consider implementing these ideas and incorporating the key elements of transformative environments. By doing so, leaders of all types can create learning spaces that inspire people to become curious, engaged, and self-directed learners. The best place for this is in the context of community, fostering academic excellence, personal growth, and the discovery of the knowledge of God. *We need immersive experiences and environments that foster encounters with God, revelation of the truth, and holistic development in order to raise up authentic disciples and warriors who can shake the world.*

PAUSE. CAPTURE. APPLY
Prompts to help you process

1. What specific insights or concepts from this chapter resonated with you the most? Why do you think these stood out to you?

_____

_____

_____

2. How can you practically apply the principles discussed in this chapter to your daily life, relationships, or ministry? Identify at least one actionable step you can take this week.

_____

_____

_____

3. What potential challenges or barriers might you face in implementing these concepts? How can you overcome them?

_____

_____

_____

4. What are 3-5 quotes or points from this chapter that capture the essence of what it's communicating? Write them down.

_____

_____

_____

_____

_____

5. How can you involve your family, small group, or church community in the practices and principles outlined in this chapter? What steps can you take to foster a culture of discipleship and transformation within your circle of influence?

_____

_____

_____

6. Spend a few moments in prayer, asking God for the wisdom, strength, and courage to live out the truths you've learned. Write down a commitment or a prayer that reflects your desire to grow as an authentic disciple and transformational leader to impact the world.

_____

_____

_____

CHAPTER 15

Fostering the "Flame of Intelligence" and the Passion of Christ

"The art of teaching is the art of assisting discovery."

—Mark Van Doren

"Between stimulus and response there is a space. In that space is our power to choose our response. In our response lies our growth and our freedom."

—Viktor E. Frankl

As I have mentioned before, many people, churches, and organizations typically fail to really have an effective or deliberate process of training and development. For many, it's not from the lack of desire (they want to), and not from the lack of effort (they are trying), they just don't know how to in a way that is effective. Most of the time they are just doing what they have seen or have been taught.

To really ground people in the word of God, helping them order their lives with Christ's principles, many lack an intentional and holistic plan and process that lays firm foundations nor an ongoing path to full maturity. Creating the right environment and structures is key with the understanding that people need to discover and internalize truth for themselves, get real understanding, learn express it in their own words, and skillfully apply it in their lives. Personal conviction and clarity in truth must come first before we can properly apply truth or obey it, which should be the point of our instruction—the obedience of faith from the heart not the mere recitation of biblical doctrine. We want to teach and educate people for faith, hope, and love, and the type of love that is practiced toward God and people (obedience) in affection and service, and not just knowledge. We must remember, we are after transformation—becoming like Christ out of love for Christ through the power of His Spirit. Learning should lead to living a life of love and service. As Christ is, we are to be in this life—loving as He loves.

A Method

A powerful tool we use to ground people in the teachings of Christ in our ordered process, is a Hebraic and Socratic method of dialog around the scriptures and key issues. The Socratic method shares similarities with ancient rabbinical and Hebraic teaching practices. They both emphasize dialogue, inquiry, and interpretation of texts, concepts, practical situations or ideas. Just as Socratic discussions encourage learners to grapple with questions and explore meanings, rabbinical teaching style involves deep examination and interpretation with their application of sacred texts like the Torah. Jesus was accustomed to this type of learning and discussion from His youth. Remember when He was in the temple as a boy listening to the rabbis and asking questions? This pattern of teaching and learning through questions and discussion continued through His ministry as well. These approaches prioritize the pursuit of wisdom and understanding through active engagement and respectful debate.

In our community we have an ecosystem of ways we are intentionally discipling households, individuals, and leaders. Each part in our community has an indispensable role in the transformational experience. This helps foster a fuller understanding of the faith lived out. But our smaller cohorts, centered around studying and applying ourselves to the scriptures are critical and far different from a typical "bible study."

The ability to ask questions and help people clarify their thoughts and the implications to an issue or truth, is essential to fostering maturity, skillful living, and comprehension. Sermons alone won't change people nor ensure that they are convinced of the truth.[136] We have to engage in more intimate conversations to know what people are really thinking and believe in their hearts. And then we help them work through their paradigms and resistance to truth. Our community relationships and shared life together should enable us to see the truth of what we actually believe expressed in our lifestyles versus what we just say we believe and fail to live. When discipleship is done in real community context we see where we really are. Conversations around the scriptures from this context can help real honest dialog happen where the gaps in our lives exits with the truths we can easily profess. Conversations like these are transformative that forge godly character and lifestyle.

Without going deep through dialogue, people's faith and understanding will remain shallow and unchallenged. Therefore, so will their level of transformation for lack of proper application of truth. Safe spaces let people process and ask questions overseen by a mature, seasoned

---

[136] Declaring and teaching the word of God can absolutely mark, convict, and change people. Anointed preaching and sound gifted teachers have a place in the discipleship process. My point is that the truths encountered in oration and instruction must be processed and properly internalized through dialogue and application.

believer with discernment and capacity who effectively ministers to those they are leading and nurturing in the faith.

The flame of intelligence is ignited when we can hover around a topic long enough to understand it from many levels (hear other people's thoughts, pray into it, study and consult other experts, and learn to live with the matter). Revelation and understanding happens—the "Ah-ha" moment occurs and forms key biblical convictions that impact how life is lived. Obedience from the heart in response to the truth is impossible without first having clarity of the truth, so we need to learn to help foster that discovery.

To disciple people, it is necessary for a transformational leader to develop a broad skill set:

- Asking open-ended questions

- Discerning and reading between the lines of people's initial comments

- Leading a conversation into a clear place of consciousness and understanding

- Offering appropriate challenge

- Helping people bridge the gap from discovered knowledge to proper response with action steps of application married to loving accountability

The temptation is to try to shortcut peoples' discovery process and just tell them the answer or teach the facts right away. This has a place but not in the Socratic method. The problem is people dont always really *"get it"* even if you tell them plain as day anyway. People need to discover things themselves. It is a skill and art to teach people through asking questions while holding the space for people to process and wrestle through it. This takes great patience.

Western education has taught people to barely think for themselves. People tend to just want to be told the answer and fill themselves with more information which they then don't use. Thinking is hard work. But again, the problem is that people are drowning in information and knowledge but lack real understanding that manifests in wisdom— the knowing what to do with knowledge they've gained and how to implement biblical truth.

Wisdom is skillful living, not just good ideas, sound principles, and insights to mysteries. Concepts and principles have to connect with concrete reality. Otherwise, we stay confused, possibly puffed up by knowledge, and self deceived. That's why the scripture tells us to not be hearers of the word only, *deceiving ourselves*, but to be doers of the word. Then we will be blessed in what we do (James 1:22).

If people don't think clearly enough, they can't apply the truth to themselves appropriately so that it bears the good fruit that wisdom does. How can we take truth and break it down into real applications for our real lives with real problems and relational dynamics without some measure of real clarity in the truth? We can't.

But when people can process, internalize and firmly grasp truth, their soul can purchase wisdom, live skillfully according to it, and eat the grace filled fruit it provides. Growth must be organic and not mechanical if it's to be authentic and last. We have to honor the struggle, be patient in the process, and teach others to do the same.

Growth and maturity in Christ takes time and will continue till the end of the age. Our culture of instant gratification does not serve us well when it comes to our development in Christ. We have to remember that God is the God of decades and generations.

The Socratic method invites people into discovery and empowers people to take responsibility for their learning, thinking, and decisions. It also equips people with the needed mental faculties and study habits to embrace thinking clearly and critically themselves. Many people have never been taught how to learn nor what it means to be a disciple of Christ. The ability to learn is the aim t of facilitating continual growth, development, and effectual service. And yes, it is hard work- intentional work.

Spiritual growth and maturity in Christ, and all real human flourishing does not happen by itself. It takes effort and intentionality in collaboration with the Holy Spirit and must be chosen, moment by moment, day by day, year after year.

We want to be able to create such relational spaces where people are being stimulated to grow, learn, and evolve. Let's be intentional to be agents of transformation and foster a culture that promotes the pursuit of wisdom and the knowledge of God. Let's help people use their brain power to develop clear and biblically enlightened minds that fuel faith, passion, and obedience to God; true wisdom.

Great leaders ask great questions. It is that very skill we must develop to ignite the flame of understanding that fuels transformation and the obedience of faith.

Are you up for the challenge?

Socratic Method and Skills

As I described, socratic discussion is a powerful pedagogical tool that holds immense value in effective teaching, especially within the context of holistic development. Most people in the west have a really hard time with this teaching style initially, especially in the church[137]. Many are afraid to give a wrong answer, look stupid, or are trying to

---

[137] In higher education, the Socratic method is often used in medical and legal education to help students understand difficult concepts. The Socratic method is also a hallmark of classical education and is used in both secondary and postsecondary schools.

appease the teacher. In the context of learning and forms of education, most people are used to just being lectured at or preached at, and tend to not have critical thinking skills developed.

When we started implementing this into our community it took a while to break past people's paradigms and fears, but the struggle to learn this skill and method was worth it. The sweet reward of transformed lives, marriages, families, and community, speaks to the wisdom of the method rolled out in community. If Jesus used it, I think we should use it too.

The Socratic method encourages critical thinking, self-discovery, intellectual humility, and the cultivation of a deep and lasting understanding of subjects, not just the scriptures. When applied skillfully in a relational context, Socratic discussion becomes a vehicle for holistic growth by fostering intellectual, emotional, and spiritual development.

Kenneth Sayre quotes out of his translations of "*Plato's Seventh Letter*", tries to summarize the achieved goal of the Socratic method when properly understood, saying, " The discipline imparted through many "conversations" with a teacher and by daily "living with the matter" itself, that is to say, is necessary not only to make the mind receptive to the "flame of intelligence", but also to marshall the resources required to maintain that elevated state once it is achieved."[138]

You may be convinced already or at least intrigued, but here is **6 values of Socratic discussion that make it powerful:**

1. **Critical Thinking with Depth & Integration:** Socratic discussion prompts learners to engage in thoughtful inquiry and analysis. If it is done well, it can bring all the pieces together in an integrated and useful way. Critical thinking helps properly analyze, synthesize, and

---

[138] Kenneth Sayre, "*Plato's Literary Garden: how to reward a Platonic Dialogue*", Notre Dame, 1995, pg 14.

curate the content so that something new is seen or understood or made useful for application. Through well-crafted questions, educators guide students to examine assumptions, evaluate evidence, and arrive at reasoned conclusions. This process nurtures critical thinking skills essential for problem-solving, formulating core convictions, innovation, and informed decision-making. When we engage in this process in a prayerful way, deeply looking into a subject, we trust and know the Spirit of God is at work to lead us into all truth as well. We mine wisdom and receive it from God through the diligent pursuit of truth. Staying on the surface and neglecting to go deep leads to nowhere good. We have to develop roots in order to bear fruit.

2. **Active Participation**: In a Socratic discussion, participants actively contribute to the exploration of ideas. Conversations become dynamic, taking on a life of their own. This active engagement deepens comprehension, enjoyment, and ownership of knowledge, enhancing both cognitive and emotional development. The Socratic teacher has to learn to intentionally engage those prone to want to sit back and just listen. Many people love to hide in plain sight but these smaller groups when led well can pull everyone into the dialog.

3. **Confidence and Communication**: Through respectful and collaborative discourse, learners build confidence in using their voice, articulating their thoughts, and listening to others. This is so crucial when it comes to raising up warriors and authentic disciples who can reach the people around them. Effective communication skills, including active listening and thoughtful expression, are honed through this process of Socratic discussion. People learn to not ramble about words to the "ruin of hearers", but to be concise, insightful, and clear. Plus, It's better to look stupid stepping out to ask questions and sharing your thoughts in pursuit of wisdom than to be silent and remain stupid.

4. **Empathy and Perspective-Taking:** Socratic dialogues encourage participants to consider multiple viewpoints. This whole process is

about discovery and growth and understands the need for interaction with others. This practice cultivates empathy, emotional intelligence, intellectual humility, and the ability to understand and respect diverse perspectives—essential qualities for holistic development and the deepening of community.

5. **Curiosity and Love of Learning**: The probing nature of Socratic questioning ignites curiosity and a genuine love of learning for most. As I said, some people until they settle into the method and process really struggle with "probing questions." Many knee jerk reactions from people, besides blank stares, are, "is that the answer you're looking for?" or "what do you want me to say?" Or they just reluctantly speak up and hope to be passed over so others can talk. But when people get it, it's awesome and rich! When learners are encouraged to question, explore, and seek deeper understanding, they develop a lifelong passion for knowledge and grow as disciples. John Maxwell says, "if you want to make discoveries, if you want to disrupt the status quo, if you want to make progress and find new ways of thinking and doing, you need to ask questions. Questions are the first link in the chain of discovery and innovation."[139]

6. **Character & Lifestyle Formation:** Socratic discussions provide opportunities for moral and ethical reflection as well. Participants engage with foundational questions about values, integrity, scriptural truths, and social responsibility, contributing to conscience and character conscience development. Similar to the point of empathy, character is also built simply by learning to engage in respectful conversation with people who have different views and ways of communicating. When things can get heated or passionate (which can be a good thing as people are being honest and they are engaged), It is a great opportunity to practice patience, compassion, self control, and active listening. Plus, the intended outcome of Socratic discussion is not just stimulating dialog and discovery of truth, it's growth,

---

[139] John Maxwell, *"Good leaders ask Great Questions: your foundation for successful leadership"*, Hachette Book Group, Inc, 2014, pg 15

character formation shaped by truth, new behaviors, practices, habits, and decisions.

Ultimately, when led properly, there will be life change, personal evolution, community development, and one mindedness with the people you're in dialogue with. The result will be the advancement of the truth and shared mission of the gospel.

The Socratic teacher is involved in more than just leading good discussions but is engaged in the process of qualitative assessment through the process. Ideally there is more connection happening with the students outside the context of the conversations, though how the students conduct themselves in conversation is key to observe as well. Much can be seen and heard in the manner and substance of what people say and how they respond to others in dialog. Also, In the heart of shepherding and discipling others, we need to be observant in how those we're leading actually practice the truths they are internalizing in life. There should be evident fruit of growth in the attitude, understanding, and lifestyle of the students. Life should be changing. The results of the process done well is authentic growth and transformation.

Most people have been trained, or are more comfortable with lecture, preaching, presentation of truth, or facts from findings of research. That has merit and is valuable, as there is a unique set of skills in effective communication. But we need to have another set of skills when it comes to leading socratically. They both have value and present their own challenges, but the truth is, an effective leader and transformational change agent should become skilled in styles of speaking, teaching, coaching, and communicating.

Some have said, preaching moves people while teaching informs people. They work together, are symbiotic, and we need both.

As we see in the life and teaching style of Jesus and His Apostles, they harnessed many methods. If we want to grow in our ability to reach the people around us and effectively disciple others in the truth, we should grow in these communication skills so they could be wielded with grace, confidence, and conviction.

Since we are talking about the power of questions and the Socratic method, here are six skills necessary for leading socratically.

6 Essential Skills of Leading Socratic Discussion:

1. **Effective Questioning**: Crafted open-ended, thought-provoking questions that stimulate critical thinking and exploration is key. These questions should challenge assumptions and encourage participants to delve deeper into the subject matter. The truth is, better questions produce better answers. It's also important to be able to rephrase the questions in different ways. This requires proper preparation for the discussions and a real sense of command on the issue. For a quality and deep conversation to be sustained for a good two hours, you will want one clear issue or topic and anywhere from three to five well designed primary questions. I've added 12 tips for crafting open-ended questions in the back of the book.

2. **Active Listening**: Teachers and students alike need to cultivate attentive listening skills, allowing participants to fully comprehend and respond to one another's ideas. For an effective and engaging time, it's important to create an environment where every voice is heard and respected.

3. **Facilitation, Not Dictation**: The role of the facilitator is to guide the discussion, not provide definitive answers. Skillful facilitation involves nudging participants toward greater insights without dominating the conversation. We do not want to lead in a way that positions us as

the expert but as a fellow traveler on the road of truth. The difference when it comes to grounding people in the faith and the truth of Scripture,, should ideally be led by a mature believer who has a firm grasp on the truth. That person is skillfully teaching as a Shepard through a Socratic method, not merely facilitating a discussion.

It could be a point by itself, but the need to bring a sense of closure and clarity to the discussion and lay a foundation for the next conversation is key. At the end of the conversation it's important to circle back around and:

- **Summarize** the progress, conclusions, and any sense of growing consensus in the group.

- **Clarify** the remaining issues and key points made.

- **Challenge** the group to further study and reflection.

- **Relate** this discussion to the main issue of the course, and review the group's overall progress.[140]

4. **Encouragement of Dialogue:** Promote a collaborative atmosphere where participants engage in a back-and-forth exchange of ideas. Avoid monologues or one-way communication. People should not respond to questions solely to the Socratic leader but should be speaking to the group, as the group should enter into responding and not just the "teacher." The Socratic leader needs to help each person clarify their thoughts, articulate their argument

5. **Patience and Reflection**: Allow for moments of silence and reflection, enabling participants to process their thoughts and arrive at meaningful responses.

---

[140] Jeff reed, "*Teaching the First principles*", learnCorp Resources, 2003. Pg 45

6. **Flexibility and Adaptation**: Be open to unexpected directions the discussion may take and adjust your approach accordingly. If you are using this method around the scripture it's important to not rush. Bbe willing to have many conversations and meetings around the same topic and issue until you feel that there is real clarity and understanding. Bunny trails can be very useful to get at the peripheral issues and thoughts of people. Bunny trails can also derail a quality conversation. It's important to discern when to bring the conversation back into focus around the issue at hand or the last important thought or question. Adapting to the needs, interests, and contributions of the participants is important and must be balanced with the topic and truth you're teaching and discussing around. Many times have conversations turned into times of prayer and ministry to someone or a few. We just continue the conversation next time.

Other Questions and Holy Clubs

Questions are powerful as we can see and help us get to the heart of things and all together help us be opened up to discover truth.

Of course, the Socratic method or rabbinical method is not the only approach, though it is a very powerful method and a needed skill that I believe every leader should develop. There are other methods that are more direct, have a different focus, and pull on more subjective heart postures and objective places of accountability.

If discipleship is about following, knowing, and obeying Christ, we need a reality check on whether we are really doing what the word says, and what we said that we are going to do. We have to look at our life, behaviors, attitudes, and habits.

The great revivalist John Wesley and his Methodist movement has a strong philosophic influence on our ministry. His ministry was responsible for planting a church a day for over 150 years straight!

That is incredible! They were a gospel preaching, disciple making, and church planting movement that carried a spirit of revival and spiritual fervor.

These were simple churches built around spiritual disciplines and devotion to Christ unto Christian maturity—the perfection of love. They would regularly gather in these small groups (known as "Bands"), in sweet fellowship, and ask each other very specific questions and share openly, honestly and with accountability to grow in grace and truth. *They watched over each other in love for the perfecting of love.* This was not some legalistic cold or dead religious practice of checking boxes—it was authentic disciples of Christ doing what disciples do out of friendship and love for one another and God.

As a community we have implemented these little holiness clubs of 3-6 people, men with men and women with women. This is a further breakdown of our micro churches called Life Groups/Life Churches. The goals are to go deep in accountability and relationships, to foster love for God and His Kingdom, to provoke one another in love and good works, and to spur each other on to earnestly pursue holiness and the perfecting of love.

Some groups meet early in the morning, others meet midday, and still others meet at night. It's whatever the small group decides. As a base line, we encourage people to ask the same core questions or ones like them that were asked in these holy clubs of the methodist movement:

1. What known sins have you committed since our last meeting?

2. What temptations have you met with?

3. How were you delivered or how did you overcome?

4. What have you thought, said, or done, of which you doubt whether it be sin or not?

5. Am I a slave to dress, friends, work or habits?

6. Am I self-conscious, self-pitying or self-justifying?

7. Did the Bible live in me today?

8. Am I enjoying prayer?

9. Do I pray about the money I spend?

10. Do I get to bed on time and get up on time?[141]

I think these are great! These questions and similar ones that touch on different areas of life, marriage, family, work, ministry, moral purity etc, can help keep the people of God sharp and aligned with truth. When meeting in small groups with the intention to grow, there may be other questions from times of personal study in the scripture, alongside some focused reflection on the previous week.

People are real and honest about their lives and try to identify how God was speaking and moving with them and the people in their meeting. Discerning the hand of God with each other is a powerful practice and should be a regular rhythm of our lives. *Read that again.*

This practice is essential to the meaning of fellowship and Christ centered community, where people discern, receive and respond to the Lord's presence and voice. To "let the words of Christ richly dwell among you" as to teach, encourage and admonish each other is the way God designed His people to interact with each other in truth

---

141 Band meetings had a core 4 questions and the Class meetings, typically made up of 12 people, had more questions. Wesley also would ask additional questions around the decision making of how money would be spent such as: 1. In spending this money, am I acting as if I owned it, or am I acting as the Lord's trustee?
What Scripture requires me to spend this money in this way?
3. Can I offer up this purchase as a sacrifice to the Lord?
4. Will God reward me for this expenditure at the resurrection of the just?
In addition, there was a list of 22 questions he would personally ask himself every day.

and love.[142] Doing that together is really fun too and part of how we experience the reality of the living God among us. This fuels renewal-hearts of gratitude, worship, praise, and thanksgiving.

Another powerful practice is to look forward to the days and week ahead to set intention and weekly goals for life. It is game changing when we focus on our responsibilities, our key relationships and disciples, our intention for prayer, the scriptures, evangelism, and personal growth. The point is about living with focus and intention and being a good steward of our lives. This is the way of authentic disciples who are oriented around growing into the fullness of Christ, living a life that is pleasing and worthy of Him in every respect. *Such warriors and disciples discipline themselves to live godly lives and maximize their personal potential; they are committed and submitted to the process of growth.*

These small bands of brothers and sisters committed to growth are a perfect context to forge such leaders and disciples.

As a coach, people have paid me thousands of dollars to do what I'm talking about because they didn't have it in their context. But ideally, the Church family could and should do this for one another. I understand the value of connecting with people outside your context and the various skill sets, anointing, and abilities of the people of God around the world, but my point is most are not connected closely enough in the local church family nor going deep in the way we are called. The Church needs reform in her ways on many levels to come into maturity by returning to God's original design for her.

Think about what this could look like in your context.

---

142 Colossians 3:16-17

Discovery Bible Study Method

Here is another method to consider that has scaled all over the world and is used in many disciple making movements: the Discovery Bible Study. (DBS)

This model of small accountability groups and discovery bible studies uses a core seven questions in their meetings. They help them "*look back*" at the previous week, "*look up to God*" for help and insight, and "*look forward*" to plan the week with intention for how they will apply the truth discovered in the Bible study and who they will share what they are learning.

When initially meeting up the group looks back at the week and each person answers the following questions:

- How have you obeyed what you've learned so far?

- Who have you trained in what you've learned?

- Who have you shared your story or God's story with since we've been together as a group?

When they shift into studying the scripture, they read the passage together and ask the following questions (questions five to seven are a time of prayer and listening to the Holy Spirit. After prayer and getting some clarity they share with each other and practice what they are going to say with those they plan to share with):

1. What did you like about this passage?

2. What did you find challenging or hard to understand?

3. What can we learn about people from this passage?

4. What can we learn about God from this passage?

5. God, how can I obey and apply what You're teaching me?

6. Who can I train from this passage so they can learn to obey and love You more?

7. Who would You have me share my testimony or Your good news of Jesus with?

This small group applies the power of questions to train and develop people. This fosters personal growth in the faith but also missional advancement of the gospel by getting people to share their faith and reach their circles of influence.

To fan the flame of intelligence, we all need to think and act likewise in terms of continual personal growth, disciple-making, and soul winning. When we live between learning and doing, we truly come to understand things in reality and grow in the wisdom of skillful application. Knowledge must become useful and productive if we are to experientially understand and be transformed by it.

In learning, discussing, and doing, the light of God and the spirit of revelation gives us key insights and understanding necessary for growth, repentance, and ultimately transformation.

Lord, help us to live in the light by practicing the truth!

BonHoeffer's Confessing Church

Dietrich Bonhoeffer was a German theologian and reformer who opposed the Nazi regime and was eventually martyred by the Gestapo. His written works have been studied for decades (and will continue for the years to come) and are a rich source of instruction for the church today.

God's intention for His people and the reality of the fellowship of believers—the Church—is that we are the visible presence of Christ on the earth. Thus, our unity is imperative to the witness of Christ, our experience of Christ, and our growth and maturity in Christ. In John 17, Jesus' priestly prayer for His people, the Lord calls us into complete unity that we would be one as the Lord is one, and so that the world would know that Jesus was indeed sent from heaven. Truly amazing! Our unity and love for one another is how the world would identify that we are indeed His disciples. What an incredible reality! This good and pleasant unity among God's people is what releases God's commanded blessing and glorious witness in the earth (Ps 133). This unity is realized when we abide and walk in the light and truth of God through humility, confession, and repentance. Without divine alignment to the word of God, we misrepresent Him and His ways to the world, but we also miss out on the experience of His greater glory and wisdom in our midst. The hidden wisdom of God is reserved for the mature and leads to greater glory and entrustment.[143]

So how do we get there?

Scripture tells followers of Christ to "Confess your faults one to another and pray for one another that you might be healed." (James 5:16). This must become a way of life. But as Bonhoeffer notes, many Christians neglect this instruction to their own detriment: "He who is alone with his sin is utterly alone," and this despite being together with others in worship, prayer and fellowship. Without confession as part of the practice of the community, its fellowship "permits no one to be a sinner... everybody must hide his sin from himself and from the fellowship." The result is people gathered together, yet living alone "in lies and hypocrisy."[144]

---

143 1 Corinthians 2:1- 3:23
144 Dietrich Bonhoeffer, "Life Together: The Classic Exploration of Christian Community ", pg 110

In cultivating an authentic Christian community, confessing sin and sharing struggles were crucial to experiencing the presence of Christ, the power of forgiveness, and freedom. They would spend all day Saturday confessing sin to each other and praying for each other, then their Sunday love feasts (communion gatherings) were explosions of joy and the power of God. The 1st John 1 walking in the light before God and each other was critical to the release of the power of God and the maturity and joy of the saints.

Open relationships, confession of sin, and the pursuit of holiness are beautiful earmarks of believers described in *"Life Together: The Classic Exploration of Christian Community"*. Written originally at age 17 (another example of a youth given to Christ and His Kingdom), we have Bonheoffer's experience of Christian community. This story of a unique fellowship in an underground seminary during the Nazi years reads like one of Paul's letters. If you have not read it, please do so.

"It is the command of Jesus that none should come to the altar with a heart that is unreconciled to his brother" (p121). It is thus appropriate (even vital) that in the worship services of the community, prayers of confession together with a declaration of forgiveness in Jesus name precede the receiving of the Lord's Supper. But even more importantly, the church that regularly practices confession person-to-person, will find true Christian community at the Lord's Table. Bonhoeffer comments:

"Here [at the Lord's Table] the community has reached its goal. Here joy in Christ and his community is complete. The life of Christians together under the Word has reached its perfection in the sacrament" (p122).

Through confession of sin, one brother to another, there is true and profound breakthrough to the authentic Christian community, and true transformation of individuals. Sin likes darkness and hiddenness, but when it is brought into the light through confession, strongholds that enslave people in sin are broken. One of the great sins that holds us enslaved to other sins is pride. But confession demands, and yields humility. In confession we die to self—we let go of self-protective false pride and come into the freedom of being reconciled to God and others. Bonhoeffer comments:

"In confession we break through to the true fellowship of the Cross of Jesus Christ. In confession we affirm and accept our cross. In the deep mental and physical pain of humiliation before a brother—which means before God—we experience the Cross of Jesus as our rescue and salvation. The old man dies, but it is God who had conquered him. Now we share in the resurrection of Christ and eternal life." (p114.)

And so it is through the death of the self-protective self that we enter into new life. "Confession is conversion...Christ has made a new beginning with us...Confession is discipleship." (p115.) On this point, Bonhoeffer quotes Proverbs: "He that covereth his sins shall not prosper; but whoso confesseth and forsaketh them shall have mercy." (Proverbs 28:13) He then states that "What happened to us in baptism is bestowed upon us anew in confession" (p115). Powerful!

To be authentic disciples who are transformational agents, this mode of transparent living in the light and truth of God must be our reality and regular rhythm in community. This confession of sin, repentance, the pursuit of holiness, and communion is critical for the authority and power of God to be released through us, toward each other, and the world around us. Spiritual health, healing, and maturity is impossible without it. If we intend to grow up in Christ, honesty, truth, and confession are a must for the saints to come to maturity and fullness.

To connect the dots here from the nature of the Socratic method to discipleship and fostering both revelation and transformation:

- The right questions lead to clarity, revelation, and conviction

- Which leads to confession and repentance

- Which leads to cleansing, authentic community and sweet fellowship

- Which leads to celebration in the gospel and its transformative power at work among us

- Which leads to a powerful witness in the earth, effective evangelism, and the type of a discipleship culture that tips the scales and can turn the tide of history one heart, one family, one community at a time.

To Wrap Up

Powerful questions in a relational context foster engagement, learning, revelation, and the obedience of faith that positions hearts and lives to know God better, experiencing His transforming power.

When the word and ways of God come alive in us and are put into practice, we not only become passionate for Christ, we experience the passion of Christ. In the pursuit of obedience to His word and the advancement of His kingdom, we share in the fellowship of His suffering and the power of His resurrection. We come to share in His heart and passion for us, His people, and the lost. To follow Jesus and truly be His apprentice requires courage and radical surrender. It requires suffering, perseverance, and endurance with hope. Jesus learned obedience by the things He suffered (Hebrews 5:7-10). His suffering to do what was right and love before God and for us, was part of His passion. As we give ourselves to the sanctifying work of God to conform us to His image and the obedience of faith, we should expect both internal and external suffering. Self denial (internal suffering) and external resistance from those around you who may not understand your obedience and righteous decisions, may persecute you. But remember, if you suffer for Christ's sake you fellowship with Him in it and His Spirit rests on you.[145]

We have to commit to be forged and transformed into His image no matter the cost, to lay hold of grace and the purpose for which His grace laid hold of us. We may come in weakness but through the power of His word and Spirit He makes us warriors who can live in His wisdom and work alongside Him to change the world.

I want to encourage you to engage in the life of the Church in a deeper way. Dive into these smaller groups where you can be known, accountable, and grow to the next level. Whatever model you choose, these smaller relational environments with the focus of discipleship is what matters most. In fact, every initiative in the church should be unto this call of discipleship and what it means to legitimately grow in Christ and advance His mission.

Remember, to go big we have to go small and deep. These simple churches, micro monastic communities, holy clubs, life groups, small groups, warrior cohorts, whatever you'd like to call them, are key to the pursuit of the Lord. You will be going deep, becoming whole, discovering the knowledge of God, while effectively making disciples in an intentional, strategic, and authentic way.

Remember, we change the world by being an authentic disciple ourselves and by making disciples who do the same. On with it!

---

145 Philippians 3, 1 Peter 2:11-25, 2 Timothy 3:12

PAUSE. CAPTURE. APPLY
Prompts to help you process

1. What specific insights or concepts from this chapter resonated with you the most? Why do you think these stood out to you?

_____

_____

_____

2. How can you practically apply the principles discussed in this chapter to your daily life, relationships, or ministry? Identify at least one actionable step you can take this week.

_____

_____

_____

3. What potential challenges or barriers might you face in implementing these concepts? How can you overcome them?

_____

_____

_____

4. What are 3-5 quotes or points from this chapter that capture the essence of what it's communicating? Write them down.

_____

_____

_____

_____

_____

5. How can you involve your family, small group, or church community in the practices and principles outlined in this chapter? What steps can you take to foster a culture of discipleship and transformation within your circle of influence?

_____

_____

_____

6. Spend a few moments in prayer, asking God for the wisdom, strength, and courage to live out the truths you've learned. Write down a commitment or a prayer that reflects your desire to grow as an authentic disciple and transformational leader to impact the world.

_____

_____

_____

CHAPTER 16

Making the Shift and Counting the Cost

"Getting over a painful experience is much like crossing monkey bars. You have to let go at some point in order to move forward."

—C.S. Lewis

How do we make the shift from where we are to where we want to be, both in terms of our own growth and in terms of making disciples? How do we build discipleship oriented cultures in our homes and communities? Sacrifice.

The law of sacrifice says, to go up we have to give up. The Kingdom of God advances through sacrifice—the sacrifice of His people who give themselves entirely to the will of God just like Jesus the Son of God did. Unless a kernel of wheat falls to the ground and dies, it remains alone.

Serving the King and His kingdom is not about convenience or comfort but costly sacrifice even in the midst of our convenient and necessary daily activities. The simple integration of discipling people along the way is where things can start, but is that always convenient? Sometimes yes and sometimes no. Is growing in self awareness, communion with the Lord, and intentional practices for continual improvement, even in small ways every day, convenient or easy? No, but sometimes yes. Discipline and delight are tensions to navigate, in the same way as inspiration and intentionality. We can't always wait to "feel " like it before we act, but we can act our way into new feelings as we gain momentum and shift our state through consistent practice.

Start somewhere, start small, start now.

Shifting into becoming an authentic disciple who makes disciples requires that you live not for yourself, but for the will of God. This must become the orientation of our lives. "Not my will but your will be done....Father, glorify your name" is the reality and weight of discipleship.

Choosing to walk the path of intentional and authentic discipleship is one of the most profound decisions a follower of Christ and leader can make. However, it's not a decision to be made lightly. As you have read throughout this book, authentic discipleship requires transformation—of the heart, mind, family, church, and community. This kind of deep, lasting change is costly, on may fronts. It asks us to examine our lives, abandon comfort zones, and reorder priorities according to God's kingdom, not the world's. In this chapter, we'll explore the transitions, decisions, and challenges involved in moving toward intentional discipleship, as well as the profound value of it.

The Call to Count the Cost

Jesus never sugarcoated the cost of following Him. In Luke 14:28-30, He illustrates this through the analogy of building a tower: "Suppose one of you wants to build a tower. Won't you first sit down and estimate the cost to see if you have enough money to complete

Making the Shift and Counting the Cost

it?" This scripture points to the necessity of counting the cost before embarking on the path of discipleship. There is a reality check, a reorientation of life and devotion that changes casual Christianity. Remember as Bonhoeffer said, "when Christ calls a man He bids him come and die." And of course, we know that it is unto life that is truly life, but nonetheless, it is a death to a self-oriented life. He calls us to deny ourselves and place Him and His call as preeminent in our hearts and lives.

Making the decision to pursue an authentic walk with Christ forces us to ask hard questions:

- What am I willing to surrender?

- What sacrifices must I make for my family, my church community, and myself?

- Am I prepared for the resistance, misunderstanding, or even opposition from those who might not understand this shift? Even from those potentially in my own household?

- Am I okay being persecuted and enduring rejection? Am I willing to endure and embrace suffering and inconvenience?

- Am I willing to be poured out in life for Christ, His Kingdom, His church, His mission?

-A'm I willing to endure to the end? Do I understand that this is a life long and eternal choice?

- Am I okay with delayed gratification?

These are difficult but necessary questions. Without honest reflection, the pursuit of discipleship can be easily derailed by challenges, comforts, the cares of this life, and disappointments along the way.

Simon Sinek says it this way, "The cost of leadership is self-interest." from his book *Leaders Eat Last* (2014).

Transition 1: Personal Transformation – Surrendering Self

The journey toward intentional discipleship begins with personal transformation. Before we can impact others, we must first be transformed ourselves. Authentic discipleship demands a fundamental shift in how we see ourselves in relation to Christ, others, and our purpose in the world.

I've been walking with the same core group of people for 25 years at the time of writing this. I'v had plenty of opportunities to take the path of least resistance and go to other communities, leave when it's been hard, accept big and exciting invitations from other ministries, and more. It takes hard choices to stay and learn to yield to God's divine process of development. So many I'v met over the years, both young and old, have short circuited their process of growth and discipleship. They simply couldn't learn the lessons of submission, faith, surrender, forgiveness, and more. People also have been so conditioned not only by culture but denominational traditions that make it so easy to hop around, church shop, and leave when they don't agree with something. Ancient paths must be recovered.

The way of the Lord is a narrow path and a small gate that few find. The cost of discipleship requires surrender and commitment. Jesus said if we are not willing to deny ourselves and forsake our own life, and even hate our mother, brother, sister, father, children, spouse, we aren't worthy to even be His disciple.[146] This is radical and requires all.

---

146 Matthew 10:34-38, 16:24-28, Luke 14:26-28 - remember to "hate", doesn't mean you need to hate them, it is in reference to allegiance and what comes first. We are called to love others with the love of Christ and lay down our lives for them. Serving Christ may cause those in your own house to oppose you and hate you, but allegiance to Christ must come first.

We humble ourselves or we get humbled. Surrendering self is a daily choice and a lifelong call. It begins with acknowledging that we are no longer our own and can do nothing of eternal value apart from Him. The Apostle Paul writes in Galatians 2:20, "I have been crucified with Christ and I no longer live, but Christ lives in me. The life I now live in the body, I live by faith in the Son of God." In choosing discipleship, we relinquish our right to define success, pursue personal ambitions without considering God's call, or make decisions based solely on comfort and convenience. We were bought with a price, the precious blood of Jesus.

This surrender involves:

- **Time**: Discipleship demands time spent in prayer, scripture, and service. This may mean rearranging schedules or sacrificing leisure activities.

- **Comfort**: Intentional discipleship often calls us to step out of our comfort zones—speaking truth in difficult situations, serving in unfamiliar capacities, or moving away from patterns that offer temporary pleasure but hinder spiritual growth.

-**Pride**: Being a disciple requires humility. We must be teachable, willing to admit our faults, and open to correction, not just from God, but from others around us.

Transition 2: Family Transformation – Leading by Example

As we are transformed, the next challenge is leading our families into the same intentional discipleship. This is no small task. Family discipleship can be difficult because it requires a reorientation of family priorities, habits, and expectations. It means modeling a Christ-centered life in every aspect—from finances to time management to conflict resolution to rest and recreation, to devotion.

Some key decisions include:

- **Creating a Culture of Prayer and Scripture**: Discipleship within the family means being intentional about:

- Fostering spiritual habits like prayer and worship.

- Engaging in Bible study and scripture reading together.

- Participating actively in church life.

- Serving the community as a family.

- Discussing faith openly at home.

- Doing anything else God asks of you.

These practices build a foundation for spiritual growth and help align the family's values with Christ's teachings.

- **Balancing Grace and Discipline**: Discipling family members—especially children—requires a balance between offering grace and instilling discipline while providing structure and tons of affirmation. Parents must lead by example, demonstrating the grace of God in their interactions, while also helping their children understand the importance of spiritual disciplines, honoring authority, and participating in the household. Consistent loving discipline is critical to model the Fatherhood of God, keeping people aligned with truth and walking together in unity. Training internal attitudes and external behaviors is necessary to produce authentic godliness and kids who truly love God. But two things must be present: the right environment within God's structure for family, and trust in the Holy Spirit to encounter our kids and spouses. We must do our part and God does

His part. The Lord Himself must capture the heart, affection, and allegiance of our families as we do our part to lead, love, and teach what is good, right, and true. Trying to overly control and "stuff" the faith into our kids or spouses only crushes their spirit and leads to rebellion and dead religion.

- **Sacrificing Personal Goals for Family Discipleship**: Many times, personal ambitions may need to be set aside to prioritize family discipleship. This might mean forgoing career advancement opportunities, changing financial priorities, or setting boundaries that protect the spiritual development of the family. Remember, discipling our kids is one of our first sacred charges. Even ministry leadership flows out of our marriages and family life. Someone who cannot manage their own house and raise their kids in a manner worthy of respect, is not fit to help manage God's house (1 Timothy 3:5). It starts in the home.

The cost of family discipleship can be particularly steep. It will require difficult conversations, possibly changing long-held family traditions, or facing the reality that not every family member will embrace the same spiritual values. However, the investment is invaluable. Leading a family toward intentional discipleship creates lasting spiritual legacy. I know that God's word is faithful and if we give ourselves to live into God's design and keep Christ and His Kingdom first, He will also take care of our families and encounter our children and spouses. We do our part and God does His part.

I understand the difficulty of single family homes, as I grew up in one for many years of my formative years. Yes, there is various difficulties and hard waters to navigate depending on the situation, but I will say that God's grace is still sufficient, and will meet you and your kids. He met me. The Church and the Lord Himself fill the gaps. I would also call the church to rise up to take note of the single parent families in their midst and come alongside them.

The Church is a family full of fathers and mothers, big brother and sisters, grandparents and more that can provide where the natural family doesn't or cant. This is my and my wife's story as well on both a receiving end and a giving end. My kids have many grandparents in the Body that relate and connect as really healthy biological grandparents would. It's beautiful! And there are kids and youth we mentor and father who don't have fathers and we seek to treat everyone as family. One single parent knows that if something were to ever happen to her that me and my wife would adopt her two boys. That is the culture we have created in the Church body.

Transition 3: Church Community Transformation – Shifting the Paradigm

Intentional discipleship goes beyond personal and family life; it requires a paradigm shift within the church community. As you can see, mentioned above is a little touch of an essence of connection and care in the family of God. This is not a program, it's family. Most churches are accustomed to a consumer-driven model, where members attend services, receive teaching, and leave without engaging in deep relationships or accountability.

Transforming a church community toward authentic discipleship involves shifting from this consumer model to a relational, disciple-making model. This shift requires vision, courage, a well crafted, prayerful strategy to transition the people with all your leaders on board, and a willingness to confront the status quo.

Key decisions in this transition include:

- **Creating a Culture of Joyful Discipleship:** A class called "discipleship" won't do it. To foster a disciple-making church, leaders must be intentional about creating environments where discipleship is prioritized and well integrated at a paradigm/mindset level. This requires a shift from programs to a presence centered life where discipleship is oriented on knowing God, becoming like Him, and doing what He does in a community context. This might involve restructuring programs, de-emphasizing large events void of a discipleship strategy, and refocusing on small groups where relationships can flourish and the joy of being conformed to His image can happen as central.

- **Equipping the Body**: Every member of the church needs to be equipped to both be discipled and disciple others. This may take the form of training, leadership development, and mentorship opportunities. It means moving from a pastor-centered model to one where every believer is empowered to be a soul winner and disciple maker.

- **Fostering Accountability**: True discipleship thrives in an environment of accountability. Churches must build systems where believers are accountable to one another in their walk with Christ, encouraging each other to grow and confront areas of spiritual weakness as they grow together in perfecting of love and holiness and being faithful to the good works they are called to.

The cost of transforming a church community can be high. It often involves letting go of programs or traditions that no longer serve the mission of making disciples. It may lead to friction within the congregation as people resist change, preferring the familiar comfort of routine over the challenge of relational discipleship. However, churches that embrace this paradigm can expect lasting, meaningful transformation that extends far beyond Sunday services. You may lose people, as unfortunate as it is, but that's okay. Start with those who are responding and hungry, then build from there. One mature believer who has the capacity to disciple others has the potential to give birth to a multiplying movement and plant new communities. Developing the few to impact the many is worth it.

Howard Snyder talks about 10 keys for a renewal strategy for a local church:

1. Begin with life: identify key people and structures God is already breathing on. See what The Father is already doing and feed the organic life.

2. Don't attack entrenched institutional patterns: move around them or reform them from within. Build organic models and community within eh "walls."

3. Seek to pastor all people: win over the resistant but focus on the core who are catching the vision.

4. Build a balance of worship, community, and witness that consists of evangelism, service, and justice.

5. Incorporate small groups and home groups: These are universal and cross cultural.

6. Affirm the ministry of all believers: leaders equip and activate the body.

7. Move toward the biblical model of leadership: Character and giftedness, pastoral leadership equals equipping, and a team modal—a plurality of leadership.

8. Help the congregation discover its own identity.

9. Work to ensure the financial stewardship authentically reflects the churches mission and identity.

10. Help the Church catch a Kingdom vision and clear understanding that the Lord reigns over all of life: The church

is to engage in real community, worship, evangelism, justice, and discipling and see this as a part of social transformation.[147]

Transition 4: Leadership Team Transformation – Changing the Practice

For those in leadership roles, the cost of intentional discipleship comes with unique challenges. Leaders must first embody the principles of discipleship before they can expect others to follow. This requires a radical reevaluation of leadership practices, values, and goals. The process of getting on the same page, clarifying vision, and defining a plan of integration is critical for healthy transitions, change, and mission success.

In our church, some of our hardest transitions and struggles with people have been with leaders who are unable to make the changes. They had been stuck in old paradigms and previous ministry training, or unwilling to go to the next level of personal growth and relational investment with others.

Some of the key shifts include:

- **From Leading Programs to Leading People**: Many church leaders are accustomed to focusing on programs, events, and administrative tasks. While these are important, discipleship-focused leadership prioritizes the development of *people over programs*. Leaders must invest in relationships, ensuring that their primary focus is the spiritual growth and maturity of those they lead. That means leaders will have to slow down enough to actually be present with people and make time in their schedule for them. Discipleship takes quality and quantity of time. It's not a 9-5pm job or only calling hours between 7-9pm Monday- Friday.

---

[147] Howard A. Snyder, "Building a Renewal Strategy for the Local Church" from *Signs of the Spirit: How God Reshapes the Church*. 1989, Zondervan publishing.

- **From Authority to Servanthood First:** Discipleship requires servant leadership. Jesus modeled this by washing His disciples' feet, illustrating that true leadership is rooted in humility and service. Church leaders must adopt a posture of humility, focusing on serving rather than wielding authority. This might mean letting go of personal agendas or visions in order to facilitate God's work in the lives of others. As a leader you win by helping others win. The authority entrusted to you as a leader is first and foremost to build up the body of Christ though this will require healthy parenting and discipline as well. This includes hard conversations, confrontation, correction, rebuke, training, assessment, coaching, and more. But relationship and servanthood first. Give more than you take and use your authority appropriately.

- **From Measuring Attendance to Measuring Transformation:** Many churches measure success by numbers—attendance, giving, and event participation. However, in a disciple-making church, the metrics of success shift to spiritual transformation as a primary. This means celebrating stories of life change, repentance, and growth, even when the outward signs of "success" may not be as visible. Those other indicators still may play a role but they are not the first set of metrics we should be looking at. Being faithful to love the one in front of you and the flock you are over, and laboring for Christ to be formed in them, is the first and core aim of a Kingdom leader and Shephard after the Lord's heart. How do you measure success in the church?

Leaders who embrace discipleship must be prepared for the weight of the task. Changing long-standing practices and expectations within leadership teams can be difficult. However, the reward of leading a church into authentic transformation far outweighs the discomfort of the transition.

The Value and Cost of Pursuing Genuine Transformation

Intentional and authentic discipleship is costly, but the value far exceeds the price. As missionary Jim Elliot said, "That man is no fool who will give up what he cannot keep in order to gain what he cannot lose." The work of discipleship transforms individuals, families, churches, and communities, leaving a lasting impact that transcends temporary successes and bears the fruit of eternal reward. The price is paid in time, effort, and sacrifice, but the return is eternal.

- **Lasting Spiritual Fruit:** The transformation that comes through discipleship results in lasting spiritual fruit. When individuals and communities commit to following Christ wholeheartedly, the fruit of the Spirit—love, joy, peace, patience, kindness, goodness, faithfulness, gentleness, and self-control—becomes evident. What also becomes evident is the use of their spiritual and natural gifts in the life of the church, and their passion to reach the lost around them. This transformation has a ripple effect, spreading beyond the walls of the church to impact neighborhoods, workplaces, and entire communities. Spontaneous expansion of the gospel has always been the fruit of active and authentic disciples.

Just recently, we hosted a week-long training in evangelism, taking teams of people out to share the gospel every day for six days straight. The activation of people in our community has been profound. In that week of outreach, we led 507 people to the lord and shared the gospel with hundreds more. But what's even better is that people have brought this into their everyday life and have been lit on fire by seeing the harvest all around them from sharing the gospel. People who haven't led one person to Christ in 10 years are leading 5-10 people to the Lord each week. Their life and the lives of those they are reaching are being changed.

- **A Legacy of Discipleship:** Pursuing authentic discipleship creates a legacy that endures for generations. When parents are discipled, they pass on spiritual values to their children and grandchildren. Churches that prioritize discipleship become training grounds for future leaders who will continue the mission of making disciples. Every lasting work of God has a generational impact. If we want to move from revival to reformation, the spiritual revolution and restoration of ancient paths will require the paradigm and culture of discipleship that runs a minimum of three to four generations deep. What God wants and what we should want is something sustainable and truly transformational that grows stronger and stronger from one generation to the next.

-**The Kingdom of God Advancing:** Ultimately, the value of discipleship is found in the advancement of God's kingdom and the Father adding to His Family the eternal Church. When disciples are made, the gospel spreads, the earth is blessed, and more people come to know and follow Jesus, becoming sons and daughters of the Most High. This is the heart of the Great Commission—to go and make disciples of all nations, baptizing them and teaching them to obey everything Jesus commanded that we might be as He is(Matthew 28:19-20). Jesus died to bring many sons to glory that we might approach the Father with confidence now and dwell with Him forever as we are being conformed to His image and walking out the preordained good works for which we were made for in Christ to the glory of the Father (Heb 2:10-11, 10:14-25, Rom 8:12-30, Eph 1-2:22, 1 Cor 3:16-22, 1 Cor 15:20-28, John 1:9-13, John 15:8, Col 1:26-29, 1 Theses 3:12-13, 2 Theses 2:13-17, 1 John 2:3-6, 3:2-3, 4:7-21 and so many more)

O what shall we say to these things? If God is for us, who can be against us? He who did not spare His own Son, but gave Him up for us all-how will He not also, along with Him, graciously give us all things? Romans 8:31-32

Conclusion: The Journey is Worth the Cost

The cost of discipleship is steep. It requires personal, familial, and communal sacrifice. It means letting go of comfort, embracing change, and committing to a lifelong process of growth. But the rewards—deep transformation, lasting impact, and the advancement of God's kingdom—are immeasurable. As we count the cost, we can take heart in knowing that the journey of discipleship, though difficult, is worth every sacrifice.

Here's a catch though, the commandments of the Lord are not burdensome.[148] Truth is, as we lay down our life we actually find our life, learn to live by divine strength, and walk in exceeding joy. Great grace is given to the "given" and humble. The humble are clothed with salvation and always filled with the oil of the Spirit. We learn to live and work in and from the rest of God as we believe in the Lord who gives us strength—His grace proves sufficient.

What starts and feels like sacrifice is transmuted into worship, praise, and gratitude as we stand in awe of the goodness of God and His mighty work in and through us and those around us. As we give ourselves to Christ and His mission, His glory becomes our greatest reward and joy. You stop thinking about what you've lost or sacrificed, in fact you don't count it at all. If anything, you count it as "dung" as the Apostle Paul said. You end up being consumed with the beauty and worth of Jesus and the deep and driving passion to know Him and please Him, in both the fellowship of His suffering and in the fellowship of His resurrection. Christ becomes all. We find that His grace is so abundantly sufficient and our cups overflow. We find ourselves in continual celebration of His mercy and goodness with nothing left but more love to give. As the scripture say, "The path of the righteous is like the morning sun, shining ever brighter till the perfect day.....[and]for the happy heart, life is a continual feast."[149]

---

148 1 John 5:3
149 Proverbs 4:18, 15:15

Mother Theresa said, "I have found the paradox that if I love until it hurts, then there is no more hurt, only more love."

You will never burn out when you do this from the right motives, from love and for Him and in Him, trusting His power and presence to obey what He has asked. Burn out is a sign of misalignment in faith and practice. There is a reality of embracing the joy-filled process of transformation on a personal level, in our families, and in our communities. Hopefully as you have read, you know that there is a better way. The ancient paths are the good way that lead to rest of soul and fruitfulness in life for the glory of God.

Remember, leading people in authentic discipleship is a way of life and means, but not limited to 7 principles that provide a balance to intentionality, flexibility, and love while fostering a culture of growth, mutuality, and multiplication:

1. Lead by Example in Shared Life and Ministry

Model Christ-like living while intentionally teaching and serving alongside others in the mission of the Church. Develop a purposeful process with clear goals and a learning, applying, reflecting process:

- *Knowing*: Biblical truth, worldview, and purpose/role-specific knowledge...etc.
- *Being*: Character formation and relational wholeness.
- *Doing*: Skills, abilities, and leadership development.

2. Begin with the End in Mind

Focus on Christ's call for every disciple and each person's unique purpose. Recognize that discipleship is not a one-size-fits-all process—we will need to be flexible to adapt methods to meet diverse needs, personalities, and calls.

3. Cultivate a Relational and Loving Approach

Be present, transparent, interruptible, and motivated by love. View the Church as a family, not a business. Prioritize relationships over programs and fuel the journey in joy, affirmation, and celebration. I like to say as Pope John XXIII, "*See everything, correct a little, praise a lot*". Yes, we are called to correct, teach, train, rebuke, but like fathers are instructed to not exasperate their kids as to discourage them or provoke them to anger, so it should be as we mentor and disciple people. Don't worry, people will get angry at you either way though. Ha!

4. Commit to Long-Term Investment

Discipleship is a journey, not a short-term program. Keep an open heart and hand—people may come, go, or shift roles, but be faithful in planting, watering, or nurturing. Trust God for the growth as you do your part unto God and in love for His people.

5. Guide Through Stages of Spiritual Maturity

To be transformational and to disciple with the heart of a healthy parent or older sibling in Christ, means meeting people where they are and helping them grow from spiritual infancy to maturity. Learn what is needed at each stage and adjust your expectations and process accordingly. It's important to embrace mutual learning from all believers, regardless of maturity level, knowing that we can contribute to one another's growth.

6. Prioritize faith, Identity, and Character Formation

Emphasize being over doing—help disciples know and live out their identity in Christ, form the character of Christ, and step into their unique purpose and calling. We have to see people and call them into their potential in Christ. Stay present-future oriented in the process even as you are dealing with the pains and sin of their past.

7. Be Missional and Reproductive

Aim for multiplication by equipping disciples to become disciple-makers. Encourage a focus on evangelism and the mission of making disciples who will also reproduce and carry on the mission. Don't wait till their "perfect" or fully prepared before they are "doing the stuff" of ministry. They learn and grow as they are doing in shared mission with you. Help guide and coach and train through the process.

As we give ourselves to the call of discipleship, remember that we GET to do this and have the PRIVILEGE of serving God. Let His joy be your strength. Immaturity will tend to focus on the sacrifice and loss and struggle whereas the mature are focused on the joy and reward of intimacy and obedience to God.

Leaders must help individuals navigate through their stages of growth and feelings of loss and offense by emphasizing the satisfaction of obedience to God's will, and reminding them that discipleship is a journey that may require parting ways with those not ready to walk the same path. We can encourage a kingdom mindset, where the cause of Christ takes precedence over personal attachments. We can also continually encourage them that laying down our lives for God's glory ultimately bears fruit in transformed hearts, churches, and societies.

PAUSE. CAPTURE. APPLY
Prompts to help you process

1. What specific insights or concepts from this chapter resonated with you the most? Why do you think these stood out to you?

_____

_____

_____

2. How can you practically apply the principles discussed in this chapter to your daily life, relationships, or ministry? Identify at least one actionable step you can take this week.

_____

_____

_____

3. What potential challenges or barriers might you face in implementing these concepts? How can you overcome them?

_____

_____

_____

4. What are 3-5 quotes or points from this chapter that capture the essence of what it's communicating? Write them down.

_____

_____

_____

_____

5. How can you involve your family, small group, or church community in the practices and principles outlined in this chapter? What steps can you take to foster a culture of discipleship and transformation within your circle of influence?

_____

_____

_____

6. Spend a few moments in prayer, asking God for the wisdom, strength, and courage to live out the truths you've learned. Write down a commitment or a prayer that reflects your desire to grow as an authentic disciple and transformational leader to impact the world.

_____

_____

_____

CHAPTER 17

Join the Mission!

"Every man dies, but not every man truly lives"
— William Wallace: Braveheart

As we come in for a landing I recognize we've covered a lot of ground and some big concepts. I hope we hear the clarion call for every believer in Jesus Christ to rise up and embrace the invitation to become an authentic disciple and transformational leader who makes an eternal impact in the places of their influence in life. I hope you are encouraged to use your gifts, passions, and abilities not only as part of your worship but for the advancement of the gospel. I hope we understand the call to make disciples and the need to approach it from a holistic and relational perspective. I hope you have been inspired to engage with the Lord in a new way to take action on your faith like never before.

Hopefully you have grasped our current era and the sobriety, excitement and possibilities before us. I hope you have gained a compelling sense that you have been called for such a time as this, to serve the Lord in unprecedented times for an unprecedented move of His Spirit. We have a part to play in this epic time of spiritual revolution and awakening. The Lord is pouring out His Spirit and reviving His People, and moving us into radical reform both in the church and in society. We are at the hinge of history and America and other nations hang in the balance.

So I invite you to set yourself apart, arise and renounce every compromise and spirit of the age. Caste off all that would dilute and dull you from being a brilliant torch of light and truth in the midst of gross darkness. Warriors and authentic disciples are countercultural agents of breakthrough, standing apart from the majority and status quo. They prepare a way for others to embrace the truth of the gospel, freeing them from the bondages of sin, ungodly tolerations, religious hypocrisy, and apostasy.

If you have read this far, I charge you to fully engage in the mission of Christ and be revived in your love and devotion to Christ Himself; return to your first love and be given wholly to the first commandment and the great commission, to know Him and make Him Known.

Some may be called to birth unconventional, fresh expressions of the church based on new testament patterns, that may not meet within the four walls of a "church" building or in the traditional pattern. We have to get out of the box of our religious thinking, old wineskins that keep us isolated and ineffective in reaching the world and making disciples. Heidi Baker, missionary to Mozambique, said "We like beautiful churches, but don't worry too much about them. A lot of the greatest services we've ever known happened under trees."

I love that!

Trust me when I say that I'm not villainizing church buildings. Our church facility has multiple buildings on 100+ acres, that are all creatively used for the mission 24/7 365. We will need facilities and hubs of gathering for equipping and training and sending. But as you go, just know the kingdom is advancing everywhere. Fresh reform is coming to the Church all over the earth. John 17 unity among churches is happening for greater Kingdom collaborations for both the building up of the Body of Christ and for greater works. It's a new day, a new era. Meaningful works can be birthed in coffee shops, restaurants, the workplace, your home, farms, the parks, the dojo, the school, the neighborhood, the internet, social media platforms, and virtual communities. The essence, nature, and function of the church is eternal and does not change, but the context and expression of those functions are diverse, and can take shape in many ways. Don't hold back, but go into all the earth and in all avenues, the highways and byways, with the glorious gospel and make it known! Preach good news, set captives free, heal the sick, do the works of the Kingdom and make disciples of all peoples!

I want to encourage you to visit each chapter and consider the questions I've asked in the text. There's questions outside the end of chapter prompts for you to answer if you saw them. I intentionally did not put chapter specific end of chapter questions, due to the length of this book and will plan to create another resource for you.

Take time to reflect, pray, and converse with those closest to you, then take fresh action. We cannot be hearers of the word only but must become effectual doers of it. Like the sons of Issachar, you must not only understand the time and season we are in but also what you must do about it. We pray and take action, we learn and we apply, we believe and we obey.

Take note of these questions:

- What has changed in your thinking?

- What has challenged you?

- What do you need to talk through more?

- What are you inspired or convinced to do?

- What are your practical next steps?

This can be just another book and information for you, or it can be a catalyst for change and transformation.

You choose what it will be.

As you have read throughout this book, I have shared that making an eternal impact starts with your own heart and life. The present and next generations desperately need good examples to follow. There has been much scandal and poor modeling of the faith but I believe God is raising a new standard and He's called you to be a part of it!

Remember, we reproduce who we are not what we teach (being precedes doing).

One of the best things you can do for others is to develop yourself, be faithful with your God-given responsibilities, and devote yourself to continual growth in Christ. That's what authentic disciples, warriors, and transformational leaders do. It's part of who they are. They're devoted to excellence, in body, soul, and spirit for the glory of God. They discipline themselves to godliness and steward their lives. They make daily consistent life improvements so that they can faithfully maximize their potential before God and add the highest value to those that they serve.

It's like what Paul exhorted his son in the faith he told Timothy, to: "Be diligent in these matters; give yourself wholly to them, so that everyone may see your progress. Watch your life and doctrine closely. Persevere in them, because if you do, you will save both yourself and your hearers." (1 Timothy 4:15-16 NIV)

You must set yourself apart unto the Lord in radical consecration and become a transformational agent that can help release God's saving work and word on the earth. You are the vessel and your life matters to Christ and His mission.

Remember

We are called to make a lasting and eternal impact on the world around us no matter what we are doing; We are called to be "fishers of men." We do this by good works, authentically living our faith, and sharing the gospel message. But also by intentionally entering into relationships to help others know Jesus, follow Jesus, become like Jesus, and join the mission of Jesus. We impact the world by our witness and by actively helping build up the body of Christ through the practice of discipleship. *This is not passive and random but rather highly intentional and proactive.* As believers and as the Church, the gates of hell will not prevail against us as we are advancing. We must advance, attack and plunder hell, save souls, and help establish people in the faith, ensuring that Christ is formed in them and they and we all come to spiritual maturity.

This Kingdom leaven must leaven everything and fill the whole world. Light must shine and overcome darkness and we must work while it is still called "today." Our labor in the gospel should be a holistic, continuous cycle of reproduction; spiritual multiplication through loving God, loving others, and making disciples. This is our mandate. You and I are called to bear fruit that remains. It starts with one individual at a time, one household at a time, one community at a time.

In the pursuit to impact the world with the gospel, we previously discussed the *path* and the *"HOW"* of development as key to the success of the mission.

The "HOW" we do it is just as important as "WHY" we need to do it. The path of development and discipleship should not be random or haphazard, but intentionally designed with the end in mind. Again, many leaders don't have an ordered, strategic, and well integrated discipleship process. Let alone one that is holistic, relational, and produces authentic disciples who love God, live in freedom, and have wholesome lifestyles that actually adorn the gospel, effectively advancing and reproducing it.

This can change and starts with you.

I'd like to remind us: If what we are doing does not produce the fruit of biblical proportions, then we need to re-evaluate our own lives and the things we are doing. Something must change so that we become and raise up the kind of people in whom " the world is not worthy of and who turn the world upside down[150]" with the love and power of God while multiplying other disciples to do the same. This is non negotiable.

We have to ask ourselves again, "do we have a plan and is that plan working?"

Our methodologies should be effective to produce the fruit of transformed lives; if our approach to training or mentoring people does not produce authentic followers and lovers of Christ who are becoming more and more like Him and doing the things He does, we are missing it! If we personally are not being continually transformed and growing more and more like Christ, we're missing it!

We cannot be passive or casual about this, we must be highly INTENTIONAL, disciplined, and diligent.

The truth is, we cannot afford to stay in spiritual infancy or extended adolescence. We need mature men and women of God who can change the world and be faithful witnesses of Jesus Christ. We must live lives worthy of the gospel; lives that inspire the next generation

---

150 Hebrews 11:38, Acts 17:6

to serve the God that they clearly see in the lives of those closest to them. We must lead by example. There is an all out assault to destroy and pervert the next generation and turn them away from the faith.

We must rise up!

We cannot have a form of godliness but deny the transforming power of God that should be continually at work in those who believe and are submitted to Christ. Nominal Christianity is no Christianity at all. We need a spiritual revolution and Kingdom warriors to arise! Creation is groaning for the sons of God and the Earth is in desperate need of authentic disciples who labor in partnership with God as redemptive catalysts. We are to be light and salt, adorning the gospel through our faithful witness and through its proclamation.

The sound of the trumpet is blowing, calling us to wake up and to return to the Lord and the ancient paths. When biblical discipleship happens in the way the Scriptures actually instruct us, It produces good fruit—people who authentically love God, live according to His word, and positivity change their world to the glory of God. The eyes of the Lord look to and fro throughout the whole earth looking for one who would be completely devoted to Him that He could fully support you and show up mighty on your behalf. (1 Chron 16:9)

Let's pray, let's act, let's move together at the sound of His voice, and know that surely victory will be had. He promised to be with us to the end of the age and gave us the battle plan. We can trust in His word and ways and take confident action on it. Even if it's in small ways to start, we must start now.

Our nation hangs in the balance. There is a sovereign summoning and calling to the people of God to hear and respond to the trumpet that's blowing in Zion. God is speaking and He is calling you.

Will you respond?

We must shake ourselves from the dust and refocus our gaze upon the Lord and His word. He goes out before us and the question is, who will follow? Who will reform their ways? Who will take command of their life in the grace of God and steer it into the purposes of God for this hour? Who will take bold and courageous action for the gospel's sake and help turn the tides of history regardless of the cost?

These questions must be asked and are far from rhetoric or hype. And even more so these questions must be answered.

The time is now.

Don't say "four months to the harvest, for the fields are white unto harvest, but pray to the Lord of the harvest, to send out laborers." Choose today whom you will serve. People are sheep without shepherds and Oh, how we need the people of God to rise up. Will you give yourself to being prepared, to be used by God to reach the lost and broken, and to disciple those around you? Will you say "yes" to Christ and His mission and help rebuild the desolations of many generations? Will you speak up and be unashamed of the gospel? Will you let His love and goodness flow through you to others?

Will you be a fisher of men? Will you contend for their souls?

We have a great work ahead of us and we have one life to live. It will be over before you know it. Let's do something in and for Jesus in our generation. You were born for such a time as this!

What say you? Are you in?

Let's pray, unite, get equipped, and mobilized for the greatest harvest of souls and move of God the earth has ever seen.

"Every reformation has one defining moment that is remembered long after the names of politicians and kings have been forgotten. At every massive shift in human history – whether political, cultural, or religious – a flash point occurs. That is the moment when a door for massive change opens. Great revolutions for good or for evil occur in the vacuums created by these openings. It is in these times that key men and women, even entire generations, risk everything to become the hinge of history, that pivotal point that determines which way the door will swing. America has been thrust into such a divine moment. In this socially convulsing era, the times demand that the church risks everything to lead the parade of history." — Lou Engle

Could this be our defining moment? Absolutely! And if not now, then when? And If not us, then who?

WARRIOR ARISE AND RETURN!

"Seek the Lord while he may be found; call on him while he is near. Let the wicked forsake their ways and the unrighteous their thoughts. Let them turn to the Lord, and he will have mercy on them, and to our God, for he will freely pardon…..Even now, declares the Lord, "return to me with all your heart, with fasting and weeping and mourning." Rend your heart and not your garments. Return to the Lord your God, for He is gracious and compassionate, slow to anger and abounding in love, and He relents from sending calamity. Who knows? He may turn and relent and leave behind a blessing— grain offerings and drink offerings for the Lord your God. (Isaiah 55:6-7, Joel 2:12-14 NIV)

I want to hear from you and connect with my fellow warriors around the globe. I want to be a resource for you, your family, your community, and a brother in arms. If you need help going to the next level, and don't have mentors or community around you, then let's work together. Reach out, let's get on the phone for a breakthrough clarity call and help you figure out your next steps. If it makes sense for us to work together, I would be honored to coach you.

If you have been stirred and challenged by this book, ask yourself who else in your circle of influence needs the message and truths in this book? Would you please share this with them?

Let's mobilize the people of God to become transformational agents, forerunners, and warriors to do His will and stand in the gap for our nation and the nations of the earth.

For such a time as this God has called you to help turn the tide in our Generation.

P.S. If you found this book helpful, and especially if you have had success and growth in implementing the content in these pages, **please leave a review on Amazon letting me know your story.**

P.S.S. Be sure to get your **Free Video Summary** and some other **exclusive resources** and content at *AriseandReturn.com*

Consider and Assess Yourself:

- Are we inconveniencing ourselves to reach others for Christ?
    - Consider, when was the last time you shared the gospel or your testimony in Christ with an unbeliever?

- Are we pursuing becoming fishers of men? Are you intentionally spending time with unbelievers and cultivating opportunities for the gospel?

- Are we pursuing mastery in the faith, to both know and live the scriptures? Do you have a plan of growth?

- Are you clear on your unique purpose in life and have a plan to live into it? Is it written down? Are there people around you aware of your plan, purpose, and course of action?

- Do you have mentors in your life? Are you being discipled? Are you really being accountable?

- Are we who should be teachers by now in need to be taught again because we have become dull in our faith and understanding?

- Are you pursuing wholeness in Christ and reconciling your past in Him and living in a sense of victory, joy, peace, with demonstrated healthy relationships?

- Are you settled in your identity as the beloved of God?

- Is your house in order according to the biblical design for the family? What needs to shift? What role are you to play?

- Are we exuding the glory and presence of God wherever we go and are we being an influence for the gospel or are we being influenced by the word?

- Are we living for the Glory of God and for the things that are eternal?

- Are you using your places of influence in life for the gospel?

- Are you developing yourself and stewarding your gifts and abilities as part of your worship to God? To be of greater service to the world around you for the glory of God?

- Are you actively engaged in the life of a local church?

- Are you intentionally discipling others? Do you have a plan or process for this?

- If you have people you are discipling, are they discipling others? Is your process of discipleship designed to multiply other disciple makers?

> **PAUSE. CAPTURE. APPLY**
> **Prompts to help you process**

1. What specific insights or concepts from this chapter resonated with you the most? Why do you think these stood out to you?

_____

_____

_____

2. How can you practically apply the principles discussed in this chapter to your daily life, relationships, or ministry? Identify at least one actionable step you can take this week.

_____

_____

_____

3. What potential challenges or barriers might you face in implementing these concepts? How can you overcome them?

_____

_____

_____

4. What are 3-5 quotes or points from this chapter that capture the essence of what it's communicating? Write them down.

_____

_____

_____

5. How can you involve your family, small group, or church community in the practices and principles outlined in this chapter? What steps can you take to foster a culture of discipleship and transformation within your circle of influence?

_____

_____

_____

6. Spend a few moments in prayer, asking God for the wisdom, strength, and courage to live out the truths you've learned. Write down a commitment or a prayer that reflects your desire to grow as an authentic disciple and transformational leader to impact the world.

_____

_____

_____

FREE VIDEO SUMMARY'S

WANT VIDEO SUMMARY'S OF EACH CHAPTER & MORE?

Transformational Tools & Resources

Think about this **FREE** resources as a training process and master class loaded with value and discussion prompts for your people and your own reflection.

ARISEANDRETURN.COM

JOIN THE MISSION!

URGENT PLEA!
THANK YOU FOR READING MY BOOK!

I really appreciate all your feedback and I love hearing what you have to say.

I need your input to make the next version of this book and my future books better.

Please take two minutes now to leave a helpful (4.5 OR 5 STAR) review on **Amazon** letting me know what you thought of the book.

If you think less of the book than a 4 star rating, i'd still love to hear from you (just not on Amazon ...ha) - just email me at josiah@ariseandreturn.com

Thanks so much!!

—Josiah Armstrong

CLAIM YOUR 75% OFF CODE:

"BOOKBONUS75XP"

YOUR STRATEGIC PATH TO BREAKTHROUGH, CLARITY, AND ABUNDANT LIFE!

Transformational Tools & Resources

Discover your unique God given purpose, breakthrough your barriers, craft a strategic and prayer plan with a rule of life that leads to fruitfulness and fulfillment. Leave a transformational legacy!

FORERUNNERFITNESS.NET/BREAKTHROUGHXP

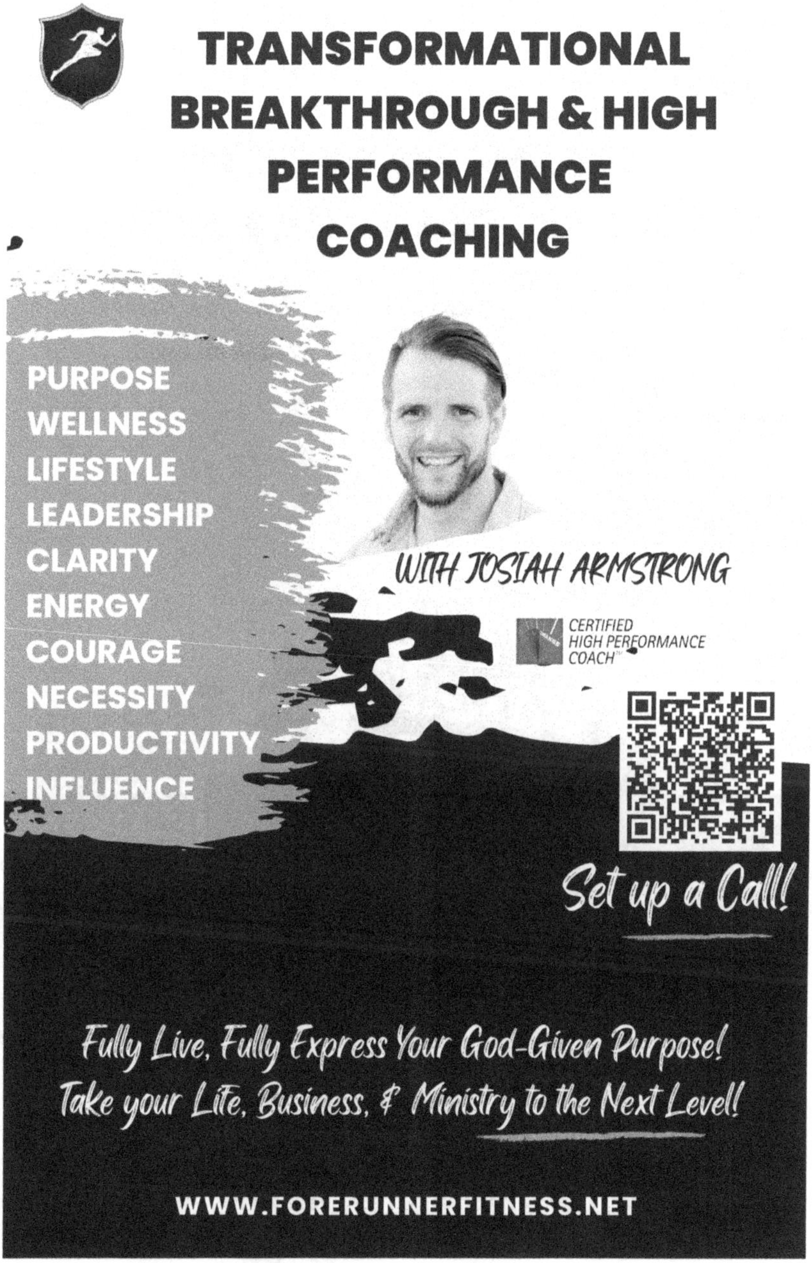

WANT ME TO COME SPEAK, TRAIN, OR EQUIP?

Serving your Church, Team, Camps, workshops, Conferences, off sights and more...

UNITING
EQUIPPING
MOBILIZING
INSPIRING
REVIVAL
AWAKENING
FREEDOM
KINGDOM
STRATEGY
TRANSFORMATION

Set up a Call!

*Equipping the Church and Impacting Culture.
Raising up the Next Generation of Authentic Disciples and Transformational Kingdom leaders*

WWW.FORERUNNERFITNESS.NET

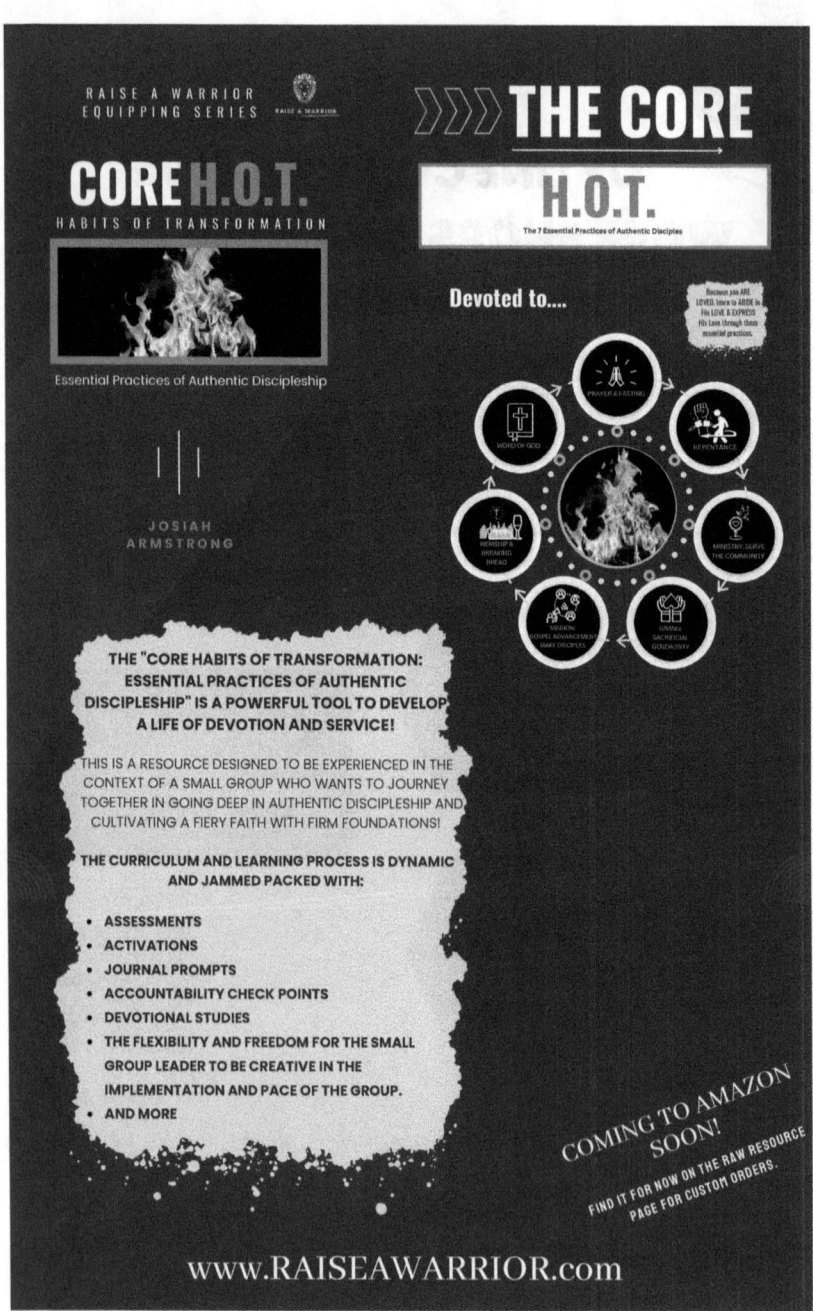

JOIN THE MISSION!

R.A.W.
RESOURCES

School of Warrior Arts presents Immersive faith based, training, and personal development resources for the young and aspiring warrior!

THE R.A.W WORKSHOP   **PODCAST**   **BOOKS**
BUSHIDOBYTES.COM   THEBUSHIDOBOOKS.COM

www.RAISEAWARRIOR.com

CERTIFIED HIGH PERFORMANCE COACH

S.O.W.A. School of Warrior Arts

Camp R.A.W.
RAISE A WARRIOR

Overnight & Day Camp options

School of Warrior Arts presents an Immersive faith based, martial art, and personal development Camp for the young and aspiring warrior!

Ages 9-17

PREMIER ANNUAL SUMMER CAMP

This is for all levels and World class training in various combative arts, weapons, fitness, character and leadership development, hard core fun, crafts, challenges, activities, biblical teaching, and more, all in the context of outdoor adventure.

- Fun activities, crafts, and games
- Karate, Boxing, Ju-Jitsu, MMA
- Weapons training (Bow staff, Kali sticks, Archery)
- Beach day and Hiking day.
- Healthy breakfast, lunch, and dinners.
- Exciting Bible based leadership lessons
- Daily Fitness & Character education
- Laws of Leadership

- Obstacle Course & Archery Tag Challenge!
- Transformation R.A.W Journals and personal Development tools!
- Dr John Maxwell Youth Impact DISC assessment and Training!
- Family Friendly Movie night!
- Bon fires & Snacks
- And more....

"This Camp is AMAZING!"

JOIN THE MOVEMENT. JOIN THE TRIBE!

www.SCHOOLOFWARRIORARTS.com

APPENDIX

12 Tips for Crafting Great Open-Ended Questions:

1. Avoid Yes/No Questions: Construct questions that require more than a simple "yes" or "no" answer. Encourage participants to elaborate on their thoughts.

2. Use Neutral Language: Craft questions without leading participants toward a specific answer. Maintain an impartial tone to promote diverse viewpoints.

3. Start with "What," "Why," "How": These question starters prompt deeper exploration and invite participants to analyze and explain their thoughts.

4. Encourage Self-Reflection: Pose questions that prompt participants to consider their beliefs, values, and experiences in relation to the topic.

5. Probe for Evidence: Ask for specific examples, evidence, or data to support participants' assertions.

6. Explore Assumptions: Challenge participants to identify and examine any underlying assumptions they may be making.

7. Encourage Critical Thinking: Craft questions that require participants to analyze, compare, contrast, and evaluate different aspects of the topic.

8. Consider Diverse Perspectives: Invite participants to think from alternative viewpoints, fostering empathy and a more holistic understanding.

9. Build on Previous Responses: Reference participants' previous contributions and ask follow-up questions that build on their ideas.

10. Use Thought Experiments: Pose hypothetical scenarios or "what if" questions to encourage participants to think creatively and speculate on different outcomes.

11. Be Patient and Give Space: Allow participants time to think and respond. Silence can be a powerful tool to encourage deeper reflection.

12. Follow the Flow: Adapt your questions based on the direction of the conversation. Listen actively and adjust your questioning strategy as needed.

By incorporating these Socratic questions and crafting open-ended inquiries thoughtfully, you can facilitate engaging and enriching discussions that lead to deeper understanding, critical thinking, and a genuine love for learning.

APPENDIX 2

AI Dynamics

One area where the people of God can lead and hold the standard of truth is in human connection, community. We can cut through the artificial and virtual vortex that traps so many. The people of God must be the living embodiment of the truth and love of God to a lost, confused, and complex world that has never been so "connected" yet so lonely, fearful, and easily manipulated.

Listen to a few words from some serial entrepreneurs in 2023 specifically about AI and how it will affect not just industry but the character of people:

According to Joe Polish, Founder of Genius Network, one of the highest level groups in the world for entrepreneurs, says,

> "You've probably heard about the rise of ChatGPT, Midjourney and other accessible AI scripts.
>
> But here's what NO ONE is talking about…
>
> The very real danger that we're going to rewrite and rewire DOPAMINE.

Because when you start "feeding the dopamine machine" so that people want everything instantaneously, patience will go out the window.

And we're NOT built for this. We simply haven't evolved quickly enough, and this complete overload of the nervous system will lead to an epidemic of people who are really disconnected.

And this shift isn't limited to interpersonal relationships. AI is going to completely reorient and reorganize the entire workforce.

We now have computer programs that can do the creative work people once did. So, what other businesses are going to be decimated?

My friend Akira Chan sent me this profound audio message that will give you some serious food for thought…

"If you can tell an AI to write a brilliant love letter to a person you're dating or write an essay for you, on top of using AI to make yourself look like a superhero and 10 years younger… that becomes an extreme addiction."

Just think about that. AI writing the perfect love letter AND fashioning the ideal visual avatar for you… who can resist?

But in a world where everything is fake, where will authenticity come from? What will people crave?

Human connection.

> In 2023, being a real person will be more critical than ever before. We have a need for human connection .
>
> 2023 (*and 2024*) is going to be insane so get prepared right now."
>
> And as another industry leader said, "2023 is going to be a bit messy as we learn to tell the difference between what's real and what's AI made-up.
>
> It's those who can maintain authenticity, truthfulness and transparency who will have the greatest chance of success, leveraging AI to help rather than reinvent themselves as something they're not."

Authenticity, truthfulness, and transparency should come from the people of God- the Church—the pillar and foundation of the truth, first. As you can see, technology is only complicating things. It will require our full engagement if we want to be effective in fulfilling our call as a disciple of Christ who will make disciples, raise warriors, and pass on a living faith to the next generation. We need to be a people of understanding, discernment, skill, and most importantly, love.

On the other hand, AI can be harnessed for many great things and tasks and generation of ideas. We should not fear it but not become dependent on it. AI cannot replace the creativity of His people, the community of His people, and the need to hear from the Holy Spirit.

In the words of ChatGPT itself (Ha Ha):

Artificial Intelligence (AI) is increasingly being integrated into church ministries, offering various opportunities and challenges. Here are the top ways AI is being harnessed by churches, along with key considerations to maintain ethical and effective use:

Top 5-10 Ways AI Is Being Harnessed by Churches:

1. **Sermon Preparation Assistance:** AI tools like ChatGPT can help pastors overcome writer's block, structure sermons, and generate illustrative content, streamlining the preparation process.

2. **Language Translation:** AI-powered translation services enable churches to make sermons and materials accessible to non-native speakers, fostering inclusivity within diverse congregations.

3. **Content Creation for Social Media:** AI can automate the creation of engaging social media posts, enhancing online presence and outreach efforts.

4. **Administrative Task Automation:** AI streamlines administrative duties such as scheduling, data management, and communication, allowing church staff to focus more on ministry work.

5. **Enhanced Worship Experiences:** AI can assist in creating multimedia content for services, including sermon illustrations, music, and videos, enriching the worship experience.

6. **Virtual Assistance and Chatbots:** AI-driven chatbots can provide immediate responses to inquiries on church websites, improving communication with congregants and visitors.

7. **Data Analysis for Congregational Insights:** AI analyzes engagement patterns, helping church leaders understand congregational needs and tailor ministries accordingly.

8. **Educational Content Development:** AI aids in creating devotionals, Bible study materials, and children's ministry content, supporting educational initiatives within the church.

9. **Fundraising Optimization:** AI can enhance fundraising efforts by analyzing donor data and suggesting personalized engagement strategies.

10. **Virtual Tours and Experiences:** AI enables the creation of virtual tours of church facilities or historical sites, broadening access and engagement.

Top 5 Considerations for Churches Using AI:

1. **Data Privacy and Security:** Ensure robust cybersecurity measures are in place to protect sensitive information, maintaining trust within the congregation.

2. **Ethical Use and Bias Mitigation:** Be vigilant about potential biases in AI algorithms and strive for responsible data use to uphold fairness and inclusivity.

3. **Maintaining Human Connection:** While AI can enhance efficiency, it should not replace the personal interactions that are foundational to pastoral care and community building.

4. **Transparency with Congregation:** Clearly communicate the use of AI within church operations to congregants, fostering openness and addressing any concerns.

5. **Theological and Ethical Reflection:** Engage in ongoing discussions about the theological implications of AI, ensuring its use aligns with the church's mission and values.

By thoughtfully integrating AI technologies and remaining mindful of these considerations, churches can leverage AI to enhance their ministries while upholding ethical standards and fostering genuine human connections.

www.ingramcontent.com/pod-product-compliance
Lightning Source LLC
Chambersburg PA
CBHW050846160426
43194CB00011B/2054